EMPIRICALLY SUPPORTED THERAPIES

BANFF INTERNATIONAL BEHAVIORAL SCIENCE Series

SERIES EDITORS

Kenneth D. Craig, *University of British Columbia*
Keith S. Dobson, *University of Calgary*
Robert J. McMahon, *University of Washington*
Ray DeV. Peters, *Queen's University*

Volumes in the **Banff International Behavioral Science Series** take the behavioral science perspective on important basic and applied challenges that confront practitioners working in the fields of the social, psychological, and health services. The editors invite leading investigators and practitioners to contribute because of their expertise on emergent issues and topics. Contributions to the volumes integrate information on themes and key issues relating to current research and professional practice. The chapters reflect the authors' personal, critical analysis of the topics, the current scientific and professional literature, and discussions and deliberations with other experts and practitioners. It is our intention to have this continuing series of publications provide an "expressive" early indicator of the developing nature and composition of the behavioral sciences and scientific applications to human problems and issues. The volumes should appeal to practitioners, scientists, and students interested in the interface between professional practice and research advances.

Volumes in This Series:

- *Anxiety and Depression in Adults and Children*   Edited by Kenneth D. Craig and Keith S. Dobson
- *Advances in Cognitive-Behavioral Therapy*   Edited by Keith S. Dobson and Kenneth D. Craig
- *Preventing Childhood Disorders, Substance Abuse, and Delinquency*   Edited by Ray DeV. Peters and Robert J. McMahon
- *Child Abuse: New Directions in Prevention and Treatment Across the Lifespan*   Edited by David A. Wolfe, Robert J. McMahon and Ray DeV. Peters
- *Empirically Supported Therapies: Best Practice in Professional Psychology*   Edited by Keith S. Dobson and Kenneth D. Craig

EMPIRICALLY SUPPORTED THERAPIES

Best Practice in Professional Psychology

Keith S. Dobson
Kenneth D. Craig
editors

BANFF **I**NTERNATIONAL **B**EHAVIORAL **S**CIENCE SERIES

SAGE Publications
International Educational and Professional Publisher
Thousand Oaks   London   New Delhi

For information:

 SAGE Publications, Inc.
2455 Teller Road
Thousand Oaks, California 91320
E-mail: order@sagepub.com

SAGE Publications Ltd.
6 Bonhill Street
London EC2A 4PU
United Kingdom

SAGE Publications India Pvt. Ltd.
M-32 Market
Greater Kailash I
New Delhi 110 048 India

Printed in the United States of America

Library of Congress Cataloging-in-Publication Data

Main entry under title:

Empirically supported therapies: Best practice in professional
psychology / edited by Keith S. Dobson and Kenneth D. Craig.
 p. cm. — (Banff international behavioral science series; v. 5)
 Includes bibliographical references and index.
 ISBN 0-7619-1075-1 (hardcover: alk. paper)
 ISBN 0-7619-1076-X (pbk.: alk. paper)
1. Psychotherapy—Evaluation—Congresses.
2. Psychotherapy—Outcome assessment—Congresses.
3. Psychotherapy—Differential therapeutics—Congresses.
I. Dobson, Keith S. II. Craig, Kenneth D., 1937- . III. Series.
 RC480.52.E43 1998
 616.89'14—ddc21   98-19759

This book is printed on acid-free paper.

98 99 00 01 02 03 10 9 8 7 6 5 4 3 2 1

Acquiring Editor:	Jim Nageotte
Editorial Assistant:	Heidi Van Middlesworth
Production Editor:	Wendy Westgate
Editorial Assistant:	Denise Santoyo
Designer/Typesetter:	Janelle LeMaster
Cover Designer:	Candice Harman

Contents

PART II: EMPIRICALLY SUPPORTED INTERVENTIONS

Preface

Empirical Support and Psychological Interventions: A Peaceable Union

Anyone who has read the psychotherapy literature will be aware of the ongoing debate about whether these treatments have any benefit beyond those attributable to the passage of time, minimal interventions, or social support (Bergin & Garfield, 1994; Lambert & Bergin, 1994). Even if psychological treatment is granted success beyond any minimal effect, the debate about "best" or "better" treatment rages, with some credible reviews suggesting that treatments are all roughly equivalent in their outcomes (Hollon, Shelton, & Loosen, 1991; Luborsky, Singer, & Luborsky, 1975). Speaking very generally, the consensus appears to be emerging that psychological treatments do work, although the precise nature of the treatment, the patient's presenting problems, and some interaction between patient's and therapist's working styles complicate the overall picture dramatically (Beutler & Clarkin, 1990; Lambert & Hill, 1994; see also Chapter 3 of this volume).

Due to the recognition of the value of psychological treatments, they are increasingly funded by both public and private health providers. At the same time, parties that pay for psychological services are increasingly strident in their demands for proven treatments. The scientist-practitioner ideal professed by psychology also implies that the interventions and services offered should have a validated basis (Hayes, Barlow, & Nelson-Grey, in press). In recent years, these two "conspiratorial" factors have led to a reexamination of therapies in terms of their empirical justification. Perhaps seen most clearly in the American Psychological Association's Division 12 Task Force on Promotion and Dissemination of Psychological Procedures (Chambless et al., 1995), there has been a specific response to the calls for empirical validation, and a list of empirically supported treatments has begun to emerge.

Almost as soon as the first list of empirically supported treatments was released, criticism erupted from within the psychological community. Questions were raised about the criteria employed by the Task Force, the body of literature that was reviewed (and not reviewed), and the implications of this type of activity. In response, the Task Force reviewed its criteria, considered further research evidence, and issued appropriate cautions about the role of empirical evidence in establishing the validity of psychological treatments (Chambless et al., 1996).

One of the controversies surrounding the Task Force's reports is the preponderance of treatments from the behavioral and cognitive-behavioral traditions. It is not a coincidence, however, that the list of validated treatments includes these treatments, for the behavioral and cognitive-behavioral therapy movements have from their beginnings made a conscious effort to document outcome and process issues with quantitative measures (Dobson, 1988). Thus, although other therapy approaches may be able to be validated, to some extent the behavioral/cognitive-behavioral movement has generally been given the benefit of "first validation" by the empirical validation efforts. This benefit will precipitate further research attention, which in turn is likely to prompt even further innovations and justifications of these approaches.

Another notable concern raised about the Task Force report is that although the adopted criteria do not specifically endorse any nosological or diagnostic system such as the *Diagnostic and Statistical Manual of Mental Disorders* (*DSM;* American Psychiatric Association, 1994), most of the treatments have been validated on diagnostically related groups of patients. Such a reliance on diagnosis to validate treatments has led some to question whether this movement will enhance the medicalization of psychotherapy and may paradoxically undermine psychological approaches in the longer term.

Other concerns about the empirical validation movement have been recognized and are beginning to receive the attention that they require (Dobson, 1996). The current volume reflects most of these concerns and in a balanced manner tries to place the empirical validation movement in its appropriate place and time.

THE CURRENT VOLUME

In recognition of the importance of the theme of empirical justification of psychological interventions, and consistent with the long-standing tradition of this conference series to examine issues from a data-based perspective, the 1996 Banff Conference on Behavioural Science set the conference theme as "Best Practice: Developing and Promoting Empirically Validated Treatments." Our goal was to consider from a theoretical perspective the benefits and cautions attendant to this development, as well as to consider the implications of this movement in several specific practice domains. Experts in different areas came together to present and discuss their work and to provide an update of recent developments in the empirical validation movement. This volume not only represents the ideas shared at the conference but also includes discussion about broader issues related to this topic.

The volume is divided into two major sections. The first considers general theoretical issues in the field; the second examines in some detail specific fields of practice and the evidence for empirical validation. The lead chapter of the first section (Chapter 1) is by one of the members of the APA Task Force, Paul Crits-Christoph. The author details the original impetus for the report, its mode of action, and recent revisions to its work. This chapter reflects one of the best overviews of this topic and is important for its careful considerations of the limitations of the empirical validation movement.

The second chapter in the book highlights the overall political context into which the empirical validation movement has been placed. Steven C. Hayes critically examines some of the negative influences on the mental health sector in contemporary United States (e.g., managed care, guild interests) and within that context suggests that simple lists of "proven" treatments may be dangerous. He articulates the need for practice guidelines based upon sound science (see also Clinton, McCormick, & Besterman, 1994; Hayes,

Follette, Dawes, & Grady, 1995), even though such guidelines will undermine some of the traditions on which the profession of psychology is built.

In Chapter 3, Larry E. Beutler and Mary Baker raise concerns about the use of randomized clinical trials as the major method to validate psychosocial treatments. They suggest that such trials misrepresent the nature of clinical work and also imply more precision about psychological treatment than may be warranted. Further, they point out that most of the research that is conducted has focused on fairly homogeneous, diagnostically defined populations. This methodology for selecting research subjects fails to take into account a number of individual-difference variables that may cut across psychotherapies but that still account for an important part of the variance in many or all psychotherapies. The authors go on to identify the need for "aptitude by treatment interaction" research, in which individual differences can be analyzed in interaction with treatment.

Chapter 4 addresses the important question of whether the criteria developed by the APA task Force are appropriate for children. John R. Weisz notes some of the differences in research between adults and children and suggests that some modifications of the criteria are important. He then further echoes Beutler and Baker by suggesting that the standard clinical research method may not be highly informative about practice in the clinic. He suggests there may be the need for a "new genre of treatment outcome research" devoted to the adaptation and exportation of laboratory-based interventions to the real world.

The fifth chapter in the volume raises concerns about the extent to which the extant lists of empirically supported therapies are sensitive to the issue of cultural diversity. Anna Beth Doyle argues that the cultural appropriateness of these treatments has been "overlooked" and that as a result a specific focus on this issue is needed before it is assumed that validated treatments are culturally appropriate.

Taken as a whole, the first section highlights the plethora of conceptual, methodological, and pragmatic concerns associated with developing lists of empirically validated therapies. Although most of the authors do not take issue with the idea of linking science and practice, the manner in which that linkage is made and the state of our current knowledge to make that link are often challenged. One conclusion that can be drawn from these chapters is that although the concept of empirically supported practice is endorsed, innovative research methods and considerable research using these methods are needed before the overall strategy will be overwhelmingly accepted.

The six remaining chapters in this book examine the existing literature in various specific areas of practice and try to make conclusions about the empirical status of these interventions. These areas were chosen by the co-chairs of this conference as those in which some of the strongest evidence for empirical validation has been suggested and those in which many of the critical questions for the empirical validation movement will need to be addressed. All of these chapters focus on a particular area of dysfunction (depression, couples therapy, schizophrenia, headache, alcohol abuse, and sexual dysfunction). They are written by noted experts in their respective areas and constitute important milestones in these various practice areas.

CONCLUSION

Any publication is defined by the time and context in which it is produced; this volume is no different. Between the generation of the chapters and the publication of the book, there will already be developments that one could argue "should" have been included in this text. We know that the list of supported treatments continues to be revised. We know that the Canadian Psychological Association's Section on Clinical Psychology is developing a formal position on empirical validation and that the Child Section of APA's Division 12 has also reviewed the literature for evidence of empirically supported therapies. The *Journal of Consulting and Clinical Psychology* has published a special issue on this topic in February 1998. For any "omissions," we as coeditors assume responsibility. We are also acutely aware that the issue of empirically supported treatments is itself in a state of dynamic development and that any effort to capture its range and scope is at best a "snapshot" of a moving target. For example, there has been a title change between the conference upon which this book is based and the issuance of book itself. Specifically, we have changed the title from "empirically validated" to "empirically supported" in recognition of the fact that treatments are not "validated" per se but are subjected to an ongoing process of validation. Thus, although it is appropriate to speak about treatments with empirical support, to imply that they are validated is to draw a conclusion that may be difficult, if not impossible, to sustain.

The Banff Conferences
on Behavioural Science

We are pleased to offer this volume as one of a long list of publications that have emerged from the Banff Conferences over the years. This series includes the following topics:

This conference series has been, and continues to be, a singular honour to host. The conference brings together a cohort of experts in the intimate setting of Banff, Canada, and combines the best of science and recreation (notably skiing) in a stimulating environment.

Bringing the Banff conferences to publication is an expectation of the conference committee. In this regard, we want to acknowledge the people we work with at Sage Publications, and in particular C. Terry Hendrix, Jim Nageotte, Nancy Hale, and Vicki Baker. Through our series contract, we are able to move conferences into press in a much more expedient manner than was previously the case, which we hope will be an overall benefit to those who read this work. We also want to acknowledge Alison Wiigs for her secretarial assistance on this volume. We want to extend our deep and formal thanks to our collaborators on this series, Drs. Bob McMahon and Ray Peters. It was a blast, as always! Finally, we want to recognize our host universities and the support that they provide to each of us: The University of Calgary for Keith Dobson and The University of British Columbia for Ken Craig.

KEITH S. DOBSON
KENNETH D. CRAIG

References

American Psychiatric Association. (1994). *Diagnostic and statistical manual of mental disorders* (4th ed.). Washington, DC: American Psychiatric Press.

Bergin, A. E., & Garfield, S. L. (Eds.). (1994). *Handbook of psychotherapy and behavior change* (4th ed.). New York: John Wiley.

Beutler, L. E., & Clarkin, J. (1990). *Systematic treatment selection: Toward targeted therapeutic interventions.* New York: Brunner/Mazel.

Chambless, D. L., Babich, K., Crits-Christoph, P., Frank, E., Gilson, M., Montgomery, R., Rich, R., Steinberg, J., & Weinberger, J. (1995). Training in and dissemination of empirically-validated psychological treatments: Report and recommendations. *Clinical Psychologist, 48,* 3-24.

Chambless, D. L., Sanderson, W. C., Shoham, V., Johnson, S. B., Pope, K. S., Crits-Christoph, P., Baker, M., Johnson, B., Woody, S., Sue, S., Beutler, L., Williams, D. A., & McCurry, S. (1996). An update on empirically validated therapies. *Clinical Psychologist, 49,* 5-18.

Clinton, J. J., McCormick, K., & Besterman, J. (1994). Enhancing clinical practice: The role of practice guidelines. *American Psychologist, 49,* 30-33.

Dobson, K. S. (Ed.). (1988). *Handbook of the cognitive-behavioral therapies.* New York: Guilford.

Dobson, K. S. (1996). Empirically validated treatments: Not the last word. *Canadian Clinical Psychologist, 7,* 3-6.

Hayes, S. C., Follette, W., Dawes, R. D., & Grady, K. (Eds.). (1995). *Scientific standards of psychological practice: Issues and recommendations.* Reno, NV: Context.

Hayes, S. C., Barlow, D. H., & Nelson-Grey, R. O. (in press). *The scientist-practitioner: Research and accountability in the age of managed care* (2nd ed.). New York: Allyn & Bacon.

Hollon, S. D., Shelton, R. C., & Loosen, P. T. (1991). Cognitive therapy and pharmacotherapy for depression. *Journal of Consulting and Clinical Psychology, 59,* 88-99.

Lambert, M. J., & Bergin, A. E. (1994). The effectiveness of psychotherapy. In A. E. Bergin & S. L. Garfield (Eds.), *Handbook of psychotherapy and behavior change* (4th ed.). New York: John Wiley.

Lambert, M. J., & Hill, E. H. (1994). Assessing psychotherapy outcomes and processes. In A. E. Bergin & S. L. Garfield (Eds.), *Handbook of psychotherapy and behavior change* (4th ed.). New York: John Wiley.

Luborsky, L., Singer, B., & Luborsky, L. (1975). Comparative studies of psychotherapy. *Archives of General Psychiatry, 32,* 995-1008.

PART I

Theoretical Issues

1

Training in Empirically Validated Treatments

THE DIVISION 12 APA TASK FORCE RECOMMENDATIONS

PAUL CRITS-CHRISTOPH

In 1993, David Barlow, as president of the Clinical Psychology Division (Division 12) of the American Psychological Association (APA), embarked on a number of initiatives designed to increase current knowledge on the effectiveness of psychological interventions. One of the initiatives was the creation of a task force, chaired by Dianne Chambless, PhD, on the promotion and dissemination of psychological interventions. Its report was published in 1995 (Task Force, 1995), and an updated report was published in 1996 (Chambless et al., 1996). A considerable amount of controversy has been generated about these reports, bringing to the fore a variety of issues related to what is known about the efficacy of psychological interventions and how and when such efficacious interventions should be disseminated.

The purpose of this chapter is first to briefly present the methods and recommendations of the task force. Because details of the original task force are available in the published version (Task Force, 1995), I will provide only some general orienting information in regard to the original report and will focus on changes that have been made to the original report and are contained in the updated report (Chambless et al., 1996). This will be followed by a discussion of the major controversial issues surrounding the report and the larger issues facing the field of psychotherapy research in the current environment of great pressure to document effectiveness and reduce costs. In this context, I will address questions related to the importance of client, therapist, and relationship factors in psychotherapy and the empirical status of psychodynamic treatments in particular.

THE TASK FORCE REPORT

Overview

The initial task force report (Task Force, 1995) presented the background and goals of the task force, the criteria for determining efficacy of treatments, a list of examples of treatments that met such criteria, and a set of recommendations to APA regarding education about empirically validated treatments. The initial task force report was widely disseminated to elicit feedback and comments. A draft version of the report was presented at the 1993 APA convention, with a lengthy discussion period. Before publication, the report was discussed by the Division 12 Board, the APA Committee on Accreditation, the Council of University Directors of Clinical Psychology, the APA Boards of Professional Affairs, Educational Affairs, and Scientific Affairs, the Association of Psychology Postdoctoral and Internship Centers, the APA Continuing Education Committee, and the APA Committee for Approval of Continuing Education Sponsors. The report was sent to all directors of APA-approved clinical internships and doctoral programs, the APA Board of Directors, state psychological associations, attendees of the APA conference on postdoctoral education, and all members of the Society for a Science of Clinical Psychology.

The updated task force report (Chambless et al., 1996) provided slight revisions to the criteria for determining efficacy, a revised list of examples of treatments, and discussion of certain important issues such as treatment of ethnic minorities, aptitude-by-treatment interactions that might be worthy of consideration, and ethical issues.

Goals

The central goal of the task force report was to facilitate education by identifying treatments with a scientific basis. Because of many misunderstandings, it is important to state what the goals of the report were not. In particular, it was not the goal of the report to make recommendations that would constrain clinical practice or training programs to certain treatment approaches. Moreover, it was not the goal of the report to convince third-party payers that only certain treatments should be reimbursed. The authors of the report explicitly attempted to avoid such misunderstandings by labeling the list of efficacious treatments as "examples" rather than a definitive list and by stating that "one should not conclude that a treatment absent from our list has not been shown to be effective" (Task Force, 1995, p. 5). Furthermore, in regard to training, the report stated, "We are not suggesting that all clinical training be restricted to these treatments" (Task Force, 1995, p. 7). The update of the task force report further clarified these issues by including an addendum that contained a resolution issued by the Board of Directors of Division 12 stating that the task force report is not intended to be viewed as practice guidelines. In addition, the updated report specified that the list of empirically validated treatments does not substitute for educators' and clinicians' own decisions about what is the most appropriate treatment with a given client.

Criteria for Efficacy

Members of the task force reviewed the psychosocial treatment literature using certain criteria to determine whether a given treatment had been "well established" scientifically or at the current time was "probably efficacious." The decision to have two categories of efficacy was made in part because of the recognition that such criteria for deciding whether empirical validation of a treatment was sufficient are somewhat arbitrary.

In reviewing different treatments, the intention of the task force was not to make claims that a certain treatment from a given theoretical orientation was in general effective. Consistent with the trend throughout the psychosocial treatment research literature, the task force focused on whether a treatment was effective for a specific problem or disorder.

The revised criteria used for the updated report are given in Table 1.1. For a treatment to be classified as "well established," there needed to be at least

TABLE 1.1   Criteria for Empirically Validated Treatments

Well-Established Treatments

I.   At least two good between-group design experiments demonstrating efficacy in one
     or more of the following ways:
     A. Superior to pill or psychological placebo or to another treatment.
     B. Equivalent to an already established treatment in experiments with adequate
         statistical power (about 30 per group). OR
II. A large series of single-case design experiments (*N* gee 9) demonstrating efficacy.
     These experiments must have:
     A. Used good experimental designs and
     B. Compared the intervention to another treatment as in I.A.

FURTHER CRITERIA FOR BOTH I AND II:
III. Experiments must be conducted with treatment manuals.
IV. Characteristics of the client samples must be clearly specified.
V.   Effects must have been demonstrated by at least two different investigators or
     investigatory teams.

Probably Efficacious Treatments

I.   Two experiments showing the treatment is more effective than a waiting-list control
     group.

OR

II. One or more experiments meeting the Well-Established Treatment criteria I, III,
     and IV, but not V.

OR

III. A small series of single-case design experiments (*N* gee 3) otherwise meeting
     Well-Established Treatment Criteria II, III, and IV.

two group design experiments showing either (a) superiority to pill or
psychological placebo treatment or (b) superiority or equivalence to an
already established treatment (assuming adequate statistical power). Alternatively, efficacy could be established via a large series of single-case
experiments. A further criterion was that all studies must use treatment
manuals. Manuals were seen as important because they allow for clearer
interpretation of study results, leading to more specific clinical recommendations and greater ease of dissemination of a treatment. One change in the
criteria was made for the updated task force report. The meaning of a "large
series" of single-case experiments was defined to be nine or more such
single-case experiments. This decision was made after consultation with a
number of experts in single-case research.

For the designation of "probably efficacious," the task force criteria specified (a) two experiments demonstrating that the treatment was more efficacious than a wait-list or (b) one or more experiments meeting all of the criteria for "well established," with the exception that the studies were not performed by at least two different investigators. For the revised report, a small series of single-case studies was defined as three or greater. One criterion contained in the original report involved downgrading a treatment to "probably efficacious" if the two or more studies were flawed by hetero-geneity of client samples. The task force used the term *heterogeneity of sample* to refer to studies that did not focus on a specific client problem or disorder (a "mixed bag" of clients) and not to samples that did focus on a target problem but also had comorbidity. Because the concept of a mixed sample was against the guiding criteria of the report (specific treatments for specific problems), this category was dropped in the revised report. The testing of effectiveness of treatments on "real-world" samples that involve comorbidity is actually very important and should be encouraged.

Examples of Empirically Validated Treatments

Using the criteria described above, the task force members reviewed the treatment outcome literature to arrive at a list of examples of treatments that were supported by scientific evidence. The updated list of treatments is given in Table 1.2. Although many of the examples within the list are described in terms of the "brand-name" labels (e.g., behavior therapy) that are used to generally characterize different psychotherapies, these examples are not meant to convey that all subvariants within the "brand name" (e.g., all types of behavior therapy) are considered effective for the particular problem specified. On the contrary, the basis for inclusion of a treatment in the list is the existence of a treatment manual that was used in the supporting efficacy studies, and it is these specific forms of treatment that have been judged to be efficacious.

The specific forms of treatments contained within the list of empirically validated treatments will not be discussed here, other than to say that various forms of cognitive and behavioral treatments predominate, because other chapters within this volume focus on specific treatments for different patient populations. Clearly, a large percentage of the efficacy studies that have been conducted have involved cognitive-behavioral treatments. Later in this chap-ter, I will return to the issue of the status of some of the treatment modalities

TABLE 1.2   Examples of Empirically Validated Treatments

Well-Established Treatments

ANXIETY AND STRESS:

    Cognitive-behavioral therapy for panic disorder with and without agoraphobia

    Cognitive-behavioral therapy for generalized anxiety disorder

    Group cognitive-behavioral therapy for social phobia

    *Exposure treatment for agoraphobia

    *Exposure treatment for social phobia

    Exposure and response prevention for obsessive-compulsive disorder

    *Stress inoculation training for coping with stressors

    Systematic desensitization for simple phobia

DEPRESSION:

    Cognitive therapy for depression

    Interpersonal therapy for depression

HEALTH PROBLEMS:

    *Behavior therapy for headache

    *Cognitive-behavioral therapy for irritable bowel syndrome

    *Cognitive-behavioral therapy for chronic pain

    *Cognitive-behavioral therapy for bulimia

    Interpersonal therapy for bulimia

PROBLEMS OF CHILDHOOD:

    *Behavior modification for enuresis

    Parent training programs for children with oppositional behavior

MARITAL DISCORD:

    Behavioral marital therapy

SEXUAL DYSFUNCTION:

    Behavior therapy for female orgasmic dysfunction and male erectile dysfunction

OTHER:

    Family education programs for schizophrenia

    Behavior modification for developmentally disabled individuals

    Token economy programs

Probably Efficacious Treatments

ANXIETY:

      Applied relaxation for panic disorder

      *Applied relaxation for generalized anxiety disorder

      *Exposure treatment for post-traumatic stress disorder (PTSD)

      *Exposure treatment for simple phobia

      *Stress inoculation training for PTSD

      *Group exposure and response prevention for obsessive-compulsive disorder

      *Relapse prevention program for obsessive-compulsive disorder

CHEMICAL ABUSE AND DEPENDENCE:

      *Behavior therapy for cocaine abuse

      *Brief dynamic therapy for opiate dependence

      *Cognitive-behavioral therapy for benzodiazepine withdrawal in panic disorder patients

DEPRESSION:

      *Brief dynamic therapy

      *Cognitive therapy for geriatric patients

      Psychoeducational treatment

      *Reminiscence therapy for geriatric patients

      *Self-control therapy

HEALTH PROBLEMS:

      *Behavior therapy for childhood obesity

      *Group cognitive-behavioral therapy for bulimia

MARITAL DISCORD:

      Emotionally focused couples therapy

      *Insight-oriented marital therapy

PROBLEMS OF CHILDHOOD:

      Behavior modification of encopresis

      *Family anxiety management training for anxiety disorders

OTHER:

      Behavior modification for sex offenders

      Dialectical behavior therapy for borderline personality disorder

      Habit reversal and control techniques

NOTE: The asterisks denote new or changed entries relative to the original task force report (Task Force, 1995).

(e.g., psychodynamic, family) that have been subjected to far fewer tests of efficacy.

Recommendations

Although the task force report made a number of recommendations related to the education of practitioners (through continuing education programs) and the public, I will focus on the central recommendations made in regard to pre- and postdoctoral clinical training.

The first recommendation was not specific to training but would affect training as well as all other recommendations. This recommendation was that a complete list of empirically supported treatments be established and updated as new evidence is accumulated. This recommendation was pursued by another Division 12 task force chaired by Peter Nathan. The end result was a scholarly edited volume (labeled *A Guide to Treatments That Work;* Nathan & Gorman, 1998). (It should be noted that this work was not published by, or specifically endorsed by, APA because there were legal concerns about a professional organization's implicitly endorsing certain treatments but not others.)

With regard to clinical training, the first step in formulating recommendations was to understand the extent to which doctoral program and clinical internship training programs were already focusing on empirically validated treatment. Accordingly, the task force undertook national surveys of training programs (both doctoral and internships). The full results of these surveys are given in Crits-Christoph, Frank, Chambless, Brody, and Karp (1995). In brief, the results of the surveys indicated that empirically supported treatments are given substantial attention in most training programs but that considerable variability across training programs is evident. Of the 167 directors of APA-approved clinical training programs that responded to the survey (81% of such programs), the average treatment within the list of empirically validated treatments created by the task force was included in didactic courses in 46% (range 0% to 96%) of doctoral programs, and the average treatment was included in practica for 44% (range 0% to 92%) of the programs. However, 22% of the programs provided didactic coverage for less than 25% of the empirically validated treatments within the list. In regard to internships, few programs actually required that interns become competent practitioners of empirically supported therapies, although the majority of programs provided formal supervision in several empirically supported therapies. These findings suggested that although many programs are teaching empirically validated treatments, there is also room for improvement in the attention given to empirically supported treatments for at least one in five APA-approved programs and many internships.

The main task force recommendation with regard to doctoral programs was that training in empirically validated treatments be made a high-priority issue for APA site visitors involved in the accreditation of such programs. This would be accomplished via examination of coverage of empirically supported treatments in the assigned reading for courses. Clinical supervisors and students could be interviewed to determine the amount of exposure to empirically validated treatments within practica.

For clinical internships, a somewhat stronger recommendation was made in that APA site visitors of internships were enjoined to make training in empirically validated treatments a criterion for APA accreditation. More specifically, it was recommended that every intern be trained to competence in at least one empirically validated treatment.

The APA Committee on Accreditation was responsive to the thrust of the task force recommendations. The February 1995 version of the *Guidelines and Principles for Accreditation of Programs in Professional Psychology* (Office on Program Consultation, 1995) contained the following statements regarding the kind of competence that students would be expected to acquire and demonstrate: "diagnosing or defining problems through psychological assessment and measurement, and formulating and implementing intervention strategies (including training in empirically supported procedures)" and, with regard to practica, "plac[ing] students in settings that . . . provide a wide range of training and educational experiences though applications of empirically supported interventions procedures" (p. 7). Similarly, with regard to internships, the guidelines read that "the program requires that all interns demonstrate an intermediate to advanced level of professional psychological skills, abilities, proficiencies, competencies and knowledge in the areas of . . . theories and methods of assessment and diagnosis, and effective intervention (including empirically supported treatments)" (p. 7).

Reactions to the Task Force Report

The task force report has thus far generated considerable interest. In addition to numerous presentations and discussions of the issues raised in the task force report at professional conferences, several published comments on the report have appeared or are forthcoming. Articles on the task force report were published in the APA *Monitor* (Sanderson, 1995) and the *Independent Practitioner* (Kovacs, 1995). A critique of the task force report by Garfield (1996) appeared in *Clinical Psychology: Science and Practice* with several commentaries. The journal *Psychotherapy Research* published a special issue on empirically validated treatments (Elliot, 1998), as did the *Journal of Consulting and Clinical Psychology* (Kendall & Chambless, 1998). Kovacs (1995) strongly criticized the report in the *Independent Practitioner,* with a condensed version in *AAP Advance* (the newsletter of the Association for the Advancement of Psychology; Kovacs, 1996). A number of critiques of the task force report appeared in the newsletter of the Clinical Section of the Canadian Psychological Association (McMullen, 1995; Pyke, 1995; Steffy, 1995).

A variety of issues have been raised by critics of the task force report and recommendations. Many of these concerns were actually anticipated within the original report in the report's epilogue and have also been discussed in commentaries (see Chambless, 1996; Crits-Christoph, 1996). The intention here is to review and provide some further discussion of the central issues raised in reaction to the task force report, particularly in terms of how these issues bear on the question of how science might inform training and clinical practice.

CAN WE DRAW ANY CONCLUSIONS
FROM THE RESEARCH LITERATURE?

Many of the criticisms of the task force report reduce to a belief that it is impossible or premature to draw any conclusions from the existing literature on the efficacy of psychosocial treatments. I will address this topic first at a broad level and then in terms of some specific methodological issues.

The Relation of Science to Practice

Following from the Boulder model of scientist-practitioner, most clinical psychologists certainly believe that research should influence practice. In fact, as reviewed in the updated task force report (Chambless et al., 1996), psychologists have an ethical responsibility to use, where possible, treatments that work. Klerman (1984), in discussing a proposed public policy in regard to psychotherapy, stated this issue strongly: "Only . . . interventions with demonstrated efficacy, safety, and efficiency should be supported financially, programatically, or educationally" (p. 348). However, even if one adopts such a policy in principle, differences emerge among psychologists in the interpretation of the existing research literature on particular substantive issues and in the process of translating research into practice.

One particular concern that is often expressed is the overreliance on randomized clinical trials as the standard for determining which treatments are efficacious. There has been extensive discussion of some of the problems of the clinical trial methodology as applied to psychotherapy, including problems of attrition and the nature of appropriate control conditions. Despite the problems with the clinical trial methodology applied to psychotherapy, this methodology has been and continues to be the overwhelming guiding approach to decisions about efficacy. Recent practice guidelines for the treatment of depression published by the American Psychiatric Association (1993) and the Agency for Health Care Policy and Research (AHCPR, 1993) were substantially influenced (particularly the AHCPR guidelines) by the clinical trials literature. It seems likely that this reliance on clinical trials, despite the inherent problems, is related to the lack of compelling rationale for basing such treatment policy recommendations on other scientific methodologies. The task force attempted to recognize the importance of other methodologies through the acknowledgment of single-case experiments as important. It remains incumbent on proponents of other approaches to the question of treatment efficacy (e.g., quasi-experimental designs) to build a compelling rationale for their use in treatment policy decisions. Even if such alternative methodologies gain wider acceptance, it may be a considerable time before enough studies have been done with these methodologies to affect policy issues related to type of treatment beyond the influence of the clinical trials methodology. Of course, other types of studies, such as quasi-experiments, can influence policy decisions related to other aspects of treatment (e.g., length) independent of the type of treatment.

Therapist and Client Variability

Several writers have questioned the focus on treatments within the task force report, given that therapist and client factors are likely to be important determinants of psychotherapy outcome (Garfield, 1996; Pyke, 1995; Steffy, 1995). Although therapist variance appears significant in more naturalistic studies, there is meta-analytic evidence that the use of treatment manuals decreases therapist variance considerably (Crits-Christoph et al., 1991). Crits-Christoph (1996) recently reanalyzed the data from the earlier meta-analysis to examine this issue directly: Studies that did not use a treatment manual had 13% of the outcome variance on average attributable to therapist differences; studies that did use a manual evidenced only 4% of outcome variance due to therapist differences. Monte Carlo simulation studies (Crits-Christoph & Mintz, 1991) have made it clear that this rather low level of therapist variance when manuals are used is not likely to be a major problem for the interpretation of treatment comparisons.

It should be clear that stating that therapist variance can be minimized in research studies is not the same as claiming that all clinicians or trainees who use a treatment manual will achieve the same positive outcomes. Many factors, including the selection of trainees, amount of training, quality of supervision, criteria for certifying a therapist as competent, and client factors, will have an impact on subsequent outcomes obtained by the trainee or experienced clinician. However, given the multitude of variables that can affect outcome, it would seem all the more important that professional organizations such as APA provide some guidance to doctoral programs about training in treatment methods that have been shown to be efficacious. By disseminating effective treatment methods, the benefits of psychotherapy to the public can be increased despite the moderating effects of other factors that may be more difficult to regulate directly.

The necessary reduction of therapist variance for treatment comparisons should also not be misunderstood as a claim that therapist variance in itself should not be studied. As part of the process of developing a new treatment package, the study of therapist variance as it naturally occurs may be a very useful strategy for identifying therapy processes that produce positive outcomes. Once identified, these therapy processes can then be put into a manual and studied experimentally.

With regard to client factors, an important distinction should be made between client factors that predict outcome across treatment types (main effects for client factors) and factors that predict differential outcome depending on treatment type (interactions of client factors and treatment types). Surprisingly few main-effect client factors show up consistently in the research literature (Garfield, 1994). Even if such main-effect predictors do emerge, they do not necessarily invalidate the results of treatment comparisons. As long as treatment groups are relatively equated on such factors, interpretation of treatment results can be made.

The study of client factors that interact with treatment type, also known as aptitude-by-treatment-interactions (ATI) research, has received considerable interest of late (Beutler, 1991). The task force initially made no statements about such ATI research because of the limited results available so far in the research literature. However, the updated task force report, though concluding that it was premature to make any recommendations from ATI research, provided a brief overview of some of the most promising findings emerging from such research and established some initial criteria for identifying ATI findings of note. More information on ATI research is given in Chapter 3 of this volume. When adequate research on client factors interacting with treatment methods exists, appropriately qualified treatment recommendations can be made. In the meantime, without any scientific basis for making recommendation regarding client factors, the best we can do is to recommend treatments with proven efficacy and allow therapists to refer clients or change the treatment if the recommended treatment does not work for a particular client.

Relationship Factors

It has been often stated that the lack of outcome differences found between psychotherapies is evidence for the power of "nonspecific" factors such as the quality of the therapeutic alliance. Indeed, a growing body of literature has tended to support the hypothesis that a favorable therapeutic alliance is associated with good outcome. In one meta-analysis, for example, Horvath and Symonds (1991) found that the average correlation of the therapeutic alliance with outcome was .26. Assuming causality of alliance to outcome, which is not actually determined in these studies, the fact that the therapeutic alliance is an important variable in many studies does not negate the establishment of a list of empirically supported treatments. Several issues are germane here.

First, it is not the case, as Garfield (1996) assumed, that factors such as the therapeutic alliance are overlooked in treatment manuals. Many of the manuals on brief dynamic therapy, for example, specifically include facilitation of the therapeutic alliance as one of the central techniques of the therapy. In terms of cognitive-behavioral treatments, Beck's cognitive therapy (see Beck & Emery, 1985, pp. 173-175) explicitly acknowledges and discusses the role of the therapeutic relationship as a necessary factor for successful treatment.

A second issue relates to a relative comparison of the importance of relationship versus technique factors. A common view is that because reviews of treatments often conclude that there are no differences between active treatments (e.g., Luborsky, Singer, & Luborsky, 1975; Smith & Glass, 1977), and because the alliance predicts outcome consistently, the relationship factors are more potent than the technique factors. However, the more appropriate comparison would be between effect sizes for treatment and control groups, not between effect sizes for active treatments versus effect sizes for relationship factors. Chambless (1996) cited agoraphobia treatment data in which the effect size for the treatment control group comparison was 57% of the outcome variance, whereas the alliance explained 9% of outcome variance.

Correlational studies of techniques in psychotherapy have also increasingly yielded positive results. For example, Crits-Christoph, Cooper, and Luborsky (1988) found that the accuracy of therapists' interventions predicted outcome more strongly than the therapeutic alliance. Barber, Crits-Christoph, and Luborsky (1996) found that the quality of expressive (exploratory) intervention in brief dynamic therapy significantly predicted outcome, controlling for the alliance and for the influence of prior symptomatic change. Within cognitive therapy, DeRubeis and Feeley (1990) found that the use of concrete cognitive-behavioral techniques predicted outcome but that the alliance was more a function of previous improvement and did not predict subsequent improvement.

The above is not to say the alliance is unimportant; on the contrary, it clearly is one important factor. Under many circumstances (certain treatments with certain client types), however, other aspects of the treatment package may have a greater impact on outcome than the alliance does. Outcome is multiply determined; the existence of one factor does not negate the role of others. By focusing on one factor (i.e., treatment), the task force was not stating that all other factors that might predict outcome are unimportant. As long as these other factors do not directly confound the treatment-condition-versus-control-condition comparison, treatment effects can be interpreted, and treatment recommendations can be made.

Though it is certainly true that more research needs to be done on client, therapist, and relationship factors in psychotherapy, it is not necessary to identify all of the potential predictors of treatment response to an efficacious treatment before recommending its dissemination. Rosenthal (1990) has described how the psychotherapy field is very conservative about its findings even though the effect sizes generally found for treatment-versus-control comparisons for psychotherapy are often much larger than effects found for other medical treatments. Even though all sources of outcome variance have not yet been identified, the effect sizes for psychotherapy treatments can translate into real public health benefits. For such public health purposes, it is often preferable to act on imperfect data. As further research confirms the role of additional factors predicting outcome, there can be dissemination of appropriate qualifications of when the treatment is most effective and when it is least effective. With regard to psychotherapy treatments, treatment manuals would need to be updated to account for such findings.

Problems With Treatment Manuals

Two very serious but common misunderstandings about the nature and application of treatment manuals are relevant. The first misunderstanding is the notion that treatment manuals are all lockstep, session-by-session, inflexible "cookbooks." Whereas some treatment manuals are highly specific guides to therapist behavior at each step of treatment, the degree to which treatment manuals reach such a level of specificity depends partly on the type of treatment and partly on the particular client problem of interest. More behaviorally oriented treatments lend themselves to a step-by-step approach. A cookbook approach is also more likely when there is greater specificity of the client problem, particularly when the problem is reflected in a single overt behavior or symptom. For example, panic control therapy (Craske & Barlow, 1993) is codified in a highly specific way. This treatment is more behavioral and addresses a highly specific client problem (panic attacks). However, the majority of commonly used treatment manuals are not cookbooks. These treatment manuals are generally characterized by three elements: (a) individualized case formulation, (b) a rather large set of techniques within the package, and (c) some degree of flexible application of the techniques. Most of the cognitive therapy treatment manuals by Beck and colleagues (e.g., Beck & Emery, 1985; Beck, Rush, Shaw, & Emery, 1979), though having a general format for topics to cover in the course of treatment, allow individualized case formulation and flexible use of techniques depending on what is most appropriate to the patient. Psychodynamic treatment manuals also allow for individualized case formulation and flexible application of techniques, with a general outline for how a course of brief dynamic therapy would typically unfold. Interpersonal therapy manuals (e.g., Klerman et al., 1984) actually consist of techniques, including supportive therapy, behavior therapy, and Sullivanian therapy, with flexible application. Thus, although a greater degree of specificity with regard to therapist actions in each session may be of value, particularly in the training of therapists, many treatment manuals have been sensitive to the clinical need to retain flexibility given the diversity of client problems and characteristics that must be taken into account with a particular case. Another reason that clinical flexibility is required is that clients' presenting target complaints often change after a few sessions (Sorenson, Gorsuch, & Mintz, 1985). However, the fact that presenting problems change does not invalidate a decision to initiate treatment targeted to the first presenting problem. In fact, it is likely that often new problems are brought into therapy because of the success of the initial treatment with the presenting problem (e.g., after initial depressive symptoms have alleviated, a client might focus more on interpersonal problems).

The second major misunderstanding about treatment manuals is the false assumption by some that in clinical practice such manuals would need to be rigidly adhered to by the therapist regardless of the special circumstances and issues that might arise with a given client. No one has ever intended treatment manuals to compromise quality of service by preventing therapists from using their clinical judgment with a particular case. This misunderstanding has been so common that the updated task force report addressed it directly: "This list does not substitute for educators' and practitioners' own decisions about what is the most appropriate treatment for a given client" (Chambless et al., 1996, p. 5). If clinicians ultimately can use their own judgment, what is the value of a treatment manual? The point is that it is better to be aware of (and trained in) a treatment manual that has been shown to produce good results with a specific patient problem than not to know anything about the efficacious treatment approach and be left with treating such patient problems only with techniques that are less efficacious or are untested. Thus, the thrust of the task force recommendations can only increase clinicians' options and enhance (on average) client outcomes, rather than decreasing the likelihood of positive outcomes through inflexible application of the approaches.

Despite the obvious need to retain clinical judgment as the ultimate decision basis, there is accumulating evidence that an "anything goes," unstructured treatment approach may not be optimal. Chambless (1996) cited data from an agoraphobia clinic in which the effects of a structured time-limited treatment were compared to those of ongoing therapy in which clinicians did whatever they thought best. The outcomes of the structured program were far superior at a 6-month evaluation, despite the therapists' own feelings that the structured program was too limiting.

Another study (Schulte, Kunzel, Pepping, Schulte-Bahrenberg, 1992) directly compared standardized therapy (exposure therapy plus retraining of self-verbalizations) with individualized therapy for patients with a *DSM-III* (*Diagnostic and Statistical Manual of Mental Disorders,* 3rd ed.; American Psychiatric Association, 1990) diagnosis of a phobia. The individualized therapy allowed the therapist to design an individual treatment plan for each patient, using any therapeutic method commonly used in cognitive or behavior therapy. The investigators hypothesized that the individualized approach would be more successful, but the standardized approach was superior.

Certainly, as clinicians, we can all remember cases in which flexibility and use of a range of techniques were important. Such flexibility is likely to be especially important with a subset of patients who have complex problems. But we must also acknowledge that we are human: that some of us might be distracted, tired, motivated by the financial gain of therapy, or attracted to certain forms of intervention because they are interesting to us rather than the most efficacious. A more structured approach has the benefits of keeping a therapist on target. A structured approach in combination with clinical judgment about when to deviate from the approach would seem to have the potential to keep therapists on target but not overly rigid to the extent of adhering to treatment that is not addressing the patient's needs and problems.

The Predominance of Cognitive and Behavioral Treatments

One concern that has been expressed is that, because cognitive and behavioral treatments predominated in the list of empirically validated therapies given in the task force report, the report was biased in favor of such cognitive and behavioral treatments. Indeed, some have even seen the report as an attempt by cognitive-behaviorally oriented psychologists to impose their perspective on the field. There is no denying that the psychotherapy arena consists of various factions and that some advocates of particular approaches are overzealous about the success of their own preferred treatment modality. Such overzealousness potentially leads to bias in the design, conduct, or interpretation of the results of research studies. For example, several authors have documented a relation between the allegiance of investigators and the results of treatment outcome research (Luborsky, Diguer, Schweizer, & Johnson, 1996). However, it seems likely that the process engaged in by the Division 12 Task Force will tend to reduce, not increase, the opportunity for such biases to influence scientific developments in psychotherapy. By establishing some criteria for categories of "well-established" and "probably efficacious," the task force provides an objective standard for consideration of any treatment modality.

Although cognitive-behavioral treatments predominate on the current list, one concern raised has been that the task force criteria are lenient and that as different psychotherapies are investigated they will all successfully meet the criteria for efficacy, leading to the politically popular but scientifically unsatisfying "Dodo Bird" verdict originally described by Luborsky et al. (1975): "Everyone has won and all must have prizes." There are several responses to this concern. First, it is unlikely that a very large number (e.g., 400) of psychotherapies will meet criteria for a specific client problem. Although in the history of psychotherapy a very large number of treatments may have been described at one time or another, only about 10 or so general types (e.g., dynamic, behavioral, cognitive, family, humanistic, Rogerian) are practiced by the vast majority of practitioners (Jensen, Bergin, & Greaves, 1990). Second, there is nothing inherently problematic about many psychotherapies' reaching established criteria for efficacy. In psychopharmacology, for example, a relative large number of antidepressant medications have received FDA approval. The large number of "approved" medications is actually seen as an asset, increasing the clinician's options. Last, nothing would prevent future committees from tightening the criteria so that if one (or more) treatment had been demonstrated to be robustly better than other treatments for a given client problem, even if all treatments met the more lenient criteria, only the treatment(s) that was superior would be recommended, cutting down on the total number of recommended treatments. This, of course, would be the logical evolution to a process that was concerned with identifying the "best" treatments.

Psychodynamic and Other
Underresearched Treatments

The relative lack of research that meets the task force criteria for dynamic therapy, as well as other modalities such as family therapy, is particularly important given the common use of these approaches in clinical practice. Jensen et al. (1990), in a survey of over 600 practitioners (psychologists, psychiatrists, and social workers), concluded that psychodynamic therapy was the most influential orientation in practice. Although Jensen et al. (1990) found that at first glance an eclectic orientation appeared most common, when eclectic practitioners were queried about the primary modality that underlay their eclectic orientation, the majority of them stated that a psychodynamic approach was the most frequently used in their practice. Because of the prevalence of psychodynamic treatment in practice, there has been particular concern that no psychodynamic treatments reached the status of "well-established" treatment and that only three reached the status of "probably efficacious" (brief dynamic therapy for opiate addiction, brief dynamic therapy for depression, and insight-oriented marital therapy). However, interpersonal therapy, which is a close cousin to many forms of psychodynamic therapy, reached the "well-established" list for depression and bulimia.

One of the problems has been that until recently (see Barber & Crits-Christoph, 1995), psychodynamic therapies were seen as general treatments and not as treatments for specific problems or disorders. Moreover, only a limited number of psychodynamic treatment manuals have been published. Examination of studies of manual-guided dynamic therapy included within meta-analytic reviews by Anderson and Lambert (1995) and Crits-Christoph (1992) revealed few studies in which dynamic therapy was targeted to a specific patient problem. Of 11 studies of manual-guided dynamic therapy contained within these reviews, 2 used mixed samples and 3 used samples not traditionally thought to be appropriate for dynamic therapy (substance abuse). No two studies have been performed using the same target client problem, with the exception of two studies on opiate addiction by the same investigators. Several studies were performed without adequate preliminary development work (e.g., no selection, training, certification, or competence monitoring) of the dynamic therapy and without adequate involvement of dynamic therapy researchers.

Despite the limited number of studies of dynamic therapy that conform to the criteria established by the task force, it is worth noting that, in general, brief dynamic therapy appears to be efficacious. Anderson and Lambert (1995) reported effect sizes (Cohen's d) of .71 in comparison to wait-list controls, .34 relative to minimal treatments, and .03 relative to other active treatments. There was no evidence that brief dynamic therapy was better, or worse, than other treatments such as cognitive-behavioral therapy. Whereas this evidence is supportive about the general effects of brief dynamic therapy, we cannot generalize these results to the treatment of all client problems and disorders. Would brief dynamic therapy be an efficacious treatment of obsessive-compulsive disorder or panic disorder? These studies have yet to be done, so no conclusions can be offered at this time.

CONCLUSION

Although the limitations of existing data on the efficacy of psychotherapy for different client problems need to be acknowledged, it is not the case that we know nothing. In terms of clinical training and practice, it is important to step back periodically and draw conclusions about what we have learned thus far. At this point, there is empirical evidence that is supportive of the use of a number of psychological interventions. This information needs to be disseminated, particularly so that psychological interventions are not viewed as unvalidated empirically relative to other treatment modalities in the clinical arena, such as pharmacotherapy. This is not to say that all of the answers are in yet or that other factors such as therapist, client, and relationship factors are unimportant. However, for public health purposes, it is often necessary to act on imperfect data. It is likely that there will always be imperfections in the research literature on psychosocial treatments. The cost of waiting until there are no imperfections would be great, both in terms of the reputation of clinical psychology and in terms of public health benefits.

Any set of recommendations concerning specific treatment modalities is likely to be controversial because clinical psychologists have traditionally aligned themselves with one school of thought or another. The fact that a list of treatments meeting certain efficacy criteria can be created, however, is of benefit to all clinical psychologists in that it documents that we have generated a growing empirical base for what we do. Through stating clearly what we do know about psychosocial treatments, it becomes even clearer what we do not know. Thus, an additional benefit of a list of empirically supported treatments is that it can generate further research. In particular, a number of widely used modalities in clinical practice need to be investigated in controlled efficacy trials.

REFERENCES

Agency for Health Care Policy and Research, U.S. Public Health Service. (1993). *Clinical Practice Guideline Number 5. Depression in primary care: Vol. 2. Treatment of major depression.* Rockville, MD: Author.

American Psychiatric Association. (1980). *Diagnostic and statistical manual of mental disorders* (3rd ed.). Washington, DC: Author.

American Psychiatric Association. (1993). Practice guideline for major depressive disorder in adults. *American Journal of Psychiatry, 150*(Suppl.), 1-26.

Anderson, E., & Lambert, M. (1995). Short-term dynamically oriented psychotherapy: A review and meta-analysis. *Clinical Psychology Review, 15,* 503-514.

Barber, J., & Crits-Christoph, P. (1995). *Dynamic therapies for psychiatric disorders (Axis I).* New York: Basic Books.

Barber, J. P., Crits-Christoph, P., & Luborsky, L. (1996). Therapist competence and treatment outcome in dynamic therapy. *Journal of Consulting and Clinical Psychology, 64,* 619-622.

Beck, A. T., & Emery, G. (1985). *Anxiety disorders and phobias: A cognitive perspective.* New York: Basic Books.

Beck, A. T., Rush, A. J., Shaw, B. F., & Emery, G. (1979). *Cognitive therapy of depression.* New York: Guilford.

Beutler, L. E. (1991). Have all won and must all have prizes? Revisiting Luborsky et al.'s verdict. *Journal of Consulting and Clinical Psychology, 59,* 226-232.

Chambless, D. L. (1996). In defense of dissemination of empirically supported psychological interventions. *Clinical Psychology: Science and Practice, 3,* 230-235.

Chambless, D. L., Sanderson, W. C., Shoham, V., Johnson, S. B., Pope, K. S., Crits-Christoph, P., Baker, M., Johnson, B., Woody, S. R., Sue, S., Beutler, L., Williams, D. A., & McCurry, S. (1996). An update on empirically validated therapies. *Clinical Psychologist, 49,* 5-18.

Craske, M. G., & Barlow, D. H. (1993). Panic disorder and agoraphobia. In D. H. Barlow (Ed.), *Clinical handbook of psychological disorders: A step-by-step treatment manual* (2nd ed., pp. 1-47). New York: Guilford.

Crits-Christoph, P. (1992). The efficacy of brief dynamic therapy: Current status and future directions. *American Journal of Psychiatry, 149,* 151-158.

Crits-Christoph, P. (1996). The dissemination of efficacious psychological treatments. *Clinical Psychology: Science and Practice, 3,* 260-263.

Crits-Christoph, P., Baranackie, K., Kurcias, J. S., Beck, A. T., Carroll, K., Perry, K., Luborsky, L., McLellan, A .T., Woody, G. E., Thompson, L., Gallagher, D., & Zitrin, C. (1991). Meta-analysis of therapist effects in psychotherapy outcome studies. *Psychotherapy Research, 1,* 81-91.

Crits-Christoph, P., Cooper, A., & Luborsky, L. (1988). The accuracy of therapists' interpretations and the outcome of dynamic psychotherapy. *Journal of Consulting and Clinical Psychology, 56,* 490-495.

Crits-Christoph, P., Frank, E., Chambless, D., Brody, C., & Karp, J. F. (1995). Training in empirically validated treatments: What are clinical psychology students learning? *Professional Psychology: Research and Practice, 26,* 514-522.

Crits-Christoph, P., & Mintz, J. (1991). Implications of therapist effects for the design and analysis of comparative studies of psychotherapies. *Journal of Consulting and Clinical Psychology, 59,* 20-26.

DeRubeis, R. J., & Feeley, M. (1990). Determinants of change in cognitive therapy for depression. *Cognitive Therapy and Research, 14,* 469-482.

Elliot, R. (Ed.). (1998). The empirically supported treatments controversy [Special issue]. *Psychotherapy, 8*(2).

Garfield, S. L. (1994). Research on client variables in psychotherapy. In A. E. Bergin & S. L. Garfield (Eds.), *Handbook of psychotherapy and behavior change* (4th ed., pp. 190-228). New York: John Wiley.

Garfield, S. L. (1996). Some problems associated with "validated" forms of psychotherapy. *Clinical Psychology: Science and Practice, 3,* 260-263.

Horvath, A. O., & Symonds, D. B. (1991). Relationship between working alliance and outcome in psychotherapy: A meta-analysis. *Journal of Counseling Psychology, 38,* 139-149.

Jensen, J. P., Bergin, A. E., & Greaves, D. W. (1990). The meaning of eclecticism: New survey and analysis of components. *Professional Psychology: Research and Practice, 21,* 124-130.

Kendall, P. C., & Chambless, D. L. (Eds.). (1998). Empirically supported psychological therapies [Special issue]. *Journal of Consulting and Clinical Psychology, 66*(1).

Klerman, G. L. (1984). Psychotherapy and public policy: What does the future hold? In J. B. W. Williams & R. L. Spitzer (Eds.), *Psychotherapy research: Where are we and where should we go?* New York: Guilford.

Klerman, G. L., Weissman, M. M., Rounsaville, B. J., & Chevron, E. S. (1984). *Interpersonal psychotherapy of depression.* New York: Basic Books.

Kovacs, A. (1995). We have met the enemy and he is us! *Independent Practitioner, 15,* 135-137.

Kovacs, A. (1996, Winter). We have met the enemy and he is us! *AAP Advance,* pp. 6, 19, 20, 22.

Luborsky, L., Diguer, L., Schweizer, E., & Johnson, S. (1996, June). *The researcher's allegiance as a "wildcard" in studies comparing the outcomes of treatments.* Paper presented at the meeting of the Society for Psychotherapy Research, Amelia Island, FL.

Luborsky, L., Singer, B., & Luborsky, L. (1975). Comparative studies of psychotherapy: Is it true that "everybody has won and all must have prizes?" *Archives of General Psychiatry, 32,* 995-1008.

McMullen, L. M. (1995, November). Newt, Tammy, and the Task Force: What's happened to common sense and moderation? *Newsletter of the Clinical Section of the Canadian Psychological Association,* pp. 5-7.

Nathan, P. E., & Gorman, J. M. (Eds.). (1998). *A guide to treatments that work.* New York: Oxford University Press.

Office on Program Consultation and Accreditation, Education Directorate. (1995). *Guidelines and principles for accreditation of programs in professional psychology.* Washington, DC: American Psychological Association.

Pyke, S. W. (1995, November). Empirically validated treatments: The baby and the bath water. *Newsletter of the Clinical Section of the Canadian Psychological Association,* pp. 7-11.

Rosenthal, R. (1990). How are we doing in soft psychology? *American Psychologist, 45,* 775-777.

Sanderson, W. C. (1995, March). Which therapies are proven effective? *Monitor,* p. 4.

Schulte, D., Kunzel, R., Pepping, G., & Schulte-Bahrenberg, T. (1992). Tailor-made versus standardized therapy of phobic patients. *Advances in Behavioral Research and Therapy, 14,* 67-92.

Smith, M. L., & Glass, G. V. (1977). Meta-analysis of psychotherapy outcome studies. *American Psychologist, 32,* 752-760.

Sorenson, R. L., Gorsuch, R. L., & Mintz, J. (1985). Moving targets: Patients changing complaints during psychotherapy. *Journal of Consulting and Clinical Psychology, 53,* 49-54.

Steffy, R. A. (1995, November). Some concerns about the listing of "manualized" therapies: Beware the procrustean bed. *Newsletter of the Clinical Section of the Canadian Psychological Association,* pp. 11-13.

Task Force on Promotion and Dissemination of Psychological Procedures. (1995). Training in and dissemination of empirically-validated psychological treatments. *Clinical Psychologist, 48,* 3-23.

2

Scientific Practice Guidelines in a Political, Economic, and Professional Context

STEVEN C. HAYES

Scientifically oriented psychologists are often cautious people, both by nature and by professional training. They learn to take a considered and thoughtful approach to their discipline and its practices. This makes it inherently more difficult for scientific psychologists to organize and to push for needed political and professional outcomes, as compared to more professionally oriented colleagues. But there are times when the circumstances are sufficiently different that the dialectical back and forth that scientific training promotes no longer prevents directed action. Applied scientific psychology seems to be in one of those times regarding scientifically oriented practice guidelines.

Several forces are coming together to make movement on this issue likely. In what follows, I will attempt to discuss the political, economic, and professional forces pushing toward and pulling away from empirically based practice guidelines. I will first discuss four major forces that tend to promote scientific practice guidelines: managed care, advances in applied psychological science, the partnership between industry and scientifically oriented societies and associations, and the competitive interests of mental health guilds.

MANAGED CARE

Managed care has seen tremendous growth in the United States. More than 124 million persons are now covered by private managed behavioral health care plans (Mechanic, 1996). The public sector is rapidly opening up to managed care as well (Frank, McGuire, Notman, & Woodward, 1996), and 37 states either have or are applying for waivers by the U.S. Health Care Financing Administration to place Medicaid patients in managed care (Manderscheid & Henderson, 1996). Managed care is becoming the normative mode of behavioral health care services delivery, and it becomes more so each day (Cummings, 1992; Trabin & Freeman, 1995).

This process of the industrialization of behavioral health care is the linchpin in the development and use of empirically based clinical practice guidelines. At first this may seem surprising. The rise of managed care has been driven by the rapidly increasing cost of health services, and the first major wave of managed-care organizations (MCOs) emphasized cost containment and "supply-side" methods of reducing the utilization of services (Manderscheid & Henderson, 1996; Sobel, 1995). Systems that are controlling costs by delaying or denying needed services would hardly be interested in the development and implementation of empirically based practice guidelines because these steps themselves are costly. Several factors reviewed below have come together, however, to change the managed-care industry. As a result, the modern U.S. health care environment MCOs are developing a financial interest in treatment that is safe, effective, and efficient.

Factors Influencing an Industrialized Health Care System

To understand how changes in the industry are leading to practice guidelines, it is necessary to understand how MCOs compete and win in the marketplace. To see some of the factors involved, an extended analogy seems useful. Suppose a computer manufacturer offers computers for sale to businesses. The value of the product offered is a combination of the capabilities of the machine, its reliability, and its cost. The buying decisions may be made both by middle management (who may, for example, put certain machines on an approved internal list) and by lower-level employees following management guidelines regarding approved machines. Additional purchases depend in part on the satisfaction of employees and management with the machines. Manufacturers can save money by lowering the quality of the product, but if the machines are unreliable, consumer satisfaction begins to go down, repurchases go down (e.g., the business may remove the vendor from the approved list of purchase options), and costs to the manufacturer go up as machines are returned for repair. The trick is to offer capabilities that consumers want, at a lower cost than competitors, but without cutting into quality in a way that reduces competitive and cost advantages.

Managed behavioral health care is an industry, no less than computer hardware, and thus the same forces are at play. MCOs offer health services for a fee. The services offered must be what the consumers want, and the fee charged must be low enough to be competitive with that of other service providers. Buying decisions are made both by employers (who usually put a given MCO on an approved list and pay part of the costs of the coverage) and by employees who want certain kinds of capabilities within a given cost range. Whether patients reenroll depends in part on the satisfaction of the employees and of management with the coverage provided. MCOs can save money by lowering the quality and availability of services, but if the perceived valued goes down, consumer satisfaction begins to go down, reenrollment goes down (e.g., the business may remove the MCO from the approved list of purchase options), and costs to the provider may go up as clients who were not treated effectively continue to demand services for continuing problems. The trick is to offer services that consumers want, at a lower cost than competitors, but without cutting into quality in a way that reduces competitive and cost advantages.

The first generation of managed care was like the early stage of any sudden industrialization within a business sector, whether automobiles, telephones, or frozen food. The computer industry analogy is a good one because industrialization within this sector is still recent enough to be fresh in our minds. In the early stages of industrialization, *vendors proliferate chaotically.* This happened in the computer industry. Firms sprung up overnight literally in garages. Thousands of firms began to offer software and hardware. *Consumers are often confused about the features of the products being offered.* In the computer industry, the capabilities of given machines were initially hard to compare because there was a bewildering array of hardware and software features that varied a great deal from machine to machine. Consumers had a hard time knowing which operating system was better—Commodore Amiga, Apple, Radio Shack, or that newcomer, MS-DOS—and standardized comparison measures did not exist. They could not tell which processor was better, or which bus, or which video card. In the early stages of industrialization, *poor-quality products succeed but then die out.* Some vendors in the computer industry learned that they could use no-name low-quality components and deliver a machine with market appeal and high-performance features. As the poor reliability of these machines became known, however, consumer satisfaction plummeted, and the cost of returns and repairs soared. Companies that abused this strategy folded.

As products become better understood, *both vendors and product lines are consolidated.* The computer industry went through a shake-out. Operating systems fell away. Platforms became standardized. The number of hardware and software manufacturers fell as larger successful firms bought out smaller successful firms and unsuccessful firms died out.

In the mature marketplace, *known firms offer known commodities of known quality, cost, and value.* The computer industry is just entering this phase. A handful or two of manufacturers are major players, offering highly predictable machines, most using name-brand components of known capability, reliability, and cost. The market is stratified into sectors based on combinations of these factors.

The managed-care industry is much earlier in this developmental sequence than is the computer industry, but it is proceeding rapidly. In a fashion typical of industrialization, vendors did indeed proliferate chaotically, and consumers were confused about the features of the products being offered. In November 1996, a Louis Harris poll showed that 55% of the United States had no understanding of what "managed care" meant and that almost half either did not know what health maintenance organizations (HMOs) were or did not know how they operated ("HMOs Remain a Mystery," 1996). The perception was widespread that poor-quality products existed and were succeeding initially, although formal evidence of this is hard to come by. Indeed, even fairly careful controlled studies showed that MCOs reduced costs at no overall decrease in health care quality (see Mechanic, 1996, for a review). It does seem to be widely agreed on, however, that quality was uneven and was not a general emphasis of the early stages of managed care (Manderscheid & Henderson, 1996). These were the features of Generation 1 of managed care (Strosahl, 1996), and many professionals and consumers now virtually identify "managed care" with the attempt to produce profits by the denial of services or the delivery of low-quality services. The managed-care industry is maturing, however, as is evidenced by several factors.

Competitive Costs of Arbitrary
Limits on Services

In mature managed-care environments, arbitrary treatment limits are increasingly being reduced. Over the last 3 years, I have consulted regularly at Group Health Cooperative, for example, the largest managed-care firm in the Northwest region of the United States. Over that period, Group Health has virtually eliminated session caps and other arbitrary limits on behavioral health services.

These caps are coming off in part because both companies and covered individuals do not like them. It irks companies to have to hear the complaints from employees that services have been denied. If the denial of services influences the employee's performance, employers may see possible economic benefit in changing the approved list of providers. In Seattle, for example, Boeing does not approve MCOs with arbitrary session caps on mental health services. Just as important for MCOs, it does little financial good to impose session caps if it means cost shifting or increases in costs due to delayed or denied necessary treatment. Arbitrary service caps thus can impose both a competitive disadvantage for the health care firm and potentially a cost disadvantage.

Shake-Out and Consolidation

Many authors have noted that the behavioral health care industry is undergoing a major shake-out (e.g., Belar, 1995). The statistics on this point are still a bit confusing because the proliferation of small MCOs is also continuing. For example, from 1975 to 1995, the number of HMOs increased from 166 to 600 (Group Health Association of America, 1995). Nevertheless, larger and larger MCOs have clearly resulted from mergers and acquisitions, and firms such as Kaiser-Permanente and Value Behavioral Health are now regional or even national powerhouses with millions of covered lives. The industrialization of health care is like a bucket of agitated water with oil in it—thousands of separate droplets have formed on the surface, but gradually the larger drops are gathering in all the smaller drops.

As this process continues, fewer companies are covering more and more lives, particularly in metropolitan areas. There are economies of scale possible in large managed-care firms, balanced somewhat by the inefficiencies of tendencies toward centralization, bureaucratization, and slowness of de-cision making. Most relevant for our present focus, however, larger plans mean that movement between plans goes down, both because large plans increasingly control important health resources, such as hospitals, and be-cause the statistical probability of movement is almost necessarily less when there are fewer major providers in a given area.

This reduction in movement has important effects. It means a considerable reduction in the cost savings that can be gained by delay and denial of coverage. If a company delays or denies needed treatment today, the person may still be covered months or years later and the costs may be higher tomorrow. To return to our computer analogy, the cost of lower quality occurs in part because machines are sent back to the manufacturer. If that were not true, only eventual low consumer satisfaction would prevent all manufactur-ers from producing poor-quality machines. In the earliest phases of health care industrialization, movement between plans meant that returns for the same problem might not go to the original (poor-quality) provider but to someone else. The cost of poor quality was shifted to someone else. Consid-ering the whole industry, this would tend to increase the costs for all MCOs, but considering one at a time, some MCOs could benefit over the short term.

As cost savings produced by delay and denial go down, the relative importance of cost savings due to other methods goes up. The major alter-native available to MCOs is cost-effective methods of increasing quality of care (Quirk et al., 1995). If services can be delivered that are effective, demands for additional services go down, consumer and employer satisfac-tion goes up, and renewal of coverage goes up. If the treatments are also efficient, the MCO can offer the capabilities that consumers want at a lower cost, but without cutting into quality.

This alternative is viable only if the system can actually identify treatment that is needed, effective, and efficient and can distinguish it from treatment that is unnecessary, ineffective, and inefficient. "Dump and run" is the best strategy, economically speaking, if the only alternative is "mindlessly treat and treat." Science is the best decision system available to identify treatment that is needed, effective, and efficient. It is this nexus that makes managed care the biggest ally of empirically based practice guidelines. Thus, MCOs are increasingly turning to evidence-based health care based on systematic reviews of empirical data (Bero & Rennie, 1995).

Increase in Fully Capitated
and Carve-In Models

HMOs are beginning to win out over preferred-provider organizations (PPOs) (Manderscheid & Henderson, 1996), especially in our larger cities in the United States. PPOs and similar network models usually do not put the provider at financial risk, and there seem to be some resulting inherent inefficiencies. Provider panels, by their very nature, create a unit of analysis that is cut off somewhat from the total health care delivered to a person. If an untreated panic-disordered client shows up in the emergency room for a "heart attack," mental health carve-out firms can hide from those shifted costs. If the person did not receive or was denied mental health treatment, the carve-out firm might have been able to keep its specific costs down, but the costs for the whole system might have gone up. Fully capitated models are inherently more likely to detect cost shifting, and the impact of behavioral health care on primary care costs can be fully managed only when the MCO controls both (Manderscheid & Henderson, 1996). In such an environment, effective and efficient treatment, even if more costly in local dollar terms, can be cheaper in total dollar terms. Conversely, ineffective and inefficient treatment, even if inexpensive in local dollar terms, can be more costly in total dollar terms.

Accreditation and Regulation

Accreditation is increasingly important to managed care. In the United States, the National Committee on Quality Assurance (NCQA) has come from nowhere over the last few years to being an essential component in the competitive position of health care organizations. The lack of NCQA accreditation can affect health care business, and managed care thus cares. If scientifically based standards of care are picked up by NCQA, MCOs will rise to meet that challenge. This could rapidly mean that unreasonable denial of service will threaten an important business necessity.

Formal regulation is also becoming an increasingly important part of the landscape of managed care (Mechanic, 1996). In part because of clear abuses and dramatic tales of woe, and in part because of the powerful political forces that have been hurt by the rise of managed care, legislators are increasingly willing to rein in MCOs. One of the major ways to avoid unreasonable regulation is to show that quality guidelines have been followed.

Accountability

Managed-care companies usually have multiple consumers, including not just individuals but also employers and other payers. Ineffective and inefficient care costs companies money in the form of worsened employee loyalty, job satisfaction, absenteeism, and job performance. Because of this, large corporations especially are beginning to rate HMOs and to encourage employees to select quality plans. Formal measures are being developed of client satisfaction (Marshall, Hays, Sherbourne, & Wells, 1993). Some of the ratings are being done on the basis of how well managed-care firms treat specified disorders, given what the literature suggests. This is recognizably the beginning of practice standards driven from outside the system.

Science and the Economics of Managed Care

By their behavior, many managed-care firms seem to believe that a better method of achieving cost control and competitive success is a serious effort to deliver effective and efficient treatment. This involves a serious effort to triage clients, funneling clients with lesser needs into cheap but effective treatment alternatives (e.g., group, bibliotherapy) and sending high-utilizing clients with treatable and serious conditions into more demanding treatment programs of known effectiveness (Strosahl, 1994). The only way to do all of that *well* is through science. This is the formula through which cost control has become linked to scientific standards of care (Strosahl, 1996). These changes put us at a unique moment in the history of applied scientific psychology because they mean that science is becoming commercially important in this area.

ADVANCES IN APPLIED SCIENCE

If we turned the clock back 20 years, scientific practice guidelines in mental health would be out of the question. The research was still too limited, and the results were still to ambiguous to be useful.

The depth of knowledge needed for completely adequate practice guidelines is impressive. In a recent paper, I listed 13 key questions that I believe practice guidelines need to address in mental health (Hayes, 1995):

- Assessment and Analysis
  1. How are these problems best assessed for purposes of prediction, monitoring, outcomes assessment, and selecting interventions?
  2. Is the specific problem associated with general areas of poorer functioning, and if so, which general outcomes should be measured in addition to specific areas in order to assess the overall effectiveness of treatment?
  3. Are there popular assessment methods that are known to be unreliable or inefficient and that should be put aside?
  4. Is this set of problems best approached as a clear syndrome, or is it known to overlap significantly with other problems?
  5. Do we know the functional processes that are characteristic of this set of problems, and do they overlap with the functional processes that affect other problem sets?
- Intervention
  6. What are the more and the most effective treatments for these problems as measured by Questions 1 and 2? Are there particular ways that these treatments should or should not be delivered (e.g., settings, therapists)?
  7. Are any of these treatments known to be slow-acting, costly, more variable in outcome, difficult to train, or dangerous? Do these characteristics suggest a reranking of those in Question 6?
  8. Are there treatments that are known not to work and should be prohibited, or long-standing or popular treatments that have little or no supportive data and should be used only under extraordinary circumstances in the context of the answer to Question 6?
  9. Can we predict which treatments are most likely to work
     a. With certain clients (e.g., are there clear subtypes of this problem, especially with treatment implications? Do things such as client personality matter? If the problem co-occurs with other problems, does that change which treatments should be used?)?
     b. With certain therapists (e.g., personality types, level of training, orientation)?
     c. In certain settings (e.g., in outpatient settings, in community-based or home-based settings)?
  10. What is known about how best to train therapists to use the treatments listed in response to Questions 6 and 7? How can these treatments be best disseminated?
  11. Why are therapists most likely to use treatments listed in response to Question 8? How can these views or conditions be changed so that these treatments can be put aside?
  12. What is the usual course and outcome of the treatments listed in response to Questions 6 and 7? Can the existing data be used as a guide by third-party payers or as a means of informing clients of likely outcomes?

13. Are there innovative assessment or treatment approaches in this area that, though not yet proven, seem promising? Under what conditions, if any, might they be used? Are there any times that they might be tried first?

In addition to these 13 questions, there are 3 additional questions of importance to the long-term adequacy of practice standards:

14. On the basis of the best available evidence, which theory or set of theories seems currently best able to explain the current data, while being precise and clear in its predictions, clear about its boundary conditions, broad in scope, coherent, useful, and consistent with what is known about these problems from various domains (psychology, biology, sociology, etc.)?

15. What kinds of research projects are most needed to advance the state of knowledge about these problems, as reflected by the ability to answer the preceding 14 questions?

16. In answering each of these questions in a specific instance, what can be said about how best to go about answering such questions in general? In other words, regardless of the specific content (e.g., the specific applied problem), are there certain research methods, sources of information, organizational schemes, and the like that could be used to guide the effort to answer such questions in other areas? Are there other questions that should be included in future lists for the development of adequate practice guidelines?

It is impressive that applied scientific psychology has progressed to the point that it can even seriously consider such a list of questions. In a number of health areas, methods for rating and gathering empirical evidence for clinical practice guidelines are maturing (e.g., Hadorn, Baker, Hodges, & Hicks, 1996). The practice guidelines developed so far in psychology, however, are limited. In psychology, they consist of little else than an approved list of treatments (Chambless et al., 1996). This ultimately will not be adequate, and there are several dangers to the adoption of approved treatment lists as a substitute for adequate practice guidelines.

PARTNERSHIPS BETWEEN INDUSTRY AND SCIENCE-BASED ORGANIZATIONS

A third force promoting the adoption of practice guidelines is the development of partnerships between and among industry and science-based applied behavioral organizations. A fairly militant wing of applied science has developed that is actively pursuing clinical practice guidelines. The American Association for Applied and Preventive Psychology (AAAPP), for example, has developed a guideline initiative (see Hayes, Follette, Dawes, & Grady, 1995, for a book-length treatment of their effort). AAAPP has now joined with the Association for Advancement of Behavior Therapy to develop this initiative further and has held a series of national summits drawing together behavioral science and professional associations with more than 400,000 members and industrial groups with more than 80 million covered lives (Hayes, 1996). This partnership could be tremendously powerful because the MCOs have the need and the professional and scientific associations have the knowledge base. It is very meaningful that the 1996 Banff conference is focused on this topic, especially given the tradition of the Banff conferences' being both science oriented and practice based.

GUILD INTERESTS

Up until quite recently, guild forces have resisted practice guidelines, foreseeing interference and restriction. Guilds have preferred to emphasize the certification of people over procedures, in part because this approach has been shown over the centuries to provide an extremely effective method of enhancing economic success and professional power of particular groups.

The certification of people is the very essence of professional licensure, for example. Licensure defines the group, limits their growth, and confines access to populations, setting, or procedures to them. Thus, for example, psychotherapy was once confined to psychiatry and then to psychology. Hospital admitting privileges have been confined to medicine, including psychiatry, and now psychology and other groups are fighting for these privileges.

The problem with certifying people is that it is an extremely ineffective way of ensuring quality. It is not by accident that although the first meaning of *license* in the dictionary is "lawful permission," the second is "excessive liberty." People with license do sometimes take license. When one's judgment is officially sanctioned, it is but a small step to disconnect judgment from careful and defensible reasoning and base it instead on mere personal preference.

Essentially, what the practice guidelines movement is doing is establishing a list of certified procedures. This is usually dangerous to a guild. For one thing, it opens the process to scrutiny and demystifies the issue at hand. For another, it gives other groups something clear to aim at by showing that this procedure can be done just as well and less expensively. For example, master's-level providers will certainly point out how they too can deliver certified procedures competently. Third, practice guidelines invite regulators to examine the content of professional behavior—a huge threat to guild activities.

The reason that things may be different now is that both the psychology and the psychiatry guilds are fighting for the survival of their members. In both groups, some see practice guidelines as a way to fight effectively.

Psychology is in a difficult spot. It became overcommitted to psychotherapy delivery, largely giving away many hard-won prizes in that process: assessment, career counseling, child development, and so on (Hayes & Heiby, 1996). Then it lost control over the supply of doctoral providers with the advent of the free-standing, tuition-dependent school. Now, as the psychotherapeutic hordes move in, psychology seems to have nothing special to offer and no way to turn down the tap.

But psychology does have something special to offer: a science-based profession. If mental health moves to guidelines-based practice, psychologists are best positioned to develop programs linked to those guidelines, to evaluate these programs, to supervise master's-level providers in these empirically established technologies, and to pick up the pieces when practice guidelines are not enough with complex cases (Belar, 1995; Hayes, Barlow, & Nelson-Grey, in press).

This is the formula that has interested some in the professional wing of organized psychology (Belar, 1995). It just may be possible that practice guidelines will provide a way for psychology to fight for survival.

Psychiatry is already busily developing practice guidelines (Zarin, Pincus, & McIntyre, 1993). Psychiatry sees a guild interest in promoting its view of mental disorders and their treatment, and practice guidelines are a good way to do this.

Ironically, the biggest point of contention between psychology and psychiatry—prescription privileges for psychologists—could help both professions to compromise on a broader approach to the practice standards issue. The push for prescription privileges is just another symptom of the changing role of psychology in the modern health care environment (Hayes & Heiby, 1996). Ironically, the success of psychiatry in establishing a syndromal and even biological model has led others to want access to biological interventions. Scientifically based practice guidelines for psychosocial interventions may provide a partial counterweight because the actual data provide strong support for nonbiological interventions. It is remotely possible that a grand compromise may be fashioned in which psychology backs off from its attempt to gain prescription privileges in exchange for support of practice guidelines that give psychology a clear and defensible role.

We may now have a unique moment in which practice standards are in the interest of both psychiatry and psychology. Practice guidelines will help put doctoral psychologists in the role of program developers, evaluators, supervisors, and trainers, with their direct service delivery focused on cases that require more than the standardized and manualized empirically validated packages or cases in which doctoral-level treatment has been shown to be more effective or efficient (Hayes, 1995). One can envision a day in which HMO accreditation criteria will require scientifically trained psychologists to administer or oversee empirically validated psychosocial treatment programs. All the mental health fields could prosper in such a world.

FORCES RESISTING SCIENTIFIC
PRACTICE GUIDELINES

Not everything is moving in the direction of practice guidelines. These same four forces each have factors that go in the opposite direction. All of these seem worth mentioning.

Proprietary Interests of Managed Care

Many managed-care companies right now have panels of their own staff (especially psychologists and psychiatrists, who, as doctoral providers, have more science training) reading the scientific literature and developing proprietary practice guidelines. Treatment guidelines are being used as proprietary strategies that differentiate managed-care companies. It is not a big step for a corporation to develop rules that ensure consistent quality. This is what corporations do in many areas. But these rules now are held closely within the company or are being sold to smaller companies (Cummings, 1996). Income from the sale of books and manuals linked to proprietary standards is becoming significant, and companies such as PsychCorp or my own company, Context Press, are actively marketing treatment guidelines.

Unfortunately, proprietary guidelines seem unlikely to protect consumers adequately and to change the practice domain consistently and fairly. The worst-case scenario is that proprietary guidelines could result in a status quo that makes nonproprietary guidelines harder to achieve.

Continuing Difficulties in Applied Science

Available science is probably not yet adequate to provide working answers for some questions important to the development of practice guidelines (Manderscheid & Henderson, 1996). For example, we know surprisingly little about how to fit interventions to clients. Our assessment procedures are usually never evaluated against this ultimate purpose of assessment (Hayes, Nelson, & Jarrett, 1987). When they are, they are often found wanting. As a result, most of the early work on standards of practice has focused on syndromes, which are too crude a unit of analysis in many cases. Similarly, we know little about how to train clinicians to do therapy well. I have argued elsewhere (Hayes, 1995) that the artistic component of therapy needs to be covered by what I have termed *process standards:* standards that specify the conditions under which effective behavior can be learned by experience and shaping. These are distinct from the more familiar type of *content standards,* which denote the description of effective and ineffective behavioral topographies. An easy example of a process rule might be a rule that specifies that certain kinds of information will be gathered about clients or that the impact of interventions will be continuously evaluated. This is not a topographical standard because doing these things does not itself constitute effective psychological practice. Rather, doing these things makes it more likely that effective behavior will be shaped—though no scientific research has yet examined this empirically.

Proprietary Interests of Guilds and Science-Based Organizations

In the present environment, each discipline and each society is still thinking too narrowly. The American Psychiatric Association wants its guidelines (Zarin et al., 1993) to be adopted by managed-care groups or NCQA, but naturally these guidelines emphasize pharmacotherapy. If each professional group pursues an individual course, we will run the risk of multiple sets of practice guidelines. But for scientific standards of care to matter, a more unified approach is needed.

THE WAY AHEAD

The bottom line is this: In the current situation, the economic interests of the industrialized health care sector and of core constituencies are linked to progress in the development of scientifically based practice guidelines. Unfortunately, managed scientific societies, individual producers, and trade associations all still see some benefit in guidelines that are local, controlled, or proprietary. Yet for guidelines to do real good, they need to be global, open, and nonproprietary.

The solution to this could come from government, but government efforts in this area are too slow, cumbersome, and politically troublesome. The Agency for Health Care Policy Research (AHCPR) has labored for years to produce unwieldy guidelines tomes (e.g., those on depression; see AHCPR, 1993a, 1993b). It ended up having Congress reduce its funding because of the political heat that this process produced.

The best alternative seems to be a process that will pull the various science groups, professional organizations, consumer groups, health care industry associations, and other stakeholders together behind cooperative efforts, trading off financial or other narrow gains for the larger good that real practice guidelines would do. Cooperation will be difficult, but the need is there. This is the model being pursued by AAAPP and the Association for Advancement of Behavior Therapy (Hayes, 1996), but it is not yet clear if it will be successful.

Ironically, this does not mean that particular groups or societies should slow or stop their individual initiatives. To the contrary, ultimate cooperation becomes more likely as individual societies forge ahead in the short term. The worst thing we could do is to stop and wait. This is because we very much need good models of practice guidelines. We need to learn how to form panels, what questions to ask of the experts, how to keep the process flexible and open, how to change guidelines, and how to present guidelines to practitioners and consumers.

But as we move ahead, we should do so with an admission of the difficulty of the task, with humility about our current efforts, with determination to make real progress, and with openness to the efforts of others. We should be ready to set aside any individual achievements that we make along this road in the service of the larger goal, which is shared and collective.

I conclude my chapter where it began, with this simple observation: There are times when an issue is so important that members of a discipline need to choose a direction and push ahead even though the future cannot be seen clearly. Applied scientific psychology is in one of those times. And scientific practice guidelines are the issue.

REFERENCES

Agency for Health Care Policy Research Depression Guideline Panel. (1993a). *Depression in primary care: Vol. 1. Detection and diagnosis* (AHCPR Pub. No. 93-0550). Rockville, MD: Author.

Agency for Health Care Policy Research Depression Guideline Panel. (1993b). *Depression in primary care: Vol. 2. Treatment of major depression* (AHCPR Pub. No. 93-0551). Rockville, MD: Author.

Belar, C. D. (1995). Collaboration in capitated care: Challenges for psychology. *Professional Psychology: Research and Practice, 26,* 139-146.

Bero, L., & Rennie, D. (1995). The Cochrane Collaboration: Preparing, maintaining, and disseminating systematic reviews of the effects of health care. *Journal of the American Medical Association, 274,* 1935-1938.

Chambless, D. L., Sanderson, W. C., Shoham, V., Johnson, S. B., Pope, K. S., Crits-Christoph, P., Baker, M., Johnson, B., Woody, S. R., Sue, S., Beutler, L., Williams, D. A., & McCurry, S. (1996). An update on empirically validated therapies. *Clinical Psychologist, 49,* 5-18.

Cummings, N. A. (1992). The future of psychotherapy: Society's charge to professional psychology. *Independent Practitioner, 12,* 126-130.

Cummings, N. (1996). Now we are facing the consequences: A conversation with Nick Cummings. *Scientist Practitioner, 6*(1), 9-13.

Frank, R. G., McGuire, T. G., Notman, E. H., & Woodward, R. M. (1996). Developments in Medicaid managed behavioral health care. In R. W. Manderscheid & M. A. Sonnenschein (Eds.), *Mental health, United States, 1996* (pp. 138-155). Washington, DC: Substance Abuse and Mental Health Services Administration.

Group Health Association of America. (1995). *Sourcebook on HMO utilization data.* Washington, DC: Author.

Hadorn, D. C., Baker, D., Hodges, J. S., & Hicks, N. (1996). Rating the quality of evidence for clinical practice guidelines. *Journal of Clinical Epidemiology, 49,* 749-754.

Hayes, S. C. (1995). What do we want from psychological standards and psychological practice? In S. C. Hayes, W. Follette, R. D. Dawes, & K. Grady (Eds.), *Scientific standards of psychological practice: Issues and recommendations* (pp. 49-66). Reno, NV: Context.

Hayes, S. C. (1996). You are not one of us: You are the enemy. *Scientist Practitioner, 6*(1), 12.

Hayes, S. C., Barlow, D. H., & Nelson-Grey, R. O. (in press). *The scientist practitioner: Research and accountability in the age of managed care* (2nd ed.). New York: Allyn & Bacon.

Hayes, S. C., Follette, W., Dawes, R. D., & Grady, K. (Eds.). (1995). *Scientific standards of psychological practice: Issues and recommendations.* Reno, NV: Context.

Hayes, S. C., & Heiby, E. (1996). Psychology's drug problem: Do we need a fix or should we just say no? *American Psychologist, 51,* 198-206.

Hayes, S. C., Nelson, R. O., & Jarrett, R. (1987). Treatment utility of assessment: A functional approach to evaluating the quality of assessment. *American Psychologist, 42,* 963-974.

HMOs remain a mystery, poll says. (1996, November 11). *Reno Gazette Journal,* p. 7A.

Manderscheid, R. W., & Henderson, M. J. (1996). The growth and direction of managed care. In R. W. Manderscheid & M. A. Sonnenschein (Eds.), *Mental health, United States, 1996* (pp. 17-26). Washington, DC: Substance Abuse and Mental Health Services Administration.

Marshall, G. N., Hays, R. D., Sherbourne, C. D., & Wells, K. B. (1993). The structure of patient satisfaction with outpatient medical care. *Psychological Assessment, 5,* 477-483.

Mechanic, D. S. (1996). Key policy considerations for mental health in the managed care era. In R. W. Manderscheid & M. A. Sonnenschein (Eds.), *Mental health, United States, 1996* (pp. 1-16). Washington, DC: Substance Abuse and Mental Health Services Administration.

Quirk, M. P., Strosahl, K., Todd, J. L., Fitzpatrick, W., Casey, M. T., Hennessy, S., & Simon, G. (1995). Quality and customers: Type 2 change in mental health delivery within health care reform. *Journal of Mental Health Administration, 22,* 414-425.

Sobel, D. (1995). Rethinking medicine: Improving health outcomes with cost effective psychosocial interventions. *Psychosomatic Medicine, 57,* 234-244.

Strosahl, K. (1994). Entering the new frontier of managed mental health care: Gold mines and land mines. *Cognitive and Behavioral Practice, 1,* 5-23.

Strosahl, K. (1996). Three "gold mine-land mine" themes in generation two of health care reform. *Behavior Therapist, 19,* 52-54.

Trabin, T., & Freeman, M. A. (1995). *Managed behavioral healthcare: History, models, strategic challenges and future course.* Tiburon, CA: CentraLink.

Zarin, D. A., Pincus, H. A., & McIntyre, J. S. (1993). Practice guidelines. *American Journal of Psychiatry, 150,* 175-177.

3

The Movement Toward
Empirical Validation

AT WHAT LEVEL SHOULD WE ANALYZE,
AND WHO ARE THE CONSUMERS?

LARRY E. BEUTLER

MARY BAKER

B ecause of public pressures to reduce health care costs, a new, critical gaze is being cast on the efficacy of mental health treatments. These social and political demands may conspire to encourage the fields of professional psychology to integrate science into practice in a way that the several disciplines that identify psychotherapy as a defining activity have been unable to do on their own in the 100 years of their existence. The survival of psychotherapy as a health care enterprise in the era of managed health care and, more specifically, the survival of doctoral training as the training standard for providers may well hinge on the demonstration that those

AUTHORS' NOTE: This chapter was developed from a keynote address given by the first author at the 28th Banff Conference on Behavioural Science in March 1996.

technical and highly specialized interventions that most require training and practice are effective in alleviating emotional and behavioral problems.

Although consumer satisfaction surveys such as that initiated by *Consumer Reports* (see Seligman, 1995) offer an important perspective on the general issue of treatment effectiveness, they do not address either the importance or the value of the many specific models and procedures that justify high levels of therapist training. To date, the most systematic (and controversial) effort to specify which of the 400+ currently available models of psychotherapy can be judged to have met scientific standards of efficacy was initiated by Division 12 of the American Psychological Association. Applying a set of minimal and relatively modest criteria to a review of psychotherapy efficacy studies, the Task Force on the Promotion and Dissemination of Psychological Procedures (1995) published an initial list of therapies, references to their manualized forms, and a list of conditions and problems for which these therapies had been found successful.

Although the task force's initial report represents a major step toward specifying the scientific basis of practice, a host of reviews have highlighted some of the dangers inherent in this approach (e.g., Beutler, Kim, Davison, Karno, & Fisher, 1996; Garfield, 1996; Kovacs, 1995; Smith, 1995). The possibilities that the list of empirically validated treatments published by the task force may be employed as a guide to determine eligibility for third-party coverage and that this practice will unduly limit the freedom that has been jealously guarded and valued by practitioners are among the concerns that are most often expressed by psychotherapists. However, there also are certain scientific limitations and dangers to the integrity of the empirical enterprise that derive from the task force's initial efforts. This chapter will briefly review some of these latter limitations. It should be noted that some of these issues have been topics of serious consideration in the continuing deliberations of the task force and have resulted in some modifications to the scope of its work. We are encouraged by the openness of the task force to consider the possibility of extending its reviews and analysis of research to uncover more specific aspects both of interventions and of patients than represented in the initial list of single-theory manuals and diagnostic qualities of patients represented in the first report.

Specifically, we believe that the definition of "empirically validated treatments" must be extended to strategies and techniques that (a) are derived from narrow observations of treatment-outcome relationships rather than broad theories, (b) allow the matching of treatments to patients across theoretical lines, and (c) include nondiagnostic patient variables when assessing "fit" of treatment rather than basing decisions on problem characteristics alone. These recommendations are founded on the presence of both conceptual limitations in the current approach and an emerging body of empirical data.

CONCEPTUAL LIMITATIONS

Limitations of the Task Force Criteria

Criteria that the Division 12 Task Force adopted, in its initial deliberations, for a treatment to be included in the list of "probably efficacious treatments" were (a) the availability of at least two well-designed—usually taken to be randomized clinical trial—studies (or a large series of systematic single-case studies), (b) in which patient characteristics—usually taken to be a diagnosis—are reliably defined, and for which (c) the interventions are conducted following manuals. For all intents and purposes, this set of criteria resulted in a list of single-theory approaches being applied to patients who are diagnostically homogeneous and not comorbid. Though necessary for specifying the nature of treatment, restricting the list of validated interventions to manualized interventions and the list of indicator patient variables to diagnostic factors occludes two fundamental factors: (a) Most therapists find it necessary both to use their interventions more flexibly than usually allowed by manuals and to draw their technology from two or more different theoretical positions to maximize efficacy, and (b) most patient qualities that are used to guide treatment are nondiagnostic in nature. Indeed, we have been unable to find a single study to indicate that the value of a psychosocial treatment is constrained by the particular diagnostic label applied to the patient; there is no evidence that differential effects of treatment are related to diagnostic dimensions. Thus, most psychotherapies, at least as defined by brand names, are applied to patients, in similar forms, across a variety of diagnostic groups.

For example, each contemporary manual is based on a single theoretical point of view and both prescribes and proscribes specific interventions and goals in accordance with that limited theory. Thus, these theoretical restrictions necessarily limit the number of interventions that are available to the therapist. For example, psychoanalytic therapies prescribe transference interpretations and proscribe against experiential, two-chair work, whereas experiential therapies eschew the value placed on the use of procedures to enhance cognitive insight by psychodynamic therapies. Moreover, within all of these manuals, prescribed interventions are applied in a relatively inflexible way, being based on characteristics of the patient's symptoms rather than their fit with the treatment demand characteristics. That is, the selection of particular strategies within the theoretical model is based on the nature of the problem and symptom, tending to ignore what may be important dispositions to respond selectively to therapeutic environments and demands. Both normal and pathological aspects of patient response styles that are not characteristically addressed in treatment manuals, such as conceptual levels, problem severity, and intellect, may be much more important as indicators/contraindicators for various interventions than the diagnosis or problem initially presented. Manuals pay scant formal attention to the implications of any patient characteristics, regardless of their empirical status, that might indicate that the patient was ill suited for the selected psychotherapy.

Among the practical limitations precipitated by the restrictiveness of the task force recommendations, one cannot ignore the danger that once a manualized form of intervention is identified and recommended, it may be practiced in name only. Many clinicians are not familiar with the manuals that have been subjected to and supported by research (Beutler, Williams, Wakefield, & Entwistle, 1995). Nonetheless, it might be assumed that they will have a pronounced tendency to become "cognitive" or "interpersonal" in orientation once they are informed that these models, but not their own, are included in a list of empirically validated treatments. In the absence of effective training and monitoring procedures that can be applied on a large scale, therapists may be disposed to adopt the course of ancient archers who, under threat of death for missing their mark, drew the bull's eye around their arrows rather than learning to precisely direct the course of the arrow itself. There is considerable danger of clinician drift and a strong possibility that the intricate balance between skill and compliance that is ensured in research studies will be lost if pure-form therapies are practiced in an unmonitored fashion among practitioners. Thus, the procedures may become diluted and unrecognizable in practice, perhaps even losing their advantage over generic psychotherapy in the process.

The Level of Analysis Needed to Plan Treatment

As noted, a focus exclusively at the level of single-theory manuals and diagnostic problems potentially loses power as a method of defining the most effective treatments for any given individual. Such a limited focus may even detract from efforts to develop a fine-grained analysis of what makes each model more and less effective. As long as the focus is simply on global theories, as operationalized in manuals, and general symptom and diagnostic dimensions, it is easy to assume that all interventions within the manual are equivalent, that all therapists practicing a given manual are interchangeable, and that all patients who share a diagnosis or problem are equally responsive to the intervention. Of course, there is no evidence that any of these assumptions are correct and much evidence to argue that they are not. The assumptions of therapist, patient, and therapy uniformity are reminiscent of Kiesler's (1966) concept of "myths" that pervade psychotherapy and psychotherapy research.

Theoretical models that share the same brand names may be assumed to be similar when in fact they may be remarkably different in application. Though sharing some principles and a theoretical model, Barlow and Cerny's (1988) manual for working with panic and anxiety is quite different from that of Beck and Emery (1985). Even more important, diagnostic or problem labels mask important, and often nonpathological, patient characteristics that may be indicators and contraindicators for the use of different manuals. All of the treatment manuals tested to date produce a wide range of effects on each diagnostic group studied. There is little to indicate that patient diagnosis is a differential indicator for selecting between any specific psychological treatment (Beutler, 1989; Follette & Houts, 1996). Nonpathological variables such as social support, socioeconomic status, distress, intelligence, rigidity, and motivation may all be of much greater importance to the effectiveness of treatment than diagnosis (Garfield, 1994). To restrict the task force's focus to the level of diagnosis or symptom, therefore, weakens its potential contributions to understanding and guiding treatment selection.

In grappling with the problem of how to plan interventions in the most useful way, Goldfried and Padawer (1982) suggested that there are three levels at which therapeutic interventions may be integrated. The most general level is that of applications based on a theoretical model. This is the level currently used as the basis both for developing manuals and for identifying empirically validated treatments. At the other end of the spectrum is the level of technique. These are specific procedures that may or may not be identified within a theoretical structure and that constitute the specific actions of the therapist. A middle level of analysis is that of strategy. The strategies of the therapist define the immediate goals and general principles that are used to guide treatment, allowing one to select specific procedures to fit these goals. Strategies may include being directive, focusing on facilitating insight, or reducing arousal. For each strategy, a set of procedures may be selected representing several different theoretical models but embodying a degree of strategic similarity.

The low correspondence between abstract theoretical formulations and the concrete activities of the therapist (Orlinsky & Howard, 1986) suggests that there are certain advantages to using therapist strategies, rather than theoretical formulations or specific procedures, as the level at which the application of interventions are planned. Validating theories is too abstract, and identifying a list of effective procedures may be too concrete to be easily adapted by most clinicians. Any technique can be applied in multiple ways, depending on the goals, objectives, and problems to which it is addressed. This malleability makes it difficult to identify a particular person or problem type for whom each technique is most effective. However, one may find a basis for selecting valid interventions by identifying the strategies and goals that distinguish effective treatments when applied to a clearly defined subset of patients or problems. That is, to identify effective strategies, we need only identify classes of therapeutic procedures whose objectives and application bear a common relationship to change and the nature of the patients for whom this relationship holds. For example, instead of asserting the value of both cognitive therapy and interpersonal psychotherapy for depression, an approach based on strategies might first determine what characterizes those depressed patients who respond differently to these two treatments (e.g., severity of problem or level of social support). We might then be able to suggest not only that these two treatments are useful for altering the symptom of depression but that one works better than the other if the patient lacks strong social supports.

The current review was designed to identify classes of intervention that have been found, through empirical study, to be differentially helpful with patients whose problems differ in systematic ways. Accordingly, we reviewed available meta-analyses and review papers in which treatments were compared. We also reviewed the treatments and corresponding articles reported in the Division 12 Task Force report, in each case identifying the nature of the patient sample and the patient qualities or conditions under which differences between treatment were and were not observed. The focus of this effort on nondiagnostic patient dimensions and relative strategies that distinguished therapies (as opposed to their brand names) paralleled, conceptually, contemporary theoretical and empirical writings that have variously been collected under the titles of "integrationist," "eclectic," and "prescriptive" therapies. A number of "prescriptive models" have gained favor among segments of the professional community. A brief review of these models and their status is warranted.

PRESCRIPTIVE MODELS OF
PATIENT-TREATMENT MATCHING

As initially formulated by Arnold Lazarus (1967), the goal of what have become "prescriptive interventions" is to apply the most empirically sound procedures available on the basis of patients' presenting problems and styles of relating. The various models of treatment that constitute "prescriptive treatment" (Beutler & Harwood, 1995) emphasize that the procedures of psychotherapy can effectively be applied independently of much, if not most, of the explanatory theory in which they are embedded. The commitment to empirical evidence over theoretical models prevails in contemporary renditions of the several approaches to prescription (Norcross & Goldfried, 1992; Striker & Gold, 1993).

Available prescriptive models vary in several ways, including (a) whether they focus on mental health treatment generally or only on the specific domain of psychotherapy; (b) the availability of a manualized form of the prescribed interventions; (c) the particular patient dimensions that are considered to direct treatment; (d) whether the focus of integration among treatments is at the level of theory, strategy, or techniques; and (e) the amount of research generated by the approach. Though neither a full summarization of these approaches nor a detailed analysis of any of them is warranted in the current context, the status of these approaches can be summarized with brevity.

Major Models

Multimodal Therapy

Three models of integrating the diversity of psychosocial treatment have achieved critical levels of visibility. The most widely recognized is that proposed by Arnold Lazarus (1981) under the name *multimodal therapy* (MMT). MMT was the original technical eclectic therapy and retains the distinction of being, among the prescriptive treatments, the most closely focused on the selection and use of specific techniques.

MMT begins with a careful and systematic assessment of the patient, the patient's strengths and weaknesses, and the context in which the problems occur. The assessment is guided by a structured procedure that systematically gathers data that are relevant to seven domains of experience. These domains, identified by the acronym *BASIC-ID,* include aspects of behavioral (B), affective (A), sensory (S), imaginal (I), cognitive (C), interpersonal (I), and biologic/neurophysiologic (D = drugs) functioning. Problems in each area are identified or ruled out, and a hypothesis is constructed, from the patient's history, regarding the relationships among the symptoms in each area or domain. From this hypothesis, a firing order or triggering process is identified that describes the relationships among the domains, and interventions are selected from across a wide range of theoretical approaches to address the symptoms in each.

Progress is monitored by systematic tracking of symptoms in each of the seven domains, and this allows the MMT therapist to develop and employ a modified treatment to coincide with progress or to redress the lack of progress. Although the procedures themselves are derived from a broad body of knowledge, their application is undertaken largely within a behavioral and cognitive-behavioral tradition.

Transtheoretical Psychotherapy

Transtheoretical psychotherapy (Prochaska, 1984) has chosen to focus on the level of strategy rather than specific technology. Thus, it is much more closely focused on a theory of behavior and behavior change than MMT. The foundation for this approach is a theoretically derived stage model of readiness to change. Initially, four levels of change were hypothesized, but this list has expanded to five with the infusion of research (Prochaska & DiClemente, 1992), each identifying a stage of progress and readiness to effect change.

From an assessment of the patient's readiness for change, the transtheoretical clinician identifies both a class of therapeutic processes that are expected to be especially useful in affecting the motivation to proceed to the next level of readiness and a level of focus for the intervention. Thus, stages vary from precontemplative through contemplative, preparation, action, and maintenance, and the corresponding 10 basic processes of change include consciousness raising (for the precontemplative patient), self-evaluation (for the contemplative patient), self-liberation (for the patient in preparation for change), and contingency management and relationship facilitation (for those in action and maintenance stages). These methods are applied to achieve desired changes in areas ranging from symptoms to interpersonal and family factors.

Systematic Treatment Selection

Systematic treatment selection (STS; Beutler & Clarkin, 1990) derived from two separate efforts to define patient indicators and contraindicators for applying a variety of treatment approaches. Frances, Clarkin, and Perry (1984) merged clinical lore with empirical knowledge to suggest guidelines for the application of a wide range of interventions, including the use of medication, short- and long-term therapies, various modes and formats of therapy, and even specific theoretical approaches. Beutler (1983), on the other hand, focused exclusively on the procedures used in individual psychotherapy, providing a fine-grained analysis of the empirical evidence that supported the use of various patient dimensions to direct the selection of techniques extracted from extant research on different psychotherapy models.

Systematic treatment selection combined the breadth of Frances et al. (1984) and the specificity of Beutler (1983) with other integrative models, including the stages of readiness embodied in transtheoretical psychotherapy (Prochaska, 1984). Empirical literature was scoured to define patient dimensions that had prognostic value, especially those that characterized research programs that had compared two or more forms of treatment. Four levels of clinician decisional processes were defined and arranged in sequence to produce a graduated and increasingly detailed set of decisions about treatment. The first level of decision making represents the assessment phase. The clinician evaluates and judges the patient's status on a series of dimensions that have predictive properties for the decisions that follow. Initially, a large number of patient characteristics were defined, but these have been reduced to a half-dozen major dimensions with the passage of time and the accumulation of research evidence (Beutler & Consoli, 1992; Gaw & Beutler, 1995).

From an assessment of initial patient variables, decisions are made regarding the context of treatment (setting, intensity, modality, format, etc.), the method of developing a working relationship (role induction, support versus confrontation, use of self-disclosure, etc.), and the particular procedures and goals to be pursued (outcomes, intermediate goals, strategies, and techniques). Particular focus has been brought to bear on the indicators and contraindicators for the use of directive and nondirective procedures, insight versus behavioral procedures, systemic versus symptomatic goals, and the use of supportive versus arousal evocation procedures.

Status of Research

Though MMT is a strong advocate of the importance of using empirical evidence, our review of literature has failed to reveal any systematic testing of the model among adult patients with clinical disorders. There is research on child and school-based behaviors, but this research provides ambiguous results, and the diversity of procedures used does not permit a concise statement of efficacy. This general trend is noted for the other two models as well, although both transtheoretical psychotherapy and systematic treatment selection have—paradoxically, in view of their later development—generated much more research than MMT.

A major contribution of the transtheoretical approach has been in the development of methods for identifying readiness for change and for identifying the nature of change processes that may be linked to each stage of readiness (Prochaska & DiClemente, 1992). It has also been applied successfully to studies of smoking cessation. Recently, it has been used to treat alcoholics in the large-scale, multisite program Project MATCH. Though promising in these areas, no systematic research has been published on general or specific populations of psychiatric patients to date.

STS has provided an organizing model for a great deal of research (Beutler & Clarkin, 1990; Beutler, Engle, Shoham-Salomon, et al., 1991). The dimensions used in this model were selected on the basis of an empirical rather than theoretical criteria, quite unlike either MMT or transtheoretical psycho-therapy (see Beutler, 1979, 1991). As such, there is reasonable post hoc support for the use of some indicators that derive from a variety of unrelated sources that has been complemented by a prospective research program (Beutler, Engle, Mohr, et al., 1991).

Research Obstacles

Unlike single-theory formulations, none of the integrative models of intervention have been tested directly. Such a test has been considered to be impractical and inappropriate to the effort of combining interventions across multiple models. The focus and priority given to the role of patient-treatment interaction effects precludes a comprehensive test because of the virtually limitless variations of treatment that are postulated to be effective with different patients. A comprehensive test would require prohibitively large and varied samples. Indeed, this requirement limits the usefulness of the task force criteria for evaluating integrative/prescriptive approaches to treatment. This concern can be illustrated by comparing a typical clinical trials meth-odology for testing single-theory versus integrative models of intervention.

In the National Institute of Mental Health (NIMH) Treatment of Depres-sion Collaborative Research Program (TDCRP; Elkin, 1994), manualized forms of cognitive therapy (CT) and interpersonal psychotherapy (IPT) were compared to placebo and imipramine contrast groups, each of which in-cluded a regimen of supportive clinical management. Each of the psycho-therapies derived from its own theoretical framework, and by virtue of that fact, the goals and procedures could be kept quite distinct. An IPT goal is different from a CT goal, and the procedures used for change are also predictably and consistently different.

Prescriptive models, in contrast, select very different goals and employ a very different set of strategies and techniques with each patient, although they retain the advantages of using precise rules of application. For some, a goal consistent with IPT may be set, but the procedures of change may include IPT, CT, and psychodynamic interventions. Though treatments fol-low a consistent and replicable logic for each patient, their variability from patient to patient is so broad as to compromise the usual comparison. Moreover, the many combinations of interventions preclude a comprehen-sive, dismantling test of efficacy. Both CT and IPT comprise a finite set of procedures, including some that are prescribed by one theory and proscribed by the other. In contrast, prescriptive models, in theory, have no procedures that are not shared with some other approach. The difference is with whom they are applied. That is, the exclusivity of the application is dependent on the patient rather than on the theory.

As the foregoing suggests, the interest of those who study or employ prescriptive procedures is at a much more detailed level than is true of contemporary comparisons of theoretical models. Indeed, such a focus is necessary to refine the broadly ranging treatment algorithms. At the level of the patient, this close focus is seen in the many dimensions that are used to define a single treatment program, contrasting with the single-diagnostic or problem area focus of single-model randomized clinical trials (RCT) research programs. Thus, although the latter approaches have used diagnosis to homogenize groups, prescriptive approaches would consider this inadequate and would seek to identify and use several dimensions of heterogeneity in defining treatment algorithms to guide application. The fine-grained analysis also characterizes the focus on the treatment itself, with the target being the strategies and specific procedures used rather than the holistic package. These sources of variation are present in traditional manual-driven research, but the theories do not consider them to be of major importance for understanding the efficacy and effectiveness of treatment.

The foregoing does not automatically preclude using an RCT methodology to assess efficacy, including a cell in which treatment procedures are combined following the logic of a systematic prescriptive manual, such as MMT, transtheoretical, or STS. However, except possibly for transtheoretical psychotherapy, the refinement of decisions within prescriptive frameworks has not yet achieved the level of specificity to support such research to date. Most of the research on prescriptive models has remained at the level of testing discrete matching dimensions in sequential, additive designs rather than in studying several combinations of characteristics at once. Focus has remained on extracting relevant and effective combinations of therapy and patients from past research and then applying these dimensions to the prospective prediction of treatment outcome within the variability of currently established, manualized treatments. Beutler, Engle, Mohr, et al. (1991), for example, studied the efficacy of two patient-treatment matching dimensions within a sample of patients with major depression. Each matching dimension initially was considered separately rather than in combination because of sample size constraints.

CRITERIA FOR SELECTING
EMPIRICALLY SUPPORTED
PRESCRIPTIVE STRATEGIES

Because of the methodological differences that distinguish research on single-theory, conventional treatment manuals from multitheory manuals, we believe that the criteria adopted initially by the Division 12 Task Force must be modified to include empirically validated combinations of treatment procedures and patient qualities. To illustrate this point, we will review a sampling of patient dimensions and differential treatment relationships using the following criteria that we have modified slightly from the criteria that guided the initial task force report. In our review, a treatment intervention is considered to be empirically established for a given patient type if there are at least two good group design studies, conducted in different laboratories (preferably by different investigators), demonstrating differential efficacy of a specific class of procedures (strategies) among patients varying on a specific dimension, and

1. The treatments are manualized so that the identity of the class of procedures reliably can be either extracted or systematically measured directly from an assessment of in-therapy activity.
2. Generalized characteristics of the therapy that identify its focus, objectives, and therapist roles can be reliably extracted from the manual or described procedures.
3. The patients/participants represent a clinical population, and the identity of other, relevant but nondiagnostic patient dimension(s) can be reliably assessed.
4. The demonstration of efficacy includes a comparison either to another treatment, in which case differential efficacy is shown, with a pill or psychological placebo, or to a previously established treatment, employing samples that ensure adequate statistical power.

It should be noted that unlike the criteria initially used by the APA Task Force, these criteria do not restrict patient samples to a clearly defined diagnostic group. However, we will comment on characteristic diagnoses that make up different samples in which findings are reported. Thus, some of our conclusions are restricted to diagnostic domains, whereas others cut across diagnostic conditions.

STATUS OF PATIENT-THERAPY
MATCHING VARIABLES

To assess the status of fitting patient characteristics to treatment strategy, we conducted an extensive but somewhat selective review of literature. To ensure a common dependent variable and to keep the review within manageable limits, we emphasized research on patients with clinical depression. This review included a reevaluation of those studies from which the original task force results derived, those underwriting the primary care guidelines for the treatment of depression; a review of recent literature through psychological abstracting services; and references from other resource books reporting research on and guidelines for the treatment of depression. Several hundred references were extracted from these sources. These sources were scoured for patient variables and the nature of the treatments. We also tabulated the nature of the study (RCT, naturalistic, quasi-experimental, etc.) and the results of treatment comparisons.

Although the body of literature surveyed will not be comprehensively reported here, we have presented in the following paragraphs a brief synopsis of conclusions that we think are supportable when the modified criteria are applied, along with references to the two index studies for each variable that support our conclusions. Because of space limitations, we have not tabulated either the specific procedures that constitute classes of therapy intervention or the measures used to define dimensions of patients. A reliable assessment of these therapy and patient factors was ensured by independent agreement of the two authors on reviewing each study.

Probably Efficacious Interventions
and Associated Patient
Indicators/Contraindicators

We will summarize the status of three sets of therapeutic strategies and the associated patient dimensions with which they are differentially effective on the basis of the modified criteria adopted. The classes of therapy intervention to be reviewed are (a) antidepressant medication plus psychotherapy versus psychotherapy alone, (b) directive versus nondirective treatments, and (c) behavioral versus insight-oriented treatments.

TABLE 3.1   Antidepressants Plus Psychotherapy Versus Psychotherapy Alone

Reference	N	Impairment Index	Treatments	Findings
Sotsky et al., 1991	23 high 9 low	HRSD ≥ 14 = high HRSD < 14 = low	Interpersonal (IPT) Cognitive (CT) Imipramine + supportive therapy (IMI) Placebo (Pla)	Among high-impairment pts.: IMI > others Among low-impairment pts.: IPT > others
Prusoff et al., 1980	81	Raskin Depression Scale, endogenous versus situational	Amitriptyline (AMI) Interpersonal (IPT) AMI + IPT Nonscheduled control treatment (CON)	Among high-impairment pts.: AMI + IPT > others Among low-impairment pts.: IPT = (AMI + IPT) > AMI > CON

NOTE: HRSD, Hamilton Rating Scale for Depression.

Antidepressant Medication Plus Psychotherapy Versus Psychotherapy Alone

Our review provided ample evidence that antidepressant medications are an effective intervention for many forms of depression. There are many classes of medication, and a plethora of effects are associated with them, but the role of antidepressant medications as an independent treatment for depression is outside the scope of the current review. Instead, this review concentrated on extracting evidence for the possibility that the concomitant use of medication and psychotherapy is more effective for some patients than for others. We addressed this issue by reviewing the results of studies in which patients given medication plus some form of psychotherapy were compared to psychotherapy-only and medication-only groups of depressed patients. We particularly looked for patient conditions and attributes in which differential effects were observed.

The results reported in Table 3.1 provided criteria-level support for the following conclusion:

1. *Patients with high levels of functional impairment tend to respond better to psychotherapies that are supplemented with tricyclic antidepressants than to psychotherapy alone (Prusoff, Weissman, Klerman, & Rousaville, 1980; Sotsky et al., 1991).*

A number of other studies, besides those referenced, bear on the foregoing conclusion, especially as applied to the alleviation of symptoms of depression. Perhaps the best single treatment of this issue has been NIMH's TDCRP (Elkin, 1994). Though certainly not providing independent evidence to support the conclusion, the several different analyses of functional impairment (external ratings of impaired functioning) suggest that among those with moderate and severe depression, tricyclic antidepressants along with supportive psychotherapy exert at least modestly superior effects to the various psychotherapies. Although the TDCRP results suggest that different models of psychotherapy may interact differently with medication, the available evidence for this conclusion is insufficient to meet the criteria required for our conclusions.

Directive Versus Nondirective Treatments

Interventions that rely on the direct transmission of knowledge or instructions from therapist to patient through such procedures as interpretations, homework assignments, and directed imagery also seem to be differentially effective when compared to procedures that are guided by or initiated by the patient. Moreover, this relationship cuts across patient diagnosis and symptom type. The patient quality with which therapist directiveness interacts is embodied in states and traits that are usually described by the terms *resistant* or *reactant*. This literature, along with the methods of measuring patient states and traits, has been recently summarized quite extensively (Beutler, Sandowicz, Fisher, & Albanese, 1996). The examples reported in Table 3.2 support the following conclusion:

> 2. *Directive interventions are indicated for patients whose resistant states and traits are low but are contraindicated for those whose resistant states and traits are high (Beutler, Engle, Mohr, et al., 1991; Beutler, Mohr, Grawe, Engle, & McDonald, 1991).*

The two references given represent the best of several studies on this topic and most clearly meet the criteria used in this report. Yet they are misleading, appearing to violate the criterion of being conducted independently. In fact, although the study by Beutler, Engle, Mohr, et al. (1991) was designed, monitored, and supervised by Beutler, the study by Beutler, Mohr, et al. (1991) was designed and conducted independently by Klaus Grawe at the

TABLE 3.2   Directive Versus Nondirective Interventions

Reference	N	Resistance Index	Treatments	Findings
Beutler, Engle, Mohr, et al., 1991	63	MMPI scale combination of "Anxious Resistance"	Directive: cognitive (CT) and gestalt (FEP) Nondirective: self-directive therapy (S/SD)	Among high-resistance pts.: S/SD > CT & FEP Among low-resistance pts.: CT > S/SD & FEP
Beutler, Mohr, et al., 1991	60	Nine German-language measures, scored for high and low resistance	Directive: behavior therapy (BT) Nondirective: client-centered therapy (C-C)	Among high-resistance pts.: C-C > BT Among low-resistance pts.: BT > C-C

NOTE: FEP, focused expressive psychotherapy.

University of Berne. The contributions of Beutler and Mohr to this study were simply to initiate a reanalysis of extant data in order to cross-validate the earlier findings and to write the published report. Although one may still question the independence of analytic procedures, there are other controlled studies that also support the conclusion in problem domains that extend far beyond that of depression (e.g., Patterson & Forgatch, 1985).

Behavioral Versus Insight-Oriented Treatments

An extensive body of literature has accumulated to support the proposition that behavioral and various nonbehavioral therapies are differentially effective for patients who are high and low on indices of impulsivity. The body of research reported in Table 3.3 suggests that the following conclusion not only applies in the narrow domain of depressive spectrum disorders but extends to other problem domains as well.

3. *Behavioral strategies are more effective than nonbehavioral ones for patients who are impulsive, and this pattern is reversed for those with well-maintained impulse controls, across a variety of patient conditions (Beutler, Engle, Mohr, et al., 1991; Kadden, Cooney, Getter, & Litt, 1989; Sloane, Staples, Cristol, Yorkston, & Whipple, 1975).*

The studies by Beutler, Engle, Mohr, et al. (1991) used a group of patients with a standardized diagnosis of major depression, whereas Sloane et al.

TABLE 3.3 Behavioral Versus Nonbehavioral Interventions

Reference	N	Impulsivity Index	Treatments	Findings
Beutler, Engle, Mohr et al., 1991	63	MMPI (Pd + Pa), covaried	Symptom therapies: cognitive-behavioral therapy (CT) Insight and awareness therapies: gestalt (FEP) and self-directed support (S/SD)	Among high-impulsivity pts.: CT > S/SD & FEP Among low-impulsivity pts.: S/SD > CT
Sloane et al., 1975	94	MMPI and EPI indices of impulsivity (post hoc)	Dynamic therapy (PT) Behavior therapy (BT)	Among impulsive pts.: BT > PT Among nonimpulsive pts.: PT ≥ BT
Kadden et al., 1989	96	CPI Socialization Scale	Behavioral coping skills training (BT) Nonbehavioral Interactional group therapy (IT)	Among high-socialization pts. (low impulsivity): IT > BT Among low-socialization pts. (high impulsivity): BT > IT

NOTE: CPI, California Personality Inventory; EPI, Eysenck Personality Inventory; FEP, focused expressive psychotherapy; Pa and Pd, Paranoid and Psychopathic Deviate subscales of the MMPI.

(1975) employed a mixed sample of clinic outpatients, most of whom had symptoms of depression and anxiety, and Kadden et al. (1989) studied individuals with alcohol dependence. The studies vary somewhat in level of control and prospective design. Both Beutler, Engle, Mohr, et al. (1991) and Kadden et al. (1989) tested a priori hypotheses, using systematic manuals, whereas Sloane et al. employed a loosely structured therapy model and a post hoc analysis of patient-treatment interactions to reach their conclusions. These results are further supported by a host of other studies varying in level of control and manualization. These studies include investigations of long-term follow-up (Cooney, Kadden, Litt, & Getter, 1991), cross-cultural populations (Beutler, Mohr, et al., 1991), psychiatric inpatients (Calvert, Beutler, & Crago, 1988), and mixed psychiatry outpatients (Beutler & Mitchell, 1981). The persistent pattern of these results reinforces the conclusion outlined above, but it should be noted that the concept of resistance traits may be related to impulsivity. The relationship between measures of impul-

TABLE 3.4 Interpersonal Versus Individually Focused Interventions

Reference	N	Social Support Index	Treatment	Findings
Sotsky et al., 1991	23 married 9 separated/ divorced	Marital status	Interpersonal focus: interpersonal (IPT) Individual focus: imipramine + case management, cognitive-behavioral (CT), placebo (Pla)	Among married pts.: CT > others Among separated/ divorced pts.: IPT > others

sivity and patient resistance states or traits, as reviewed in the earlier paragraphs, is still uncertain, and the two dimensions probably cannot be considered to be independent.

Promising but Tentative Interventions

To date, one other class of intervention has emerged from our review of literature as a promising differential treatment. The value of interpersonally focused interventions for individuals who have disrupted social support systems is promising, but not to the degree necessary to receive an endorsement at this time.

1. *Disrupted family functioning (lack of social support) may be indicative of the relative value of interpersonally and intrapersonally focused interventions (Sotsky et al., 1991).*

As reflected in Table 3.4, Sotsky et al. (1991) determined that among those patients in the TDCRP who were divorced or separated (an index of low family functioning), interpersonal psychotherapy (IPT) was more effective than pharmacological, cognitive, and placebo treatments. These effects disappeared among both those in stable marital relationships and those with nonfamilial social disturbances. In the first instance, cognitive therapy was more effective than IPT, and in the latter instance, medication plus supportive therapy was more effective than IPT.

Low familial support may also be a predictor of treatment intensity or length. Moos (1990) provided an example of a study that suggests this conclusion. In a mixed sample of major and minor depressions, he found that those with poor family support and high disruption tended to respond better to long-term treatment, whereas those with low levels of family conflict responded quite well to brief therapy.

CONCLUSION

Contemporary efforts to identify treatments that are empirically validated (e.g., Chambless et al., 1996) are important to the advancement of the mental health field. However, progress in identifying these treatments requires that we reach some agreement on the difficult issue of what constitutes a reasonable and acceptable criterion of a treatment's validity (Beutler, Kim, et al., 1996). The nature of "acceptable" evidence varies between academic researchers and clinical practitioners. Whereas scientists tend to rely on quantitative, empirical evidence based on controlled research, clinicians are often unpersuaded by these criteria, favoring instead those based on clinical experience and qualitative judgments. Indeed, there are logical, if not empirical, reasons to reject controlled clinical trials as the only basis for assessing the efficacy of a treatment.

The assumptions of treatment and patient uniformity that are embodied in RCT research programs are not justified, for example, either because these assumptions do not translate to how treatments are planned and implemented in clinical practice or because they do not adequately represent important empirical evidence regarding differential treatment effects. Specifically, neither single-theory formulations nor the treatment manuals that derive from them are typically employed in clinical practice. Moreover, the diagnostic criteria that are used to define homogeneous patient groups in most comparisons of manualized treatment paradigms have little relevance for how clinicians typically select among available psychotherapeutic strategies. To accurately represent the empirical status of clinical treatment, therefore, a more fine-grained analysis of interventions and patients must be considered. Variables that limit and mediate between treatment type and outcome deserve consideration in assessing treatment effects.

In this chapter, we have provided evidence for the importance of various patient characteristics, such as defensive tendencies, coping styles, levels of social support, and problem severity, as mediators of treatment effects. Importantly, none of these patient qualities are captured well within research paradigms that rely on diagnoses to ensure patient homogeneity. We have provided evidence that some of these patient variables mediate treatment effects. In a parallel fashion, it seems likely that when these patient variables are matched to corresponding, cross-cutting characteristics of treatment, such as therapist directive style, focus (insight vs. symptomatic), and modality (individual vs. family) of the treatment, the power of intervention may be improved. Many of the most promising of these treatment characteristics are quite independent of the theory of psychopathology on which most treatment models are based.

In response to the dilemma of selecting the level of analysis needed to determine the efficacy of treatment, therefore, we conclude that the most helpful analysis will include evidence from effectiveness and matching research. It must be supportive of a process that parallels that used for the selection and integration of treatments in clinical settings. Although treatments whose evidence for efficacy is based on controlled-trials research and assessments of the efficacy of manualized treatment models are important to consider, the identification of effective treatments must also include a differential determination of patient-treatment fit that is relevant to the integrative way in which treatments are usually practiced. Constraining the criteria of "empirical validation" to studies of manualized treatments and diagnostically homogeneous patient groups is likely to be relatively uninformative for clinicians who want to use this information in planning treatment.

REFERENCES

Barlow, D. H., & Cerny, J. A. (1988). *Psychological treatment of panic.* New York: Guilford.

Beck, A. T., & Emery, G. (1985). *Anxiety disorders and phobias: A cognitive perspective.* New York: Basic Books.

Beutler, L. E. (1979). Toward specific psychological therapies for specific conditions. *Journal of Consulting and Clinical Psychology, 47,* 882-897.

Beutler, L. E. (1983). *Eclectic psychotherapy: A systematic approach.* Elmsford, NY: Pergamon.

Beutler, L.E. (1989). Differential treatment selection: The role of diagnosis in psychotherapy. *Psychotherapy, 26,* 271-281.

Beutler, L. E. (1991). Have all won and must all have prizes? Revisiting Luborsky et al.'s verdict. *Journal of Consulting and Clinical Psychology, 59,* 226-232.

Beutler, L. E., & Clarkin, J. (1990). *Systematic treatment selection: Toward targeted therapeutic interventions.* New York: Brunner/Mazel.

Beutler, L. E., & Consoli, A. J. (1992). Systematic eclectic psychotherapy. In J. C. Norcross & M. R. Goldfried (Eds.), *Handbook of psychotherapy integration* (pp. 264-299). New York: Basic Books.

Beutler, L. E., Engle, D., Mohr, D., Daldrup, R. J., Bergan, J., Meredith, K., & Merry, W. (1991). Predictors of differential response to cognitive, experiential and self-directed psychotherapeutic procedures. *Journal of Consulting and Clinical Psychology, 59,* 333-340.

Beutler, L. E., Engle, E., Shoham-Salomon, V., Mohr, D. C., Dean, J. C., & Bernat, E. M. (1991). University of Arizona: Searching for differential treatments. In L. E. Beutler & M. Crago (Eds.), *Psychotherapy research: An international review of programmatic studies.* Washington, DC: American Psychological Association.

Beutler, L. E., & Harwood, T. M. (1995). How to assess clients in pretreatment planning. In J. N. Butcher (Ed.), *Clinical personality assessment* (pp. 59-77). New York: Oxford University Press.

Beutler, L. E., Kim, E. J., Davison, E., Karno, M., & Fisher, D. (1996). Research contributions to improving managed health care outcomes. *Psychotherapy, 33,* 197-206.

Beutler, L. E., & Mitchell, R. (1981). Psychotherapy outcome in depressed and impulsive patients as a function of analytic and experiential treatment procedures. *Psychiatry, 44,* 297-306.

Beutler, L. E., Mohr, D. C., Grawe, K., Engle, D., & McDonald, R. (1991). Looking for differential effects: Cross-cultural predictors of differential psychotherapy efficacy. *Journal of Psychotherapy Integration, 1,* 121-141.

Beutler, L. E., Sandowicz, M., Fisher, D., & Albanese, A. L. (1996). Resistance in psycho-therapy: What conclusions are supported by research? *In Session, 2,* 77-86.

Beutler, L. E., Williams, R. E., Wakefield, P. J., & Entwistle, S. R. (1995). Bridging scientist and practitioner perspectives in clinical psychology. *American Psychologist, 50,* 984-994.

Calvert, S. C., Beutler, L. E., & Crago, M. (1988). Psychotherapy outcome as a function of therapist-patient matching on selected variables. *Journal of Social and Clinical Psychology, 6,* 104-117.

Chambless, D. L., Sanderson, W. C., Shoham, V., Johnson, S. B., Pope, K. S., Crits-Christoph, P., Baker, M., Johnson, B., Woody, S. R., Sue, S., Beutler, L. E., Williams, D. A., & McCurry, S. (1996). An update on empirically validated therapies. *The Clinical Psychologist, 49*(2), 5-14.

Cooney, N. L., Kadden, R. M., Litt, M. D., & Getter, H. (1991). Matching alcoholics to coping skills or interactional therapies: Two-year follow-up results. *Journal of Consulting and Clinical Psychology, 59,* 598-601.

Elkin, I. (1994). The NIMH treatment of depression collaborative research program: Where we began and where we are. In A. E. Bergin & S. L. Garfield (Eds.), *Handbook of psychotherapy and behavior change* (4th ed., pp. 114-139). New York: John Wiley.

Follette, W. C., & Houts, A. C. (1996). Models of scientific progress and the role of theory in taxonomy development: A case study of the DSM. *Journal of Consulting and Clinical Psychology, 64,* 1128-1132.

Frances, A., Clarkin, J., & Perry, S. (1984). *Differential therapeutics in psychiatry.* New York: Brunner/Mazel.

Garfield, S. L. (1994). Research on client variables in psychotherapy. In A. E. Bergin & S. L. Garfield (Eds.), *Handbook of psychotherapy and behavior change* (4th ed., pp. 190-228). New York: John Wiley.

Garfield, S. L. (1996). Some problems associated with "validated" forms of psychotherapy. *Clinical Psychology: Science and Practice, 3,* 218-229.

Gaw, K. F., & Beutler, L. E. (1995). Integrating treatment recommendations. In L. E. Beutler & M. Berren (Eds.), *Integrative assessment of adult personality* (pp. 280-319). New York: Guilford.

Goldfried, M. R., & Padawer, W. (1982). Current status and future directions in psychotherapy. In M. R. Goldfried (Ed.), *Converging themes in psychotherapy* (pp. 3-49). New York: Springer.

Kadden, R. M., Cooney, N. L., Getter, H., & Litt, M. D. (1989). Matching alcoholics to coping skills or interactional therapies: Posttreatment results. *Journal of Consulting and Clinical Psychology, 57,* 698-704.

Kiesler, D. J. (1966). Some myths of psychotherapy research and the search for a paradigm. *Psychological Bulletin, 65,* 110-136.

Kovacs, A. (1995). We have met the enemy and he is us! *Independent Practitioner, 15*(3), 135-137.

Lazarus, A. A. (1967). In support of technical eclecticism. *Psychological Bulletin, 21,* 415-416.

Lazarus, A. A. (1981). *The practice of multimodal therapy.* New York: McGraw-Hill.

Moos, R. H. (1990). Depressed outpatients' life contexts, amount of treatment, and treatment outcome. *Journal of Nervous and Mental Disease, 178,* 105-112.

Norcross, J. C., & Goldfried, M. R. (Eds.). (1992). *Psychotherapy integration.* New York: Basic Books.

Orlinsky, D. E., & Howard, K. I. (1986). The psychological interior of psychotherapy: Explorations with the therapy session reports. In L. S. Greenberg & W. M. Pinsof (Eds.), *The psychotherapeutic process: A research handbook* (pp. 477-501). New York: Guilford.

Patterson, G. R., & Forgatch, M. S. (1985). Therapist behavior as a determinant for client noncompliance: A paradox for the behavior modifier. *Journal of Consulting and Clinical Psychology, 53,* 846-851.

Prochaska, J. O. (1984). *Systems of psychotherapy: A transtheoretical analysis* (2nd ed.). Homewood, IL: Dorsey.

Prochaska, J. O., & DiClemente, C. C. (1992). The transtheoretical approach. In J. C. Norcross & M. R. Goldfried (Eds.), *Handbook of psychotherapy integration* (pp. 300-334). New York: Basic Books.

Prusoff, B. A., Weissman, M. M., Klerman, G. L., & Rounsaville, B. J. (1980). Research diagnostic criteria subtypes of depression: Their role as predictors of differential response to psychotherapy and drug treatment. *Archives of General Psychiatry, 37,* 796-801.

Seligman, M. E. P. (1995). The effectiveness of psychotherapy: The *Consumer Reports* study. *American Psychologist, 50,* 965-974.

Sloane, R. B., Staples, F. R., Cristol, A. H., Yorkston, N. J., & Whipple, K. (1975). *Psychotherapy versus behavior therapy.* Cambridge, MA: Harvard University Press.

Smith, E. W. L. (1995). A passionate, rational response to the "manualization" of psychotherapy. *Psychotherapy Bulletin, 30*(2), 36-40.

Sotsky, S. M., Glass, D. R., Shea, T. M., Pilkonis, P. A., Collins, J. F., Elkin, I., Watkins, J. T., Imber, S. D., Leber, W. R., Moyer, J., & Oliveri, M. E. (1991). Patient predictors of response to psychotherapy and pharmacotherapy: Findings in the NIMH Treatment of Depression Collaborative Research Program. *American Journal of Psychiatry, 148,* 997-1008.

Striker, G., & Gold, J. R. (Eds.). (1993). *Comprehensive handbook of psychotherapy integration.* New York: Plenum.

Task Force on the Promotion and Dissemination of Psychological Procedures. (1995). Training in and dissemination of empirically validated psychological treatments. *Clinical Psychologist, 48,* 3-23.

4

Empirically Supported Treatments
for Children and Adolescents

EFFICACY, PROBLEMS, AND PROSPECTS

JOHN R. WEISZ

Although the debate over empirically supported treatments has primarily revolved around adult psychotherapy thus far, nearly all the themes of the debate are relevant to the treatment of child and adolescent dysfunction. In fact, a focus on the treatment of young people may shed new light on some of the key issues. To place these issues in an appropriate perspective, it is useful to consider the state of knowledge in the field. Thus, the chapter begins with a review of research findings on psychotherapy effects with young people. This is followed by a critique of the field and a number of suggestions

AUTHOR'S NOTE: The research program described in this chapter was supported through a Research Scientist Award (K05 MH01161) and research grants (R01 MH34210, R01 MH38450, R01 MH38240) from the National Institute of Mental Health, which I gratefully acknowledge. I also appreciate the important contributions made to this work by faculty and graduate student colleagues, clinic administrators and therapists, and the many children and parents who have participated in the research before, during, and after treatment.

for future work addressing the main criticisms. The suggestions are aimed at making the child psychotherapy research that produces empirically supported treatments (a) more relevant to actual clinical practice and (b) more closely connected to core research and theory in developmental psychology. The last part of the chapter focuses on a question of special relevance to those who are now developing lists of empirically supported treatments: How ready are these treatments to make the transition from laboratory into clinical settings and clinical training programs? To illustrate some of the challenges that such a transition will pose, examples will be offered of the kinds of accommodations that may be needed to make these treatments maximally useful outside the laboratory settings where most of them were developed. Throughout this chapter, the term *children* will represent the age period from early childhood through adolescence, except where we need to draw a distinction between children and adolescents.

PREVALENCE OF CHILD PSYCHOPATHOLOGY
AND USE OF PSYCHOTHERAPY

Although there are pronounced individual differences in particular patterns of dysfunction, large numbers of children suffer from significant behavioral, emotional, or mental health problems. Several epidemiologic studies in the late 1980s (summarized by Costello, 1989) indicated that at least 17% of children in the general population met criteria for at least one diagnosis in the third edition of the *Diagnostic and Statistical Manual of Mental Disorders* (*DSM-III;* American Psychiatric Association, 1980); preliminary findings suggest that prevalence rates will be considerably higher for the most recent edition of the diagnostic manual (*DSM-IV;* American Psychiatric Association, 1994). Not evident in these rates of formal diagnosis are the many children who have very significant problems and who may well need help. Not all disturbed children receive psychotherapy, but many do. The most recent estimates available in the United States indicate that about 2.5 million American children receive treatment each year (Office of Technology Assessment, 1986) and that the annual cost in this country alone is more than $1.5 billion (Institute of Medicine, 1989). How effective is the treatment received by so many children at such significant cost?

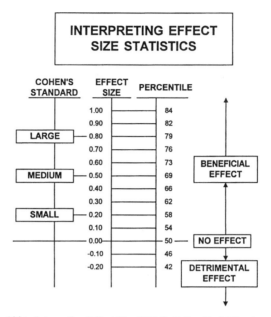

Figure 4.1. An Aid to Interpreting Effect Size (ES) Statistics. Each ES value can be thought of as reflecting a corresponding percentile value (i.e., the percentile standing of the average treated child, after treatment, averaging across outcome measures, relative to the untreated group).

SOURCE: From "Bridging the Gap Between Laboratory and Clinic in Child and Adolescent Psychotherapy," by J. R. Weisz, G. R. Donenberg, S. S. Han, & B. Weiss, 1995, *Journal of Consulting and Clinical Psychology, 63*, pp. 688-701. Copyright (1995) by the American Psychological Association. Reprinted with permission.

CLINICAL TRIALS EVIDENCE ON
CHILD PSYCHOTHERAPY EFFECTS

Answers to this question have come primarily from clinical trials research, outcome studies comparing behavioral and psychological functioning in treatment groups of children who received a candidate intervention with control groups who did not. In addition to testing the significance of post-treatment group differences in such studies, investigators may also compute *effect size* (ES), an index of the size and direction of treatment effects. For typical outcome studies, ES is the post-treatment mean on some outcome measure for the treated group minus the mean for the control group, with the difference divided by the standard deviation of the outcome measure. Figure 4.1 is a guide to interpreting ES values. As the figure indicates, ES values may be positive, indicating treatment benefit, or negative, indicating a harmful treatment effect. Each ES value corresponds to some percentile standing of the average treated child on the outcome measure(s) if that child were placed in the control group after treatment: For example, an ES of 0.90 would indicate that the average treated child scored better after treatment than 82% of the control group. As an aid to interpretation, Cohen's (1992) guidelines suggest that an ES of 0.20 may be considered a "small" effect, 0.50 a "medium" effect, and 0.80 a "large" effect.

Clinical trials research findings on psychotherapy effects can be pooled via a technique called meta-analysis, using ES as the unit of analysis (see Mann, 1990; Smith, Glass, & Miller, 1980; but see also critiques, e.g., by Wilson, 1985). By averaging across the various outcome measures used, a meta-analyst may compute a single mean ES for each study (or each treatment group) in the collection to be reviewed. This permits computation of an overall mean ES for the entire collection of studies; it also permits comparison of mean ES across studies differing in potentially important ways—for example, in the type of therapy employed, the target problem being treated, or the age or gender of the children involved.

Findings From Meta-Analyses of
Child Psychotherapy Research

To date, there have been four broad-based child psychotherapy meta-analyses—that is, meta-analyses imposing minimal limits on the kinds of treated problems or types of intervention that are included. In all, these four meta-analyses encompass more than 300 separate treatment outcome studies. In the earliest of the four, Casey and Berman (1985) surveyed outcome studies published between 1952 and 1983 and focused on children aged 12 and younger. Mean ES was 0.71 for the studies that included treatment-control comparisons; in percentile terms, the average treated child scored better after treatment than 76% of control-group children, averaging across outcome measures. In a second meta-analysis, Weisz, Weiss, Alicke, and Klotz (1987) included outcome studies published between 1952 and 1983 on children aged 4 to 18. Mean ES was 0.79; following treatment, the average treated child was at the 79th percentile of control-group peers.

In a third broad-based meta-analysis, Kazdin, Bass, Ayers, and Rodgers (1990) included studies published between 1970 and 1988 on children aged 4 to 18. For the subset of studies that compared treatment groups and *no-treatment control groups*, the mean ES was 0.88, indicating that the

average treated child scored higher after treatment than 81% of the no-
treatment comparison group. For studies in the Kazdin et al. collection that
involved comparison of treatment groups to *active control groups,* the mean
ES was 0.77, indicating that the average treated child was functioning better,
post treatment, than 78% of the control group. The fourth broad-based
meta-analysis was carried out by Weisz, Weiss, Han, Granger, and Morton
(1995); it included studies published between 1967 and 1993, involving
children aged 2 to 18. The mean ES of 0.71 indicated that after treatment,
the average treated child was functioning better than 76% of control group
children. (For more detailed descriptions of the procedures and findings of
both broad-based and more narrowly focused meta-analyses, see Weisz &
Weiss, 1993.) The findings of these four broad-based meta-analyses point to
rather consistent beneficial treatment effects; ES values ranged from 0.71 to
0.84 (0.84 is the estimated overall mean for Kazdin, Bass, et al., 1990), near
Cohen's (1988) threshold of 0.80 for a "large" effect. (Recent analyses, in
Weisz, Weiss, et al., 1995, suggest that true ES means, adjusting for heterogeneity of variance, may be closer to "medium" effects.) Figure 4.2 shows
findings from the four child meta-analyses, together with findings from two
frequently cited meta-analyses with older groups—namely, Smith and Glass's
(1977) analysis of primarily adult psychotherapy outcome studies and
Shapiro and Shapiro's (1982) analysis of exclusively adult outcome studies.
As the figure indicates, mean effects found in child meta-analyses fall
roughly within the range of effects found in these two adult meta-analyses.

In addition to generating overall mean ES values, meta-analyses may
produce estimates of the impact of various therapy, therapist, and client
factors on treatment outcome. Such comparative estimates need to be interpreted with caution because of the confounding among factors that is common in meta-analyses. Some of the confounding can be addressed via
statistical control and testing of interaction effects (see, e.g., Weisz et al.,
1987; Weisz, Weiss, et al., 1995), although this is only a partial solution. In
the two meta-analyses from our lab (Weisz et al., 1987; Weisz, Weiss, et al.,
1995), studies involving behavioral treatments (e.g., behavioral contracting,
modeling, cognitive-behavioral therapy) were found to produce larger effects than studies using nonbehavioral treatments (e.g., insight-oriented therapy, client-centered counseling). (The Casey-Berman, 1985, meta-analyses
showed the same effect, at $p = 0.06$; Kazdin, Bass, et al., 1990, did not make
this comparison.) By contrast, meta-analyses have generally not found

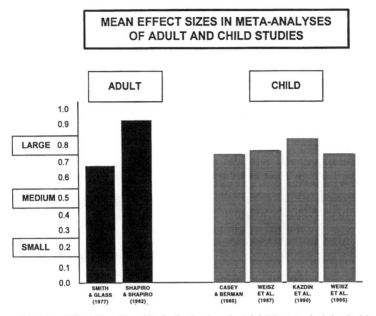

Figure 4.2. Mean Effect Sizes Found in the Predominantly Adult Meta-Analysis by Smith and Glass (1977), in the Exclusively Adult Meta-Analysis by Shapiro and Shapiro (1982), and in Four Broad-Based Meta-Analyses of Psychotherapy Outcome Studies With Children and Adolescents.

SOURCE: From "Bridging the Gap Between Laboratory and Clinic in Child and Adolescent Psychotherapy," by J. R. Weisz, G. R. Donenberg, S. S. Han, & B. Weiss, 1995, *Journal of Consulting and Clinical Psychology, 63*, pp. 688-701. Copyright (1995) by the American Psychological Association. Reprinted with permission.

treatment outcomes to differ reliably for different types of treated problems (e.g., internalizing vs. externalizing; for one exception, see Casey & Berman, 1985, pp. 392-393). The relation between age and treatment outcome has been variable across meta-analyses. However, the meta-analysis involving the most recent collection of studies (Weisz, Weiss, et al., 1995) found mean ES to be larger for adolescents than for children. This main effect was qualified by the age × gender interaction illustrated in Figure 4.4; mean ES for samples of predominantly or exclusively adolescent girls was twice as large as mean ES for adolescent boys and for children of both genders. In principle, one possible interpretation might be that adolescent girls are more likely to be treated for internalizing problems than are younger children or adolescent boys; however, we found no reliable difference in mean ES for internalizing versus externalizing problems, and in any event, the age ×

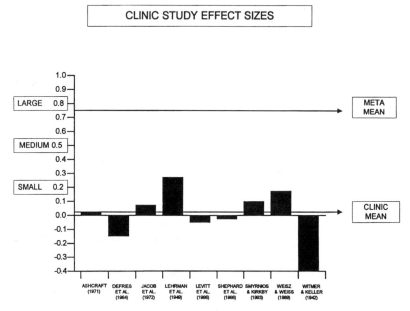

Figure 4.3. Estimated Effect Sizes for Nine Studies of Clinic-Based Psychotherapy With Children and Adolescents. Horizontal arrows show mean effect size for four broad-based meta-analyses of laboratory outcome studies (top) and averaging across the nine clinic-based studies (bottom).

SOURCE: From "Bridging the Gap Between Laboratory and Clinic in Child and Adolescent Psychotherapy," by J. R. Weisz, G. R. Donenberg, S. S. Han, & B. Weiss, 1995, *Journal of Consulting and Clinical Psychology, 63,* pp. 688-701. Copyright (1995) by the American Psychological Association. Reprinted with permission.

gender interaction shown in Figure 4.3 was not qualified by type of treated problem (internalizing vs. externalizing), type of treatment (behavioral vs. nonbehavioral), or level of therapist training (professional vs. clinical trainee vs. paraprofessional). Perhaps there is something about the recent generation of treatments reflected in this 1995 meta-analytic collection of studies that fits the characteristics and needs of adolescent girls particularly well, but we are left to our speculations about what that elusive quality may be.

We will close this section with two other findings, illustrating two additional ways that meta-analytic data can be used. First, meta-analysis can be used to assess the holding power of intervention effects. We have found in both our meta-analyses (Weisz et al., 1987; Weisz, Weiss, et al., 1995) that treatment effects measured immediately after treatment are quite similar to effects measured at follow-up assessments, which average about 6 months after treatment termination. This suggests that treatment benefits tend to be durable, at least within typical follow-up time frames.

A second finding (from Weisz, Weiss, et al., 1995) concerns the specificity of treatment effects. Obviously, children differ markedly from one another in the particular problems that they manifest, and various therapies differ from one another in the problems that they are designed to address, but do these individual differences actually have any impact on treatment outcome? Some (e.g., Frank, 1973) have proposed that psychotherapy has general, "nonspecific" effects, such as helping people with diverse problems through such unfocused means as promoting a feeling of being understood or inducing an expectancy of relief. An alternative view is that therapies help in specific ways, having their most pronounced influence on the specific problems that they are designed to address.

This controversy was addressed in Weisz, Weiss, et al. (1995) by testing whether effect sizes were larger for the specific problem domains targeted by a treatment than for other, more incidental domains. For example, we asked whether a treatment designed to reduce anxiety produced bigger changes in anxiety levels than in related but more peripheral problems such as depression. Across multiple comparisons such as these, our analyses showed that ES means were about twice as large for the specific problems addressed in treatment as for related problems that were not specifically addressed. This suggests that these tested child psychotherapies are not merely producing global or nonspecific good feelings that influence diverse outcomes equally; instead, the treatments appear to have rather precise, focused effects consistent with the particular objectives of the therapy.

In sum, evidence from broad-based meta-analyses of child psychotherapy outcome studies points to positive, problem-specific, and durable effects of mental health interventions for a variety of child problems. Clearly, child psychotherapy research is generating a number of encouraging findings. On the other hand, certain limitations in conceptualization and methodology make research in this area less valuable than it might otherwise be, particularly as a source of developmentally sensitive interventions for use with children in clinical settings in the real world. The concern is particularly salient in light of the current emphasis on moving empirically supported treatments into clinical practice and clinical training programs. We turn our attention now to some of these limitations and concerns and to associated suggestions for future research.

Limitation 1: Most Child Psychotherapy
Research Is Not Very Developmental

One limitation of current research on psychotherapy is its relative isolation from the growing base of theory and evidence on human development. Despite obvious overlap in their populations of interest, and despite their shared emphasis on the study of *change,* research on developmental psychology and research on child psychotherapy have remained surprisingly separate, insular enterprises. In introductions to journal articles on the various child treatments, it is unusual to see either theories or empirical findings of developmental psychology cited as a basis for the treatment program. The results sections of the articles are frequently notable for relative inattention to developmental factors (even age!) that may relate to treatment effects.

One cause of this state of affairs may be the very success that these relatively adevelopmental treatment efforts have had in generating beneficial effects. Success, unlike failure, may lead to confidence that one is on the right track and may thus undermine motivation to seek input from other subdisciplines. This may be unfortunate because treatment effects, though positive in current studies, might plausibly be improved through closer ties to the study of development. This statement builds on the assumption that treatment benefit will be enhanced to the extent that treatments fit the developmental characteristics of the treated individuals; a knowledge of relevant developmental literature should enhance treatment planners' capacity to produce a good fit.

In addition to treatment planning, developmental concerns may be relevant to outcome assessment. Because outcome research provides much of the feedback needed to guide the development and refinement of treatment procedures, outcome researchers may need to consider ways to attune such research to developmental questions so as to stimulate clinical-developmental cross-pollination. Accordingly, the following section addresses developmental issues that bear on both child treatment planning and outcome assessment.

Age as a Summary Variable

Most outcome researchers report the age range and mean for their samples, but the potential moderating effect of age is rarely assessed. Such within-study assessment could provide an initial step toward developmental outcome research. As noted above, broad-based meta-analyses such as those described earlier can address the relation between mean sample age and outcome, but this pooled approach lacks the precision and control of within-study analyses, or even more narrowly focused meta-analyses. The problem in broad-based meta-analyses is that age effects may differ as a function of several factors, including type of therapy employed, and each broad meta-analytic collection of studies differs from every other in its particular array of therapies. This limitation was partially addressed in a meta-analysis by Durlak, Fuhrman, and Lampman (1991) focusing on 64 treatment outcome studies, all involving cognitive-behavioral therapy (CBT). Durlak et al. predicted that effect sizes would be larger with adolescents than with pre-adolescent children because adolescents are more likely to be functioning at a formal operational level and thus are more likely to learn the cognitive skills involved in CBT, such as the use of cognitive strategies to guide behavior. The prediction was supported; mean ES was 0.92 for adolescents (ages 11-13) but only 0.55 for ages 7 to 11 and only 0.57 for ages 5 to 7.

This kind of meta-analysis deserves replication with forms of treatment other than CBT; more important, the findings suggest the potential importance of assessing the potential moderating role of age in each individual outcome study. Age is the one developmental variable to which all treatment researchers should have ready access. However, it must also be noted that the age variable is, at best, a rough summary index of multiple, diverse developmental factors—cognitive, social, and contextual—each of which deserves attention in its own right. Examples follow.

Cognitions About the Therapy Process
and the Role of the Therapist

In adult psychotherapy, it is usually safe to assume that the individuals being treated understand the concept of psychotherapy and its purpose and have some sense of what a therapist is. Young children, by contrast, may have little grasp of the nature or purpose of therapy, what a therapist is or does, or how to construe their relationship with the therapist. The concepts that children at various developmental levels apply to the process, the therapist, and the relationship are apt to be partly a function of their cognitive developmental level, in interaction with their previous experience in mental health care. There is a great need for basic inquiry into children's cognitions about these concepts; treatment planners and outcome researchers could both profit from such inquiry. The ways that children understand the concepts related to the therapy process may well influence their response to treatment and, quite possibly, their ultimate treatment outcome.

Ability to "Decenter" and View Oneself From the Perspective of Others

Piaget (e.g., 1929, 1962) wrote extensively about the development of "decentration," the ability to detach from one's own point of view and perceive objects or events from an alternate perspective. Although early work on this theme dealt with visual perception, the notion was eventually extended to social contexts and the ability to recognize the perspective of others on activities, events, and even oneself. Limited ability to decenter, in this sense, may set limits on the impact of treatments (e.g., cognitive-behavioral, psychodynamic) that involve efforts to help children see events, conditions, and even themselves from the perspective of others.

Language Ability

Developmental variations in children's ability to encode and decode language may set limits on the success of therapies that rely heavily on specific verbal content. Low-level encoding skills may limit children's ability to convey their thoughts and feelings to the therapist and may thus limit the therapist's ability to plan interventions well tailored to the child's inner state. As a simple example, both cognitive-behavioral and psychodynamic treatments for anxiety may require that the young client describe his or her anxious state in terms of both physiological arousal (e.g., "I feel tense, and I have a knot in my stomach") and psychological state (e.g., "It feels like everyone is staring at me; I'm afraid if I make a mistake, they'll think I'm stupid"). Children whose encoding facility is too limited to permit such descriptions may not be able to help their therapist understand their anxious states fully enough so that the therapist can tailor interventions with precision.

Limited ability to decode therapist comments that are intended to be helpful may limit how helpful those comments actually can be. Highly prescriptive, manual-driven therapies that are language rich and rigidly scripted may not provide sufficient flexibility for therapists to adjust language to fit their young client's capacities. And, of course, lack of assessment of language skills may hamper our ability to detect language-related reasons for variations in treatment outcome.

Finally, considerable developmental theory and research, dating to the work of Piaget (1955/1923) and Vygotsky (1962/1934), points to developmental differences in the ability to use "private speech" or "inner speech" to inhibit or guide behavior (see also Kohlberg, Yaeger, & Hjertholm, 1968, and Zivin, 1979). Piaget and Vygotsky made different predictions about the developmental course of this phenomenon, and subsequent evidence has been equivocal and complexly linked to the specific type of inner speech involved (see, e.g., Meichenbaum & Goodman, 1979). However, it seems clear that developmental differences in the use of language to guide behavior might well foster differences in responsiveness to those therapies that stress language as a means of self-control. In cognitive-behavioral therapy, for example, children are taught to use "self-talk" to make themselves less impulsive, less anxious, less depressed, less aggressive, and/or more prosocial. Use of self-talk in these ways assumes a well-developed connection between language and action, and this assumption may not be equally valid across developmental levels.

Comprehension of Concepts or
"Lessons" of the Treatment Program

Closely related to language ability is another phenomenon that seems likely to vary with developmental level: understanding of the conceptual content and central principles of a therapy program. Many child therapies are, to some extent, educational programs. For example, some treatment programs for depression are aimed at teaching children the basic components of depression plus strategies for alleviating depressed mood, and some programs for anxiety try to teach the building blocks of anxiety (e.g., fear, physiological arousal, habitual avoidance, relief that rewards the avoidance) plus specific techniques for promoting exposure to the feared situation. Are there developmental differences in children's acquisition of these concepts and skills, and might such differences influence treatment outcome? For most child therapies, so little relevant evidence has been collected that we simply cannot provide an empirically respectable answer. Indeed, one of the most striking limitations of research in this field is the infrequency with which outcome researchers test which "lessons" of their treatment were actually learned.

Abstract Reasoning

The developmental literature indicates that certain kinds of abstract thinking, including hypothetico-deductive reasoning, may emerge with formal operations, typically in adolescence. Yet some treatment programs for *preadolescent* children appear to require considerable abstract reasoning. As an example, consider social skills training programs that encourage children to generate hypothetical stressful social situations, think of various ways that they might respond, envision ways that others in the situation might respond to their response, and imagine various possible outcomes of the hypothetical interactions that might ensue. Consider also the movement from concrete instances to abstract categories required by many cognitively oriented therapies. For instance, some therapies for depression involve efforts to teach young clients to recognize such categories of depressogenic thinking as *overgeneralization* and *catastrophizing*, as well as a number of other broad categories of cognition (see examples in Cicchetti, Rogosch, & Toth, in press). Outcome research has the potential to guide treatment developers in the use of such procedures by providing information on the extent to which clients at various developmental levels do indeed achieve some grasp of the relevant concepts and categories.

Cognition-Behavior Connections

Developmentally oriented outcome research might also be used to test one of the basic tenets of cognitive behavioral intervention—that is, the notion that cognitive changes will lead to behavior changes. This may not be an equally safe assumption for youth at all ages. In the meta-analysis by Durlak et al. (1991) cited above, the authors found that in their pool of cognitive-behavioral treatment outcome studies, changes in cognitive processes and changes in behavior were essentially uncorrelated ($r = -.22$, *ns*). This painful finding reminds us that positive effects of treatment based on a particular model do not necessarily validate the model. That fact is especially important in the child treatment domain, given the significant extent to which child treatments have been downloaded from the adult psychotherapy literature. An important element of future child outcome research should be the search for true mediators of therapeutic change among treated children at different developmental levels.

Organization and the "Orthogenetic Principle"

The early developmental theorist Heinz Werner (1957) proposed an *orthogenetic principle,* the notion that "wherever development occurs it proceeds from a state of relative globality and lack of differentiation to a state of increasing differentiation, articulation, and hierarchic integration" (p. 126). One interpretation of this rather broadly worded principle is that the developing individual is continually assimilating new skills and information and integrating them into an increasingly coherent system. This notion overlaps partly with Piaget's (1970) concept of *organization,* the process by which the developing system integrates cognitive building blocks into an operating structure. In Piaget's view (supported by evidence), even memories of past experience can be reorganized to integrate such experience with newly developed cognitive structures.

One implication of these principles for intervention researchers is that some of the skills and information taught as part of a treatment program may eventually be integrated into the developing child's cognitive system but that this may not necessarily occur within the time frame of a typical child outcome study. If such thinking were taken seriously by treatment researchers, one result might be a significant shift in both goals and outcome assessment methods. Instead of focusing on proximal outcomes induced by their treatment programs alone and seen at the end of those 8- to 24-week programs, treatment planners might construe their interventions partly as perturbations designed to interact with the child's ongoing development such that some of the most profound outcomes might be evident only months or years after termination of treatment. Extending outcome research beyond the traditional follow-up periods (which are now rarely longer than 6 to 9 months) might permit detection of slow-blooming improvements or "sleeper effects" as the child's developing system integrates the lessons of therapy with other developmental inputs. Extending follow-up assessments would have at least one additional benefit: enhanced capacity to detect a falling off of treatment benefit over time, when that occurs.

Looking to the Future

Overall, the preceding sampling of developmental issues suggests that there is much work to be done in future research. Breaking down the traditional insularity of child psychotherapy research and developmental research may be useful to both enterprises. Benefits for those who study child psychotherapy may include richer and more fully informed models of child dysfunction, readiness for treatment, and intervention processes, as well as a broader picture of how outcome assessment may be conducted and employed in the process of treatment development.

Limitation 2: Most Child Psychotherapy
Research Is Not Very Context Sensitive

A second limitation of child psychotherapy research is that most of the studies focus on interventions that are rather removed from the contexts in which children live their lives. Most researchers would agree that children do not develop as solitary beings in a sterile environment, but rather as active participants in complex, multifaceted physical and social systems. Yet most treatment outcome research with children involves primarily interactions with a single therapist, or sometimes with a small group of unfamiliar children, in the sterile environment of the therapist's office or therapy room. Pretherapy assessment and treatment planning typically involve very limited sampling of the child's life circumstances and behavior at home, at school, or with familiar peers. This would seem to place significant limits on the capacity of the therapist to focus interventions in ways that fit individual children optimally; in the worst cases, it may tilt treatment development in the direction of "one size fits all" or "cookie-cutter" therapies.

Numerous theorists and researchers (e.g., Bronfenbrenner, 1979; Masten, Best, & Garmezy, 1991) have emphasized the context-boundedness of development and have discussed implications for adaptation and dysfunction. Others (e.g., Cicchetti & Toth, in press; Mash & Dozois, 1996) have noted the diverse ways in which the child's contexts and ecological systems can influence the development and expression of dysfunctional behavior and emotional states. Still others (e.g., Forehand, Lautenschlager, Faust, & Graziano, 1986; Kazdin, 1989) have noted that even what parents report (e.g., to assessors and therapists) regarding deviance and dysfunction in their children can be influenced by such diverse factors as parental psychopathology, marital discord, stress in the home, and even an intent to conceal harmful parental practices (e.g., abuse or neglect). Finally, it seems self-evident that the impact of psychotherapy with children may vary depending on the extent to which significant others in the child's contexts (e.g., parents, teachers) are involved and supportive of the process. The power of all the influences noted in this paragraph may be felt disproportionately in childhood, in part because children have such limited ability to select the contexts in which their development unfolds.

The message for treatment planners and treatment outcome researchers is that contextual factors and key individuals in the child's social environment (e.g., parents, teachers, siblings, peers) may need to figure significantly in pretreatment assessment, in treatment planning, in treatment delivery, and in outcome assessment. In general, these steps have been taken only in very limited and tentative ways in child psychotherapy research to date. There are some exceptions to this generalization, however, and noting a few of these may help illustrate what is possible in future child psychotherapy research.

In one approach, Lewinsohn and colleagues (see Lewinsohn, Clarke, Hops, & Andrews, 1990; Lewinsohn, Rohde, Clarke, Hops, & Seeley, 1994; Rohde, Lewinsohn, & Seeley, 1994) have created a parent counterpart to their Adolescent Coping With Depression group intervention. The objective is to promote parental understanding and acceptance of what is being taught to the adolescents and to reduce family conflict by teaching parents some of the same communication and problem-solving skills that their adolescents are learning. In another approach, such investigators as Szapocznik and colleagues (e.g., Szapocznik et al., 1989) treat problem behavior in Hispanic boys by means of structural family therapy. Webster-Stratton and colleagues (e.g., Webster-Stratton, Kolpacoff, & Hollinsworth, 1988) have developed a self-administered videotape therapy for families with conduct-problem children. And Henggeler and colleagues (e.g., Borduin et al., 1995; Henggeler, Melton, & Smith, 1992), in perhaps the most context-sensitive approach yet developed, send therapists into the settings where juvenile offenders live their lives, working with them to develop treatments tailored to the strengths and limitations of their family, school, peer group, and neighborhood. Each of the intervention approaches cited here has shown positive effects relative to control groups, although Lewinsohn and colleagues have not yet found that adding parent training alone to their adolescent intervention improves benefits over and above treatment of adolescents only. Perhaps procedures that delve more deeply into the child's social systems are required to produce benefits greater than those of individually administered interventions.

Looking to the Future

Moving in the directions illustrated by these research teams certainly does complicate the work of treatment development and outcome assessment. On the other hand, such efforts seem essential if we are to assess the benefits of context-sensitive treatment. We need to know, from future research, what may be gained if we push beyond a narrow focus on child characteristics and toward a broader focus on potentiating and inhibiting forces in the social systems within which the child is growing up.

Limitation 3: Most Child Psychotherapy Research Is Not Very Representative of Clinical Practice Cases or Conditions

A third limitation of child psychotherapy research is that much of it has been conducted with nonreferred children and under conditions that are more carefully orchestrated than may be possible in most clinical settings. Most of the 300-plus studies in the meta-analyses reviewed above (particularly the recent and behavioral studies) involved children, interventions, and/or treatment conditions that are not very representative of what typically happens in conventional clinical practice with referred children. In many of the studies, (a) children were recruited for treatment and were not actual clinic cases; (b) homogeneous samples were selected, with therapy addressing only one or two focal problems (e.g., a specific phobia); (c) therapists received rather extensive pretherapy training and between-session supervision in the specific intervention techniques that they would use; and/or (d) the therapy involved adherence to those specific techniques. In addition, (e) therapy was frequently highly structured, often guided by a manual and/or monitored for its adherence to a treatment plan.

These features of the experimental studies tend to coalesce around an abstract category that my colleagues and I (Weisz, Weiss, & Donenberg, 1992) have called *research therapy,* as distinguished from conventional *clinic therapy.* Table 4.1 summarizes some illustrative differences between the two therapy genres. The two are best thought of as two poles of a multidimensional continuum; certainly no single feature listed in the table under "Research Therapy" is present in all laboratory outcome studies, nor is any single feature listed under "Clinic Therapy" present in all clinic-based treatment. However, differences between child therapy in clinics and child therapy in outcome studies are common enough that it is fair to ask whether the positive outcomes generated in the research therapy studies and summarized in the meta-analyses above are representative of the outcomes achieved in actual clinical practice with children.

TABLE 4.1   Some Common Characteristics of Research Therapy and
Clinic Therapy

Research therapy	Clinic therapy
Recruited cases (less severe, study volunteers)	Clinic-referred cases (more severe, some coerced into treatment)
Homogeneous groups	Heterogeneous groups
Narrow or single-problem focus	Broad, multiproblem focus
Treatment in lab, school settings	Treatment in clinic, hospital settings
Researchers as therapists	Professional career therapists
Very small caseloads	Very large caseloads
Heavy pretherapy preparation for therapists	Little/light pretherapy preparation for therapists
Preplanned, highly structured treatment (manualized)	Flexible, adjustable treatment (no treatment manual)
Monitoring of therapist behavior	Little monitoring of therapist behavior
Behavioral methods (e.g., operant, respondent, modeling, CBT)	Nonbehavioral methods (e.g., psychodynamic, eclectic)

Evidence on the Effects of Clinic Therapy

To address the question of what outcomes are achieved in clinical practice, we carried out a search (described in Weisz, Donenberg, Han, & Weiss, 1995) for published outcome studies that focused on what might fairly be called clinic therapy. We aimed for studies that involved (a) treatment of clinic-referred (i.e., not "analogue" or recruited) children; (b) treatment in service-oriented clinics or clinical agencies, not in research settings (e.g., not public schools or university labs); (c) therapy carried out by practicing clinicians (as opposed to trained research assistants); and (d) therapy that was part of the regular service provided by the clinic, not a treatment program designed specifically for research. We required that the studies involve direct comparison between children who received treatment and a control group who received no treatment or a placebo condition.

One of the first lessons we learned was this: Clinic studies that meet the criteria outlined above are very rare. We had done one such study (Weisz & Weiss, 1989), but we found only eight others (spanning 50 years) that seemed to fit; most of these had been published years earlier. The studies all

CHILDREN   ADOLESCENTS

Figure 4.4. Mean Effect Size for Samples of Predominantly Male and Female Children (11 Years of Age and Younger) and Adolescents (12 Years and Older)

SOURCE: From "Effects of Psychotherapy With Children and Adolescents Revisited: A Meta-Analysis of Treatment Outcome Studies," by J. R. Weisz, B. Weiss, B., S. S. Han, D. A. Granger, & T. Morton, 1995, *Psychological Bulletin, 117,* pp. 450-468. Copyright (1995) by the American Psychological Association. Reprinted with permission.

compared treatment and control groups, but several different methodologies were used (for details, see Weisz, Donenberg, Han, & Kauneckis, 1995). To facilitate comparison of findings from these nine studies with the meta-analytic findings, we computed an ES or ES estimate for each of the nine studies (for studies that did not report the statistics needed for standard ES calculation, we used estimation procedures described by Smith et al., 1980, and Glass, McGaw, & Smith, 1981). As shown in Figure 4.4, ES values ranged from −0.40 to +0.29, with mean ES for the nine clinic studies (0.01) falling well below the mean ES of the four broad-based meta-analyses discussed earlier (0.77). This certainly suggests that the outcomes of clinic therapy may be less positive than the outcomes of research therapy.

It is useful to consider these findings in the light of recent evidence on "system of care" or "continuum of care" programs for children—that is, efforts to provide an array of conventional mental health services to children, with the services frequently organized and coordinated by a case manager (see e.g., Stroul & Friedman, 1986). In one of the most recent and ambitious of these efforts, the Fort Bragg Project (see Bickman, in press; Bickman et al., 1995), the U.S. Army spent $80 million to provide an organized continuum of mental health care for children in the Ft. Bragg (North Carolina) catchment area and to test its cost-effectiveness relative to more typical fragmented services in a matched comparison site. The Fort Bragg program apparently did produce well-integrated services. It was judged by the American Psychological Association's section on Child Clinical Psychology and the Division of Child, Youth, and Family Services Joint Task Force to be "the most comprehensive program to date, integrating many of the approaches demonstrated by other service programs . . . integrated and flexibly constructed, yet comprehensive, [with] services available to be adapted to meet the needs of children and their families, rather than a simplistic application of a single approach" (Roberts, 1994, p. 215). There is good evidence (see Bickman et al., 1995) that the program produced better access to treatment, but it also cost more than services in the comparison site, and unfortunately, clinical outcomes were no better among Fort Bragg children than among children in the comparison site. Fort Bragg children received more mental health intervention, but their mental health outcomes were not improved by the increase.

Similar null findings have emerged from other studies designed to modify, link, or otherwise improve delivery of conventional clinical services (see, e.g., Evans et al., 1994; Lehman, Postrado, Roth, McNary, & Goldman, 1994). A number of alternative interpretations of this general pattern of findings may be plausible, but one interpretation that must be considered is that the various treatments that are linked and coordinated in these continua of care are simply not very effective, individually or in combination. Because there is no indication that the individual interventions employed in these various continua of care have been shown to be effective in clinical trials (or approximations thereto), it is possible that the various interventions are simply not very helpful to children. By extension, it is also possible that an array of relatively ineffective services will not produce much true benefit, regardless of the extent to which they are multiplied, coordinated, or organized into continua of care.

To summarize findings on representative clinical interventions with children, (a) the evidence on conventional clinical treatments provides little support for their effectiveness, and (b) the evidence on effects of integrating conventional interventions into systems or continua of care also shows little evidence of treatment benefit.

Looking to the Future

The findings on clinic- and community-based interventions suggest a number of useful directions for future research. First, we need a richer base of information on outcomes of treatment under representative clinical conditions. Research on this question is difficult but certainly not impossible, as the nine studies shown in Figure 4.4 demonstrate (for a discussion of the pros and cons of various methods, see Weisz & Weiss, 1993). Our base of information on psychotherapy effects in public clinics is quite thin, but the situation is even worse for other treatment contexts. As best I can determine, there is currently no methodologically sound study of treatment effects in such now-common treatment configurations as individual and group private practice and HMOs. We need evidence on the child outcomes generated by these forms of practice if we are to know how outcomes across the range of today's clinic therapies compare to the outcomes of laboratory interventions. Moreover, without such information, we will lack the baseline data needed to assess the impact of such changes as introduction of managed care or implementation of empirically validated treatments (see below).

Second, assuming that further research on conventional clinical treatment continues to show rather poor effects, we need research that will help us identify factors that account for the difference between the strong positive effects of therapy in lab studies and the weak effects in clinical settings. We have made two attempts to address this issue (Weisz, Donenberg, Han, & Kauneckis, 1995; Weisz, Donenberg, Han, & Weiss, 1995). In both, we used our meta-analytic data sets to assess which, if any, of the factors that distinguish research therapy from clinic therapy (e.g., of those shown in Table 4.1) might account for substantial variance in treatment outcome. In our most recent effort, using our most complete sample (Weisz, Donenberg, Han, & Weiss, 1995), we examined eight potentially relevant factors and found that two were significantly related to treatment outcome: (a) Behavioral treatments generated better outcomes than nonbehavioral treatments, and (b) analogue cases had better outcomes than clinic-referred children. The first finding suggests that effects of clinic treatment might be enhanced if more behavioral treatments were used in those settings; recent evidence does indicate that behavioral therapies are not the first choice of most practitioners (see Kazdin, Siegel, & Bass, 1990). The second finding suggests that even the lab-tested treatment methods may be less successful in treating truly clinic-referred children than in treating the less disturbed children who are so often the subjects in lab studies. We return to this issue in the next section.

There is a third useful direction for future research, but before we can discuss it properly, we need to consider an important question related to empirically supported treatments.

CAN EMPIRICALLY SUPPORTED
TREATMENTS SAVE THE DAY?

The question arises, Can empirically supported treatments solve the problem of negligible effects in clinic and community treatment? At first glance, it would seem that the array of findings presented above points to a clear need to emphasize empirically supported treatments in clinical practice. The logic would be this: (a) The evidence from clinical trials research with children shows that the treatments represented in this literature generally produce positive effects; (b) the evidence on conventional treatments in clinical settings shows little indication of positive effects; thus, (c) to generate beneficial effects in clinical settings, we should identify those treatments that have been supported in clinical trials and export them to clinics. This logic may be appealing to many who support the efforts of the APA Task Forces (adult and child) on empirically validated treatments, and the logic may prove to be valid in the long term; however, it may be a mistake to assume that the empirically supported treatments are ready for immediate export.

The problem is that the subjects and treatment conditions involved in tests of the empirically supported treatments tend to differ so much from everyday clinic cases and conditions that it is not entirely clear how workable or effective the supported treatments will be in practicing clinics. Some of the relevant differences are those noted earlier, in our discussion of Table 4.1. At the very least, these differences make it unlikely that the treatment developers could simply mail their manuals to the clinics and safely assume that beneficial treatment effects would follow.

A quick review of Table 4.1 offers several good reasons for concern. For example, consider the samples frequently employed in clinical trials research. We cannot be certain that treatments supported in clinical trials studies with subclinical samples recruited from schools would be equally effective with seriously disturbed children referred to clinics. Indeed, in a recent analysis (Weisz, Donenberg, Han, & Weiss, 1995, p. 695), we found that mean ES in even the clinical trials research was significantly lower for studies using clinic-referred children than for those using analogue samples. As a second example, clinical trials studies frequently focus on homogeneous groups, selected for the presence of one or two target problems, and with exclusionary criteria applied to exclude children who have additional unwanted problems. We cannot be sure that treatments supported with such samples will be equally effective with the heterogeneous groups of multiple-problem children frequently seen in everyday clinical practice. As a final example from Table 4.1, the simple fact that most empirically supported treatments are behavioral (including cognitive-behavioral) may pose problems in clinics where most of the therapists are strongly psychodynamic or are unfamiliar with the behavioral perspective.

Going beyond Table 4.1, numerous practical problems arise. To illustrate, consider the simple question of how many sessions may be needed to produce beneficial effects. In our previous and present research in child mental health clinics (Weisz, in press; Weisz & Weiss, 1989), we have found that the average child in community clinic outpatient treatment receives 5 to 10 sessions. By contrast, most of the manuals used to guide empirically supported treatments require more than 15 sessions, and these are typically focused on a single focal problem. This simple contrast raises a question as to what will happen to multiple-problem children treated in clinics where the typical number of sessions is fewer than the number of manualized sessions required *for only one of their problems.* In an era of managed care in the private sector and modest capitated budgets in the public sector, strict session limits are apt to be the rule rather than the exception. Thus, it is fair to ask whether the kinds of manualized treatments that now prevail in the empirical literature can be made to work in clinics with session limits that did not prevail during the supportive clinical trials.

What these concerns suggest is that before manualized treatments from the empirical literature are implemented in our clinics and clinical training programs, we may need a new genre of treatment outcome research. This research would involve taking empirically supported treatments out of the laboratories where they were developed and experimenting with them in the crucible of clinical practice. The idea would be to find out what modifications are needed to make the treatments effective with the clientele, and under the real-life constraints, of clinical practice. Several investigators have taken steps in this direction—for example, by treating truly disturbed children in university-based lab clinics (see, e.g., Kendall, 1994; Lovaas, 1987). However, more extensive attempts may be needed to incorporate lab-tested treatments into clinical practice and to test their effects before we can know just how exportable the experimentally derived treatment methods are and what changes will be needed to make them work with seriously disturbed children.

REFERENCES

American Psychiatric Association. (1980). *Diagnostic and statistical manual of mental disorders* (3rd ed.). Washington, DC: American Psychiatric Press.

American Psychiatric Association. (1994). *Diagnostic and statistical manual of mental disorders* (4th ed.). Washington, DC: American Psychiatric Press.

Bickman, L. (in press). A continuum of care: More is not always better. *American Psychologist.*

Bickman, L., Guthrie, P. R., Foster, E. M., Lambert, E. W., Summerfelt, W. T., Breda, C. S., & Heflinger, C. A. (1995). *Evaluating managed mental health services: The Fort Bragg experiment.* New York: Plenum.

Borduin, C. M., Mann, B. J., Cone, L. T., Henggeler, S. W., Fucci, B. R., Blaske, D., & Williams, R. A. (1995). Multisystemic treatment of serious juvenile offenders: Long-term prevention of criminality and violence. *Journal of Consulting and Clinical Psychology, 63,* 569-578.

Bronfenbrenner, U. (1979). *The ecology of human development.* Cambridge, MA: Harvard University Press.

Casey, R. J., & Berman, J. S. (1985). The outcome of psychotherapy with children. *Psychological Bulletin, 98,* 388-400.

Cicchetti, D., Rogosch, F. A., & Toth, S. L. (in press). Ontogenesis, depressotypic organization, and the depressive spectrum. In S. S. Luthar, J. A. Burack, D. Cicchetti, & J. R. Weisz (Eds.), *Developmental psychopathology: Perspectives on adjustment, risk, and disorder.* New York: Cambridge University Press.

Cicchetti, D., & Toth, S. L. (in press). Transactional ecological systems in developmental psychopathology. In S. S. Luthar, J. A. Burack, D. Cicchetti, & J. R. Weisz (Eds.), *Developmental psychopathology: Perspectives on adjustment, risk, and disorder.* New York: Cambridge University Press.

Cohen, J. (1988). *Statistical power analysis for the behavioral sciences* (2nd ed.). Hillsdale, NJ: Lawrence Erlbaum.

Cohen, J. (1992). A power primer. *Psychological Bulletin, 112,* 155-159.

Costello, E. J. (1989). Developments in child psychiatric epidemiology. *Journal of the American Academy of Child and Adolescent Psychiatry, 28,* 836-841.

Durlak, J. A., Fuhrman, T., & Lampman, C. (1991). Effectiveness of cognitive-behavior therapy for maladapting children: A meta-analysis. *Psychological Bulletin, 110,* 204-214.

Evans, M. E., Armstrong, M. I., Dollard, N., Kuppinger, A. D., Huz, S., & Wood, V. M. (1994). Development and evaluation of treatment foster care and family-centered intensive case management in New York. *Journal of Emotional and Behavioral Disorders, 2,* 228-239.

Forehand, R., Lautenschlager, G. J., Faust, J., & Graziano, W. G. (1986). Parent perceptions and parent-child interactions in clinic-referred children: A preliminary investigation of the effects of maternal depressive moods. *Behavior Research and Therapy, 24,* 73-75.

Frank, J. D. (1973). *Persuasion and healing: A comparative study of psychotherapy.* Baltimore: Johns Hopkins University Press.

Glass, G. V., McGaw, B., & Smith, M. L. (1981). *Meta-analysis in social research.* Beverly Hills, CA: Sage.

Henggeler, S. W., Melton, G. B., & Smith, L. A. (1992). Family preservation using multisystemic therapy: An effective alternative to incarcerating serious juvenile offenders. *Journal of Consulting and Clinical Psychology, 60,* 953-961.

Institute of Medicine. (1989). *Research on children and adolescents with mental, behavioral, and developmental disorders.* Washington, DC: National Academy Press.

Kazdin, A. E. (1989). Developmental psychopathology: Current research, issues, and directions. *American Psychologist, 44,* 180-187.

Kazdin, A. E., Bass, D., Ayers, W. A., & Rodgers, A. (1990). Empirical and clinical focus of child and adolescent psychotherapy research. *Journal of Consulting and Clinical Psychology, 58,* 729-740.

Kazdin, A. E., Siegel, T. C., & Bass, D. (1990). Drawing on clinical practice to inform research on child and adolescent psychotherapy: Survey of practitioners. *Professional Psychology: Research and Practice, 21,* 189-198.

Kendall, P. C. (1994). Treating anxiety disorders in children: Results of a randomized clinical trial. *Journal of Consulting and Clinical Psychology, 62,* 100-110.

Kohlberg, L., Yaeger, J., & Hjertholm, E. (1968). The development of private speech: Four studies and a review of theories. *Child Development, 39,* 691-736.

Lehman, A. E., Postrado, L. T., Roth, D., McNary, S. W., & Goldman, H. H. (1994). Continuity of care and client outcomes in the Robert Wood Johnson Foundation program on chronic mental illness. *Milbank Quarterly, 72,* 105-122.

Lewinsohn, P. M., Clarke, G. N., Hops, H., & Andrews, J. A. (1990). Cognitive-behavioral treatment for depressed adolescents. *Behavior Therapy, 21,* 385-401.

Lewinsohn, P. M., Rohde, P., Clarke, G. N., Hops, H., & Seeley, J. R. (1994). *Cognitive-behavioral treatment for depressed adolescents: Treatment outcome and the role of parental involvement.* Unpublished manuscript, Oregon Research Institute. Eugene, OR.

Lovaas, O. I. (1987). Behavioral treatment and normal educational and intellectual functioning in young autistic children. *Journal of Consulting and Clinical Psychology, 55,* 3-9.

Mann, C. (1990). Meta-analysis in the breech. *Science, 249,* 476-480.

Mash, E. J., & Dozois, D. J. A. (1996). Child psychopathology: A developmental-systems perspective. In E. J. Mash & R. A. Barkley (Eds.), *Child psychopathology* (pp. 3-60). New York: Guilford.

Masten, A., Best, K., & Garmezy, N. (1991). Resilience and development: Contributions from the study of children who overcome adversity. *Development and Psychopathology, 2,* 425-444.

Meichenbaum, D., & Goodman, S. (1979). Clinical use of private speech and critical questions about its study in natural settings. In G. Zivin (Ed.), *The development of self-regulation through private speech* (pp. 325-360). New York: John Wiley.

Office of Technology Assessment. (1986). *Children's mental health: Problems and services— A background paper* (Pub. No. OTA-BP-H-33). Washington, DC: Government Printing Office.

Piaget, J. (1929). *The child's conception of the world.* Totowa, NJ: Littlefield, Adams.

Piaget, J. (1955). *The language and thought of the child.* New York: Meridian. (Original work published 1923)

Piaget, J. (1962). *Play, dreams, and imitation.* New York: Norton.

Piaget, J. (1970). Piaget's theory. In P. H. Mussen (Ed.), *Carmichael's manual of child psychology* (Vol. 1, pp. 703-732). New York: John Wiley.

Roberts, M. C. (1994). Models for service delivery in children's mental health: Common characteristics. *Journal of Clinical Child Psychology, 23,* 212-219.

Rohde, P., Lewinsohn, P. M., & Seeley, J. R. (1994). Responses of depressed adolescents to cognitive-behavioral treatment: Do differences in initial severity clarify the comparison of treatments? *Journal of Consulting and Clinical Psychology, 62,* 851-854.

Shapiro, D. A., & Shapiro, D. (1982). Meta-analysis of comparative therapy outcome studies: A replication and refinement. *Psychological Bulletin, 92,* 581-604.

Smith, M. L., & Glass, G. V. (1977). Meta-analysis of psychotherapy outcome studies. *American Psychologist, 32,* 752-760.

Smith, M. L., Glass, G. V., & Miller, T. L. (1980). *Benefits of psychotherapy.* Baltimore: Johns Hopkins University Press.

Stroul, B. A., & Friedman, R. (1986). *A system of care for children and youth with severe emotional disturbances* (Rev. ed.). Washington, DC: Georgetown University Child Development Center, CASSP Technical Assistance Center.

Szapocznik, J., Rio, A., Murray, E., Cohen, R., Scopetta, M., Rivas-Vasquez, A., Hervis, O., Posada, V., & Kurtines, W. (1989). Structural family versus psychodynamic child therapy for problematic Hispanic boys. *Journal of Consulting and Clinical Psychology, 57,* 571-578.

Vygotsky, L. (1962). *Thought and language.* Cambridge, MA: MIT Press. (Original work published 1934)

Webster-Stratton, R., Kolpacoff, M., & Hollinsworth, T. (1988). Self-administered videotape therapy for families with conduct-problem children: Comparison with two cost-effective treatments and a control group. *Journal of Consulting and Clinical Psychology, 56,* 558-566.

Weisz, J. R. (in press). *Studying clinic-based child mental health care.* Ongoing research project, University of California at Los Angeles.

Weisz, J. R., Donenberg, G. R., Han, S. S., & Kauneckis, D. (1995). Child and adolescent psychotherapy outcomes in experiments versus clinics: Why the disparity? *Journal of Abnormal Child Psychology, 23,* 83-106.

Weisz, J. R., Donenberg, G. R., Han, S. S., & Weiss, B. (1995). Bridging the gap between laboratory and clinic in child and adolescent psychotherapy. *Journal of Consulting and Clinical Psychology, 63,* 688-701.

Weisz, J. R., & Weiss, B. (1989). Assessing the effects of clinic-based psychotherapy with children and adolescents. *Journal of Consulting and Clinical Psychology, 57,* 741-746.

Weisz, J. R., & Weiss, B. (1993). *Effects of psychotherapy with children and adolescents.* Newbury Park, CA: Sage.

Weisz, J. R., Weiss, B., Alicke, M. D., & Klotz, M. L. (1987). Effectiveness of psychotherapy with children and adolescents: A meta-analysis for clinicians. *Journal of Consulting and Clinical Psychology, 55,* 542-549.

Weisz, J. R., Weiss, B., & Donenberg, G. R. (1992). The lab versus the clinic: Effects of child and adolescent psychotherapy. *American Psychologist, 47,* 1578-1585.

Weisz, J. R., Weiss, B., Han, S. S., Granger, D. A., & Morton, T. (1995). Effects of psychotherapy with children and adolescents revisited: A meta-analysis of treatment outcome studies. *Psychological Bulletin, 117,* 450-468.

Werner, H. (1957). The concept of development from a comparative and organismic point of view. In D. Harris (Ed.), *The concept of development.* Minneapolis: University of Minnesota Press.

Wilson, G. T. (1985). Limitations of meta-analysis in the evaluation of the effects of psychological therapy. *Clinical Psychology Review, 5,* 35-47.

Zivin, G. (Ed.). (1979). *The development of self-regulation through private speech.* New York: John Wiley.

5

Are Empirically Validated Treatments Valid for Culturally Diverse Populations?

ANNA BETH DOYLE

An important issue in the development and promulgation of empirically valid psychological treatment procedures (EVTs) is the generalizability of treatment effectiveness. The focus of the present chapter is on the effectiveness of EVTs for ethnic and cultural minority individuals. Although *ethnicity* and *culture* are not synonymous, members of an ethnic minority are likely to share cultural values, beliefs, and customs that diverge markedly from those of the white, majority population on which the EVTs were validated. We review the ethnic diversity of North America and theoretical views of the role of culture in psychotherapeutic change processes, identifying the prevailing assumption of cultural universality. Data are then presented showing that there is a dearth of evidence on the effectiveness of empirically validated treatments for diverse populations. The few available studies are reviewed, including some disquieting findings, and impediments to be overcome in obtaining more valid data are discussed.

AUTHOR'S NOTE: This research was supported by grants from the Quebec Fonds pour la Formation des Chercheurs et l'Aide à la Recherche.

93

DIVERSITY IN NORTH AMERICAN
ETHNIC MINORITY GROUPS

In the United States, concern is almost exclusively with visible ethnic minorities. They make up approximately 25% of the population, with the largest group being African American, followed by Asian (Chinese, Japanese, Korean, etc.), Hispanic, and Native American (Hammond & Yung, 1993). Data from Canada indicate a similar overall percentage of minorities, but the composition is somewhat different. The Canadian population of non-European origin totals 16%, with the largest group being Asian, followed by East Indian, North American Indian, and black. An additional 7% are South European (predominantly Italian, Portuguese, or Greek), about half of whom speak primarily the language of their country of origin at home, thus retaining their minority culture to a significant extent (Statistics Canada, 1993a, 1993b). In both Canada and the United States, the vast proportion of ethnic minority individuals, excepting Aboriginal peoples, are concentrated in major cities. In Canada, for example, culturally distinct groups indicated by speaking a language other than English or French at home make up 23% of the 3.8 million inhabitants of Toronto, 18% of the 1.5 million inhabitants of Vancouver, and 12% of the 3 million inhabitants of Montreal, but only 4% of the rest of the population. These substantial numbers, especially in urban centers, underline the importance of assessing the degree to which psychological treatments are effective with diverse groups.

THE CULTURAL UNIFORMITY ASSUMPTION
AND PSYCHOLOGICAL INTERVENTION

Given the attention paid in clinical psychology over the last 15 years to cultural and individual differences, reflected in requirements for the accreditation of clinical training programs (American Psychological Association [APA], 1986, 1996; Canadian Psychological Association, 1991), it is surprising that the impact of ethnicity and culture on treatment outcome has received such scant research attention. Reviews by Hays (1995), Sue (1991), and Yutrzenka (1995) substantiate the lack of data, in particular on the applicability of specific treatment procedures to culturally diverse populations. For example, in a recent review of the cognitive-behavioral therapy literature (Hays, 1995), only two studies are cited, one with Puerto Rican women (Comas-Diaz, 1981) and one with Native Americans (Renfry, 1992). It is to be noted that the prevailing theories underlying psychological treatments in clinical psychology are universalistic; culture plays almost no role as a variable (Tharp, 1991). This theoretical viewpoint leads to the assumption that treatments are equally effective with diverse cultural groups. Research on cross-cultural psychology or ethnic or racial issues implies, however, that culture would play an important role in the assessment, etiology, symptoms, and treatment of mental disorders (Sue, Zane, & Young, 1994). An alternative hypothesis, therefore, is that of cultural specificity: that is, that effective interventions differ across cultures and that the most effective may be specific to certain cultures or groups of cultures depending on their values, beliefs, and attitudes (Tharp, 1991). Unfortunately, the data are not yet in to decide between these competing hypotheses.

CONCERN WITH ETHNICITY AND CULTURE
IN PSYCHOLOGICAL TREATMENT

The 1993 APA "Guidelines for Providers of Psychological Services to Ethnic, Linguistic and Culturally Diverse Populations" do not take a clear position with reference to the hypotheses of cultural uniformity *versus* cultural specificity, requiring only that "psychologists consider . . . the cultural beliefs and values of the client and his/her community in providing intervention" (APA, 1993, p. 46). This requirement has been interpreted widely as necessitating cultural sensitivity, knowledge, and skill in the adaptation of treatment program delivery style to the communication patterns of culturally diverse groups. It has not been interpreted as necessitating investigation of treatment-population interactions: that is, investigations of differential treatment effectiveness with different cultural groups.

Thus, the bulk of available literature focuses on multicultural counseling (e.g., Atkinson, Morten, & Sue, 1989; D'Andrea, Daniels, & Heck, 1991; Sodowsky, Taffe, Gutkin, & Wise, 1994; Sue & Sue, 1990). The limited treatment outcome research available deals primarily with nonspecific treatment effects such as the effectiveness of psychotherapy in general with ethnic minority individuals and the importance of therapist-client ethnic match. Despite a reasonable number of studies, conclusions remain unclear (Sue,

1988). It has been suggested that factors proximal to treatment process (e.g., therapist credibility; similarity in client-therapist attitudes and values) are more important than distal factors such as client-therapist ethnicity (Sue & Zane, 1987). In line with this view, the case has been made that psychological interventions that are adapted to the culture of Hispanic clients are more effective (Rosado & Elias, 1993). However, more empirical evidence is needed. At least one of the studies cited in this review (Comas-Diaz, 1981), albeit well designed to show the efficacy of cognitive and behavioral treatment for depression in Puerto Rican women, could not attest to the utility of adapted treatment because this was neither compared to nonadapted treatment nor applied to different ethnic groups. More encouraging is literature suggesting that training in these aspects of multicultural service delivery increases treatment efficacy with minority-group clients (Yutrzenka, 1995), specifically in terms of use of treatment services, reduction of dropout (Lefley & Bestman, 1984), and minority clients' self-report measures of treatment outcome (Evans, Acosta, Yamamoto, & Skilbeck, 1984).

In terms of specific treatment approaches, a few articles set out principles and particulars for adapting these to diverse populations (Hays, 1995; Renfry, 1992; Wood & Mallinckrodt, 1990). Both these literatures focus almost exclusively on the major, U.S. ethnic and racial visible minority groups. A notable exception is McGoldrick, Pearce, and Giordano's book *Ethnicity and Family Therapy* (1982), which provides information on the family dynamics of a wide variety of visible and nonvisible North American ethnic groups, including, for example, those of Irish, Jewish, and Italian heritage.

EVIDENCE FOR THE EFFECTIVENESS
OF SPECIFIC TREATMENTS WITH
CULTURALLY DIVERSE POPULATIONS

There are almost no empirical studies assessing the effectiveness of specific treatments with cultural, ethnic, or racial minority populations. A review of 33 empirically valid treatment studies published since 1985 (Task Force, 1995) reveals that only 15% mentioned the ethnicity or race of their sample. In these 15%, comprising 248 subjects, the ethnic composition of the samples was 92% white, precluding any analyses of ethnic or racial differences. In the 1996 revision of the task force report (Chambless et al., 1996), 24% of the 21 additional post-1985 studies stated the ethnicity of participants, a minor increase. However, in these studies, subjects were again primarily white (86%), precluding examination of differential treatment effectiveness across ethnicity.

For the present chapter, a broader search, of *Psychological Abstracts* from 1974 to 1989 and from 1990 to 1995, was conducted. Only six relevant studies were found between 1974 and 1989; one was found between 1990 and 1995, and a further three studies were published in the last year. In six of the studies, treatment effectiveness for a minority ethnic group and a Caucasian group was compared; in three of these studies there were no differences, and in three there were differences between the groups. Specifically, no ethnic differences were found for sex therapy with Asians compared to Caucasians (Bhugra & Cordle, 1988), for client-therapist ethnic match in individual psychotherapy with black and white clients (Jones, 1982), or for the effectiveness of ethnic-specific community mental health services to Asian Americans compared to white Americans in the same setting (Zane, Hatanka, Park, & Akutsu, 1994). On the other hand, family and individual therapies were found to be less effective with black than with white child clients (Oliver, Searight, & Lightfoot, 1988), and black clients were less satisfied than white clients with psychotherapy outcome (Wolkon, Moriwaki, & Williams, 1973). In a third study, the symptom severity and responsiveness to *in vivo* exposure of African Americans and white agoraphobic outpatients were compared (Chambless & Williams, 1995). Black clients were found to be initially more phobic than white clients on several measures and to improve somewhat less after treatment or follow-up. However, the authors reported that the racial difference in initial symptom severity was inconsistent with another study (Friedman & Paradis, 1991) and that the black clients were lower in education, occupation, and income than the white clients, lived under more stressful conditions, were more likely to require home-based treatment, and if not requiring it, had to travel further to the clinic, which was located at a university in an upper-middle-class, predominantly Caucasian area of Washington, D.C. The authors surmised that only black clients who were severely disabled by agoraphobia would be motivated to seek treatment under these circumstances and that they were likely to be initially more severely disabled than the white clients. Thus, any conclusions about racial differences in response to treatment for agoraphobia seem premature. This study illustrates the considerable design issues to be overcome in conducting the studies needed to provide data on treatment effectiveness with different ethnic groups.

In another set of four studies, one or more empirically validated treatments were compared to a control condition for a particular minority ethnic group. As noted earlier, both cognitive and behavioral treatments for depression were demonstrated to be effective for Puerto Rican women (Comas-Diaz, 1981). On the other hand, training Hong Kong Chinese parents in behavioral techniques for modifying children's behavior was reported to be difficult because the techniques (play with their children and the use of contingent praise and ignoring) violated parents' customary modes of child rearing and beliefs about childhood problems (Lieh-Mak, Lee, & Luk, 1984). In a third study, the effectiveness of behavioral family management (BFM) was compared to standard case management (CM) in preventing exacerbation and relapse in schizophrenia in low-income unacculturated Hispanic families of Mexican, Guatemalan, and Salvadoran descent (Telles et al., 1995). In contrast to results of studies of majority-group Americans (Falloon et al., 1982), among the less acculturated Hispanic clients, BFM was associated with negative rather than positive outcome—that is, a significant exacerbation of symptoms—and among the more acculturated Hispanic clients was no more effective than CM. Because of its disquieting results, this study merits more discussion. Unlike white families with a member with schizophrenia, very few Hispanic families had initial high levels of expressed emotion (EE), which BFM is designed to reduce, and several treated by BFM shifted from low to high EE following treatment. Though the treatment materials were described as translated and adapted by bicultural clinicians to be socioculturally appropriate, Telles et al. (1995) suggested that the highly structured, active intervention program included specific exercises (e.g., establishing eye contact or expressing negative feelings) that were perceived as inappropriate with paternal authority figures and thus may have been stressful for patients, contributing to the exacerbation of symptoms. In a fourth and final study, again of the effectiveness of BFM and conducted in China, BFM was found to benefit family members with schizophrenia significantly more than CM (Xiong et al., 1994). Though the intervention procedures were reported to be adapted culturally, the nature of the adaptation was not clearly specified, and the frequency and duration of clinical contact were much greater for families receiving BFM than for those receiving CM. The inconsistency in these articles, however, highlights the need for more definitive research, as well as the need for practitioners to be cautious in the use of family therapy techniques with minority cultural groups.

IMPLICATIONS FOR CLINICAL PRACTICE

Though the available studies are limited in number and design, some tentative conclusions are possible. It is likely that some adapted treatments can be effective and that adapted treatments are more effective than unadapted treatments (Rosado & Elias, 1993; Xiong et al., 1994). It is distressing, however, that in the most recent studies, some treatments or adaptations were found to be less effective with or even harmful to minority-group members (Chambless & Williams, 1995; Lieh-Mak et al., 1984; Telles et al., 1995). Though design and sampling problems in many of these studies preclude firm conclusions, either positive or negative (Chambless & Williams, 1995; Xiong et al., 1994), further investigation of the parameters of successful cultural adaptation of treatment components is clearly needed. In the meantime, clinicians are left with a dilemma when treating ethnic minority clients. Even if they are sensitive to and knowledgeable about the values and beliefs of the particular culture, and skilled in communicating with ethnic group members, information on treatment effectiveness is likely to be lacking. It is probably appropriate to undertake treatments demonstrated to be effective with majority-group clients, under the hypothesis that these are most likely to generalize, especially if communication style is culturally appropriate, but to exercise vigilance for and openness to unexpected effects that may be unique to the ethnic group, not just the particular client.

OVERCOMING RESEARCH OBSTACLES
TO OBTAINING CROSS-CULTURAL
TREATMENT EFFECTIVENESS DATA

If treatment effectiveness information is to be forthcoming, difficulties in obtaining such information must be addressed. In the revised task force report, the authors stressed the need for more rigorous research on the effectiveness of empirically validated treatments with minority cultural groups (Chambless et al., 1996). This information is important both so that practitioners with a diverse clientele can meet the mental health needs of minority-group members and, for the sake of good science, so that the limits of generalizability of our current empirically validated treatments can be known. In the task force report, incentives for researchers to study the topic, a requirement that all studies report the ethnic makeup of their participants, and the reporting of effect sizes for different ethnic groups, even if samples are too small to reach conventional levels of significance, are recommended. This latter suggestion is particularly intriguing and innovative in that it permits the accumulation of evidence over time and the use of meta-analysis.

Besides incentives for the researchers through targeted grants, encouragements for ethnic minority participants are needed. Though the numbers of ethnic minority individuals appear large, especially in urban centers, they are countered by a lower rate of utilization of outpatient mental health services by ethnic minority individuals, in part because of greater social supports from family and community and in part because of cultural differences between Eurocentric service delivery style and minority-group expectations/values (Snowden & Cheung, 1990). That is, many minority-group members find it antithetical to their values and beliefs to seek professional help for mental distress and to participate fully in treatment. These differences in values and style between clients and researchers are even more likely to impede minority clients' willingness to participate in randomized controlled clinical trials of treatment effectiveness. Overcoming this obstacle will necessitate extraordinary efforts from greater numbers of researcher/ clinicians who are not only sensitive to cultural differences but knowledgeable of the particular values, customs, and language of the major local cultural minority groups and skilled in treating members of those groups. Thus, professional training in multicultural aspects of clinical psychology and recruiting of more ethnic minority professionals are important both for practice and for research.

Because of the need to avoid the confounds that have characterized many of the earlier studies, specific research design efforts are also needed from skilled researchers to ensure that different ethnic groups are equivalent on relevant variables such as severity of symptoms. The cross-cultural validity of assessment instruments and diagnostic categories must also be ascertained. Sue and colleagues (Sue et al., 1994) provided suggestions for overcoming these practical and methodological problems.

A question worthy of consideration for both research and practice is why concern should be restricted to visible minorities. Most government programs in the United States and Canada have been restricted to these groups, reflecting a concern with discrimination. However, with psychological treatment, when differential effectiveness is found across culture, we assume that treatment has interacted with cultural attitudes, beliefs, and values that differ from those of the majority culture. Such differences are not restricted to visible minorities, though discrimination may contribute to the development of particular attitudes in minority individuals.

In conclusion, with the concern for promoting psychological treatments of demonstrated effectiveness, the need to specify the degree to which such effectiveness generalizes to diverse populations—in particular, culturally different populations—has been overlooked. Data on which to base treatment decisions are severely limited. It is important to address directly the issue of cultural differences in treatment effectiveness by focusing research on minority-group members. It is also necessary to explicitly describe and investigate the principles and specifics of cultural adaptations of treatment procedures. Though fraught with difficulties, such research is currently feasible in our increasingly diverse society.

REFERENCES

American Psychological Association. (1986). *Accreditation handbook.* Washington, DC: Author.

American Psychological Association. (1993). Guidelines for providers of psychological services to ethnic, linguistic and culturally diverse populations. *American Psychologist, 48,* 45-48.

American Psychological Association. (1996). *Guidelines and principles for accreditation of programs in professional psychology.* Washington, DC: Author.

Atkinson, D. R., Morten, G., & Sue, D. W. (1989). *Counseling American minorities.* Dubuque, IA: William C. Brown.

Bhugra, D., & Cordle, C. (1988). A case-control study of sexual dysfunction in Asian and non-Asian couples. *Sexual and Marital Therapy, 3,* 71-76.

Canadian Psychological Association. (1991). *Accreditation Manual.* Ottawa: Author.

Chambless, D., Sanderson, W., Shoham, V., Johnson, S., Pope, K., Crits-Christoph, P., Baker, M., Johnson, B., Woody, S., Sue, S., Beutler, L., Williams, D., & McCurry, S. (1996). An update on empirically validated therapies. *Clinical Psychologist, 49,* 5-18.

Chambless, D., & Williams, K. E. (1995). A preliminary study of African Americans with agoraphobia: Symptom severity and outcome of treatment with in vivo exposure. *Behavior Therapy, 26,* 501-515.

Comas-Diaz, L. (1981). Effects of cognitive and behavioral group treatment on the depressive symptomatology of Puerto Rican women. *Journal of Consulting and Clinical Psychology, 49,* 627-632.

D'Andrea, M., Daniels, J., & Heck, R. (1991). Evaluating the impact of multicultural counsellor training. *Journal of Counseling and Development, 70,* 143-148.

Evans, L. A., Acosta, F. X., Yamamoto, J., & Skilbeck, W. M. (1984). Orienting psychotherapists to better serve low income and minority patients. *Clinical Psychologist, 40,* 90-96.

Falloon, I. R. H., Boyd, J. L. T., McGill, C. W., Ranzani, J., Moss, H. B., & Gilderman, A. M. (1982). Family management in the prevention of exacerbation of schizophrenia: A controlled study. *New England Journal of Medicine, 306,* 1437-1440.

Friedman, S., & Paradis, C. (1991). African-American patients with panic disorder and agoraphobia. *Journal of Anxiety Disorders, 5,* 35-41.

Hammond, W. R., & Yung, B. (1993). Minority student recruitment and retention practices among schools of professional psychology: A national survey and analysis. *Professional Psychology: Research and Practice, 24,* 3-12.

Hays, P. (1995). Multicultural applications of cognitive-behavior therapy. *Professional Psychology: Research and Practice, 26,* 309-315.

Jones, E. (1982). Psychotherapists' impressions of treatment outcome as a function of race. *Journal of Clinical Psychology, 38,* 722-731.

Lefley, H. P., & Bestman, E. W. (1984). Community mental health and minorities: A multiethnic approach. In S. Sue & T. Moore (Eds.), *The pluralistic society: A community mental health perspective* (pp. 116-148). New York: Human Sciences.

Lieh-Mak, F., Lee, P., & Luk, S. (1984). Problems encountered in teaching Chinese parents to be behavior therapists. *Psychologia, 27,* 56-64.

McGoldrick, M., Pearce, J., & Giordano, J. (1982). *Ethnicity and family therapy.* New York: Guilford.

Oliver, J. M., Searight, R., & Lightfoot, S. (1988). Client characteristics as determinants of intervention modality and therapy progress. *American Journal of Orthopsychiatry, 58,* 543-551.

Renfry, G. (1992). Cognitive-behavior therapy and the Native American client. *Behavior Therapy, 23,* 321-340.

Rosado, J. W., & Elias, M. J. (1993). Ecological and psychocultural mediators in the delivery of services for urban, culturally diverse Hispanic clients. *Professional Psychology: Research and Practice, 24,* 450-459.

Snowden, L. R., & Cheung, F. K. (1990). Use of inpatient mental health services by members of ethnic minority groups. *American Psychologist, 45,* 347-355.

Sodowsky, G. R., Taffe, R. C., Gutkin, T. B., & Wise, S. (1994). Development of the multicultural counselling inventory: A self-report measure of multicultural competencies. *Journal of Counseling Psychology, 41,* 137-148.

Statistics Canada. (1993a). *Ethnic origin* (Catalogue 93-315). Ottawa: Government of Canada.

Statistics Canada. (1993b). *Home language and mother tongue* (Catalogue 93-317). Ottawa: Government of Canada.

Sue, D. W., & Sue, D. (1990). *Counseling the culturally different: Theory and practice.* New York: John Wiley.

Sue, S. (1988). Psychotherapeutic services for ethnic minorities: Two decades of research findings. *American Psychologist, 43,* 301-308.

Sue, S. (1991). Ethnicity and culture in psychological research and practice. In J. D. Goodchilds (Ed.), *Psychological perspectives on human diversity in America* (pp. 47-85). Washington, DC: American Psychological Association.

Sue, S., & Zane, N. (1987). The role of culture and cultural techniques in psychotherapy. *American Psychologist, 42,* 37-45.

Sue, S., Zane, N., & Young, K. (1994). Research on psychotherapy with culturally diverse populations. In A. Bergin & S. Garfield (Eds.), *Handbook of psychotherapy and behavior change* (pp. 783-817). New York: John Wiley.

Task Force on the Promotion and Dissemination of Psychological Procedures. (1995). Training in and dissemination of empirically validated psychological treatments. *Clinical Psychologist, 48,* 3-23.

Telles, C., Karno, M., Mintz, J., Paz, G., Arias, M., Tucker, D., & Lopez, S. (1995). Immigrant families coping with schizophrenia. *British Journal of Psychiatry, 167,* 473-479.

Tharp, R. (1991). Cultural diversity and the treatment of children. *Journal of Consulting and Clinical Psychology, 59,* 799-812.

Wolkon, G., Moriwaki, S., & Williams, K. (1973). Race and social class as factors in the orientation toward psychotherapy. *Journal of Counseling Psychology, 20,* 312-316.

Wood, P. S., & Mallinckrodt, B. (1990). Culturally sensitive assertiveness training for ethnic minority clients. *Professional Psychology: Research and Practice, 21,* 5-11.

Xiong, W., Phillips, M. R., Hu, X., Wang, R., Dai, Q., Kleinman, J., & Kleinman, A. (1994). Family-based intervention for schizophrenic patients in China. *British Journal of Psychiatry, 165,* 239-247.

Yutrzenka, B. (1995). Making a case for training in ethnic and cultural diversity in increasing treatment efficacy. *Journal of Consulting and Clinical Psychology, 63,* 197-206.

Zane, N., Hatanka, H., Park, S., & Akutsu, P. (1994). Ethnic-specific mental health services: Evaluation of the parallel approach for Asian-American clients. *Journal of Community Psychology, 22,* 68-81.

PART II

Empirically Supported
Interventions

6

Common Determinants in Empirically Supported Psychosocial Treatments for Depression

PETER D. McLEAN

KENT W. ANDERSON

New psychological treatments for clinical depression have matured over the past 20 years to the point that they perform as well as, or better than, antidepressant medications (Antonuccio, Danton, & DeNelsky, 1995; Young, Beck, & Weinberger, 1993), regardless of depression severity (Jacobson & Hollon, 1996; McLean & Taylor, 1992). These treatments are largely, but not exclusively, the product of experimentally evolved theory, a feature that differentiates them from earlier psychological therapies for depression. Attempts to standardize these theory-derived treatments and to elucidate their active ingredients have, quite naturally, given rise to specific treatment manuals. Although there are pros and cons associated with such detailed declarations of the treatment process (Dobson & Shaw, 1988), recent evidence has found that manual-driven treatments can outperform clinicians operating on the basis of clinical wisdom, unfettered by the constraints imposed by treatment manuals (Wilson, 1996). At the same time, changes in mental health policy, evidenced in the form of managed-care competition in the United States (Barlow, 1994), have sparked the development of an American Psychological Association (APA) task force (APA, 1995) to disseminate information to clinical psychologists, third-party payers, and the public about empirically validated psychological treatments and the manuals detailing their delivery (Sanderson & Woody, 1995). It seems clear that clinical psychology has entered an evidence-based era in which empirically validated treatments will compete for health care resources.

This chapter will examine the uniqueness of the three best known psychological interventions for clinical depression for which there is an empirical tradition. The effectiveness and limitations of these three therapies—cognitive therapy, behavioral therapy, and interpersonal therapy—will be considered. New directions that hold promise for making psychological treatments for depression more competitive will also be reviewed. First, however, it may be useful to review the nature of clinical depression.

THE NATURE OF DEPRESSION

Depression, as referred to in this chapter, is regarded as dimensional, ranging from mild and transient symptoms at one end of the continuum to the severe symptom presentation of major depressive disorder at the other. Our discussion of depression in this chapter does not include bipolar or psychotic manifestations, which typically require distinct treatment considerations. The phenomenology of major depression can be appreciated by considering the criteria in the fourth edition of the *Diagnostic and Statistical Manual of Mental Disorders* (*DSM-IV;* American Psychiatric Association, 1994) for a major depressive episode. The essential requirement of this diagnosis is to be rendered significantly distressed or impaired in function by a specific density of depressive symptoms (at least five out of nine), which have endured for at least 2 weeks and which cannot be attributable to other specific causes (see Table 6.1). Major depressive disorder extends the diagnosis of major depressive episode by recognizing the possibility of multiple episodes and by precluding causation due to schizoaffective disorder or a variety of related disorders.

Major depression is more than twice as prevalent in women than in men. The point prevalence for major depression in Western industrialized nations is 2.3% to 3.2% for men and 4.5% to 9.3% for women, and lifetime

TABLE 6.1 Criteria for *DSM-IV* Major Depressive Episode

A. Five or more symptoms for same two-week period, including (1) or (2) below:

  (1) Depressed mood most of day, nearly every day.

  (2) Markedly diminished interest in all, or most, activities.

  (3) Weight loss or weight/gain without intent.

  (4) Insomnia or hypersomnia.

  (5) Psychomotor agitation or retardation.

  (6) Fatigue or loss of energy.

  (7) Feelings of worthlessness, or excessive or inappropriate guilt.

  (8) Diminished ability to think or concentrate, or indecisiveness.

  (9) Recurrent thoughts of death or suicidal ideation.

B. No prior manic or hypomanic episode.

C. Symptoms cause clinically significant distress or impairment in functioning.

D. Symptoms not due to substance abuse or general medical condition.

E. Symptoms not better accounted for by bereavement.

SOURCE: American Psychiatric Association (1994).

prevalence is 7% to 12% for men and 20% to 25% for women (U.S. Department of Health and Human Services [USDHHS], 1993a). The course of major depression is variable. Forty-five percent of those who experience one episode of major depression never experience another. However, two episodes are associated with a 70% chance of having a subsequent episode, and three or more episodes are associated with a 90% risk of reoccurrence, often separated by years of normal functioning (USDHHS, 1993a).

Of clinical importance is the high rate of comorbidity between depressive disorder and other Axis I disorders, general medical conditions, and Axis II disorders. For example, 74% of the National Institute of Mental Health (NIMH) Treatment of Depression Collaborative Research Program sample was comorbid with an Axis II disorder (Shea et al., 1990). The presence of comorbidity complicates treatment delivery, usually results in a poorer treatment outcome, and should be considered to be more the rule than the exception in clinical assessment and case formulations. Furthermore, most clinical depressions are never treated. Approximately 70% of psychiatric hospitalizations and 60% of suicides are associated with mood disorders (USDHHS, 1993a). Multiple studies report that primary care practitioners fail to detect at least 50% of clients who have major depressive disorder (e.g., Gullick & King, 1979; Johnson, 1974). A reanalysis of the multisite Epidemiologic Catchment Area Study involving some 18,000 community

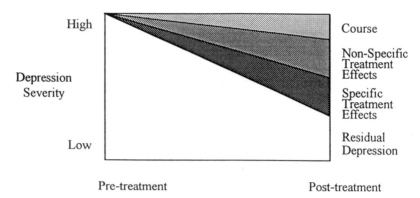

Figure 6.1. Theoretical Sources of Improvement in Depression Symptoms

interviews by the Depression Guideline Panel responsible for the development of clinical practice guidelines for the treatment of depression in primary care (USDHHS, 1993b) found that 40% still qualified for a diagnosis of major depressive disorder 1 year after initial diagnosis and that an additional 20% retained some symptoms of depression.

It is apparent that major depression is typically comorbid with other disorders, frequently recurrent, often undetected or inadequately treated, and associated with considerable mortality. Given this perspective, the emergence of psychological therapies for major depression that are judged to be effective by scientific standards is meaningful.

PSYCHOLOGICAL TREATMENTS

Claims of treatment-related improvements in uncontrolled treatment studies of major depression have always been difficult to interpret and can give rise to unjustified confidence in often inadequate treatments. In fact, such improvements can be due to the passage of time (i.e., course effects) or a caring therapist (e.g., therapeutic alliance), as well as to the "active ingredients," represented as treatment procedures derived from specific schools of therapy. Good experimental designs control for course and nonspecific effects associated with symptom improvement. As can be seen in Figure 6.1, there are three theoretical sources of improvement in major depression: (a) spontaneous improvement due to the episodic nature of depression, referred to as "course effects" (remember that clients often enroll in clinical

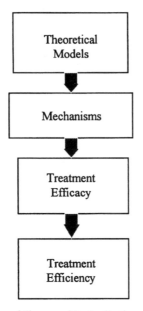

Figure 6.2. Logical Progression of Theory and Its Applications

trials when they are approaching or are already at their most severe symptom levels); (b) "nonspecific effects," which are common to any good therapeutic alliance and generally account for more outcome variance than the theory-derived treatments; and (c) specific treatment effects attributable to procedures that effectively target theory-relevant mechanisms thought to be responsible for the development and maintenance of depression. Although the relative proportions of symptom change identified in Figure 6.1 are speculative, these three sources of treatment outcome variance need to be kept in mind when comparing the results of theory-driven treatments and when trying to identify their active ingredients.

As seen in Figure 6.2, there is a logical progression from theory to treatment efficiency. Theoretical models postulate mechanisms that can be experimentally evaluated. If these are found to be valid, subsequent treatment programs attempt to manipulate such mechanisms in order to outperform competing treatments under strict (i.e., ideal) experimental conditions. If treatment efficacy is established, then ways of delivering the therapeutic effect most efficiently can be addressed. In a time of increasing market pressure to empirically demonstrate treatment efficacy for psychological treatments, understanding mechanisms allows for increased flexibility and treatment efficiencies. In contrast, one of the reasons that treatments such as electroconvulsive shock therapy have not progressed remarkably as a treatment for major depression is that they lack both a theoretical base and clearly understood mechanisms of action. Below, we review three prominent psychological theories of depression and their respective therapies.

Cognitive Therapy

Although several theorists were involved in the development of cognitive models of depression, Beck's cognitive theory of depression (Beck, Rush, Shaw, & Emery, 1979) is the most widely researched and recognized. In Beck's cognitive model, dysfunctional attitudes and automatic negative thoughts mediate the relationship between negative life events and depressive symptoms. The focus is therefore on the cognitive disturbances in depression (see Figure 6.3). Specifically, the theory highlights the manner in which cognitive structures (i.e., schemas) guide the processing and filtering of emotional information, which in turn predispose individuals to depression and serve to maintain this affective state through a relatively high concentration of situation-specific, self-referenced automatic thoughts. The more persistent schemas, alternatively referred to as *dysfunctional attitudes, dysfunctional beliefs, underlying assumptions,* or *cognitive schemas* (Dobson & Shaw, 1986), are represented as the cognitive structures that organize, filter, and differentially attend to stimuli. Beck's model represents a diathesis-stress or cognitive vulnerability model in that the person's deeper cognitive structures, or core schemas, represent a vulnerability to depression when activated by particular life events (Miranda, Persons, & Byers, 1990; Teasdale & Dent, 1987). The cognitive model maintains that many maladaptive schemas can be developed as early as childhood (e.g., failure to achieve, emotional inhibition, mistrust/abuse, defectiveness/shame, insufficient self-control/self-discipline) and become stable, enduring themes that are elaborated on over the life course (Young et al., 1993). Normal, but stressful, life events become distorted during the cognitive appraisal process by the maladaptive schemas and activate depressogenic automatic thoughts, which in turn foster depressive affect and behavior. Although there has been an impressive amount of research supporting the presence and nature of cognitive schemas and automatic thoughts, the causal relationship between these cognitive phenomena and depressive affect remains controversial (DeRubeis & Feeley, 1990; Sullivan & Conway, 1991).

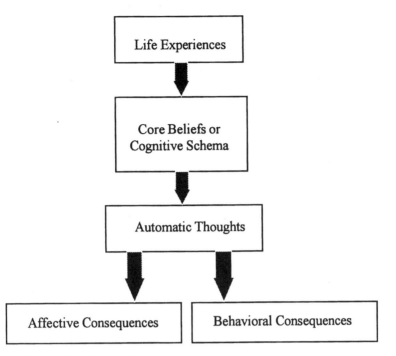

Figure 6.3. Cognitive Theory of Depression

In practice (see Table 6.2), cognitive theory involves an educational process in which the therapist supplies a rationale for cognitive therapy that clarifies the relationship between thoughts, feelings, and behaviors and then proceeds to identify and challenge the cognitive errors that stem from faulty appraisals and beliefs. Clients are taught how to generate alternative interpretations and solutions and to test both automatic and alternative thoughts for evidence of accuracy. Engagement in pleasant activities and the use of homework assignments, including graded task assignments, are standard features of cognitive therapy. Throughout therapy, the therapist and client collaborate as an investigative team to unravel and challenge dysfunctional cognitions and to promote the agenda of this short-term therapy. A number of self-help manuals for the cognitive treatment of depression are available (e.g., Greenberger & Padesky, 1995). The popular book by Burns (1980) has been shown to be an effective form of cognitive bibliotherapy (Jamieson & Scogin, 1995), thus demonstrating that cognitive therapy can be delivered efficiently.

TABLE 6.2   Cognitive Therapy Methods

Rationale: Depression explained by maladaptive or depressogenic cognitions and beliefs

Specific Techniques:

    (1) Cognitive rationale

    (2) Monitoring and identifying cognitive errors

    (3) Testing and changing beliefs

    (4) Mastery and pleasure activity scheduling

    (5) Homework assignments

    (6) Collaboration

    (7) Following an agenda in therapy

Behavior Therapy

Historically, Skinner (1953) and Ferster (1966) conceptualized depression as the weakening of behavior due to interruptions in positive reinforcement available for well-established behaviors. This extinction model accounted for the reduction of adaptive behaviors characteristic of depression. Lewinsohn and his colleagues have been the most systematic and influential contributors to the development and refinement of behavioral theory of depression. Lewinsohn (1974) postulated that a low rate of response-contingent positive reinforcement in significant life areas, and/or a high rate of aversive experiences can induce dysphoric affect. Three factors are thought to lead to a low rate of response-contingent reinforcement (Lewinsohn & Gotlib, 1995; Lewinsohn, Lobitz, & Wilson, 1973): (a) deficits in an individual's behavioral repertoire, or skills, thus precluding the attainment of positive reinforcement; (b) lack of available reinforcers in the individual's environment, or a surplus of aversive experiences; and (c) a decreased ability for an individual to enjoy positive experiences, or increased sensitivity to negative experiences. The ensuing dysphoric affect and depressive behavior, however, can evoke a sympathetic response from one's social environment, which has the effect of maintaining/reinforcing both the dysphoric affect and depressed behavior (see Figure 6.4).

The Lewinsohn team has produced experimental evidence, particularly on the relationship of positive events to mood and interpersonal interactions, that lends support to the mechanisms they have identified. They have also developed a 12-session, small-group treatment program called the Coping With Depression Course (Lewinsohn, Antonuccio, Steinmetz, & Teri, 1984),

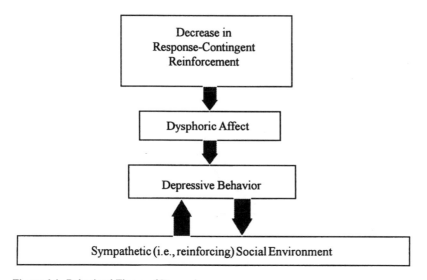

Figure 6.4. Behavioral Theory of Depression

designed to help clients achieve a satisfactory level of response-contingent reinforcement. Table 6.3 identifies the specific techniques used in this treatment approach.

The behavioral approach to understanding depression has led to a number of related formulations to account for the etiology of depression. Coyne (1976) has suggested that depression is maintained through attempts by depressed individuals to gain sympathy from their increasingly hostile and alienated social field. Rehm (1977) has developed a self-control theory and treatment for depression in which selective attention to negative events and the immediate consequences of one's behavior, perfectionistic expectations, and failure to provide oneself with positive recognition are considered sufficient to cause depression. Others, such as Nezu (1987), have proposed that ineffectual problem-solving skills applied to difficult life events lead to unsatisfactorily resolved problems and negative outcomes, resulting in depression. As Lewinsohn and Gotlib (1995) pointed out, behavioral theories and treatments of depression have clearly moved beyond stimulus-response formulations of reinforcement contingencies and have embraced more complex concepts, including the nature of one's social environment, self-awareness, and internal standards for acceptable performance.

TABLE 6.3   Behavioral Therapy Methods

Rationale: Depression explained by inadequate reinforcement

Specific Techniques:
   (1) Relaxation training
   (2) Structuring and scheduling pleasant events
   (3) Methods of constructive thinking
   (4) Social skills training
   (5) Homework assignments
   (6) Development of a life plan

Interpersonal Psychotherapy

Although interpersonal psychotherapy (IPT) can conceptually be traced to the therapeutic practices of Harry Stack Sullivan and Adolf Meyer, it was developed by Klerman, DiMascio, Weissman, Prusoff, and Paykel (1974) as a short-term supportive psychotherapy that reflected the general psychotherapy practices of the 1970s. It was initially developed to test relapse prevention in a pharmacological treatment trial. Since the IPT manual was refined and published (Klerman, Weissman, Rounsaville, & Cheveron, 1984), it has been widely implemented and assessed as a treatment for major depression (see Frank & Spanier, 1995, for a review). The goal of IPT is to reduce depressive symptoms by improving the client's social competence and the quality of social relationships. IPT techniques were developed to address four standard problem areas (see Figure 6.5), any one of which could be the basis for depression. The therapist collaborates with the client in IPT to determine which of the four problem areas best coincides with the onset of the current depression episode. Once the problem area is identified, the therapist works with the client to improve the client's current social roles and interpersonal relationships, consistent with the particular problem area. A listing of specific IPT techniques is provided in Table 6.4.

The interpersonal approach to understanding and treating depression views problematic social relations as pathogenic and causally linked to depression. IPT is not considered to be unique by its founders but rather to integrate perspectives from psychoanalytic to cognitive-behavioral schools to improve interpersonal functioning and reduce current psychosocial stressors in very practical ways. As Frank and Spanier (1995) explained, IPT represents "grandmother's wisdom."

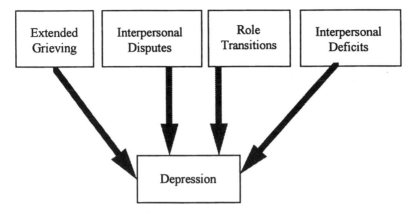

Figure 6.5. Interpersonal Theory of Depression

TABLE 6.4   Interpersonal Psychotherapy Methods

Rationale: Depression causally linked to interpersonal context

Identification of major problems area(s): (grief, interpersonal disputes, role transitions, interpersonal deficits)

Specific Techniques:
   (1) Exploratory
   (2) Encouragement of affect
   (3) Clarification
   (4) Communication analysis
   (5) Use of therapeutic relationship
   (6) Behavior change techniques

SOURCES OF TREATMENT EFFECTS IN COGNITIVE, BEHAVIORAL, AND INTERPERSONAL THERAPIES

Because symptom improvement concurrent with treatment may be attributable to various factors, it is incumbent on the field to consider the magnitude of course effects and nonspecific treatment effects in order to accurately identify actual differences between specific treatments. Of course, good experimental designs control for these factors. However, not all treatment studies are optimal, so these factors are often confounded within gross pre-post symptom improvement figures. The discerning reader will compare net treatment effects across studies and will use this information as a basis for interpreting results from uncontrolled outcome studies.

Course Effects

The Agency for Health Care Policy and Research, under the U.S. Department of Health and Human Services, recently developed empirically derived clinical practice guidelines for the treatment of depression by primary care physicians (USDHHS, 1993b). They reviewed treatment outcome studies and found that 60% of the gain in symptom improvement was attributable to a combination of treatment effects and course effects, with the theory-driven treatment effects accounting for only 40% of the improvements. It is difficult to estimate the course effects for moderately to severely depressed clients over the usual 3-month treatment period because ethical reasons limit studies including a substantial wait-list control period with this population. In a recent comorbidity study investigating treatment effects when panic and major depression disorders occurred alone or together, we found that clients with major depression alone evidenced symptom improvement over 3 months on the order of 15% to 20% (McLean, Woody, Taylor, & Koch, 1996). These clients were seen weekly under the auspices of continued assessment in order to provide an attention control condition and monitor suicidal risk. Assuming spontaneous improvements to be around 20% for outpatients with major depression over a 3-month period, the remaining 80% of the treatment outcome variance can be attributed between nonspecific and specific treatment effects.

Nonspecific Treatment Effects

It is well known that nonspecific treatment effects fail to receive their due credit relative to theory-driven effects and tend to receive passing, but not honorable, mention. We are aware of very few training programs that offer a course in nonspecific treatment effects, provide competency-based guidelines to exploit this source of influence, or even address the issue at all. Instead, it seems to be incorrectly assumed that nonspecific treatment skills are akin to good manners and that all therapists should have them before they present for professional training.

Hollon (1984) developed an audiotape rating system to evaluate treatment content in NIMH's collaborative depression treatment program. A subsample

TABLE 6.5   Sources of Nonspecific Treatment Effects

Psychiatric history
Professional manner
Symptoms inquiry
Encouragement
Convey expertise
Warmth
Optimistic reassurance
Empathy
Receptive listening
Reflective listening
Involvement/interest
Genuineness
Rapport
Exploring personal meaning

SOURCE: Adapted from Hollon (1980).

of the "nonspecific strategies" identified by Hollon is given in Table 6.5. In our internship training and treatment evaluation programs, we scale each of these strategies, which are descriptively anchored at either end of a 7-point scale, for both nonspecific treatment and specific treatment (e.g., cognitive-behavioral) strategies. This allows therapists to be aware of and to rehearse both sets of strategies before their treatment sessions, to rate their own performance subsequently, and to be rated by peers or supervisors. In this case, strategies such as warmth, empathy, and genuineness can be operationally defined, discussed, illustrated, and targeted for delivery. Keeping in mind that variance in treatment-related improvements in short-term psychological, acute-phase treatments for depression can be attributed to spontaneous improvement or to course effects (20%), nonspecific effects (40%), and theory-specific effects (40%), we can now return to a comparative review of treatment outcome.

Theory-Specific Effects

Since Dobson's (1989) meta-analysis of various psychotherapies for depression, which disclosed superior efficacy for cognitive therapy, most subsequent studies and reviews have reported no significant differences in treatment efficacy between cognitive therapy, behavior therapy, and interpersonal psychotherapy (Barlow, 1994; Elkin et al., 1989; Ogles, Lambert, & Sawyer, 1995; Shapiro et al., 1994). Typically, these treatments are significantly better than wait-list control or placebo conditions yet are equivalent to each other and to pharmacological treatments in terms of efficacy. The most compelling study of comparative effects was recently reported by Jacobson et al. (1996). The purpose of this large treatment trial was to examine the independent contribution made by various treatment components of the overall cognitive-behavioral therapy program. This component analysis was composed of three treatment groups: (a) behavioral activation, (b) behavioral activation and skill training in managing automatic thoughts (addressing core schemas was prohibited), and (c) the full cognitive-behavioral program. The therapists involved were experienced cognitive therapists, and adherence to treatment protocols was demonstrated. All treatment conditions improved equally during acute treatment and maintained these gains when reevaluated at 6-month follow-up. As in previous studies, changes in specific response domains were not unique to any particular treatment. That is, improvements in negative thinking and dysfunctional attributional styles were associated with all three treatment conditions, regardless of whether they were addressed in treatment or not.

The above finding raises key theoretical questions about causal mechanisms versus treatment coeffects. As Lazarus (1996) pointed out, "It is techniques, not theories, that are actually used on people" (p. 59). Taken together, the evidence on treatment efficacy suggests that although these three psychological treatments are efficacious, they are not unique in terms of their effects on overall symptom improvement or changes in theory-related domains.

Common Therapeutic Features

If theory-derived treatments are equally successful and if treatment response does not depend on the modality of treatment technique used, we must assume that these treatments share active ingredients. Setting aside theoretical claims, a close examination of cognitive, behavioral, and IPT treatment protocols indicates that, compared to the techniques employed by many other schools of therapeutic thought, these three treatment approaches share a number of therapeutic features. It is likely that clients are responding more to the common features of these therapies than to their theoretical differences. The nine features common to the techniques of behavioral, cognitive, and interpersonal therapies are listed and discussed below. However, it is important to note that these common features are not the same as nonspecific effects. *Nonspecific factors* refers to features that contribute to improvement although they are neither mandated nor specified by either the theoretical rationale or the therapy techniques of the theoretical orientation. They represent the commonsense foundation that we expect from any effective clinician, irrespective of theoretical orientation. In contrast, the therapeutic features common to cognitive, behavioral, and interpersonal therapies are explicit in their treatment methods.

Treatment Process Is Collaborative

The client and therapist act as a team, working together in an egalitarian manner to explore, experiment, rehearse, and reevaluate issues and strategies related to the client's symptoms and functional behavior. This partnership involves a high degree of active collaboration and is established by the therapist as an operating style at the onset of therapy.

Focus Almost Exclusively on Present and Future

Improvement of current functioning is a primary focus of the three therapies. The future receives prominent attention in terms of goal setting, problem anticipation, and general planning. The past is considered etiologically relevant, but problems are normally addressed in the present tense. This is somewhat less true for IPT, given its psychoanalytic roots and adherence to attachment theory. Nonetheless, there is little focus on reprocessing perceptions and emotions associated with past grievances. These are not ignored but are conceptualized as vulnerability factors. Negative emotions are cast as downstream effects of current performance and perception problems.

Therapist Active, Not Passive

Therapists are active and directive in these therapies, often alternating between the roles of collaborator and coach. Accordingly, the rates of mutual problem-solving interchanges and generation of alternate options for coping are relatively high, unlike those of more traditional therapies, in which the therapist assumes a less active role.

High Treatment Structure

These three therapies are highly structured as cumulative learning programs. The agendas for treatment sessions are reviewed, goals are identified, homework is assigned and reviewed, progress is routinely assessed, and behavioral experiments, rehearsal by role playing, and the identification and preparation for anticipated problematic encounters are all normal components of treatment sessions. This structure should not result in the client feeling hurried, the treatment session appearing to be busy, or the agenda being perceived as too rigid. The intent of the treatment structure across these therapies is to give clients a "hands-on" approach to efficient problem solving and learning and to help focus treatment interventions on symptom reduction.

Detailed Treatment Protocols

These three therapies have led the field in the standardization of quality treatment manuals. This manualization enables replication of outcome studies and data sharing across sites and now is considered a requirement to meet scientific standards in psychological practice. There are also published client guides available for all three therapies that are coordinated with the published therapist's manuals. This level of organization and information sharing moves these therapies away from traditional therapies toward a self-development educational course format.

Development of Personal Competencies

The stated goals of these treatments include the development of personal competencies in social, cognitive, and behavioral realms. The focus is on self-mastery, goal achievement, emotional independence, and the normalization of cognitive appraisals. Consequently, increases in perceived self-efficacy may mediate therapeutic change in these treatments.

Ongoing Empirical Assessment (CT and BT)

Continuous empirical assessment of symptoms, homework, hypothesis testing, and response to behavioral experiments is integral to both behavioral and cognitive treatment traditions. Empirical assessment allows the client-therapist team to make continuous course adjustments in treatment. IPT does not use empirical assessment as a treatment technique.

Homework Assignments
(Especially CT and BT)

The use of assigned homework promotes the generalization of treatment through practice in natural settings. Homework is characteristic of both behavioral and cognitive therapies and is assigned in virtually every session, although its use in IPT is much less frequent. Ilardi and Craighead (1994) have identified the assignment of homework in cognitive-behavioral therapy for depression to be one of the two most potent treatment factors in mediating clinical improvement.

Time-Limited Treatment

All three treatments are designed for short-term, acute treatment, on the order of 12 to 16 individual or group sessions. Thereafter, clients can be seen monthly for maintenance treatment but typically do not receive maintenance sessions. There is no standard duration for maintenance treatment.

LIMITATIONS OF THEORY-DRIVEN
TREATMENTS OF DEPRESSION

Lack of Treatment Specificity

An examination of treatment manuals for cognitive, behavioral, and interpersonal therapies reveals clear procedural overlapping in terms of areas addressed and techniques used, despite theoretical claims of unique mediators in the pathogenesis and treatment of depression. It appears that the three treatments differ primarily in the degree of emphasis placed in specific areas. For example, all three therapy schools consider interpersonal, cognitive, and behavioral domains to be interactive, as indicated in Figure 6.6, but place increased therapeutic emphasis on the domain most relevant to their particular theory. The issue of a unique mechanism of action in these therapies has not been supported. Many therapies produce cognitive change (Jacobson et al., 1996: Persons & Miranda, 1995; Whisman, 1993), and the endorse-

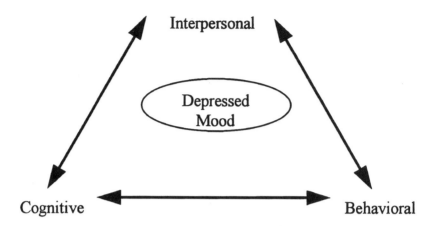

Figure 6.6. Reciprocal Influences of Cognitive, Behavioral, and Interpersonal Functioning

ment of dysfunctional beliefs apparently depends on one's present mood state (Miranda et al., 1990). In summary, treatment response is not mode specific (e.g., behavioral change can produce cognitive change), mechanisms of change remain controversial, and treatment techniques overlap considerably.

Subject Homogeneity

Treatment efficacy studies have traditionally excluded clients who are comorbid with another Axis I or Axis II disorder in order to conduct treatment trials under relatively ideal conditions, thereby reducing subject variation attributable to factors not under study. Comparative treatment efficiency trials using clinically referred clients, unselected for comorbidity, have yet to be undertaken. Such selection practices create doubts regarding the generalizability of these procedures to more prototypical depressed patients, who typically present with comorbid diagnoses.

Preoccupation With Acute Phase

It has become an industry standard to deliver treatment once a week for 10 to 20 weeks, although there is little empirical support for this convention (Frank & Spanier, 1995). In fact, there is ample evidence that many clients remain undertreated on the conclusion of standard treatment trials. A review

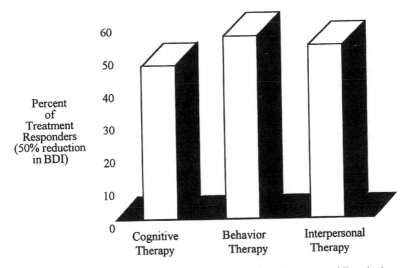

Figure 6.7. Comparative Efficacy of Cognitive, Behavioral, and Interpersonal Functioning

of studies by the Depression Guideline Panel (USDHHS, 1993b) showed that 40% to 50% of clients did not experience at least a 50% symptom reduction after receiving either cognitive, behavioral, or interpersonal therapy (see Figure 6.7). Further, it is known that over 50% of the major depression population experiences at least one subsequent episode, and all three schools of therapy refer to vulnerabilities as traitlike qualities, implying long-term risk for symptomatic recurrence among those who have had a major depressive episode. Preoccupation with acute-phase treatment and short-term follow-up creates a snapshot view of depression that may not easily reconcile with the realities of mental health service delivery.

These factors limit the practical implications of theory-based efficacy studies because such studies are not representative of actual clinical practice and because the benefits realized from them delivered in this format appear to be maximized.

NEW DIRECTIONS

Health care reform is influencing the way psychotherapy is being delivered and who provides the services. Further, there is increased pressure for pharmacological treatment of depression based on economic grounds. Where will further treatment gains come from in psychological therapies? We suggest that further gains are probable if treatments are tailored to the individual client. Recent research has indicated opportunities for customizing treatment to individual clients that go beyond the previous unfruitful attempts to match client characteristics to theory-driven treatments in order to get a better treatment outcome. It is proposed that adjustments to treatment delivery on the basis of personality factors, course characteristics, and contextual factors will improve the efficiency of theory-derived treatments.

Personality

It has been argued that the modest main effect sizes in psychotherapy research are diluted due to mismatches between clients and treatment (Beutler, 1991, 1995; Smith & Sechrest, 1991; Whisman, 1993). Though previous research has generally found minimal support for the utility of aptitude × treatment considerations, various methodological and statistical flaws routinely noted in these studies seriously limit the power of these studies to detect true interaction effects (Shoham-Salomon, 1991). Treatment matching based on patient attributes promises to provide a better fit between moderators (i.e., client characteristics) and choice of psychotherapy approach. The presence of aptitude × treatment interactions is a basis for optimism in that the treatment is shown to work better for some persons under some conditions than for others (Smith & Sechrest, 1991). Beutler and Clarkin (1990) have pioneered the search for prescriptive indicators of specific therapeutic interventions based on aptitude × treatment interaction research. This search has been aided by developments in personality research, particularly the development of the NEO five-factor personality inventory, which reduces the large number of personality trait descriptors to five orthogonal domains (Costa & McCrae, 1992). The utility of such a comprehensive yet efficient summarization of personality constructs can help to standardize aptitude × treatment interaction research, for researchers can now use these factorially derived personality constructs to quantify the personality domain in a consistent manner across research sites (Anderson, 1997).

To illustrate the potential of aptitude × treatment research in matching clients to various treatments, we will consider several of the "big five" personality dimensions: neuroticism, extroversion, and conscientiousness. Anxious individuals are apprehensive, fearful, prone to worry, nervous and tense, whereas those who score low on neuroticism are calm, relaxed, and unworried (Costa & McCrae, 1992). Beutler and Clarkin (1990) reported evidence that patients high in neuroticism fare poorer in conflict-focused therapies, and Elkin (1994) found high neuroticism to be a poor prognostic indicator for IPT. Shea et al. (1992) found that extroverts benefit from IPT more than introverts, presumably because they have more interpersonal skills and a preexisting orientation toward interpersonal activity that allows them to benefit more from IPT. Extroverts also tolerate group treatment, brief treatment, and less structured therapy better than introverts. Costa and McCrae (1992) described the personality dimension of conscientiousness as reflecting orderliness and organization, persistence and dependability, achievement striving, efficiency and effectiveness, and deliberation and planning. In contrast, low conscientiousness represented an undisciplined approach to life. In a study of depressed clients in receipt of maintenance treatment following discharge from inpatient psychiatric care, we found that problematic alcohol use, satisfaction with one's level of social support, major life stressors, and initial depression severity (i.e., on discharge from inpatient care) together accounted for 7% of the variance on the Depression subscale of the SCL-90-R (Derogatis, 1983) 6 months after discharge. However, conscientious scale ratings on the NEO-Personality Inventory (NEO-PI; Costa & McCrae, 1985) at Time 1 accounted for 28% of the variance on the SCL-90-R Depression subscale at 6 months follow-up (Anderson & McLean, 1997). From a clinical perspective, clients low on conscientiousness would be likely to benefit most from behavior therapy techniques, which emphasize daily goal setting, self-pacing, graduated goal attainment, and highly speci-fied homework assignments. In examining the relative endurance of four depression treatments over a $2\frac{1}{4}$-year follow-up period, we found that behavior therapy was uniquely effective in improving personal productivity (McLean & Hakstian, 1990). Finally, there are indications that depressed, perfectionistic individuals respond better to long-term, less structured treat-ment (Blatt, 1995). For a full review of the role of personality variables in psychotherapy aptitude × treatment research, see Anderson (1997).

Course Characteristics

The goal of acute-phase treatment is primarily symptom reduction. Cog-nitive and behavioral therapies typically include preparation for relapse as part of acute-phase treatment but unlike IPT do not usually switch to maintenance treatment on the conclusion of acute-phase treatment. Although cognitive therapy has been shown to be more effective in reducing relapse rates relative to pharmacotherapy (Evans et al., 1992; Miller, Norman, & Keitner, 1989), many clients remain symptomatic (Shea et al., 1992; USDHHS, 1993b) and vulnerable following treatment. For these reasons, maintenance programs might prove to be cost-effective. Visits may range from monthly to quarterly sessions, depending on a client's symptom severity, functional performance, and degree of vulnerability. Similarly, prevention programs targeted to at-risk populations, such as children with poor social skills (Cole, Martin, Powers, & Truglio, 1996), teenage boys experiencing academic failure and social rejection (Patterson & Stoolmiller, 1991), individuals with subsyndromal levels of depression (Wells et al., 1989), children of depressed parents (Beardslee, 1990), women on public assistance (Tableman, 1987), and the elderly (Teri, Curtis, Gallagher-Thompson, & Thompson, 1994), are proving to be effective but are in the junior stage of development. Now that the best acute-phase treatment results are likely to have been achieved, adapting the knowledge and skills involved in treatment to optimize prevention and maintenance programs seems an appropriate public health goal.

Contextual Factors

In client-tailored treatment for depression in which client characteristics help determine the choice of treatment, increased importance needs to be placed on functional assessment, including assessment of vulnerabilities and social support. The APA National Task Force on Women and Depression (McGrath, Keita, Strickland, & Russo, 1990) made it clear that the rate of sexual and physical abuse of women is higher than previously suspected and identified poverty as "the pathway to depression." Such abuse and adversity need to be thoroughly assessed to make the best treatment selection choices. Similarly, current social stressors, level of social skills, and degree of social support can inform treatment selection, which can vary in terms of individual or group delivery, degree of structure, confrontation, and degree of training in functional problem solving. For example, Elkin et al. (1995) found that functional impairment significantly predicted differential treatment effects and noted treatment group interactions on this variable. Further, Sotsky et al. (1991) reported that social dysfunction predicted poor response to treatment, and McLean and Hakstian (1990) found that behavior therapy was more effective in improving the rate of social activity over a 2¼ year follow-up period than alternative therapies. As assessment practices expand to include more information on predisposing factors, and as protocol-driven therapies are applied to a wider range of special populations, there will be an even better scope of variables by which clients can be matched to specific intervention techniques for optimal treatment results. These new directions have the potential to advance the gains made by the well-established, empirically validated treatments but are likely to do so only to the extent that scientific standards are rigorously applied to research efforts.

REFERENCES

American Psychiatric Association. (1994). *Diagnostic and statistical manual of mental disorders* (4th ed.). Washington, DC: Author.

American Psychological Association. (1995). Training in and dissemination of empirically-validated psychological treatments: Report and recommendations. *Clinical Psychologist, 48*, 3-24.

Anderson, K. W. (1997). Utility of the five-factor model of personality in psychotherapy aptitude-treatment interaction research. *Psychotherapy Research, 8*, 373-389.

Anderson, K. W., & McLean, P. D. (1997). Conscientiousness in depression: Tendencies, predictive utility, and longitudinal stability. *Cognitive Therapy and Research, 2*, 223-238.

Antonuccio, D. O., Danton, W. G., & DeNelsky, G. Y. (1995). Psychotherapy versus medication for depression: Challenging the conventional wisdom with data. *Professional Psychology: Research and Practice, 26*, 574-585.

Barlow, D. H. (1994). Psychological interventions in the era of managed competition. *Clinical Psychology: Science and Practice, 1*, 109-122.

Beardslee, W. P. (1990). Development of a clinician-based preventive intervention for families with affective disorders. *Journal of Preventive Psychiatry and Allied Disciplines, 4*, 39-61.

Beck, A. T., Rush, A. J., Shaw, B. F., & Emery, G. (1979). *Cognitive therapy of depression.* New York: Guilford.

Beutler, L. E. (1991). Have all won and must all have prizes? Revisiting Luborsky et al.'s verdict. *Journal of Consulting and Clinical Psychology, 59*, 226-232.

Beutler, L. E. (1995). Common factors and specific effects. *Clinical Psychology: Science and Practice, 2*, 79-82.

Beutler, L. E., & Clarkin, J. (1990). *Systematic treatment selection: Toward targeted therapeutic interventions.* New York: Brunner/Mazel.

Blatt, S. J. (1995). The destructiveness of perfectionism: Implications for the treatment of depression. *American Psychologist, 50*, 1003-1020.

Burns, D. D. (1980). *Feeling good: The new mood therapy.* New York: Signet.

Cole, D. A., Martin, J. M., Powers, B., & Truglio, R. (1996). Modeling causal relations between academic and social competence and depression: A multitrait-multimethod longitudinal study of children. *Journal of Abnormal Psychology, 105*, 258-270.

Costa, P. T., & McCrae, R. R. (1985). *The NEO Personality Inventory manual.* Odessa, FL: Psychological Assessment Resources.

Costa, P. T., & McCrae, R. R. (1992). *Revised NEO Personality Inventory (NEO-PI-R) and NEO Five-Factor Inventory (NEO-FFI) professional manual.* Odessa, FL: Psychological Assessment Resources.

Coyne, J. C. (1976). Toward an interactional description of depression. *Psychiatry, 39,* 28-40.

Derogatis, L. R. (1983). *SCL-90-R manual.* Towson, MD: Clinical Psychometric Research.

DeRubeis, R. J., & Feeley, M. (1990). Determinants of change in cognitive therapy for depression. *Cognitive Therapy and Research, 14,* 469-482.

Dobson, K. S. (1989). A meta-analysis of the efficacy of cognitive therapy for depression. *Journal of Consulting and Clinical Psychology, 57,* 414-419.

Dobson, K. S., & Shaw, B. F. (1986). Cognitive assessment with major depressive disorders. *Cognitive Therapy and Research, 10,* 13-29.

Dobson, K. S., & Shaw, B. F. (1988). The use of treatment manuals in cognitive therapy: Experience and issues. *Journal of Consulting and Clinical Psychology, 56,* 673-680.

Elkin, I. (1994). The NIMH treatment of depression collaborative research program: Where we began and where we are. In A. E. Bergin & S. L. Garfield (Eds.), *Handbook of psychotherapy and behavior change* (4th ed., pp. 114-139). New York: John Wiley.

Elkin, I., Gibbons, R. D., Shea, M. T., Sotsky, S. M., Watkins, J. T., Pilkonis, P. A., & Hedeker, D. (1995). Initial severity and differential treatment outcome in the National Institute of Mental Health treatment of depression collaborative research program. *Journal of Consulting and Clinical Psychology, 63,* 841-847.

Elkin, I., Shea, M. T., Watkins, J. T., Imber, S. D., Sotsky, S. M., Collins, J. F., Glass, D. R., Pilkonis, P. A., Leber, W. R., Docherty, J. P., Fiester, S. J., & Parloff, M. B. (1989). National Institute of Mental Health treatment of depression collaborative research program. *Archives of General Psychiatry, 46,* 971-982.

Evans, M. D., Hollon, S. D., DeRubeis, R. J., Piasecki, J. M., Grove, W. M., Garvey, M. J., & Tuason, V. B. (1992). Differential relapse following cognitive therapy and pharmacotherapy for depression. *Archives of General Psychiatry, 49,* 802-808.

Ferster, C. B. (1966). Animal behavior and mental illness. *Psychological Record, 16,* 345-356.

Frank, E., & Spanier, C. (1995). Interpersonal psychotherapy for depression: Overview, clinical efficacy, and future directions. *Clinical Psychology: Science and Practice, 2,* 349-369.

Greenberger, D., & Padesky, C. A. (1995). *Mind over mood: A cognitive therapy treatment manual for clients.* New York: Guilford.

Gullick, E. L., & King, L. J. (1979). Appropriateness of drugs prescribed by primary care physicians for depressed outpatients. *Journal of Affective Disorders, 1,* 55-58.

Hollon, S. D. (1984). *System for rating psychotherapy audiotapes* (Final report to National Institute of Mental Health, Contract No. 278-81-0031[ER]). Rockville, MD: U.S. Department of Commerce, National Technical Information Service.

Ilardi, S. S., & Craighead, W. E. (1994). The role of nonspecific factors in cognitive-behavior therapy for depression. *Clinical Psychology: Science and Practice, 1,* 138-156.

Jacobson, N. S., Dobson, K. S., Truax, P. A., Addis, M. E., Koerner, K., Gollan, J. K., Gortner, E., & Prince, S. E. (1996). A component analysis of cognitive-behavioral treatment for depression. *Journal of Consulting and Clinical Psychology, 64,* 295-304.

Jacobson, N. S., & Hollon, S. D. (1996). Cognitive-behavior therapy versus pharmacotherapy: Now that the jury's returned its verdict, it's time to present the rest of the evidence. *Journal of Consulting and Clinical Psychology, 64,* 74-80.

Jamieson, C., & Scogin, F. (1995). The outcome of cognitive bibliotherapy with depressed adults. *Journal of Consulting and Clinical Psychology, 63,* 644-650.

Johnson, D. (1974). Study of the use of antidepressant medication in general practice. *British Journal of Psychiatry, 125,* 186-212.

Klerman, G. L., DiMascio, A., Weissman, M., Prusoff, B., & Paykel, E. (1974). Treatment of depression by drugs and psychotherapy. *American Journal of Psychiatry, 131,* 186-191.

Klerman, G. L., Weissman, M. M., Rounsaville, B. J., & Cheveron, E. (1984). *Interpersonal psychotherapy of depression.* New York: Basic Books.

Lazarus, A. A. (1996). The utility and futility of combining treatments in psychotherapy. *Clinical Psychology: Science and Practice, 3,* 59-68.

Lewinsohn, P. M. (1974). A behavioral approach to depression. In R. J. Friedman & M. M. Katz (Eds.), *The psychology of depression: Contemporary theory and research* (pp. 157-185). New York: John Wiley.

Lewinsohn, P. M., Antonuccio, D. O., Steinmetz, J. L., & Teri, L. (1984). *The Coping With Depression course: A psychoeducational intervention for unipolar depression.* Eugene, OR: Castalia.

Lewinsohn, P. M., & Gotlib, I. H. (1995). Behavioral therapy and treatment of depression. In E. E. Becker & W. R. Leber (Eds.), *Handbook of depression.* New York: Guilford.

Lewinsohn, P. M., Lobitz, W. C., & Wilson, S. (1973). "Sensitivity" of depressed individuals to aversive stimuli. *Journal of Abnormal Psychology, 81,* 259-263.

McGrath, E., Keita, G. P., Strickland, B. R., & Russo, N. F. (Eds.). (1990). *Women and depression: Risk factors and treatment issues.* Washington, DC: American Psychological Association.

McLean, P. D., & Hakstian, A. R. (1990). Relative endurance of unipolar depression treatment effects: Longitudinal follow-up. *Journal of Consulting and Clinical Psychology, 58,* 482-488.

McLean, P. D., & Taylor, S. (1992). Severity of unipolar depression and choice of treatment. *Behaviour Research and Therapy, 30,* 443-451.

McLean, P. D., Woody, S., Taylor, S., & Koch, W. J. (1998). Comorbid panic disorder and major depression: Implications for cognitive-behavioral therapy. *Journal of Consulting and Clinical Psychology, 66,* 240-247.

Miller, I. W., Norman, W. H., & Keitner, G. I. (1989). Cognitive-behavioral treatment of depressed inpatients: Six- and twelve-month follow-up. *American Journal of Psychiatry, 146,* 1274-1279.

Miranda, J., Persons, J. B., & Byers, C. N. (1990). Endorsement of dysfunctional beliefs depends on current mood state. *Journal of Abnormal Psychology, 99,* 237-241.

Nezu, A. M. (1987). A problem-solving formulation of depression: A literature review and proposal of a pluralistic model. *Clinical Psychology Review, 7,* 121-144.

Ogles, B. M., Lambert, M. J., & Sawyer, J. D. (1995). Clinical significance of the National Institute of Mental Health treatment of depression collaborative research program data. *Journal of Consulting and Clinical Psychology, 63,* 321-326.

Patterson, G. R., & Stoolmiller, M. (1991). Replications of a dual failure model for boy's depressed mood. *Journal of Consulting and Clinical Psychology, 59,* 491-498.

Persons, J. B., & Miranda, J. (1995). The search for mode-specific effects of cognitive and other therapies: A methodological suggestion. *Psychotherapy Research, 5,* 102-112.

Rehm, L. P. (1977). A self-control model of depression. *Behavior Therapy, 8,* 787-804.

Sanderson, W. C., & Woody, S. (1995). Manuals for empirically validated treatments: A project of the Task Force on Psychological Interventions. *Clinical Psychologist, 48,* 7-11.

Shapiro, D. A., Barkham, M., Rees, A., Hardy, G. E., Reynolds, S., & Startup, M. (1994). Effects of treatment duration and severity of depression on the effectiveness of cognitive-behavioral and psychodynamic-interpersonal psychotherapy. *Journal of Consulting and Clinical Psychology, 62,* 522-534.

Shea, M. T., Elkin, I., Imber, S. D., Sotsky, S. M., Watkins, J. T., Collins, J. F., Pilkonis, P. A., Beckham, E., Glass, D. R., Dolan, R. T., & Parloff, M. B. (1992). Course of depressive symptoms over follow-up. *Archives of General Psychiatry, 49,* 782-787.

Shea, M. T., Pilkonis, P. A., Beckham, E., Collins, J. F., Elkin, I., Sotsky, S. M., & Docherty, J. P. (1990). Personality disorders and treatment outcome in the NIMH treatment of depression collaborative research program. *American Journal of Psychiatry, 147,* 711-718.

Shoham-Salomon, V. (Ed.). (1991). Client-therapy interaction research [Special section]. *Journal of Consulting and Clinical Psychology, 59*(2).

Skinner, B. F. (1953). *Science and human behavior.* New York: Free Press.

Smith, B., & Sechrest, L. (1991). Treatment of aptitude × treatment interactions. *Journal of Consulting and Clinical Psychology, 59,* 233-244.

Sotsky, S. M., Glass, D. R., Shea, M. T., Pilkonis, P. A., Collins, J. F., Elkin, I., Watkins, J. T., Imber, S. D., Leber, W. R., Moyer, J., & Oliveri, M. E. (1991). Patient predictors of response to psychotherapy and pharmacotherapy: Findings in the NIMH treatment of depression collaborative research program. *American Journal of Psychiatry, 148,* 997-1008.

Sullivan, M. J. L., & Conway, M. (1991). Dysphoria and valence of attributions for others' behavior. *Cognitive Therapy and Research, 15,* 273-282.

Tableman, B. (1987). Stress management training: An approach to the prevention of depression in low-income populations. In R. F. Muñoz (Ed.), *Depression prevention: Research directions* (pp. 171-184). Washington, DC: Hemisphere.

Teasdale, J. D., & Dent, J. (1987). Cognitive vulnerability to depression: An investigation of two hypotheses. *British Journal of Clinical Psychology, 26,* 113-126.

Teri, L., Curtis, J., Gallagher-Thompson, D., & Thompson, L. W. (1994). Cognitive-behavior therapy with depressed older adults. In L. S. Scheider, C. S. Reynolds, B. Lebowitz, & A. Friedhoff (Eds.), *Diagnosis and treatment of depression in the elderly: Proceedings of the NIH Consensus Development Conference* (pp. 279-291). Washington, DC: American Psychiatric Press.

U.S. Department of Health and Human Services. (1993a). *Depression in primary care: Vol. 1. Detection and diagnosis.* (AHCPR Pub. No. 93-0550). Rockville, MD: Author.

U.S. Department of Health and Human Services. (1993b). *Depression in primary care: Vol. 2. Treatment of major depression.* (AHCPR Pub. No. 93-0551). Rockville, MD: Author.

Wells, K. B., Stewart, A., Hays, R. D., Burnam, A., Rogers, W., Daniels, M., Berry, S., Greenfield, S., & Ware, J. (1989). The functioning and well-being of depressed patients: Results from the Medical Outcomes Study. *Journal of the American Medical Association, 262,* 914-919.

Whisman, M. A. (1993). Mediators and moderators of change in cognitive therapy of depression. *Psychological Bulletin, 114,* 248-265.

Wilson, G. T. (1996). Manual-based treatments: The clinical application of research findings. *Behaviour Research and Therapy, 34,* 295-314.

Young, J. E., Beck, A. T., & Weinberger, A. (1993). Depression. In D. H. Barlow (Ed.), *Clinical handbook of psychological disorders* (2nd ed.). New York: Guilford.

7

Acceptance and Change
in Couples Therapy

ANDREW CHRISTENSEN

NEIL S. JACOBSON

In the late 1960s and 1970s, several clinicians and researchers began applying behavioral principles to the treatment of couples. Richard B. Stuart (1969), Gerald Patterson and Robert L. Weiss (Weiss, Hops, & Patterson, 1973), and Robert Liberman (1970) were the first to describe and illustrate such treatments. Neil S. Jacobson (1977) performed the first randomized clinical trial comparing behavioral treatment to a control condition. Since those early beginnings over 25 years ago, several books describing behavioral treatment of couples (e.g., Jacobson & Margolin, 1979) and dozens of empirical studies examining the effectiveness of those treatments (e.g., Christensen & Heavey, in press) have been conducted.

In this chapter, we will first describe traditional behavioral couples therapy (TBCT), some of the research documenting its effectiveness, and some of its limitations. Then we will spend most of the chapter discussing our integrative behavioral couples therapy (IBCT), which we developed to improve on the effectiveness of TBCT. We will describe some of the preliminary data from a research project comparing TBCT with IBCT. Finally, we will end with a discussion of the empirical validation of psychological treatments, particularly couples therapy.

TRADITIONAL BEHAVIORAL COUPLES THERAPY

The focus of TBCT is to create positive changes in couples' interaction through behavioral principles. TBCT typically begins with an assessment phase in which problems as well as strengths in the relationship are evaluated. Following this assessment, TBCT therapists present their findings and recommendations for treatment in a feedback session with the couple. Then treatment begins. Two major treatment strategies constitute TBCT: behavior exchange and communication/problem-solving training. Behavior exchange (BE) procedures are the clearest and most direct application of behavioral principles. The therapist tries to instigate positive behaviors in each partner in order to enrich the level of positive reinforcement that each receives. Behavioral therapists using BE may direct couples to generate lists of positive actions that might be pleasing to each. They may have couples monitor the frequency of these positive actions and take specific steps to increase the frequency of these actions. For example, therapists may have couples set aside special times such as "caring days" (Stuart, 1980) or "love days" (Weiss et al., 1973) during which they will make a special effort to increase positive events. Behavioral therapists are careful to debrief these experiences to be sure that couples carried out the assignments, to help couples acknowledge and express appreciation for what the other did, and to resolve any difficulties that they experienced. The idea is that BE should be used early in treatment because it can create relatively rapid positive change in couples. With some immediate positive improvement, the therapist can then focus on the major difficulties that brought the couple into treatment.

The focus of communication/problem-solving training (CPT) is on developing skills in couples that they can use to solve not only their immediate conflicts but also future problems. Thus, CPT is not expected to produce the rapid improvement of BE, but it is expected to produce more enduring improvement that will hopefully last long after therapy has ended. To describe CPT, we should distinguish between the content of what is taught and the procedures used to teach this content. Three types of content are typically the focus of CPT: (a) general communication skills, (b) problem definition skills, and (c) problem-solving skills. *General communication skills* refers to both expressive speaking skills and receptive listening skills. *Expressive speaking skills* are abilities such as speaking for oneself rather than for the other, speaking in behavioral specifics rather than in character generalities, speaking about specific situations rather than globally, and speaking about one's feelings rather than making judgments or evaluations. Thus, one would be taught to say, "I feel angry when you make weekend plans without consulting me" rather than "You are selfish and never consider my feelings." *Receptive listening skills* refers to abilities such as attending to the other nonverbally, paraphrasing or summarizing the other's message (and thus demonstrating that you have listened), and reflecting the other's feelings (thus demonstrating emotional understanding of the other). *Problem definition skills* refers to abilities such as focusing on one problem at a time, defining the problem in behaviorally specific terms, and acknowledging one's role in the problem. *Problem-solving skills* refers to abilities such as brainstorming possible solutions, withholding evaluations of solutions until most or all possible ones have been generated, providing pro and con arguments for possible solutions, negotiating possible solutions, and implementing solutions. These skills are deemed valuable for good interpersonal communication and for the management of virtually all interpersonal problems.

Behavioral principles are used in the training of these communication and problem-solving skills. TBCT therapists first provide instruction in these skills. Couples may be asked to read material about the skills (e.g., readings on communication skills from Gottman, Notarius, Gonso, & Markman, 1976; readings on problem solving from Jacobson & Margolin, 1979), or the therapist may present information about the skills. TBCT therapists may supplement instruction with modeling of some of the skills. Couples are typically asked to practice the skills in the session and at home. Therapists provide feedback and positive reinforcement. However, it is assumed that as the skills develop, they will facilitate naturalistic, spontaneous reinforcement because the couple will be able to communicate and solve problems more effectively.

TBCT has been researched more extensively than any other approach to couples therapy. Approximately two dozen clinical trials, conducted in several countries, have consistently shown TBCT to be more effective than control conditions (Hahlweg & Markman, 1988). In fact, TBCT is the only marital treatment that is listed as "empirically validated" in the latest update on such treatments by the Division 12 Task Force of the American Psychological Association (Chambless et al., 1996). In the task force report, the treatment is labeled as *behavioral marital therapy;* however, we prefer to call it *traditional behavioral couples therapy.* We use the word *traditional* to distinguish it from our newer treatment; we prefer *couples therapy* to *marital therapy* because we have used this treatment with unmarried couples (unmarried heterosexual couples as well as homosexual couples) and believe that it is applicable to their problems.

This is not to say that TBCT is the only treatment that has received empirical support. Johnson and Greenberg's emotionally focused couples therapy (Greenberg & Johnson, 1988; Johnson & Greenberg, 1985) and Snyder and Wills's insight-oriented marital therapy (Snyder & Wills, 1989; Snyder, Wills, & Grady-Fletcher, 1991) have been supported in clinical trials and are both listed as "probably efficacious treatments" in the Division 12 report (Chambless et al., 1996). There has not been enough research on these treatments alone or in comparison to TBCT to indicate if any one is generally more effective. For example, one otherwise excellent study that compared TBCT to insight-oriented treatment was challenged by Jacobson as not being an adequate reflection of TBCT or of insight-oriented therapy (Jacobson, 1991a).

Although clearly successful, TBCT fails to reach about one third of the couples it treats. These couples represent clear-cut treatment failures (Jacobson & Follette, 1985). Furthermore, of the couples who respond positively to TBCT, about 30% relapse over a 1- to 2-year period following treatment (Jacobson, Schmaling, & Holtzworth-Munroe, 1987). Thus, despite the marked success of TBCT, only about 50% of couples improve and maintain their improvement over the long run.

Not surprisingly, the couples who do not do well in TBCT are in more severe marital distress than those who do well. Beyond this general finding, Jacobson and his group identified five specific couple factors that discriminated between successful and unsuccessful couples in their research (Jacobson, Follette, & Pagel, 1986; Jacobson et al., 1987). First, couples who were more committed to staying together were more likely than couples who were less committed to benefit from TBCT. Second, younger couples responded more positively to the approach than did older couples. This age effect was not an artifact of marital duration. Couples in their 50s who had been married only a short time were more difficult to treat than couples in their 40s who had been married longer. Third, couples who were emotionally engaged with each other were more likely to show improvement with TBCT than were couples who were less emotionally engaged. Emotional engagement was indexed in part by sexual interaction and activity. The cessation of all sexual contact was a bad prognostic sign for couples. Emotional engagement was also indexed by withdrawal. Couples were better off if they still argued than if they had withdrawn in anger. Fourth, TBCT was more successful with egalitarian marriages than with traditional marriages. Traditional marriages were indexed by three factors: (a) whether the husband was the sole bread-winner or whether both partners worked, (b) whether the housework was the responsibility of the wife or whether it was shared with the husband, and (c) whether the emotional well-being of the family was the primary respon-sibility of the wife or whether the husband was willing to discuss difficult, emotional topics without waiting for his wife to bring them up. Finally, couples did better in TBCT when they had convergent goals for their marriage. Not surprisingly, couples with incompatible goals, such as those in which she wanted children but he did not, were more difficult to treat.

TBCT's approach to therapy emphasizes change through collaboration, negotiation, and compromise. In BE, this emphasis on change is specific and direct. Partners identify particular behaviors that would be pleasing to the other and, through a variety of strategies, are directed by the therapist to change those behaviors. In CPT, the emphasis is on change through negotia-tion and compromise. Partners are taught skills of problem identification and problem solving that emphasize deliberate, rational, negotiated change.

Clinically, this emphasis on change can be limiting. First of all, many couples have some areas of genuine incompatibility in which they are unable or unwilling to accommodate. Second, even if couples do make changes in some areas of disagreement, these changes often do not maintain. Couples revert back to their old ways. Finally, the entire approach often does not fit in with many couples' notions of love. Having to specify what you want, negotiate with a partner who wants something different, compromise on issues of importance, and make written agreements or contracts to carry out a negotiated plan simply does not feel like love to many couples. It has too many business and legal metaphors that imply two self-interested partners trying to get the best deal possible from the other. In addition, these proce-dures often fall flat when some kind of emotional responsiveness is a goal. For example, these rational procedures might work well with discussions of who does what housework, but they do not work so well with discussions around sexual responsiveness, interest in the other, or physical affection.

Fred might well agree to clean the toilets every week and follow through in ways that please Irene. But can Fred agree to be more sexually interested in Irene and follow through in ways that are satisfying to both?

Skinner's (1966) important distinction between rule-governed and contingency-shaped behavior seems important here. In the former, one matches one's behavior to a rule and gets reinforced for that. In the latter, the immediate contingencies of the situation shape and condition behavior. Although behaviors elicited under the two conditions might look quite similar, the latter is liable to feel more "right," "genuine," and "authentic." Fred's best efforts to show more sexual interest in Irene might feel forced and unsatisfying to both.

Because of these empirical and clinical limitations of TBCT, we developed an alternative approach to couples that emphasizes emotional acceptance in addition to change. To understand what we mean by *emotional acceptance,* consider the problematic behavior of criticism. Positive change would mean that the criticizer would lower the frequency or intensity of this behavior. Emotional acceptance would mean that the recipient of the criticism would react differently to it. If the recipient was less hurt and angered by the criticism and perhaps was even able to see some value in it, then we would say that emotional acceptance of this problematic behavior had occurred. It is important to point out that emotional acceptance is in fact a change—a change in emotional responsiveness to behavior. However, we use the term *change* to refer to the alterations in the frequency and intensity of behavior that a complainant desires and reserve the term *acceptance* to refer to the complainant's emotional reactions to that behavior.

An essential premise of our approach is that change and acceptance are mutually facilitating and that a combination of the two is more powerful than either alone in promoting relationship satisfaction. For example, if the recipient of criticism experiences the criticizer as being less critical, than the recipient may be more inclined to accept the criticism that does exist. Similarly, if the recipient is more accepting of the criticism, than the criticizer may be more open to lowering the frequency or intensity of the criticism. Sometimes the pressure to change is one of the biggest barriers to change. Clearly, if both change and acceptance occur with the criticism, then relationship satisfaction will be more likely.

Except in extreme cases such as violence, our approach does not specify what should be changed and what should be accepted. Instead, we try to create the conditions that will facilitate acceptance and change. In our view, an essential condition is that therapists themselves be accepting and validating. They do not preach acceptance or push for change. They cannot hope that couples will be accepting of each other if they are not accepting of their couples.

But what, then, can therapists do, beyond being accepting themselves, to create conditions that facilitate acceptance and change in couples? We will try to provide some of this information in the remainder of this chapter by describing the assessment and treatment strategies of integrative behavioral couples therapy (IBCT). We will end with a brief description of some preliminary data evaluating this treatment in comparison with TBCT.

INTEGRATIVE BEHAVIORAL
COUPLES THERAPY (IBCT)

Christensen and Jacobson developed IBCT (Christensen & Jacobson, in press; Christensen, Jacobson, & Babcock, 1995; Jacobson & Christensen, 1996a). The description here is of necessity brief. The interested reader can consult a more detailed chapter describing the treatment (Christensen et al., 1995), a book for therapists that provides the most detailed description (Jacobson & Christensen, 1996a), or a book for couples that is designed to be used with IBCT (Christensen & Jacobson, in press).

Evaluation and Feedback

IBCT begins with an evaluation and feedback phase that lasts approximately four sessions. During this period, the couple is seen together, and each partner is seen individually for some or all of a session. Questionnaires are also given. In the fourth session, feedback about the evaluation and a plan for treatment is shared with the couple. At this point, the couple makes a decision to pursue treatment.

IBCT therapists address six questions during the evaluation:

1. How distressed is this couple?
2. How committed is this couple to this relationship?
3. What are the issues that divide them?
4. Why are these issues such a problem for them?
5. What are the strengths holding them together?
6. What can treatment do to help them?

An answer to the first question regarding distress is necessary to determine how therapy will proceed. If couples are extremely distressed, therapists may need to forgo further assessment and intervene immediately. For example, if couples are ready to separate, if there is a danger of violence, or if one member is having a serious psychiatric episode such as a manic or psychotic state, immediate intervention may be required.

Because of the prevalence of violence in married couples who seek therapy (O'Leary, Vivian, & Malone, 1992), we believe that marital therapists should routinely assess for violence. This can be simply and easily done with a questionnaire such as the Conflict Tactics Scale (Strauss, 1979) and a follow-up individual interview with each spouse. If there is moderate or severe violence, we do not believe that conjoint couples therapy is appropriate. The focus of couples therapy is often on conflictual issues that could precipitate a violent episode. Furthermore, seeing the couple in therapy provides an official sanction that a relationship with serious violence is okay—a view we do not wish to promote. We will see couples in which there are mild levels of violence, but even here we usually insist on a no-violence contract as a prerequisite for treatment (see Jacobson & Christensen, 1996b, for more information on our work with violent couples).

We have few automatic exclusions from couples therapy based on psychiatric diagnosis. Certainly, we cannot treat couples who are actively psychotic. Also, couples in which one or both are abusing substances may need to have treatment for this problem before couples therapy or, at the very least, in conjunction with couples therapy. Finally, we do not think that our approach is appropriate for couples in which one partner has a severe Axis II disorder, such as antisocial, borderline, or schizotypal personality disorder. Apart from these obvious cases, we do not routinely exclude couples from therapy on the basis of psychiatric criteria.

Distress level of the couple can be easily assessed in an interview format. However, it is often helpful to have a standardized measure of relationship satisfaction, such as the Dyadic Adjustment Scale (Spanier, 1976) or the Marital Satisfaction Inventory (Snyder, 1979). In addition to providing a normative measure of satisfaction, it can serve as a simple measure of outcome.

The second question, which concerns commitment, is similar to but different from the question regarding distress. Although distress level and commitment are often correlated, some couples can be seriously distressed but still have a high commitment to the relationship. Likewise, some couples may be only mildly distressed but may have little commitment to the relationship. Commitment level can dramatically determine the course that couples therapy should take. If one or both partners have little commitment to maintaining the relationship, a period of therapy to facilitate decision making may be necessary, or separation counseling may be appropriate. If one partner has had an affair, therapy may first need to focus on any damage that has been created.

Commitment can be assessed with questionnaire measures. For example, the Marital Status Inventory (Weiss & Cerreto, 1980) assesses the steps that a couple has taken toward divorce, and the Dyadic Adjustment Scale (Spanier, 1976) has a rating of commitment. However, commitment should also be assessed in an individual interview. Here, each partner can talk more freely without the other's possibly inhibiting presence. This advantage of an individual session also presents some difficulties. If one partner reveals a secret affair, the therapist is left holding on to confidential information that is perhaps crucial to the relationship but that cannot be revealed to the other. We handle this issue by informing partners before the individual session that information in the individual session is confidential but that if the information is important to the relationship, the therapist will encourage, and in the extreme insist, that partners share this information with the other. For example, if one partner will not terminate a secret affair, the therapist will insist that the partner share information about the affair with the other before couples therapy begins.

Answers to the third and fourth questions, which concern the issues that divide the couple and why these issues are so problematic for them, provide information for the therapist's formulation of the couple's problem. The issues that divide the couple are typically areas of incompatibility between them. For example, one member of the couple may want greater closeness in the relationship—more time together, more sharing of feelings, and more emotional support—whereas the other wants greater autonomy in the relationship—more independence, more time alone, and more privacy (see Christensen & Heavey, 1993). This major area of incompatibility we sometimes call the theme in the couple's distress (Christensen et al., 1995; Jacobson & Christensen, 1996b). Any area of incompatibility may present challenges for a couple, but couples who end up in therapy often have engaged in struggles around this theme that have accentuated rather than ameliorated their differences. They have polarized around the theme (Christensen & Walczynski, 1997; Jacobson & Christensen, 1996b). As a result, partners often feel trapped—helpless and desperate because their best efforts to solve the problem seem to only make the problem worse. Our formulation of the couple's problem, based on the answers to the third and fourth questions, emphasizes these three components: the theme of their struggle (the incompatibility over which they fight), the polarization process (the efforts to solve the problem that often make the incompatibility even greater), and the mutual trap (the feelings that nothing will make the problem better).

The fifth question about strengths refocuses the couple away from their struggles and toward the positive features of their relationship that attracted them to each other in the first place and that now hold them together despite the difficulties. The process as well as the content of this inquiry into strengths can be revealing about a couple. If partners have a difficult time naming positive features of the other or the relationship, or if they state positive features begrudgingly or framed as an absence of negative ("At least he's not a drunk"), the therapist may learn, for example, that the couple's struggles have overwhelmed any sense of appreciation between the pair or that each member is competitively portraying him- or herself as the most injured party (i.e., "I receive all negative and no positive from him/her").

The last question, how can treatment help, requires an assessment of the couple's capacity for change. The goals of therapy in IBCT almost always involve both change and acceptance; IBCT has strategies for promoting both. However, because promoting acceptance can also generate spontaneous change, IBCT treatment usually starts with an emphasis on promoting acceptance rather than using direct strategies for promoting change. An assessment of the couple's "collaborative set" (Jacobson & Margolin, 1979)—whether they have a shared perspective on their problems that emphasizes mutual responsibility for them—can provide an indication of their capacity for change and determine whether therapy should begin with an emphasis on change instead of acceptance.

We believe that assessment of the collaborative set can best be done in the individual interview. Useful questions are "What role do you see yourself playing in this problem?" and "What changes might you make that would help the relationship?" If partners reply in such a way as to indicate that they are simply the victim of the other's malicious acts, then they clearly do not have a collaborative set. Even if partners give lip service to notions of joint responsibility ("It takes two to tango"), they may not be very collaborative because they voice only general notions rather than specific ideas about how they contribute to the marital distress.

As we shall see below, our means of promoting acceptance requires that we often focus on specific incidents that are manifestations of the couple's problematic pattern as well as on the broad pattern itself. By hearing specific examples of conflicts during assessment, the therapist learns what kind of incidents typically happen and thus what to focus on during treatment.

At the end of the evaluation phase, the therapist provides the couple with feedback about the assessment. The questions listed above can be used as the format for sharing assessment feedback. The most important part and most lengthy part of the feedback is the formulation of the couple's problems. Presentation of this formulation is really the first step in promoting acceptance for the couple because the formulation portrays each partner in a sympathetic and understandable way. When IBCT therapists present the theme of the couple's struggles, they carefully avoid any judgment that one side of the struggle is any better or more right than the other. They present both people's positions as reasonable. In describing the polarization process between the pair, IBCT therapists show how each partner's actions, even though painful to the other, were motivated from his or her own difficult position. Finally, IBCT therapists describe the trap that each partner feels in the current situation. Each is frustrated and discouraged because his or her best efforts seem to lead nowhere.

As an example, consider a shortened version of how an IBCT therapist might provide feedback about a responsibility issue for a couple, Jeff and Dora:

> I see the two of you as quite different in this area of responsibility. Jeff, I think a major strength you bring to the relationship is your consistency and steadiness in carrying out your responsibilities—whether those responsibilities involve money, housework, or career. Dora, I think a strength you bring to the relationship is your spontaneous, fun-loving approach to life. These differences create a problem when it comes to housework and finances. Given your approach to life, Dora, you aren't upset if the housework backs up a while or if spontaneous purchases put you behind a bit financially. However, Jeff, you want to keep things in order, so you take care of the housework and watch the finances. But then you get angry that you are having to take all of the responsibility in this area—doing the dishes, cleaning up the apartment, putting money into savings—and you want it to be shared. At times you get really angry at Dora, which then calls the problem to her attention. Dora, when you see he is angry, you are concerned. You really don't want him to have all the load, so you put all of your considerable energy into cleaning up the house

or going over your finances, etc. Yet you resent the way Jeff treats you when he is angry. So this solution—Jeff getting angry and Dora doing work—is at best a limited success. Neither of you likes the idea of solving the problem only through emotional upset. You in particular, Jeff, have expressed concern that you would become a nag to Dora. And Dora, you have acknowledged that the work you do in response to Jeff's anger is only short lived. You mentioned that you have a hard time maintaining consistency even on projects very dear to you, such as writing your novel, so it is not surprising that you are not consistent with the housework. The result is that both of you feel stuck. You, Jeff, don't want to nag or get angry at Dora, but nothing seems to happen unless you do. Dora, you want to do your fair share and to please Jeff, but your style of taking care of things is so different from Jeff's. You would of course take care of housework and bills as you did when you lived alone—but the point at which you take action is long after Jeff has taken care of it himself or gotten very angry at you.

Strategies for Promoting
Acceptance in Couples

In IBCT, there are three broad strategies that are used to promote acceptance: empathic joining, unified detachment, and tolerance building. The first two attempt to use the conflicts of couples as vehicles for promoting intimacy. When they work, they promote not only acceptance but also greater closeness. The last strategy, tolerance building, has a less lofty goal—namely, to decrease the sensitivity of each partner to the other's negative behavior. Although all three strategies have as their focus greater acceptance, they often promote spontaneous change as well. Partners may change their own behavior, for example, because they experience more compassion for the pain that their behavior causes the other. These spontaneous changes are thought to be more enduring because they are controlled by natural contingencies rather than by the therapist-structured contingencies often used in IBCT.

Promoting Acceptance Through Empathic Joining

In this strategy, IBCT therapists create conditions in the therapy session that foster compassion in each partner for the other. To do this, IBCT therapists must themselves model compassion for each partner's position. They focus on the pain that each experiences in the relationship without any judgment toward the other partner who does the behavior that causes the pain. They make no recommendations for change in either. When partners blame the other or insist that the other should change, IBCT therapists redirect them to the distress behind the blame and pressure for change.

The formulation described above is the first step toward empathic joining in that it describes the mutual trap that both experience in the relationship. After the feedback session, there may be further discussions that refine the formulation, increase its sophistication as a description of the problem, and further promote each partner's understanding that they are both victims of the problem they share. Although these general discussions are helpful in promoting acceptance, what is more important is discussion of concrete incidents in the lives of the couples that exemplify this pattern.

IBCT therapists engage couples in discussion of three kinds of incidents: negative incidents of the problem, positive incidents in which the problem was handled better than usual, and future incidents in which the problem is anticipated to occur. Negative incidents tend to predominate the discussion, particularly in the early stages of therapy. There may be few positive incidents at that point. However, when positive or even partially positive incidents occur, it is important to debrief them. Discussions of anticipated incidents are especially helpful because they offer the promise of prevention of a negative incident.

The goal of these discussions is to identify the emotions, particularly the painful emotions, that each partner experiences during the incident and then to show how these understandable emotions motivate each partner's behavior, no matter how problematic that behavior is for the other. In the discussion of negative incidents, it is most helpful to focus on the beginnings of the interaction because it may be easier for partners to understand each other at the beginning of a conflict than later in the conflict. Consider, for example, an incident between Dora and Jeff. After experiencing a build-up of resentment for several days because Dora has done very little around the house, Jeff forces himself to say something to her. He doesn't want to be mean or nagging, so he tries to say it in a joking manner. Dora accepts it in the joking manner that he intended, at some level hears his request for help, and makes a well-intentioned assurance to him that she will get to the housework. She doesn't do so immediately, so Jeff can no longer contain his resentment and criticizes her lack of response. At this point, she is upset because it seems to her that Jeff is demanding that she jump into action at his command. They may escalate from there and call each other names, threaten each other, and bring in other issues unrelated to the problem. It may be much more difficult for each to be sympathetic to what the other does during this escalation phase than during the opening phase.

Discussion of the ending of an incident, particularly how people get back to normal again, may also be productive. These discussions can highlight the emotional barriers that each experiences in getting back together and the mixed feelings with which each leaves a conflict. For example, after a conflict Dora may feel guilty that she doesn't do more and angry with Jeff for making such a big deal about the housework. She puts out a major effort to clean up the house but is disappointed that he is not more appreciative of her efforts. This disappointment is a barrier to her return to normal. On his side, Jeff may feel both upset with himself for making such a big deal out of the housework and angry that Dora doesn't do her share. He doesn't feel good about her housework in response to his anger and doesn't want to give her the impression that the problem is all solved if she does some housework at this point, so he is not very appreciative of her efforts.

During these discussions of specific incidents, IBCT therapists emphasize the expression of "soft" thoughts and feelings over "hard" ones. By "hard" feelings and thoughts, we mean those experiences that portray the self in a dominant, powerful, and invulnerable position. Feelings of anger and disgust and thoughts of revenge and control ("No one is going to get away with treating me like that" or "I won't allow myself to be manipulated") are examples. By "soft" feelings and thoughts, we mean experiences that portray the self in a less powerful, less dominant, and more vulnerable position. Feelings of disappointment and hurt and thoughts of doubt and uncertainty ("I didn't know how to handle the situation" and "I wasn't sure how you would respond") are examples. Most couples in therapy focus on their "hard" feelings and thoughts. Although IBCT therapists do not minimize or dismiss these experiences, they look for, suggest, and encourage the expression of "softer" experiences because these are more likely to promote compassion within the couple. For example, with Dora and Jeff, an IBCT therapist might focus on Jeff's attempts to restrain himself and his concern about being a nag as well as his resentment at Dora for not doing her share. Similarly, an IBCT therapist would focus on Dora's guilt about her lack of participation as well as her anger at the way Jeff treats her.

When this intervention works well, partners experience compassion for each other through these discussions in the session and, as a result, feel closer and more intimate with each other than they have in some time. The conflicts have served as a vehicle for greater intimacy. This intimacy and compassion will also promote more emotional acceptance of the other's behavior. Dora may still feel stung by Jeff's anger, and Jeff may still feel upset at Dora's lack of participation, but the sting may not be as intense or as prolonged. They may be able to recover more quickly when they do experience one of these negative incidents. Finally, the increased compassion will encourage each to change. Dora may take a more active role in housework, and Jeff may not be so angry and critical when she does not. Of course, the strategy of empathic joining does not often produce these ideal outcomes. It may generate some compassion, some intimacy, some acceptance, or some spontaneous change. But other strategies are also needed.

Promoting Acceptance Through Unified Detachment

In contrast to empathic joining, which emphasizes a close-up, emotionally sensitive view of the pain that each person experiences, unified detachment emphasizes an objective, distanced, intellectual analysis of the problem. The idea is that if couples see their problems in more objective terms as a reciprocal and circular interplay of their behavior, they will be less likely to blame each other for the problem and more likely to accept their stuckness. This acceptance may lead them to do "less of the same" and thus to diminish the problem indirectly.

In unified detachment, IBCT therapists emphasize the differences between partners and the patterns of behavior that result from these differences. For example, therapists might engage Dora and Jeff in a discussion of the origins of their differences. Jeff was always an organized, orderly person, even as a child. Dora was always a "do it at the last minute" person whose life and possessions were at the edge of chaos. When they began going together, they spent much more time at Jeff's rather than Dora's place because there was always room to sit or lie, the refrigerator was always stocked, and things that were needed could be found. Then IBCT therapists might engage Dora and Jeff in a discussion of the patterns in their conflicts, identifying the triggers that touch off emotional reactions and the conditions that exacerbate or ameliorate the problem. For example, stress in Jeff and Dora's life has opposite effects on each: It makes Jeff more organized but Dora less so. Although Jeff can tolerate some clothes lying around on a stressless day, he cannot on a stressful day.

As in empathic joining, there is an emphasis on concrete incidents in unified detachment. However, in unified detachment, the goal is to identify the sequence of behavior and the triggers for emotional upset in specific incidents. Often incidents are contrasted and compared. Dora did nothing about the dishes on Wednesday night because she was stressed out about a presentation at her job the next day. However, on Friday she responded to Jeff's joking question, "Where is the counter?" by doing all the dishes. Light reminders work better for her than tense demands.

When possible, IBCT therapists inject metaphor and humor into the situation to help partners create some emotional distance from their problems. For example, an IBCT therapist might label Jeff's efforts, when he is stressed, to check whether Dora has left any of her dirty clothes lying around as the "dirty clothes patrol." As another example, an IBCT therapist would try to create conditions in which the couple could mutually laugh at Dora's well-honed balancing abilities, in that she would rather place trash high on the trash container than empty it and would rather balance dishes on top of dishes in the sink than clean any of them. Therapists must be careful not to ridicule either partner or minimize his or her concerns. But when couples can smile or laugh at their difficulties, they achieve a distance from them that may make the problems more acceptable to them. They may feel more connected with each other as they view their problems from a unified distance.

Often empathic-joining and unified-detachment interventions are mixed during a discussion of specific incidents. For example, a therapist might contrast two different incidents and show what triggers occurred in each but also focus on the strong feelings that were aroused in each incident. Humor, lightness, and detachment can be a break from the intensity of empathic joining interventions.

Promoting Acceptance Through Tolerance Building

The final strategy has less lofty goals than the first two. There is no attempt to create greater closeness between the pair. Rather, the attempt is to somewhat desensitize partners to the pain of the other's problematic behavior. A number of strategies can work to reduce each one's sensitivity to the other.

One strategy is to engage the couples in a discussion of the positive features of each one's negative characteristics. The point is not to deny the negative features of those characteristics but to create greater complexity in the view that each has of the other by pointing to the attractive features of these same characteristics. For example, Jeff was attracted to Dora in part because of her carefree, fun-loving, spontaneous style. He had more fun with her than with any of his previous girlfriends. Yet it is precisely this style that contributes to her neglect of responsibilities. Although Jeff's responsible, orderly lifestyle was not a major attraction for Dora, she did get many benefits from it. She hated doing paperwork (paying bills, doing taxes, balancing checkbooks) and maintenance (taking the car in for maintenance, getting the vacuum cleaner fixed), but Jeff enjoyed and excelled in these tasks. He gladly took most of them over for her. Yet his willingness to take on responsibility also contributed to his demands that she take on some responsibility also.

A second strategy to promote tolerance is to role-play negative behavior in the session. Because these role plays are done in a different context than usual—a therapist is present, a provocative incident does not elicit the behavior—they rarely have their usual upsetting effects. Thus, the experience may make each partner's behavior more tolerable. These role plays can also be combined with the previous two interventions. For example, if they elicit strong feelings in either, the therapist can debrief those feelings as in empathic joining. Sometimes the therapist can encourage the partners to exaggerate their role plays and create humor, as in unified detachment.

A third strategy, which follows a clear desensitization rationale, is to ask couples to fake negative behavior during the week at home. The therapist asks one partner to do the negative behavior when he or she is not feeling it so that he or she can see, without his or her own emotions clouding their picture, how the other reacts painfully to this behavior. The therapist comments to the other partner that this week he or she may receive some faked negative behavior. Because he or she won't know for sure whether the behavior is real or faked, he or she may not respond so automatically to the behavior. This question about the authenticity of the behavior may make a new, less reactive, response more likely. Sometimes this intervention has paradoxical effects; none of the problematic behavior occurs. That is okay, but it is not the goal that is desired. An IBCT therapist wants the couple to experience the negative behavior in a different context so that a different and more tolerating response is likely.

A final strategy for promoting tolerance is to promote self-care in each. If partners can take care of themselves more effectively, they may not be so badly stung by their partner's behavior. In one version of this strategy, the therapist engages each partner in a discussion of the alternatives that he or she has in the presence of the other's negative behavior. Such actions as taking a time out, assertively voicing one's feelings, or seeking solace elsewhere are possibilities. It is important in these discussions to consider the effects of these self-care actions on the other because they can in some cases escalate the ongoing conflict. In a second version of this strategy, therapists engage one or both partners in a discussion of alternative means of need fulfillment. If they do not get enough intimate talk with their partner, is it possible to get it with a friend? As with the first version, one needs to consider the effects on the partner. One doesn't want to encourage acts that could punish or threaten the partner. Also, therapists do not want to enter these discussions with any implication that the partner has no responsibility to meet the needs of the other. A spouse may not be willing to discuss alternative means of need fulfillment if he or she thinks that this lets the partner off the hook for any responsibility in meeting these needs. Even if neither of these strategies comes up with alternative behaviors that the partner actually employs, the discussion promotes acceptance because it promotes the notion that these negative behaviors will happen and that one's partner will not be able to meet all of one's needs.

These are the major strategies used to promote acceptance. As we have noted throughout, these strategies may also stimulate spontaneous change. Of course, they do not necessarily produce change or enough change to satisfy partners. Therefore, the change strategies of TBCT described above (BE and CPT) can also be used in IBCT. These change strategies are often conducted in a more flexible, less structured fashion than in TBCT. If they meet resistance, IBCT therapists often revert back to acceptance strategies. However, it is our belief that the use of acceptance strategies first makes the change strategies of TBCT more effective. Of course, only data can validate that belief.

COMPARISONS BETWEEN TBCT AND IBCT

We are currently conducting a clinical trial comparing IBCT with TBCT. Couples were recruited through newspaper advertisements and had to meet a criterion of distress based on the Dyadic Adjustment Scale. A group of five therapists is treating cases in both conditions. At this point, 16 couples have completed therapy (8 in TBCT and 8 in IBCT), and their data have been analyzed.

We have conducted measures of adherence to each treatment. On the basis of ratings of taped sessions, we have demonstrated substantial differences between treatments, with much more acceptance-oriented treatments taking place in IBCT and more change-oriented treatments taking place in TBCT. Also, we have had an expert in TBCT, Don Baucom at the University of North Carolina, rate the competence with which our TBCT cases have been conducted. He has given high ratings for TBCT competence, describing the therapist's work with these cases as "state of the art."

On our primary outcome measure, the Global Distress Scale (GDS) of the Marital Satisfaction Inventory (Snyder, 1979), we conducted repeated-measures ANOVAs with treatment condition (IBCT vs. TBCT) as the between-subjects factor and time (pre vs. post) as the within-subjects factor. Even with the small sample size, there was a significant interaction between time and treatment for husbands and an almost significant interaction for wives. IBCT husbands and wives showed greater increases in marital satisfaction than did their counterparts in TBCT. Furthermore, there were large effect sizes favoring IBCT (1.28 for husbands and 1.46 for wives). Other analyses showed that IBCT was having the impact that we expected. On a measure of acceptability of a partner's negative behavior, wives in IBCT scored higher than wives in TBCT. Ratings by IBCT husbands were in the same direction but were not statistically significant.

When we assessed the data with the yardstick of clinical significance rather than merely statistical significance, we also found evidence favoring IBCT. The criteria for improvement and recovery that we used were developed by Jacobson and associates (Jacobson, Follette, & Revenstorf, 1984; Jacobson & Truax, 1991) and included (a) reliable change in the appropriate direction (the clients' scores have improved more than would be expected by chance) and (b) greater similarity to a nondistressed group than to a distressed group. We set a criteria of 58 on the GDS as a cutoff point between "happily married" and "still distressed" couples. In IBCT, 50% ($\frac{4}{8}$) of husbands and wives met both criteria and were considered recovered, whereas only 38% ($\frac{3}{8}$) of wives and 13% ($\frac{1}{8}$) of husbands in TBCT recovered. One additional wife in IBCT made reliable change but did not reach the cutoff (improvement but no recovery). A majority of husbands ($\frac{7}{8}$ or 87%) and wives ($\frac{5}{8}$ or 63%) did *not* make reliable change in TBCT, whereas a minority of wives (⅜ or 38%) and half of husbands (⁴⁄₈ or 50%) did *not* make reliable change in IBCT.

Data at treatment termination, even buttressed by analysis of clinical significance, are not enough to evaluate the outcome of a treatment. Follow-up data are needed. Our 6-month and 1-year follow-up data suggest that the differences between groups are even stronger at follow-up than they were at post-test. By the 1-year follow-up, three of the eight TBCT couples had separated, whereas none of the IBCT couples had separated. IBCT wives continued to show greater improvement at the 6-month follow-up than TBCT wives ($t(5) = 5.27$, $p = .004$, effect size $= 3.79$). Husbands showed similar results, again with very large effect sizes ($t(4) = 2.97$, $p = .04$, effect size $= 2.25$). Change was maintained at the 6-month follow-up for both husbands ($t(2) = 11.50$, $p = .007$) and wives ($t(2) = 6.20$, $p = .025$) in IBCT, based on pretest to 6-month follow-up paired t tests. However, neither wives ($t(3) = 0.00$, *ns*) nor husbands ($t(3) = 1.00$, *ns*) showed significant change from pretest to follow-up in TBCT. Finally, when we look just at change between post-test and 6-month follow-up, IBCT wives actually showed significant improvement, $t(2) = 8.00$, $p = .015$. For IBCT husbands as well as for husbands and wives in TBCT, there were no significant changes in marital satisfaction between post-test and follow-up.

We must interpret these data cautiously because they are based on so few couples. We continue to gather pilot data on the comparative effectiveness of the two treatments. On the basis of our pilot data, we hope to conduct a larger study with a more diverse population of married couples. Our efforts alone will not be sufficient to validate IBCT as a more powerful treatment for couples. Other investigators will need to try our treatment, using our manuals, to see if they can replicate our findings.

However, at this point we are optimistic about the effectiveness of IBCT given the current data. A combination of acceptance and change in couples therapy may be more powerful than either alone.

EMPIRICAL EVALUATION OF PSYCHOTHERAPY, PARTICULARLY COUPLES THERAPY

We certainly agree with the scientific motives behind the Division 12 Task Force report and are supportive of the idea of developing guidelines for determining the level of empirical support that a treatment has received

(Chambless et al., 1996). However, we have a number of concerns about this report. First, we have some issues with the term *empirically validated treatment*. This term implies a level of completion that we do not believe exists with any psychological treatments and certainly not TBCT, even though the report describes it as such. Much research remains to be done before psychologists can brush off their hands and say, "We have now validated this particular treatment. We know how much it works, who it works for, and how it works." It is interesting to us that the task force acknowledges this issue in a footnote and indicates that the term *empirically supported treatments* might be more "felicitous" (p. 15) but that they kept the term *empirically validated treatments* to avoid confusion. We think that more confusion is liable to occur from keeping misleading terms than from replacing them with more appropriate terms.

Second, we believe that an emphasis on clinical significance should play a more prominent part in the evaluation of empirical support for treatments. The task force report mentions the issue only in passing. We believe that data on clinical significance, such as data on the percentage of clients who made reliable change and the percentage who were more similar to a normative group than to a disordered group at the end of treatment, are essential to evaluate treatment effectiveness. Similarly, data on long-term follow-up are essential for the evaluation of treatments.

Third, data on how the treatment works with a diverse population of clients are essential to evaluating treatment effectiveness. The task force is to be commended for addressing the issue of treatment for ethnic minority clients in its report. However we find it difficult to label a treatment as empirically valid when the task force reports that "we know of no psychotherapy treatment research that meets basic criteria important for demonstrating treatment efficacy for ethnic minority populations" (Chambless et al., 1996, p. 7).

Fourth, we believe that data on effectiveness as well as efficacy are needed to evaluate treatment effectiveness (Jacobson & Christensen, 1996b). The purpose of an "efficacy" study is to demonstrate the existence of an effect; an "effectiveness" study, on the other hand, examines the generalizability, feasibility, and cost-effectiveness of a treatment. Just because a treatment has an effect in a pristine study using a select sample of clients who are treated by a select sample of well-supervised therapists does not mean that the treatment will be effective when used in real-world clinical settings. Weisz, Weiss, and Donnenberg (1992) have shown that child and adolescent psychotherapy treatments are generally effective in laboratory studies but are not generally effective in clinic settings.

There are some special, additional considerations when evaluating the effectiveness of couples therapy. We will mention two. First, one must consider outcome at the level of the unit (the couple) as well as at the level of the individual. Although a particular treatment may improve stability (couples separate and/or divorce less frequently than in comparison conditions) and mean satisfaction (partners' average level of satisfaction improves relative to control conditions), these changes may be a result of changes in satisfaction for one member primarily. For example, one could imagine a treatment that helps husbands primarily or wives primarily. Thus, it is important that researchers report data on individuals (e.g., data on husbands and data on wives) as well as on the couple unit.

Second, outcome criteria are more complicated in couples therapy than in individual therapy, in which symptomatic improvement is a universal goal. Stability and satisfaction in the relationship are the appropriate goals for most couples. However, separation or divorce may be a more realistic and preferable outcome for some couples. Of course, the researcher cannot have it both ways so that any outcome is a successful outcome. Then how can one deal with this dilemma? One possibility is to measure individual well-being in addition to relationship stability and satisfaction. Consider a possible outcome. Couples Treatments A and B create roughly equivalent levels of improved satisfaction in those couples that stay together, but Treatment A leads to more separation and divorce than Treatment B. We would normally consider Treatment B a better treatment. However, if we had data that measures of individual well-being were higher in Treatment A than in Treatment B, we might modify our conclusions. If the couples in our treatments had children, we might want to also examine child functioning in the two treatments. That data might also temper our conclusions. Thus, although measures of relationship stability and satisfaction are essential to the evaluation of couples therapy, measures of individual adult and child functioning are also important. We recommend the inclusion of these measures.

The field is learning how difficult it is to evaluate the impact of psychological treatments. However, such evaluations are essential for guiding the field of mental health and its well-intentioned but often misguided efforts to alleviate human suffering. Certainly, the importance of the evaluation enterprise justifies the efforts.

REFERENCES

Chambless, D. L., Sanderson, W. C., Shoham, V., Johnson, S. B., Pope, K. S., Crits-Christoph, P., Baker, M., Johnson, B., Woody, S. R., Sue, S., Beutler, L., Williams, D. A., & McCurry, S. (1996). An update on empirically validated therapies. *Clinical Psychologist, 49*(2), 5-18.

Christensen, A., & Heavey, C. L. (1993). Gender differences in marital conflict: The demand-withdraw interaction pattern. In S. Oskamp & M. Costanzo (Eds.), *Gender issues in contemporary society.* Newbury Park, CA: Sage.

Christensen, A., & Heavey, C. L. (in press). Intervention in couples. *Annual Review of Psychology, 50.*

Christensen, A., & Jacobson, N. S. (in press). *When lovers make war: Building intimacy from conflict through acceptance and change.* New York: Guilford.

Christensen, A., Jacobson, N. S., & Babcock, J. C. (1995). Integrative behavioral couple therapy. In N. S. Jacobson & A. S. Gurman (Eds.), *Clinical handbook of couples therapy* (pp. 31-64). New York: Guilford.

Christensen, A., & Walczynski, P. T. (1997). Conflict and satisfaction in couples. In R. J. Sternberg & M. Hojjat (Eds.), *Satisfaction in close relationships.* New York: Guilford.

Gottman, J., Notarius, C., Gonso, J., & Markman, H. (1976). *A couple's guide to communication.* Champaign, IL: Research Press.

Greenberg, L. S., & Johnson, S. M. (1988). *Emotionally focused couples therapy.* New York: Guilford.

Hahlweg, K., & Markman, H. J. (1988). The effectiveness of behavioral marital therapy: Empirical status of behavioral techniques in preventing and alleviating marital distress. *Journal of Consulting and Clinical Psychology, 56,* 440-447.

Jacobson, N. S. (1977). Problem solving and contingency contracting in the treatment of marital discord. *Journal of Consulting and Clinical Psychology, 45,* 92-100.

Jacobson, N. S. (1991). Behavioral versus insight-oriented marital therapy: Labels can be misleading. *Journal of Consulting and Clinical Psychology, 59,* 142-145.

Jacobson, N. S., & Christensen, A. (1996a). *Integrative couple therapy.* New York: Norton.

Jacobson, N. S., & Christensen, A. (1996b). Studying the effectiveness of psychotherapy: How well can clinical trials do the job? *American Psychologist, 51,* 1031-1039.

Jacobson, N. S., & Follette, W. C. (1985). Clinical significance of improvement resulting from two behavioral marital therapy components. *Behavior Therapy, 16,* 249-262.

Jacobson, N. S., Follette, W. C., & Pagel, M. (1986). Predicting who will benefit from behavioral marital therapy. *Journal of Consulting and Clinical Psychology, 54,* 518-522.

Jacobson, N. S., Follette, W. C., & Revenstorf, D. (1984). Psychotherapy outcome research: Methods for reporting variability and evaluating clinical significance. *Behavior Therapy, 15,* 336-352.

Jacobson, N. S., & Margolin, G. (1979). *Marital therapy: Strategies based on social learning and behavior exchange principles.* New York: Brunner/Mazel.

Jacobson, N. S., Schmaling, K. B., & Holtzworth-Munroe, A. (1987). A component analysis of behavioral marital therapy: Two-year follow-up and prediction of relapse. *Journal of Marital and Family Therapy, 13,* 187-195.

Jacobson, N. S., & Truax, P. (1991). Clinical significance: A statistical approach to defining meaningful change in psychotherapy research. *Journal of Consulting and Clinical Psychology, 59,* 12-19.

Johnson, S. M., & Greenberg, L. S. (1985). Differential effects of experiential and problem-solving interventions in resolving marital conflict. *Journal of Consulting and Clinical Psychology, 53,* 175-184.

Liberman, R. P. (1970). Behavioral approaches to family and couple therapy. *American Journal of Orthopsychiatry, 40,* 106-118.

O'Leary, K. D., Vivian, D., & Malone, J. (1992). Assessment of physical aggression against women in marriage: The need for multimodal assessment. *Behavioral Assessment, 14,* 5-14.

Skinner, B. F. (1966). *The behavior of organisms: An experimental analysis.* Englewood Cliffs, NJ: Prentice Hall.

Snyder, D. K. (1979). Multidimensional assessment of marital satisfaction. *Journal of Marriage and the Family, 41,* 813-823.

Snyder, D. K., & Wills, R. M. (1989). Behavioral vs. insight oriented marital therapy: A controlled comparative outcome study. *Journal of Consulting and Clinical Psychology, 57,* 39-46.

Snyder, D. K., Wills, R. M., & Grady-Fletcher, A. (1991). Long-term effectiveness of behavioral versus insight-oriented marital therapy: A 4-year follow-up study. *Journal of Consulting and Clinical Psychology, 59,* 138-141.

Spanier, G. B. (1976). Measuring dyadic adjustment: New scales for assessing the quality of marriage and similar dyads. *Journal of Marriage and the Family, 38,* 15-28.

Straus, M. A. (1979). Measuring intrafamily conflict and violence: The conflict tactics (CT) scales. *Journal of Marriage and the Family, 41,* 75-88.

Stuart, R. B. (1969). Operant-interpersonal treatment for marital discord. *Journal of Consulting and Clinical Psychology, 33,* 675-682.

Stuart, R. B. (1980). *Helping couples change: A social learning approach to marital therapy.* New York: Guilford.

Weiss, R. L., & Cerreto, M. C. (1980). The marital status inventory: Development of a measure of dissolution potential. *American Journal of Family Therapy, 8,* 80-85.

Weiss, R. L., Hops, H., & Patterson, G. R. (1973). A framework for conceptualizing marital conflict, a technology for altering it, some data for evaluating it. In L. A. Hamerlynck, L. C. Handy, & E. J. Mash (Eds.), *Behavior change: Methodology, concepts, and practices* (pp. 309-342). Champaign, IL: Research Press.

Weisz, J. R., Weiss, B., & Donenberg, G. R. (1992). The lab versus the clinic: Effects of child and adolescent psychotherapy. *American Psychologist, 47,* 1578-1585.

8

Family Intervention for Schizophrenia

KIM T. MUESER

SHIRLEY M. GLYNN

Over the past three decades, astounding progress has been made in the psychosocial treatment of schizophrenia. In this chapter, we provide a synthesis of the advances made in one of the most widely studied areas, family intervention. We begin with an historical overview of factors leading to the development of family interventions for schizophrenia, followed by discussion of different models of family therapy. We summarize the core ingredients of effective family interventions and discuss the educational curriculum taught in many family programs. Next, we summarize the empirical research supporting family intervention for schizophrenia. We present a model for individually tailoring family interventions of this population and conclude with a discussion of future directions for clinical work and research in this area.

HISTORICAL OVERVIEW

Between the 1950s and the 1970s, a variety of factors converged to pave the way toward new approaches to working with families of persons with schizophrenia. Some of the most important factors included the deinstitutionalization movement, the growth in support for biological rather than psychogenic theories of the etiology of schizophrenia, research on family expressed emotion and relapse, and the rise in the family advocacy movement.

Deinstitutionalization

Before the deinstitutionalization movement, which began in the 1950s and has continued up until today, the vast majority of persons with schizophrenia in the 20th century spent their lives in psychiatric hospitals. The spiraling economic costs of institutional care (Johnson, 1990), combined with the discovery of antipsychotic medications and strategies for community-based care of serious psychiatric illnesses (e.g., assertive community treatment programs; Stein & Test, 1980) all played a role in shifting the focus of treatment for schizophrenia away from the hospital and into the community. A natural consequence of this shift was that many people with schizophrenia returned from institutions to live with family members and that many others continued to live with relatives while receiving their psychiatric care in the community. Though estimates vary, most surveys suggest that over 60% of patients with schizophrenia either live with family members or maintain regular contacts with them (Goldman, 1984; Talbott, 1990). Thus, families play an important role in the lives of persons with schizophrenia because of their frequent contact and the caregiving that they provide.

Etiologic Theories of Schizophrenia

From the 1920s until the 1950s, increasing numbers of theorists speculated that the origins of schizophrenia could be traced back to problematic family relationships, such as contradictory communication patterns or marital schism. Psychogenic theories of schizophrenia, such as those proposed by Sullivan (1962), Fromm-Reichmann (1948), Rosen (1953), Bateson, Jackson, Haley, and Weakland (1956), Searles (1965), Winnicott (1965), and Bion (1967), dominated psychiatric treatment in America, and spawned a variety of individual and family interventions based on these theories.

Despite their popularity, the prominence of these theories decreased in subsequent years for a number of reasons. First, individual or family-based interventions based on psychogenic theories failed to demonstrate any beneficial clinical effects (Massie & Beels, 1972). Second, research on family interaction in schizophrenia failed to support the theory that family communication could lead to schizophrenia and instead suggested that the presence of schizophrenia in a relative could disrupt communication patterns between family members (Waxler, 1974). Finally, the dramatic effects of antipsychotic medications on the symptoms of schizophrenia, combined with genetic research using either twin or high-risk methodologies, rendered purely psychogenic theories of schizophrenia less plausible and increased the attractiveness of more biologically based models. Interestingly, the prominence of these biological paradigms meant that professionals no longer had to "protect" patients from the deleterious impact of interaction with their relatives. On the contrary, professionals began to view family members as potential collaborators in treatment, and interest in engaging and working with them increased.

Expressed-Emotion Research

Expressed emotion (EE) refers to communications on the part of a relative that are critical, hostile, or emotionally overinvolved (e.g., extremely dramatic or intrusive; Leff & Vaughn, 1985). Following a serendipitous finding that patients with schizophrenia who returned home after treatment of an acute symptom exacerbation had a worse outcome than similar patients returning to live in other environments (Brown, Carstairs, & Topping, 1958), a semistructured interview was devised to measure attitudes on the part of relatives that were hypothesized to be related to stressful communication styles. Over 20 studies conducted with over 1,300 patients with schizophrenia have shown that living with a high-EE relative substantially increases the risk for relapse as compared to living with a low-EE relative (Bebbington & Kuipers, 1994). Furthermore, differences in relapse rates cannot be attributed to symptom or chronicity differences between patients living with high- or low-EE relatives.

The discovery of a predictive relationship between family EE and relapse in schizophrenia generated a strong interest among clinical researchers in developing family intervention programs designed to reduce stress in the overall family and promote more effective coping. A common feature of most family intervention programs for schizophrenia is that they embrace a stress-vulnerability-family coping skills model for improving the prognosis of schizophrenia. According to this model, illustrated in Figure 8.1, the

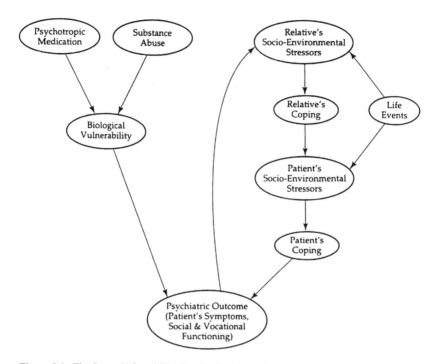

Figure 8.1. The Stress-Vulnerability-Family Coping Skills Model of Adaption to Psychiatric Disorders

SOURCE: From "Behavioral Family Therapy for Schizophrenia," by K. T. Mueser and S. M. Glynn, 1990, *Progress in Behavior Modification, 26,* 129, copyright © 1990 by Sage Publications, Inc. Reprinted by Permission of Sage Publications, Inc.

outcome of schizophrenia can be improved by reducing stress within the family, improving the coping skills of patients and relatives to manage stress effectively, and reducing biological vulnerability by encouraging medication adherence and lowering substance abuse. Thus, although EE research has been a source of some controversy (Mintz, Liberman, Miklowitz, & Mintz, 1987), it has been a valuable heuristic in the development of family intervention programs.

The Family Advocacy Movement

Caring for a mentally ill relative is associated with extraordinarily high levels of distress, including both emotional costs and financial hardship. In the wake of the deinstitutionalization movement, these difficulties were often compounded by mental health professionals who were ignorant of the needs of relatives, were outright suspicious of their motives, or believed that they had contributed to the development of the illness (Terkelsen, 1983). The frustrations of caregiving family members, with both their own and their ill relatives' treatment from professionals, gave rise to the family advocacy movement, exemplified by organizations such as the National Alliance for the Mentally Ill (NAMI). On a national level, the primary objective of family advocacy organizations has been to encourage more research in mental illness, to encourage parity of insurance coverage with medical illnesses, to decrease the stigma of mental illness through public education, and to support the allocation of more resources to the treatment of persons with severe mental illness. NAMI, whose membership numbered over 140,000 in 1996, distributes written and video educational materials, supports a toll-free telephone line for support and information, and directs lobbying and letter-writing campaigns to help achieve its legislative objectives. Family members, consumers, mental health professionals, and others can join the organization for a nominal fee and attend annual national and statewide conventions. In addition, many communities also support local affiliates, who typically meet monthly, using both educational and support group formats.

Although family advocacy organizations have generally not been strong proponents of family intervention, they have nevertheless contributed to the formation of such programs in several ways. By eloquently describing the turmoil of living with a relative who has schizophrenia and the difficulty of learning to navigate the complex and often incompetent mental health system, family members have helped professionals understand how schizophrenia affects the lives of all family members, not just the patient (Backlar, 1994). By expressing a clear desire to be involved in treatment and by advocating for better treatment themselves from professionals, family members have sent a clear message that they have a role to play in the long-term rehabilitation of their relative. Last, the family advocacy movement has helped professionals to understand the importance of social support for relatives who are managing a long-term illness. Although professional family intervention programs are one source of such support, the widespread availability of family support groups on a local level (e.g., chapters of NAMI) has made these groups a viable alternative to formal treatment programs.

MODELS OF FAMILY INTERVENTION

A wide variety of models of family treatment have been developed in recent years. Several models developed and validated by professionals are briefly mentioned here. Anderson, Reiss, and Hogarty (1986) developed a model of family intervention that combines techniques from family systems therapy and psychoeducation. Kuipers, Leff, and Lam's (1992) model involves providing education about psychiatric illnesses in both a group and an individual family format. In McFarlane's (1990) program, families meet in multiple-family groups to provide mutual family support and to resolve common difficulties. Schooler et al. (1997) developed a variation of the multiple-family group format in which meetings are divided between education about schizophrenia and how to cope with it and group support and discussion.

Although behavioral techniques may sometimes be used in the models developed by Anderson et al. (1986), Kuipers et al. (1992), McFarlane (1990), and Schooler et al. (1997), none are explicitly behavioral in their overall approach to assessment and intervention. Two other models have a strong behavioral orientation. Barrowclough and Tarrier's (1992) model combines education about psychiatric disorders with training in stress management, relapse prevention, and goal attainment. Falloon, Boyd, and McGill's (1984) model (see also Mueser & Glynn, 1995) combines education with communication skills and problem-solving training in a program designed to enable family members to manage the illness better without the assistance of professionals.

In addition to the differences between models of family intervention described above, family programs may also differ along a number of other dimensions, including theoretical orientation, format, intensity, duration, setting, and leadership. Differences between family models along each of these dimensions are briefly discussed below.

Theoretical Orientation

Some family interventions are explicitly behavioral in focus and incorporate the traditional elements of cognitive-behavioral therapies, such as assessment, skills teaching, homework, and time-limited treatment (Barrowclough & Tarrier, 1992; Falloon et al., 1984). McFarlane (1990) incorporates

TABLE 8.1   Advantages of Single- and Multiple-Family Group Formats of
Family Intervention Programs

Single-Family Format	Multiple-Family Format
Easier to conduct outreach to families	More economical
More suitable for addressing specific problem areas, training skills, etc.	More social support provided by other families
More flexible	Less vulnerable to effects of staff turnover
Easier to engage family, especially early in illness	Easier to provide multiple sources of input to family members

problem solving into his multiple-family group approach, but its main purpose is to provide a vehicle for families to share solutions to common problems and generate social support, with relatively less emphasis on teaching a formal problem-solving strategy. Anderson et al.'s (1986) model is broadly based on a family systems approach, with great emphasis placed on counseling to encourage patient autonomy. Other programs, such as Kuipers et al. (1992), are more supportive and eclectic.

Single- Versus Multiple-Family Format

One of the most critical differences between models of family intervention is whether treatment is provided in a single-family or a multiple-family group format. The relative advantages and disadvantages of each format are summarized in Table 8.1. Some family interventions combine both single- and multiple-family group formats. For example, in Anderson et al.'s model (1986), relatives were first engaged in a multiple-family group "survival workshop," which was followed by single-family therapy sessions. Kuipers et al. (1992) also combined single- with multiple-family groups, as did Schooler et al. (1997).

The models also vary according to whether the patient is included in multiple-family group sessions. Patients do not participate in Anderson et al.'s (1986) initial survival workshop or in Kuiper et al.'s (1992) multiple-family groups, but they do participate in the models developed by McFarlane et al. (1991, 1993) and Schooler et al. (1997). Also, patients may participate in psychoeducational family support groups developed by members of family advocacy organizations (Hatfield, 1990), although their level of participation in such groups is unclear and varies dramatically by locality.

Some have raised concerns about managing confidentiality of patient information in these formats. Obviously, when the patient is included in the therapy, he or she can decide how much information he or she wishes to disclose to the family, and breach of confidentiality by the therapist is rarely a concern. In some multiple-family formats, the patient is not included (e.g., Kuipers et al., 1992). The issue of patient confidentiality here can be handled in a variety of ways. Sometimes, these sessions are content driven, similar to classes, and facilitated by a professional who may have little or no contact with the patient. In such a case, limited or no access to information about the patient renders the confidentiality issue moot. When the facilitator does have more interaction with the patient, he or she can discuss, in advance, the topic of confidentiality of information and may ask for consent to a limited release of information (discussed below) to permit the facilitator to respond to specific questions from relatives.

Intensity

Most single-family intervention models begin with weekly sessions and then decrease the frequency of sessions over time. For example, in Falloon et al.'s (1984) model, family sessions are conducted weekly for approximately 3 months, biweekly for 6 months, and then monthly thereafter until the end of treatment. Multiple-family groups, on the other hand, tend to be conducted less frequently, such as biweekly (McFarlane, 1990) or monthly (Schooler et al., 1997). As we will discuss later in this chapter, it is not clear whether more intensive family interventions contribute to better patient outcomes.

In the largest study of family intervention for schizophrenia conducted to date, Zhang et al. (1993) compared the effects of a multiple-family educational intervention with effects of standard treatment on 3,092 patients in China. The intervention consisted of a series of 10 lectures and three discussions provided on a declining-contact basis over a 1-year period. Between 20 and 40 participants attended each lecture and discussion group. Despite the relatively low intensity of the intervention, positive results of the intervention were demonstrated across a range of different domains.

Duration

Family programs may be brief and time limited, long term (at least 6 months) and time limited, or long term and time unlimited. Many short-term programs focus primarily on education and are aimed at relatives, not patients (e.g., Abramowitz & Coursey, 1989). Some short-term programs involve the entire family and aim at educating family members about mental illness, helping them to accept the diagnosis and prepare for the patient's return home (e.g., Glick et al., 1985).

The behavioral approaches developed by Barrowclough and Tarrier (1992) and Falloon et al. (1984) are time-limited, longer-term interventions. These approaches focus on changing the behavior of families, on the basis of the assumption that improved coping, communication, and problem-solving skills will enable families to continue to benefit from therapy after it has ended. Time-limited treatment is also recommended by Anderson et al. (1986) and Kuipers et al. (1992), although the duration of treatment tends to be somewhat less prescribed than the 9 months to 1 year initially recommended by Barrowclough and Tarrier (1992) and Falloon et al. (1984). In particular, treatment duration appears to be longer for Anderson et al.'s (1986) approach, often lasting several years.

In contrast to the time-limited philosophy of most professionally developed intervention programs, McFarlane (1990) has suggested that continued social support is crucial to the long-term success of family treatment; therefore, in their model, multiple-family groups are provided on an ongoing, time-unlimited basis. An important distinction between McFarlane's (1990) model and the other approaches described is that this model achieved significantly better effects in a multiple-family group format.

Setting

Family intervention programs have been provided in a number of different settings, although the most common setting is a clinic located in the community. Falloon et al. (1984) originally designed their intervention to be conducted in the home of the family, in line with some earlier exploratory approaches to home-based care for schizophrenia (Passamanick, Scarpitti, & Dinitz, 1967). Both the Falloon et al. (1985) and Schooler et al. (1997) studies, which employed Falloon's model, were conducted at home. However, Randolph et al. (1994, 1995) demonstrated that this model was also beneficial when provided at the clinic.

The relative merits of home- versus clinic-based family intervention are often debated. Proponents of home-based care argue that fewer appointments are missed, more family members can be engaged, and clinicians are provided with a more informative picture of family life. On the other hand, home visits require extra clinician time, many families are willing (and even prefer) to attend appointments at the clinic, and many agencies are reluctant to permit home-based care except for emergencies or for patients who are unable to transport themselves. Clinically, a combination of home-based and clinic-based sessions is often feasible. Several home-based sessions may successfully engage the family in treatment, which can be subsequently shifted into the clinic (Mueser & Glynn, 1995).

Fewer family programs have been conducted on an inpatient basis. Glick et al. (1985) developed a 6-week inpatient therapy program for inpatients. Long-term results of the program, like those for other short-term family interventions, were mixed. Anderson et al. (1986) and Tarrier (1991) have pointed out that families can often be engaged in treatment during a patient's brief inpatient stay for an acute symptom exacerbation. Thus, the inpatient setting may be more valuable for engagement of the family than actual intervention aimed at educating families or teaching specific skills.

Leadership

Most family programs that have been systematically studied have been developed and led by mental health professionals. A notable exception to this has been a series of educational programs developed by the Training and Education Center Network of Philadelphia (Mannion & Meisel, 1993; Meisel & Mannion, 1990). This group has developed a program that involves multiple-family groups cofacilitated by a trained family member and a mental health professional. Preliminary findings from this approach have been promising (Mannion, Mueser, & Solomon, 1994), and a controlled trial of the intervention has recently been completed (Solomon, Draine, Mannion, & Meisel, 1996a, 1996b).

Most local chapters of NAMI conduct support groups on a monthly basis that are led by family members. Many family members use the materials entitled "The Journey of Hope" (Burland, 1993; Burland & Mayeux, 1995) in leading these groups. Anecdotally, many participants report that these

TABLE 8.2   Common Ingredients of Effective Family Intervention Programs

1. Educate families about psychiatric illnesses and their management.
2. Show concern, sympathy, and empathy to family members who are coping with mental illness.
3. Avoid blaming the family or pathologizing their efforts to cope.
4. Foster the development of all family members.
5. Enhance adherence to medication and decrease substance abuse and stress.
6. Improve communication and problem-solving skills in family members.
7. Provide treatment that is flexible and tailored to the individual needs of families.
8. Encourage family members to develop social supports outside their family network.
9. Instill hope for the future.
10. Take a long-term perspective.

meetings are very helpful (Lefley, 1996). However, the effects of these groups have not been systematically studied.

COMMON INGREDIENTS OF
FAMILY INTERVENTIONS

Despite the many differences in models of family intervention for schizophrenia, effective interventions are similar in more ways than they differ (Glynn, 1993; Lam, 1991). For example, all family interventions educate families about schizophrenia, strive to reduce stress, and encourage the development of all family members. Ten common core ingredients of effective family interventions are summarized in Table 8.2. The positive effects of a variety of family treatment models (reviewed below) suggest that these common ingredients are most critical for improving outcomes.

EFFICACY OF FAMILY INTERVENTION

Family treatment of schizophrenia has been one of the most extensively studied rehabilitation strategies in recent years. Many short-term educational programs, lasting 1 to 3 months, have been developed, and these often yield sustained improvements in relative knowledge of and sense of mastery over the psychiatric illness. However, the lack of evidence supporting their efficacy for patient outcomes over 1 or 2 years has tempered enthusiasm for these approaches (e.g., Glick et al., 1985; Vaughn et al., 1992). Goldstein, Rodnick, Evans, May, and Steinberg (1978) reported favorable effects on relapse rates at 6 months for a 6-week family educational program, but this finding has not been replicated. Despite the lack of effects on long-term patient outcomes, short-term interventions have been found to have beneficial effects on family burden, distress, and self-efficacy (Abramowitz & Coursey, 1989; Birchwood, Smith, & Cochrane, 1992; Glynn, Pugh, & Rose, 1993; Mills & Hansen, 1991; Sidley, Smith, & Howells, 1991; Smith & Birchwood, 1987; Solomon et al., 1996a, 1996b). Because most short-term family programs have failed to produce (or often even search for) positive effects on patient functioning, we confine our review to long-term (i.e., over 6 months) family interventions.

In part because of the focus of EE research on relapse rates in schizophrenia, most of the controlled research on family intervention has examined relapse (or rehospitalization) as the main outcome measure. Table 8.3 summarizes all of the controlled, random-assignment studies comparing long-term single-family intervention with routine treatment and reporting outcomes over at least 18 months. Table 8.4 includes those controlled studies comparing single-family intervention models with multiple-family groups for schizophrenia over at least 18 months. Most studies employed a treatment manual to guide the family interventions and provided family treatment for a period ranging between 9 and 24 months. In most cases, the patients in these studies had recently been treated for a symptom exacerbation (and thus were at higher risk for a relapse), were in regular contact with their families, and were living in the community. In all the studies, patients received routine treatment for schizophrenia, including antipsychotic medications, regular monitoring, case management, and access to other rehabilitation programs.

Several trends are apparent in Table 8.3. All of the studies reported lower relapse (or rehospitalization) rates for the single-family intervention programs compared to routine treatment. Specifically, cumulative relapse rates for family intervention ranged between 14% and 44% (unweighted mean across studies of 24%), compared to a range of 40% to 83% for routine treatment (unweighted mean of 64%). Furthermore, the difference in relapse rates between family treatment and usual care was statistically significant in each of these studies.

Examination of the studies summarized in Table 8.4 provides additional support for the beneficial effects of multiple-family group interventions. Three controlled studies comparing multiple-family groups with single-

TABLE 8.3 18- to 24-Month Cumulative Relapse Rates of Controlled Studies Comparing Long-Term Single-Family Therapy With Routine Treatment

Study	Theoretical Orientation	Treatment Manual	Duration of Family Treatment (Months)	Follow-Up Period (Months)	Sample Size	Relapse Rates (%)	
						Family Therapy	Routine Treatment
Falloon et al. (1985)	Behavioral	Falloon et al. (1984)	24	24	32	17	83
Leff et al. (1985)	Supportive[a]	Kuipers et al. (1992)	24	24	24	14	78
Tarrier et al. (1989)	Behavioral	Barrowclough & Tarrier (1992)	9	24	42	33[b]	59
Hogarty et al. (1991)[c]	Family systems	Anderson et al. (1986)	24	24	57	32	66
Xiong et al. (1994)	Educational/behavioral[a]	?	18	18	63	44	64
Zhang et al. (1994)	Supportive[a]	?	18	18	78	15[d]	54[d]
Randolph et al. (1995)	Behavioral	Falloon et al. (1984)	12	24	41	10	40
Total/mean (unweighted)					337	24	64

NOTE: ? = treatment manual unknown.

a. Single-family treatment combined with multiple-family groups.

b. Results combined from two treatment groups that received either a "symbolic" or "enactive" variant of the family intervention (which did not differ significantly).

c. This study also included a family treatment and social skills training group ($N = 23$, 35% relapse rate over 24 months) and a group that received social skills training but not family treatment ($N = 23$, 57% relapse rate over 24 months).

d. Based on rehospitalization rates.

TABLE 8.4 18- to 24-Month Cumulative Relapse Rates of Controlled Studies Comparing Long-Term Single-Family Therapy With Multiple-Family Groups

Study	Theoretical Orientation	Treatment Manual	Duration of Family Treatment (Months)	Follow-Up Period (Months)	Sample Size	Relapse Rates (%) Single-Family Therapy	Relapse Rates (%) Multiple-Family Therapy
Leff et al. (1990)	Supportive	Kuipers et al. (1992)	24	24	23	33	36
McFarlane, Link, et al. (1995)[a]	Supportive	Multiple family: McFarlane et al. (1991) Single family: Anderson et al. (1986)	24	24	34	44	25
McFarlane, Lukens, et al. (1995)	Supportive	Multiple family: McFarlane et al. (1991) Single family: Anderson et al. (1986)	24	24	172	27	16
Schooler et al. (1997)	Behavioral (single family)[b] Supportive (multiple family)	Falloon et al. (1988) Schooler & Keith (1985)	12 24	24 24	157 156	29[c]	35[c]
Total/mean (unweighted)					542	30	29

a. A third treatment group, based on psychodynamic approaches (*N* = 7) was initiated in this study, but randomization to this group was stopped because of the high relapse rates. This study provided treatment and follow-up for 4 years; to compare with other studies, only 2-year relapse rates are summarized here.
b. Single-family therapy participants also received family groups.
c. Based on rehospitalization rates.

family programs have reported remarkably similar outcomes in relapse or rehospitalizations, with weighted means of 30% and 29% respectively. The relapse rates reported in these studies for single-family programs are quite similar to those reported in studies comparing single-family intervention with routine (no family treatment) care (Table 8.3). McFarlane, Lukens, et al. (1995) reported that the multiple-family format resulted in significantly lower relapse rates than the single-family approach, whereas the difference between the two formats was not significant for the Leff et al. (1990) or Schooler et al. (1997) studies. Taken together, the studies summarized in Tables 8.3 and 8.4 provide strong evidence that manualized family intervention programs, using either a single- or a multiple-family group format and providing treatment for at least 9 months, significantly reduce relapse or rehospitalization rates over 18 to 24 months. Furthermore, a longer-term follow-up of the Tarrier et al. (1989) study reported that the patients who received 9 months of family treatment still had fewer relapses 5 and 8 years later (Tarrier, Barrowclough, Porceddu, & Fitzpatrick, 1994).

Family Interventions That
Did Not Yield Significant Benefits

Despite the overall positive findings described above, several controlled studies of family interventions have not found significant benefits. Here, treatment philosophy, underpowered tests of hypotheses, and unaddressed cultural differences limiting generalizability may all have played a role in negative or null results. For example, Köttgen, Sönnichsen, Mollenhauer, and Jurth (1984) employed a psychodynamic approach and failed to find significant differences in relapse rates over 9 months for patients in families who received treatment compared to routine treatment (33% vs. 53%, respectively). Although Köttgen et al.'s intervention, like the psychoeducational and behavioral models studied in Tables 8.3 and 8.4, was aimed at reducing stress in families and fostering social support, it differed in its use of insight-oriented techniques and attempts to focus on the past, such as delving into the origins of patients' and relatives' critical and hostile overinvolvement with each other. The negative results of this study suggest that psychodynamic techniques aimed at developing insight among family members are less helpful than strategies designed to address practical problems and teach more effective coping strategies; however, small sample size ($N = 49$; only 29 were from high expressed-emotion families) and the resulting underpowered tests of hypotheses may also play a role in the null results. Interestingly, McFarlane, Link, Dushay, Marchal, and Crilly (1995) also reported such negative outcomes with a comparison-group psychodynamic family treatment that randomization to this cell in their controlled trial was stopped before conclusion of the study. Thus, more insight-oriented family interventions would not be recommended for this population.

Zastowny, Lehman, Cole, and Kane (1992) compared the effects of behavioral family therapy (Falloon et al., 1984) with an equally intensive supportive family intervention based on psychoeducational principles outlined by Hatfield (1990) and Bernheim and Lehman (1985). This study evaluated the effects of family intervention on 30 "treatment-resistant" patients with schizophrenia who were being prepared for discharge to the community from long-term inpatient treatment. Families (including patients) received weekly sessions for 16 weeks while the patient received inpatient treatment in a specially designed rehabilitation unit. Following this, 24 of the 30 patients were discharged and received monthly family sessions for an additional 12 months. Rehospitalization rates over 12 months post discharge were in the moderate range for both the behavioral family (44%) and the supportive family (33%) interventions but did not differ significantly from each other. Although these rates of rehospitalization appear higher per year than the rates reported in other studies, the patient sample was more severely ill than that used in most other controlled studies and thus, presumably, was at greater risk for relapse and rehospitalization. The authors noted that stronger effects might have been achieved if more intensive family intervention had been provided following discharge from the hospital; obviously, small sample size is also a concern. These results do provide cautious optimism that some type of family intervention may be beneficial in facilitating the transition of severely ill patients from institutional care back into community settings, however.

Linszen et al. (1996) reported the results of an investigation of family intervention for recent-onset cases of schizophrenia. During a psychiatric hospitalization, patients were randomly assigned to receive either standard treatment (ST: pharmacological management and intensive individual therapy) or standard treatment plus behavioral family therapy (ST + BFT) based on the Falloon et al. (1984) model following their discharge into the community. At 9 months, cumulative relapse rates were quite low for both groups (ST: 15%; ST + BFT: 16%); the low relapse rates in the control group rendered it almost impossible to find other additive effects. These findings are encouraging but shed little light on the efficacy of family intervention at this point. It is unclear whether the low relapse rates and lack of differences between the treatments are due to the less chronic nature of the patients, the benefits of the intensive individual therapy, or the lack of benefit due to family intervention.

Finally, in a recently published investigation, Telles et al. (1995) reported the results of a controlled study comparing behavioral family therapy (Falloon et al., 1984) with standard treatment for 42 Hispanic patients with schizophrenia. In contrast to the other studies comparing this family model with standard treatment (Table 8.3), cumulative relapse rates at 1 year did not differ between the family intervention and standard treatment groups (50% and 41%, respectively; J. Mintz, personal communication, November 1996). In fact, post hoc analyses indicated that poorly acculturated patients fared significantly *worse* in the family intervention program than when they received only standard treatment, whereas for well-acculturated patients the program had no effect. On the basis of these negative findings, the authors suggested that cultural factors may influence the effects of family intervention on schizophrenia.

It is interesting to note that Xiong et al. (1994) also described the need to adapt Falloon et al.'s (1984) model of behavioral family therapy to the Chinese population and obtained positive results. In their report, 32% of the patients who received the family intervention relapsed over the year, compared to 60% of the patients who received standard treatment. It should be noted, however, that in the analyses of the results, only those patients whose families had attended at least five lectures were included in the family intervention group (90.3% of patients randomized to that condition), a condition that may have biased the results against the standard treatment group, in which a higher percentage of patients were included in the follow-up (97.2%). Nevertheless, this study, in combination with the findings reported by Xiong et al. (1994) and Zhang, Wang, Li, and Phillips (1994), suggests that the benefits of family intervention programs may not be limited to Western cultures.

Effects of Family Treatment
on Other Outcome Domains

There is a broad consensus among clinicians and researchers that functioning and outcome in schizophrenia are best conceptualized as multidimen-

sional, interactional processes (Avison & Speechley, 1987; Carpenter, Heinrichs, & Hanlon, 1981). Common domains of functioning in outcome research include clinical symptomatology, service utilization and community
tenure, quality of social relationships, self-care skill, and vocational functioning. Despite the importance of these different areas, most of the published findings describe only the effects of family intervention on relapse or
rehospitalization. Therefore, other than the ample evidence indicating that a
variety of family programs reduce relapse rates in schizophrenia, their effects
on other domains of functioning are largely unknown.

    Although the findings are limited, several investigations have evaluated
the effects of family treatment on other areas of functioning. Falloon,
McGill, Boyd, and Pederson (1987) reported that behavioral family therapy
resulted in significant improvements in social relationships, household tasks,
work activity, and leisure activities over the 2-year treatment period compared to the standard treatment. These authors observed that many of the
improvements in social functioning occurred during the second year and
suggested that the emphasis in the first year on developing problem-solving
skills may have contributed to the longer-term benefits.

    Barrowclough and Tarrier (1990) reported that their 9-month family
intervention resulted in significantly greater improvements at the 2-year
follow-up than standard treatment in social withdrawal, prosocial activities,
and overall social adjustment. Both groups improved significantly in interpersonal functioning. Zhang et al. (1993) reported, in their large study,
benefits of family intervention over 1 year across a broad range of social
functioning variables, such as living ability, social role functioning, and
work. Hogarty et al. (1991) described the effects of family intervention on
social functioning at 2 years post treatment, but their findings are difficult
to interpret because data were not collected on patients who had previously
relapsed, resulting in low sample sizes.

    The few available studies suggest that family intervention may improve
social functioning in schizophrenia, although more research is needed in this
area. Similarly, the three studies that have examined the effects of long-term
family treatment on caregivers have reported benefits in areas such as
subjective and objective burden, coping, and knowledge of schizophrenia
(Falloon & Pederson, 1985; Xiong et al., 1994; Zhang et al., 1993), in line
with the findings of briefer family intervention programs (e.g., Abramowitz
& Coursey, 1989; Solomon et al., 1996a). Last, two studies suggest that
family intervention programs result in lower overall mental health costs

compared to standard care (Cardin, McGill, & Falloon, 1995; Tarrier, Lowson, & Barrowclough, 1991). Considering the high cost of inpatient psychiatric treatment, it is not surprising that the positive effects of family intervention on reducing relapse and rehospitalization also translate into economic benefits.

Quasi-Experimental, Exploratory, and Other Studies

Hahlweg et al. (1994) compared the effects of standard neuroleptic dosage with targeted medication (i.e., provided only when symptoms worsen) combined with behavioral family therapy (Falloon et al.'s 1984 model). All patients received the family intervention. Cumulative relapse rates at 18 months were significantly lower for the standard medication group (4%) than for the targeted medication group (34%). Although family intervention was not directly studied, the low relapse rates of both groups in this study are consistent with the 18- to 24-month relapse rates of other studies of behavioral family therapy (Tables 8.3 and 8.4).

Brooker et al. (1994) conducted a quasi-experimental study in the context of a program designed to train community nurses in behavioral family therapy (based on Falloon et al.'s 1984 model). Using a within-subjects design, the study placed families either on a "waiting list" for 6 months, followed by 12 months of family intervention, or in a "delayed-treatment" group for whom family treatment was initiated 1 year later. Families were assigned to either the waiting-list or delayed-treatment group on the basis of when the community nurse received training in behavioral family therapy (i.e., either early or late in the course of the study). Family intervention was associated with a range of positive outcomes compared to standard treatment, including reductions in positive and negative symptoms, improved social functioning, and improvements in relatives' distress and knowledge of medication.

Rund et al. (1994) reported the results of a study evaluating the effects of a long-term (2-year) family intervention program for patients with early-onset schizophrenia (ages 13-18). Experimental patients were compared with matched patients who had been treated in the same clinic in previous years. Compared to standard treatment, family intervention both reduced relapses and was less costly. Interestingly, the authors reported that patients with poor premorbid social functioning benefited the most from the family intervention.

It is unclear why the patients with poor premorbid adjustment fared better with family treatment. It is possible that this differential rate of improvement reflected the fact that poor premorbid patients functioned worse than others and therefore had more room to improve. This interpretation may be particularly pertinent because premorbid adjustment tends to be related to more severe negative symptoms after the onset of schizophrenia (Mueser, Bellack, Morrison, & Wixted, 1990; Pogue-Geile & Zubin, 1988), and family intervention may have arrested the worsening in negative symptoms that tends to occur during the first 5 years of the illness (McGlashan & Fenton, 1992).

There is evidence that the amount of time that elapses between the emergence of psychotic symptoms and first antipsychotic treatment predicts the time required to stabilize the patient and long-term prognosis (Loebel et al., 1992; Wyatt, 1991). The Rund et al. (1994) and Linszen et al. (1996) studies suggest that early intervention at the first episode may be especially critical for improving the long-term prognosis of schizophrenia. However, these studies do not point to the unique benefits of family intervention for recent-onset patients but rather suggest the importance of relatively intensive psychosocial treatment.

A final exploratory study that hints at the potential preventative effects of family intervention was reported by Falloon (1992). In an uncontrolled investigation, Falloon trained British family practitioners to detect prodromal signs of an initial psychotic disorder and to refer patients for a more intensive psychiatric assessment if these symptoms were so identified. When the presence of these signs was confirmed, patients were prescribed minimal doses of neuroleptic medication, and patients and relatives were provided with education about schizophrenia and home-based stress management in a structured program. Participation in these interventions appeared to lower the documented first-incidence rate of schizophrenia in the local catchment area, although the lack of a randomized comparison group makes these results very tentative.

STATUS OF FAMILY INTERVENTION AS AN EMPIRICALLY VALIDATED TREATMENT

The weight of evidence indicates that family intervention programs for schizophrenia that are provided for at least 9 months and that focus on education, stress reduction, and enhancement of coping skills meet the criteria of the American Psychological Association (APA) Task Force on Promotion and Dissemination of Psychological Procedures (Division of Clinical Psychology) for a "well-established treatment" (APA Task Force, 1995). As summarized in Table 8.3, seven studies conducted by a variety of different investigators demonstrated that single-family intervention programs (provided in combination with antipsychotic medication) were more effective than medication alone. Furthermore, as summarized in Table 8.4, four additional studies have shown that multiple-family group interventions are as effective as, or more effective than, the single-family treatment programs summarized in Table 8.3. Almost every study was conducted on the basis of a treatment manual, and many of these manuals are readily available to practitioners (Anderson et al., 1986; Barrowclough & Tarrier, 1992; Falloon et al., 1984, 1988; Kuipers et al., 1992; McFarlane et al., 1991).

In addition to these studies, one study with 1-year follow-up data reported lower relapse rates for patients who received family intervention (Zhang et al., 1993). However, three studies of long-term family intervention with 1-year follow-up data failed to report positive effects for family treatment compared to no treatment. Each of these studies is significantly different from the longer follow-up studies in terms of either the type of family intervention or the population studied. Köttgen et al. (1984) examined a psychodynamic model of family intervention, compared to the more psychoeducational and stress reduction-oriented treatment models used by other investigators. Linszen et al. (1996) compared family intervention to an intensive individual therapy program for recent-onset patients and found that both treatments resulted in very low relapse rates. Finally, Telles et al. (1995) reported no overall effects of family intervention for Mexican American patients, the only study that has been conducted with this population. Thus, although some negative findings have been reported, there is ample support for the efficacy of family intervention for schizophrenia.

Research on family therapy at this time suggests benefits primarily in the area of prevention of relapses and rehospitalization, although the risk reduction is quite substantial (approximately 50% reduced risk of relapse over 2 years). Several controlled studies also indicate improvements in social functioning (Barrowclough & Tarrier, 1990; Falloon et al., 1987; Hogarty et al., 1991; Zhang et al., 1993). However, the findings are inconsistent across these studies, and insufficient data are available to draw any firm conclusions.

TAILORING FAMILY INTERVENTIONS
TO INDIVIDUAL NEEDS

Moving from the environment of controlled clinical trials to the "real world" of mental health treatment is always a challenge. Controlled trials involve defining a homogenous sample meeting specific inclusion and exclusion criteria and determining whether there are outcome differences attributable to contrasting interventions. Within the experimental paradigm, individual differences are seen as sources of error variance rather than as prompts for individual intervention tailoring. In contrast, optimal clinical intervention in the community is predicated on individual tailoring. Thus, many clinicians are left with the question "How can I use this information on the importance of family intervention to best provide treatment for patients with schizophrenia?"

Based on the literature detailing families' needs in coping with a relative with schizophrenia (Bloch, Szmukler, Herrman, Benson, & Colussa, 1995; Fadden, Bebbington, & Kuipers, 1987; Lefley, 1989; Mueser, Bellack, Wade, Sayers, & Rosenthal, 1992; Winefield & Harvey, 1994), the heuristic scheme outlined in Figure 8.2 would seem to offer some guidance. In essence, we are recommending that all families have access to an agency that recognizes their burden and distress and acts to offer some assistance in an increasingly intensive manner (see Marsh, 1992). At a most basic level, the agency should be family friendly—that is, it should routinely provide information on local support groups, provide at least some access to staff in the evening for working relatives, and provide comfortable meeting rooms large enough for a family.

One of the biggest impediments to family involvement is concern over protecting patient confidentiality and autonomy. It is clearly outside the scope of this chapter to discuss this issue in great depth, but, in addressing this concern, it can be helpful for the professional first to acknowledge that family members will often have some ongoing interaction and responsibility for the patient long after the professional has terminated—a collaboration similar to that required of family members when a relative is recovering from a heart attack or cancer. Thus, keeping lines of communication and support open among family members, patients, and staff is often in the severely ill psychiatric patient's best interest. Rather than assuming a reflexive stance that all patient information is best kept confidential, the professional is encouraged to evaluate, with each patient, whether a sharing of limited basic

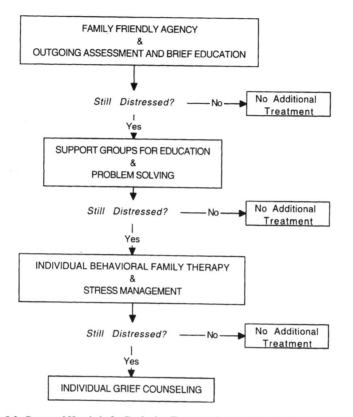

Figure 8.2. Proposed Heuristic for Designing Treatment Interventions for Relatives of Persons with Schizophrenia

information among the patient and his or her loved ones might maximize the likelihood that the patient can stay out of the hospital and develop a richer quality of life. This information might include symptoms, recommended treatment plan, realistic family expectations, signs of exacerbation, and proactive consensual interventions if they occur. Note that this information does not have to include topics that might be personally distressing for the patient to disclose and more typical of conventional psychotherapy, such as sexual preferences. Provided with a compelling rationale, many patients are willing to consent to this limited release of information, and forms for a written agreement to this end have been developed by Marsh (1992).

If either the family or the patient still exhibits high levels of distress after agency support and brief education, then more formal intervention may be required. As of yet, we have little information on the specific types of interventions that might work best for specific types of families and patients (Dixon & Lehman, 1995). Thus, the likely positive patient outcomes, reductions in family distress, and cost-effectiveness accruing from multiple-family groups emphasizing education, support, and problem solving, such as those designed by McFarlane (1990) or Schooler et al. (1997), render them a good option for the next level of intervention.

Some families and patients continue to exhibit high levels of distress even while attending groups or are reluctant to attend them. Often, these are families with more limited financial resources, unique family issues (e.g., severe psychiatric illness in multiple members), or extreme levels of shame about the schizophrenia; they often can still benefit from individual consultation with a mental health professional. In such cases, individual psychoeducational therapy (Anderson et al., 1986) or behavioral family therapy (Falloon et al., 1984) with a special emphasis on tailoring problem solving to meet the specific needs of the family would be likely to be optimal.

Finally, many family members have written eloquently about their own struggles to accept severe psychiatric illness in their loved ones (e.g., Backlar, 1994). Individual grief counseling (Miller, Dworkin, Ward, & Barone, 1990), in which family members can openly discuss their own sadness about their relatives' situation without the presence of the patient and can clarify any cognitive distortions that they might have about their contribution to the etiology of the problem, can be very helpful.

FUTURE DIRECTIONS AND CONCLUSIONS

Despite the burgeoning literature on family treatment for schizophrenia, there are still many critical questions to answer.

We do not have sufficient data to know whether one type of intervention is superior to another or to match interventions to specific family or patient characteristics. The optimal length of treatment is yet to be determined, and the clinician is often confronted with resolving the conflict between findings of studies such as McFarlane, Link, et al.'s (1995), which highlight the benefits of extended treatment, and findings such as Tarrier et al.'s (1989, 1994), which suggest that time-limited family therapy may have long-lasting effects. In addition, most of these interventions have been tested primarily on families of origin, yet with the growth of community care, more and more patients are likely to be in relationships with spouses (or their equivalents) or children, and the models may need to be revised accordingly (see Manion et al., 1994). Cultural differences in perceived optimal levels of patient autonomy and shared decision making may render these interventions unsuitable as originally designed for some contexts; systematic modifications may be required. Finally, at a most basic level, delivery of these interventions is predicated on the presence of a family, yet a substantial proportion of persons with schizophrenia (perhaps as many as 40% of severely ill patients) indicate they have little or no contact with their relatives (Goldman, 1984; Talbott, 1990). More assertive outreach to engage (or reengage) families with an offer of effective support and assistance may ultimately increase the positive social network available to the patient.

Although there is still much to be learned, family treatment is the most widely studied and empirically validated psychological treatment for schizophrenia. More work is needed to better understand how to tailor treatment to meet the individual needs of families. In addition, it is possible that some of the principles of family intervention can be adapted to other social environments in which patients reside, such as board-and-care homes and inpatient settings, improving adjustment and outcome. It is encouraging that even in this time of dramatic advancements in pharmacologic treatment in schizophrenia, psychological interventions can play a key role in psychiatric rehabilitation and recovery.

REFERENCES

Abramowitz, I. A., & Coursey, R. D. (1989). Impact of an educational support group on family participants who take care of their schizophrenic relatives. *Journal of Consulting and Clinical Psychology, 57,* 232-236.

American Psychological Association (Division of Clinical Psychology) Task Force on the Promotion and Dissemination of Psychological Procedures. (1995). Training and dissemination of empirically-validated psychological treatments: Report and recommendations. *Clinical Psychologist, 48,* 3-24.

Anderson, C. M., Reiss, D. J., & Hogarty, G. E. (1986). *Schizophrenia and the family.* New York: Guilford.

Avison, W. R., & Speechley, K. N. (1987). The discharged psychiatric patient: A review of social, social-psychological, and psychiatric correlates of outcome. *American Journal of Psychiatry, 144,* 10-18.

Backlar, P. (1994). *The family face of schizophrenia: Practical counsel from America's leading experts.* New York: G. P. Putnam's Sons.

Barrowclough, C., & Tarrier, N. (1990). Social functioning in schizophrenic patients: I. The effects of expressed emotion and family intervention. *Social Psychiatry and Psychiatric Epidemiology, 25,* 125-129.

Barrowclough, C., & Tarrier, N. (1992). *Families of schizophrenic patients: Cognitive behavioral intervention.* London: Chapman & Hall.

Bateson, G., Jackson, D. D., Haley, J., & Weakland, J. (1956). Toward a theory of schizophrenia. *Behavioral Science, 1,* 251-264.

Bebbington, P., & Kuipers, L. (1994). The predictive utility of expressed emotion in schizophrenia: An aggregate analysis. *Psychological Medicine, 24,* 707-718.

Bernheim, K. F., & Lehman, A. F. (1985). *Working with families of the mentally ill.* New York: Norton.

Bion, W. R. (1967). *Second thoughts.* London: William Heinemann.

Birchwood, M., Smith, J., & Cochrane, R. (1992). Specific and non-specific effects of educational intervention for families living with schizophrenia. *British Journal of Psychiatry, 160,* 806-814.

Bloch, S., Szmukler, G. I., Herrman, H., Benson, A., & Colussa, S. (1995). Counseling caregivers of relatives with schizophrenia: Themes, interventions, and caveats. *Family Process, 34,* 413-425.

Brooker, C., Falloon, I., Butterworth, A., Goldberg, D., Graham-Hole, V., & Hillier, V. (1994). The outcome of training community psychiatric nurses to deliver psychosocial intervention. *British Journal of Psychiatry, 165,* 222-230.

Brown, G. W., Carstairs, G. M., & Topping, G. (1958). Post hospital adjustment of chronic mental patients. *Lancet, 2,* 685-689.

Burland, J. (1993). *The Journey of Hope Family Education Course.* Baton Rouge: Louisiana Alliance for the Mentally Ill.

Burland, J., & Mayeux, D. (1995). The Journey of Hope: A family to family self-help education and support group program. *Journal of the California Alliance for the Mentally Ill, 6*(3).

Cardin, V. A., McGill, C. W., & Falloon, I. R. H. (1995). An economic analysis: Costs, benefits and effectiveness. In I. R. H. Falloon (Ed.), *Family management of schizophrenia* (pp. 115-123). Baltimore: Johns Hopkins University Press.

Carpenter, W. T., Heinrichs, D. W., & Hanlon, T. E. (1981). Methodologic standards for treatment outcome research in schizophrenia. *American Journal of Psychiatry, 138,* 465-471.

Dixon, L. B., & Lehman, A. F. (1995). Family interventions for schizophrenia. *Schizophrenia Bulletin, 21,* 631-643.

Fadden, G., Bebbington, P., & Kuipers, L. (1987). The burden of care: The impact of functional psychiatric illness on the patient's family. *British Journal of Psychiatry, 150,* 285-292.

Falloon, I., Mueser, K., Gingerich, S., Rappaport, S., McGill, C., & Hole, V. (1988). *Behavioural family therapy: A workbook.* Buckingham, UK: Buckingham Mental Health Service.

Falloon, I. R. H. (1992). Early intervention for first episodes of schizophrenia: A preliminary exploration. *Psychiatry, 55,* 4-15.

Falloon, I. R. H., Boyd, J. L., & McGill, C. W. (1984). *Family care of schizophrenia: A problem-solving approach to the treatment of mental illness.* New York: Guilford.

Falloon, I. R. H., Boyd, J. L., McGill, C. W., Williamson, M., Razani, J., Moss, H. B., Gilderman, A. M., & Simpson, G. M. (1985). Family management in the prevention of morbidity of schizophrenia: Clinical outcome of a two year longitudinal study. *Archives of General Psychiatry, 42,* 887-896.

Falloon, I. R. H., McGill, C. W., Boyd, J. L., & Pederson, J. (1987). Family management in the prevention of morbidity of schizophrenia: Social outcome of a two-year longitudinal study. *Psychological Medicine, 17,* 59-66.

Falloon, I. R. H., & Pederson, J. (1985). Family management in the prevention of morbidity of schizophrenia: The adjustment of the family unit. *British Journal of Psychiatry, 147*, 156-163.

Fromm-Reichmann, F. (1948). Notes on the development of treatment of schizophrenics by psychoanalytic psychotherapy. *Psychiatry, 11*, 263-273.

Glick, I., Clarkin, J., Spencer, J., Haas, G., Lewis, A., Peyser, J., DeMane, N., Good-Ellis, M., Harris, E., & Lestelle, V. (1985). A controlled evaluation of inpatient family intervention: I. Preliminary results of a 6-month follow-up. *Archives of General Psychiatry, 42*, 882-886.

Glynn, S. M. (1993). Family-based treatment for major mental illness: A new role for psychologists. *California Psychologist, 25*, 22-23.

Glynn, S., Pugh, R., & Rose, G. (1993). Benefits of attendance at a state hospital family education workshop. *Psychosocial Rehabilitation Journal, 16*, 95-101.

Goldman, H. H. (1984). The chronically mentally ill: Who are they? Where are they? In M. Mirabi (Ed.), *The chronically mentally ill: Research and services* (pp. 33-44). New York: Spectrum.

Goldstein, M., Rodnick, E., Evans, J., May, P., & Steinberg, M. (1978). Drug and family therapy in the aftercare of acute schizophrenics. *Archives of General Psychiatry, 35*, 1169-1177.

Hahlweg, K., Wiedemann, G., Müller, U., Feinstein, E., Hank, G., & Dose, M. (1994). *Effectiveness of behavioral family management in combination with standard dose or targeted medication to prevent relapse in schizophrenia.* Unpublished manuscript.

Hatfield, A. B. (1990). *Family education in mental illness.* New York: Guilford.

Hogarty, G. E., Anderson, C., Reiss, D., Kornblith, S., Greenwald, D., Ulrich, R., & Carter, M. (1991). Family psychoeducation, social skills training, and maintenance chemo-therapy in the aftercare treatment of schizophrenia: II. Two year effects of a controlled study on relapse and adjustment. *Archives of General Psychiatry, 48*, 340-347.

Johnson, A. B. (1990). *Out of Bedlam: The truth about deinstitutionalization.* New York: Basic Books.

Köttgen, C., Sönnichsen, I., Mollenhauer, K., & Jurth, R. (1984). Group therapy with the families of schizophrenic patients: Results of the Hamburg Camberwell-Family Inter-view Study III. *International Journal of Family Psychiatry, 5*, 84-94.

Kuipers, L., Leff, J., & Lam, D. (1992). *Family work for schizophrenia: A practical guide.* London: Gaskell.

Lam, D. H. (1991). Psychosocial family intervention in schizophrenia: A review of empirical studies. *Psychological Medicine, 21*, 423-441.

Leff, J., & Vaughn, C. (1985). *Expressed emotion in families: Its significance for mental illness.* New York: Guilford.

Leff, J. P., Berkowitz, R., Shavit, N., Strachan, A., Glass, I., & Vaughn, C. (1990). A trial of family therapy versus a relatives' group for schizophrenia. Two-year follow-up. *British Journal of Psychiatry, 157*, 571-577.

Leff, J. P., Kuipers, L., Berkowitz, R., & Sturgeon, D. (1985). A controlled trial of social intervention in the families of schizophrenic patients: Two-year follow-up. *British Journal of Psychiatry, 146*, 594-600.

Lefley, H. P. (1989). Family burden and family stigma in major mental illness. *American Psychologist, 44*, 556-560.

Lefley, H. P. (1996). *Family caregiving in mental illness.* Thousand Oaks, CA: Sage.

Linszen, D., Dingemans, P., Van der Does, J. W., Nugter, A., Scholte, P., Lenior, R., & Goldstein, M. J. (1996). Treatment, expressed emotion and relapse in recent onset schizophrenic disorders. *Psychological Medicine, 26*, 333-342.

Loebel, A. D., Lieberman, J. A., Alvir, J. M. J., Mayerhoff, D. I., Geisler, S. H., & Szymanski, S. R. (1992). Duration of psychosis and outcome in first-episode schizophrenia. *American Journal of Psychiatry, 149,* 1183-1188.

Mannion, E., & Meisel, M. (1993). *Teaching manual for spouse coping skills workshops.* Philadelphia: Mental Health Association of Southeastern Pennsylvania.

Mannion, E., Mueser, K., & Solomon, P. (1994). Designing psychoeducational services for spouses of persons with serious mental illness. *Community Mental Health Journal, 30,* 177-190.

Marsh, D. T. (1992). *Families and mental illness: New directions in professional practice.* New York: Praeger.

Massie, H. N., & Beels, C. C. (1972). The outcome of the family treatment of schizophrenia. *Schizophrenia Bulletin, 6,* 24-36.

McFarlane, W. R. (1990). Multiple family groups and the treatment of schizophrenia. In M. I. Herz, S. J. Keith, & J. P. Docherty (Eds.), *Handbook of schizophrenia: Vol. 4. Psychosocial treatment of schizophrenia* (pp. 167-189). Amsterdam: Elsevier.

McFarlane, W. R., Deakins, S. M., Gingerich, S. L., Dunne, E., Horan, B., & Newmark, M. (1991). *Multiple-family psychoeducational group treatment manual.* New York: New York State Psychiatric Institute.

McFarlane, W. R., Dunne, E., Lukens, E., Newmark, M., McLaughlin-Toran, J., Deakins, S., & Horen, B. (1993). From research to clinical practice: Dissemination of New York State's Family Psychoeducation Project. *Hospital and Community Psychiatry, 44,* 265-270.

McFarlane, W. R., Link, B., Dushay, R., Marchal, J., & Crilly, J. (1995). Psychoeducational multiple family groups: Four-year relapse outcome in schizophrenia. *Family Process, 34,* 127-144.

McFarlane, W. R., Lukens, E., Link, B., Dushay, R., Deakins, S. A., Newmark, M., Dunne, E. J., Horen, B., & Toran, J. (1995). Multiple-family groups and psychoeducation in the treatment of schizophrenia. *Archives of General Psychiatry, 52,* 679-687.

McGlashan, T. H., & Fenton, W. S. (1992). The positive-negative distinction in schizophrenia: Review of natural history validators. *Archives of General Psychiatry, 49,* 63-72.

Meisel, M., & Mannion, E. (1990). *Teaching manual for coping skills workshops* (Rev. ed.). Philadelphia: Mental Health Association of Southeastern Pennsylvania.

Miller, F., Dworkin, J., Ward, M., & Barone, D. (1990). A preliminary study of unresolved grief in families of seriously mentally ill patients. *Hospital and Community Psychiatry, 41,* 1321-1325.

Mills, P. D., & Hansen, J. C. (1991). Short-term group interventions for mentally ill young adults living in a community residence and their families. *Hospital and Community Psychiatry, 42,* 1144-1149.

Mintz, L. I., Liberman, R. P., Miklowitz, D. J., & Mintz, J. (1987). Expressed emotion: A call for partnership among relatives, patients, and professionals. *Schizophrenia Bulletin, 13,* 227-235.

Mueser, K. T., Bellack, A. S., Morrison, R. L., & Wixted, J. T. (1990). Social competence in schizophrenia: Premorbid adjustment, social skill, and domains of functioning. *Journal of Psychiatric Research, 24,* 51-63.

Mueser, K. T., Bellack, A. S., Wade, J. H., Sayers, S. L., & Rosenthal, C. K. (1992). Educational needs assessment of chronic psychiatric patients and their relatives. *British Journal of Psychiatry, 160,* 674-680.

Mueser, K. T., & Glynn, S. M. (1990). Behavioral family therapy for schizophrenia. *Progress in Behavior Modification, 26,* 122-149.

Mueser, K. T., & Glynn, S. M. (1995). *Behavioral family therapy for psychiatric disorders.* Boston: Allyn & Bacon.

Passamanick, B., Scarpitti, F. R., & Dinitz, S. (1967). *Schizophrenics in the community.* New York: Appleton-Century-Crofts.

Pogue-Geile, M. F., & Zubin, J. (1988). Negative symptomatology and schizophrenia: A conceptual and empirical review. *International Journal of Mental Health, 16,* 3-45.

Randolph, E. T., Eth, S., Glynn, S., Paz, G. B., Leong, G. B., Shaner, A. L., Strachan, A., Van Vort, W., Escobar, J., & Liberman, R. P. (1994). Behavioural family management in schizophrenia: Outcome from a clinic-based intervention. *British Journal of Psychiatry, 144,* 501-506.

Randolph, E. T., Glynn, S. M., Eth, S., Paz, G. G., Leong, G. B., & Shaner, A. L. (1995, May). *Family therapy for schizophrenia: Two year outcome.* Paper presented at the annual meeting of the American Psychiatric Association, Miami.

Rosen, J. N. (1953). *Direct analysis: Selected papers.* New York: Grune & Stratton.

Rund, B. R., Moe, L., Sollien, T., Fjell, A., Borchgrevink, T., Hallert, M., & Naess, P. O. (1994). The Psychosis Project: An efficiency study of a psychoeducational treatment programme for schizophrenic adolescents. *Acta Psychiatrica Scandinavica, 89,* 211-218.

Schooler, N. R., & Keith, S. J. (1985). *National Institute of Mental Health/Pharmacologic and Somatic Treatments Research Branch Treatment Strategies in Schizophrenia Study: Working protocol.* Unpublished document.

Schooler, N. R., Keith, S. J., Severe, J. B., Matthews, S. M., Bellack, A. S., Glick, I. D., Hargreaves, W. A., Kane, J. M., Ninan, P. T., Frances, A., Jacobs, M., Lieberman, J. A., Mance, R., Simpson, G. M., & Woerner, M. G. (1997). Relapse and rehospitalization during maintenance treatment of schizophrenia: The effects of dose reduction and family treatment. *Archives of General Psychiatry, 54,* 453-463.

Searles, H. (1965). *Collected papers on schizophrenia and related subjects.* New York: International Universities Press.

Sidley, G. L., Smith, J., & Howells, K. (1991). Is it ever too late to learn? Information provision to relatives of long-term schizophrenia sufferers. *Behavioural Psychotherapy, 19,* 305-320.

Smith, J., & Birchwood, M. (1987). Specific and non-specific effect of educational interventions with families of schizophrenic patients. *British Journal of Psychiatry, 150,* 645-652.

Solomon, P., Draine, J., Mannion, E., & Meisel, M. (1996a). Impact of brief family psychoeducation on self-efficacy. *Schizophrenia Bulletin, 22,* 41-50.

Solomon, P., Draine, J., Mannion, E., & Meisel, M. (1996b). The impact of individualized consultation and group workshop family psychoeducation interventions on ill relative outcomes. *Journal of Nervous and Mental Disease, 184,* 252-255.

Stein, L. I., & Test, M. A. (1980). Alternative to mental hospital treatment: I. Conceptual model, treatment program, and clinical evaluation. *Archives of General Psychiatry, 37,* 392-397.

Sullivan, H. S. (1962). *Schizophrenia as a human process.* New York: Norton.

Talbott, J. A. (1990). Current perspectives in the United States on the chronically mentally ill. In A. Kales, C. N. Stefanis, & J. Talbott (Eds.), *Recent advances in schizophrenia* (pp. 279-295). New York: Springer-Verlag.

Tarrier, N. (1991). Some aspects of family interventions in schizophrenia. I: Adherence to intervention programmes. *British Journal of Psychiatry, 159,* 475-480.

Tarrier, N., Barrowclough, C., Porceddu, K., & Fitzpatrick, E. (1994). The Salford Family Intervention Project for schizophrenic relapse prevention: Five and eight year accumulating relapses. *British Journal of Psychiatry, 165,* 829-832.

Tarrier, N., Barrowclough, C., Vaughn, C., Bamrah, J., Porceddu, K., Watts, S., & Freeman, H. (1989). Community management of schizophrenia: A two-year follow-up of a behavioral intervention with families. *British Journal of Psychiatry, 154,* 625-628.

Tarrier, N., Lowson, K., & Barrowclough, C. (1991). Some aspects of family interventions in schizophrenia: II. Financial considerations. *British Journal of Psychiatry, 159,* 481-484.

Telles, C., Karno, M., Mintz, J., Paz, G., Arias, M., Tucker, D., & Lopez, S. (1995). Immigrant families coping with schizophrenia: Behavioral family intervention v. case management with a low-income Spanish-speaking population. *British Journal of Psychiatry, 167,* 473-479.

Terkelsen, K. G. (1983). Schizophrenia and the family: II. Adverse effects of family therapy. *Family Process, 22,* 191-200.

Vaughn, K., Doyle, M., McConaghy, N., Blaszcynski, A., Fox, A., & Tarrier, N. (1992). The Sydney Intervention Trial: A controlled trial of relatives' counselling to reduce schizophrenic relapse. *Social Psychiatry and Psychiatric Epidemiology, 27,* 16-21.

Waxler, N. E. (1974). Parent and child effects on cognitive performance: An experimental approach to the etiological and responsive theories of schizophrenia. *Family Process, 13,* 1-22.

Winefield, H. R., & Harvey, E. J. (1994). Needs of family caregivers in chronic schizophrenia. *Schizophrenia Bulletin, 20,* 557-566.

Winnicott, D. W. (1965). *The maturational processes and the facilitating environment.* New York: International Universities Press.

Wyatt, R. J. (1991). Neuroleptics and the natural course of schizophrenia. *Schizophrenia Bulletin, 17,* 235-280.

Xiong, W., Phillips, M. R., Hu, X., Ruiwen, W., Dai, Q., Kleinman, J., & Kleinman, A. (1994). Family-based intervention for schizophrenic patients in China: A randomized controlled trial. *British Journal of Psychiatry, 165,* 239-247.

Zastowny, T. R., Lehman, A. F., Cole, R. E., & Kane, C. (1992). Family management of schizophrenia: A comparison of behavioral and supportive family treatment. *Psychiatric Quarterly, 63,* 159-186.

Zhang, M., Hequin, Y., Yao, C., Ye, J., Yu, Q., Chen, P., Guo, L., Yang, J., Qu, G., Wong, Z., Cai, J., Shen, M., Hou, J., Wang, L., Zhang, Y., Zhang, B., Orley, J., & Gittelman, M. (1993). Effectiveness of psychoeducation of relatives of schizophrenic patients: A prospective cohort study in five cities of China. *International Journal of Mental Health, 22,* 47-59.

Zhang, M., Wang, M., Li, J., & Phillips, M. R. (1994). Randomized-control trial of family intervention for 78 first-episode male schizophrenic patients: An 18-month study in Suzhou, Jiangsu. *British Journal of Psychiatry, 165,* 96-102.

9

Psychological Management of Recurrent Headache Disorders

EMPIRICAL BASIS FOR CLINICAL PRACTICE

KENNETH A. HOLROYD

GAY L. LIPCHIK

DONALD B. PENZIEN

The use of psychosocial interventions in the management of chronic medical disorders has grown rapidly in recent years. One reason is that psychological interventions have been shown to significantly enhance the management of some disorders that are often not effectively managed with standard medical therapies alone. The use of psychological interventions in the management of recurrent headache disorders illustrates many of the possibilities and problems that are encountered when developing and evaluating psychosocial interventions for the management of chronic medical

AUTHORS' NOTE: Support for preparation of this chapter was provided in part by NS32374 from the National Institute of Neurological Disorders and Stroke.

187

disorders. In this chapter, we evaluate three decades of empirical evidence bearing on the effectiveness of psychological interventions in the management of recurrent headache disorders and then use this evidence to formulate clinical guidelines for practice. We argue that clinically useful treatment guidelines will require not just the identification of empirically supported interventions but also empirically supported treatment algorithms that can guide the selection of the most appropriate psychological and pharmacological interventions for a particular patient at a particular point in therapy. Preliminary treatment algorithms of this sort are offered here for their heuristic value. First, we provide basic background information about the classification, diagnosis and social impact of recurrent headache disorders. Then we discuss behavioral interventions and common clinical problems encountered in using these interventions. Finally, we describe an empirically based treatment strategy that integrates drug and nondrug therapies.

HEADACHE DISORDERS:
IMPACT AND CLASSIFICATION

Epidemiology

Most people occasionally experience headaches but are not disabled by recurring headaches. However, epidemiological studies indicate that more than 8 million women and 2 million men in the United States are disabled with some frequency by migraine headaches alone (Stewart, Lipton, Celentano, & Reed, 1992). Approximately 20% to 30% of the population experiences tension-type headaches more than once a month, and about 4% have a tension-type headache more than half of the time (Rasmussen, Jensen, Schroll, & Olesen, 1991). Differences in headache prevalence according to gender are significant, with a female-to-male ratio of 3:1 for migraine and 5:4 for tension-type headache (Rasmussen et al., 1991). Headache disorders are thus quite prevalent and are a significant source of disability, especially for women.

Economic and Social Cost

Untreated or ineffectively treated recurrent headache disorders cost billions of dollars each year in the United States alone. The indirect costs, such as lost wages and decreased productivity, are substantial. In the United States, migraineurs spend more than 3 million days bedridden each month (Stang & Osterhaus, 1993). Employed males experience approximately 2.7 million days per year of restricted activity, and employed females suffer 18.8 million days per year of restricted activity due to migraine (Stang & Osterhaus, 1993). The estimated annual cost of lost labor due to migraine disability in the United States is between $5.6 and $17.2 billion (Osterhaus, Gutterman, & Plachetka, 1992). Because the incidence of tension-type headache is greater than that of migraine (Rasmussen et al., 1991), tension-type headaches probably account for a significant proportion of the population disability due to headache. A Danish population study, noteworthy for its careful diagnosis of headache, found that 820 workdays were lost per year per 1,000 employees due to tension-type headache compared to 270 workdays lost per year per 1,000 employees due to migraine (Rasmussen, Jensen, & Olesen, 1992).

Family, social, and recreational activities may be more disrupted by recurrent headaches than is work performance. About 19% of migraine sufferers miss work, although a larger percentage discontinue normal activities (50%) or cancel family (31%) or social activities (30%) (Pryse-Phillips et al., 1992). Recurrent headache sufferers also report greater impairments in mental health than patients with other chronic diseases (hypertension, myocardial infarction, arthritis, diabetes, gastrointestinal disorders) that have been examined (Osterhaus, Townsend, Gandek, & Ware, 1994). Nonetheless, only a small proportion of recurrent headache sufferers seen in general practice settings exhibit frank psychopathology (Penzien, Rains, & Holroyd, 1993).

Health Care Utilization

Estimates of the direct costs of recurrent headache disorders, such as medical expenditures, are sparse. Nonetheless, the impact of recurrent headaches on health care utilization appears to be substantial. Headache is one of the 10 most common reasons for a visit to a physician in the United States, accounting for more than 18.3 million outpatient visits annually (Ries, 1986). Women are more likely than men to seek medical care and receive prescription medication for their headaches. A significant number of migraineurs (up to 20% of females and 13% of males) use emergency room or urgent care clinic services for headache episodes, and 8% of them will be hospitalized at least once for their migraines (Stang & Osterhaus, 1993). However, available measures of health care utilization or medical expenses underestimate the true cost of headaches because a large proportion of people with severe headaches do not seek medical treatment (Lipton, Stewart, Celentano, & Reed, 1992; Stang, Osterhaus, & Celentano, 1994).

Classification and Diagnosis

The Headache Classification Committee of the International Headache Society (IHS; Olesen, 1988) has recently updated diagnostic criteria for all headache disorders. The classification system is summarized in Table 9.1. The vast majority of patients (probably over 95%) who seek medical assistance have benign, idiopathic headaches such as migraine and tension-type headache. The diagnostic criteria for migraine without aura, migraine with aura, and tension-type headache are presented in Tables 9.2 and 9.3.

Migraine

The prototypic migraine is characterized by pulsating pain of moderate to severe intensity (sufficient to inhibit or prohibit daily activities) that is aggravated by routine physical activities (e.g., climbing stairs). The migraine episode lasts 4 to 72 hours and is accompanied by nausea or vomiting or both and by a heightened sensitivity to light and sound. Thought, memory, and concentration may be impaired, and the sufferer may also experience light-headedness, irritability, anorexia, diarrhea, and scalp tenderness. The head pain is often unilateral and frequently originates behind or around the eyes and then radiates to the frontal and temporal regions. For the minority of headache sufferers who experience migraine with aura, the pain is preceded by temporary focal neurological symptoms that are most often visual disturbances (e.g., bright spots or stars, a scintillating scotoma) but may include sensory disturbances (e.g., parathesias), motor weakness, or syncope.

Tension-Type Headache

The prototypic tension-type headache is characterized by bilateral nonthrobbing (pressing/tightening, dull, bandlike) pain of mild to moderate intensity that may inhibit, but not prohibit, daily activities. The prototypic tension-type headache may last 30 minutes to 7 days and is usually not

TABLE 9.1 Headache Classifications of the International Headache Society's Headache Classification Committee

---

Migraine and Tension-Type Headache
1. Migraine
    1.1 Migraine without aura
    1.2 Migraine with aura
        1.2.1 Migraine with typical aura
        1.2.2 Migraine with prolonged aura
        1.2.3 Familial hemiplegic migraine
        1.2.4 Basilar migraine
        1.2.5 Migraine aura without headache
        1.2.6 Migraine with acute onset aura
    1.3 Ophthalmoplegic migraine
    1.4 Retinal migraine
    1.5 Childhood periodic syndromes that may be precursors to or associated with migraine
        1.5.1 Benign paroxysmal vertigo of childhood
        1.5.2 Alternating hemiplegia of childhood
    1.6 Complications of migraine
        1.6.1 Status migrainosus
        1.6.2 Migrainous infarction
    1.7 Migrainous disorder not fulfilling above criteria
2. Tension-type headache
    2.1 Episodic tension-type headache
        2.1.1 Episodic tension-type headache associated with disorder of pericranial muscles
        2.1.2 Episodic tension-type headache unassociated with disorder of pericranial muscles
    2.2 Chronic tension-type headache
        2.2.1 Chronic tension-type headache associated with disorder of pericranial muscles
        2.2.2 Chronic tension-type headache unassociated with disorder of pericranial muscles
    2.3 Headache of the tension-type not fulfilling above criteria

Additional Classifications:
3. Cluster headache and chronic paroxysmal hemicrania
4. Miscellaneous headaches unassociated with structural lesion
5. Headache associated with head trauma
6. Headache associated with vascular disorders
7. Headache associated with non-vascular intracranial disorders
8. Headache associated with substances or their withdrawal
9. Headache associated with non-cephalic infection
10. Headache associated with metabolic disorder
11. Headache or facial pain associated with disorder of the cranium, neck, eyes, ears, sinuses, teeth, mouth, or other facial or other cranial structures
12. Cranial neuralgias, nerve trunk pain, and deafferentiation pain

---

SOURCE: Olesen (1988).

TABLE 9.2   Diagnostic Criteria of the International Headache Society's
Headache Classification Committee for Migraine

---

1. Migraine
   1.1 Migraine without aura
      A. At least 5 attacks fulfilling B-D
      B. Headache attacks lasting 4-72 hours (untreated or unsuccessfully treated)
      C. Headache has at least two of the following characteristics
         1. Unilateral location
         2. Pulsating quality
         3. Moderate or severe intensity (inhibits or prohibits daily activity)
         4. Aggravated by walking stairs or similar routine physical activity
      D. During headache at least one of the following
         1. Nausea and/or vomiting
         2. Photophobia and phonophobia
   1.2 Migraine with aura
      A. At least 2 attacks fulfilling B
      B. At least 3 of the following characteristics
         1. One or more fully reversible aura symptoms indicating focal cerebral
            cortical and/or brain-stem dysfunction
         2. At least one aura symptom develops gradually over more than 4 minutes,
            or 2 or more symptoms occur in succession
         3. No aura symptom lasts more than 60 minutes. If more than one aura
            symptom is present, accepted duration is proportionately increased
         4. Headache follows aura with a free interval of less than 60 minutes
            (It may also begin before or simultaneously with the aura)
   1.7 Migrainous disorder not fulfilling above criteria
        Headache attacks which are believed to be a form of migraine, but which
        do not quite meet the operational diagnostic criteria for any of the forms
        of migraine.

SOURCE: Olesen (1988).

aggravated by routine activities, accompanied by nausea or vomiting, or preceded by focal neurological symptoms.

*Headache Associated With
Substances or Their Withdrawal*

The IHS system also includes a new diagnostic category, "headache associated with substances or their withdrawal" (e.g., analgesics-abuse headache, ergotamine-induced headache, narcotics abstinence headache). Prescription and nonprescription analgesic and abortive medications (combination analgesics, opiates, nonopioid analgesics, barbiturates, ergots, and

TABLE 9.3 Diagnostic Criteria of the International Headache Society's Headache Classification Committee for Tension-Type Headache

---

2. Tension-type headache
- 2.1 Episodic tension-type headache
  - A. At least 10 previous headache episodes fulfilling B-D
    Number of days with such headache < 180 year (< 15 month)
  - B. Headache lasting from 30 minutes to 7 days
  - C. At least 2 of the following
    1. Pressing/tightening (nonpulsating) quality
    2. Mild or moderate intensity (may inhibit, but does not prohibit daily activity)
    3. Bilateral location
    4. No aggravation by walking stairs or similar routine physical activity
  - D. Both of the following
    1. No nausea or vomiting (anorexia may occur)
    2. Photophobia and phonophobia are absent, or one but not the other is present
- 2.2 Chronic tension-type headache
  - A. Average headache frequency ≥ 15 days/month (180/year) for ≥ 6 months fulfilling B-C
  - B. At least 2 of the following
    1. Pressing/tightening
    2. Mild or moderate severity (may inhibit, but does not prohibit daily activity)
  - C. Both of the following
    1. No vomiting
    2. No more than one of the following
      Nausea, photophobia or phonophobia
- 2.3 Headache of the tension-type not fulfilling the above criteria
  Headache which is believed to be a form of tension-type headache, but which does not quite meet the operational diagnostic criteria for any of the forms of tension-type headache.

SOURCE: Olesen (1988).

other abortive agents) have been implicated in the development of drug-induced headaches (see Diener & Tfelt-Hansen, 1993; Diener & Wilkinson, 1988; Markley, 1994; Rapoport & Sheftell, 1993).

Drug-induced headaches (often referred to as "rebound headaches") may be difficult to distinguish from tension-type or migraine headaches. Though presenting symptoms vary, patients commonly report near-constant, diffuse head pain that may be accompanied by nausea or vomiting. Although patients are seldom pain-free, their pain level may vary throughout the day. These patients often awaken with a headache. Sleep disturbances, dysphoria, irritability, restlessness, and difficulty concentrating are also commonplace (Rapoport & Sheftell, 1993).

TABLE 9.4   Diagnostic Criteria for Headaches Aggravated by Chronic
Medication Use

International Headache Society Criteria[a]	*2nd International Workshop Criteria*[b]
Headache Characteristics	
1. More than 14 headache days/month	1. More than 20 headache days/month
2. Headache is diffuse, pulsating, and distinguished from migraine by absent attack pattern and/or absent associated symptoms for ergotamine-induced headache	2. Daily headache duration exceeds 10 hours
Relationship to Medication Use	
1. Ergotamine a. Onset is preceded by daily ergotamine intake (oral $\geq$ 2 mg., rectal $\geq$ 1 mg.)	1. Intake of analgesics or abortive medication on more than 20 days per month
2. Analgesics a. At least 50 grams of aspirin or equivalent/month b. At least 100 tablets/month of analgesics combined with barbiturates or other non-narcotic compounds c. Narcotic analgesic use	2. Regular intake of analgesics and/or ergotamine in combination with barbiturates, codeine, caffeine, antihistamines, or tranquilizers
3. Headache disappears within 1 month after withdrawal of substance	3. Increase in the severity and frequency of headaches after discontinuation of drug intake

a. Olesen (1988).
b. Diener and Wilkinson (1988).

Patients with rebound headaches commonly have had a long history of intermittent headache episodes. Headache medications often provide only partial or short-lived relief, leading to an increase in medication intake. Over time, headaches gradually transform from being intermittent to being daily and unremitting as medication use increases. Furthermore, these headaches may become refractory to treatment (Mathew, 1990). It should be kept in mind, however, that susceptibility to rebound headache varies widely across patients.

Both the IHS (Olesen, 1988) and the Second International Workshop on Drug-Induced Headache (Diener & Wilkinson, 1988) have proposed criteria for drug-induced headache (see Table 9.4). The IHS criteria use the quantity of medication consumed as the primary indicator of excessive use, whereas the Second International Workshop criteria use the number of days on which medication is consumed as the primary indicator. The Second International Workshop criteria require a less detailed report of medication consumption and are thus easier to assess than the IHS criteria. We suggest that the possibility that medication use is aggravating headache problems be entertained if an individual meets or comes close to meeting the Second International Workshop criteria. Unfortunately, a definitive diagnosis can be made only retrospectively when headaches improve following the withdrawal of the offending medication.

Chronic Daily Headache

At present, there is an ongoing debate regarding the adequacy with which the IHS nosology addresses the classification and diagnosis of patients who report continuous or nearly continuous headaches that are referred to by some as *chronic daily headache* (CDH) or *chronic daily migraine* (Mathew, 1993; Penzien & Rains, 1995; Rains et al., 1994; Sanin, Mathew, Bellmeyer, & Ali, 1994; Silberstein, Lipton, Solomon, & Mathew, 1994). Specialty headache centers have reported that from 30% to 40% of patients presenting for treatment suffer from CDH (Mathew, Reuveni, & Perez, 1987; Rains et al., 1994) and that the majority of patients with CDH report symptoms of both migraine and tension-type headache. A significant proportion of CDH sufferers also meet IHS criteria for drug-induced headache. For example in one study, 72% of CDH patients with features of migraine and 56% of CDH patients with features of tension-type headache were at risk for overusing headache medications.

Many investigators and clinicians maintain that the IHS classification system does not adequately address the diagnosis of CDH patients (Silberstein et al., 1994). Others contend that there is no convincing evidence that CDH merits consideration as a distinct classification. Rather, they maintain that CDH patients can be classified through the use of multiple diagnoses, which facilitates management in that each type of headache may require a different therapeutic intervention (Olesen & Rasmussen, 1996). Both camps agree, however, that chronic daily headaches typically are refractory to standard monotherapy with either drug or nondrug therapies and thus create special problems for treatment.

TREATMENT

Behavioral Interventions

Over the past 15 years, three types of behavioral interventions have come into widespread use in the management of recurrent migraine and tension-type headaches: relaxation training, biofeedback training, and stress management training or cognitive-behavioral therapy.

Relaxation Training

Relaxation training skills are believed to enable individuals with recurrent headache disorders to exert control over headache-related physiological responses. The practice of relaxation exercises assists patients in achieving a sense of mastery or self-control over their headaches, provides a brief hiatus from everyday stress, and may also enable headache sufferers to manage everyday stressors. Three types of relaxation training techniques have been used in the treatment of headache: (a) progressive muscle relaxation—alternately tensing and relaxing specific muscle groups throughout the body (Bernstein & Borkovec, 1973; Jacobsen, 1938); (b) autogenic training—the use of self-statements of feelings of warmth and heaviness to achieve a state of deep relaxation (Schulz & Luthe, 1969); and (c) meditative exercises or passive relaxation techniques—the use of a silently repeated word or sound to promote mental calm and relaxation (Benson, 1975). Often these various relaxation training procedures are combined in a treatment package.

Biofeedback Training

Biofeedback training refers to procedures that provide information about physiological processes (usually through the use of electronic instrumentation) in the form of an observable display (typically an audio tone or visual display). This information or "feedback" is used by the patient in learning to self-regulate the response being monitored. Two types of biofeedback are most frequently employed in the treatment of recurrent headache: (a) electromyographic (EMG) biofeedback—feedback of electrical activity from muscles of the scalp, the neck, and sometimes the upper body—most often used in the treatment of tension-type headache to reduce muscle tension; and

(b) thermal or hand-warming biofeedback—feedback of skin temperature from a finger, and less frequently from a toe or foot—most often used in the treatment of migraine. Both EMG and thermal biofeedback are commonly administered in combination with relaxation training. Currently cephalic vasomotor biofeedback is not widely used in the treatment of recurrent headache disorders because it has not been shown to produce better outcomes than other therapies that are technically less cumbersome to administer.

Stress Management Training (Cognitive-Behavioral Therapy)

The rationale for stress management training derives from the observation that the way individuals cope with everyday stressors can precipitate, exacerbate, and maintain headache episodes or can increase headache-related disability and distress. Stress management therapy focuses on the cognitive and affective components of headaches and is typically administered in conjunction with relaxation and biofeedback interventions that focus primarily on the physiological component. Stress management interventions are used to teach patients (a) to identify stressful circumstances that precipitate or aggravate headaches and to employ effective strategies for coping with these stressors; (b) to cope more effectively with pain and distress associated with headache episodes; and (c) to limit negative psychological consequences of recurrent headaches (e.g., depression and disability).

Patients are first asked to record in a headache diary the sensations, feelings, thoughts, and behaviors associated with both stressful events and headache episodes. This information is then used to assist the client in identifying relationships between (a) situational variables (e.g., work pressure or family conflict); (b) thoughts; and (c) emotional, behavioral, and symptomatic responses (e.g., anger, resentment, muscle tension) that often lead to headache. Stress management training then focuses on altering the psychological antecedents and correlates of headache. Cognitive coping skills are tailored to the specific stressful situations that confront the patient and the particular difficulties that the patient experiences in these situations. The cognitive coping skills taught to the patient may include (a) the use of self-statements to guide coping efforts and reduce anxiety-arousing rumination, (b) the production of calming imagery, (c) the application of rational problem-solving skills to practical problems (e.g., time management), and (d) the use of self-assertion skills for negotiating interpersonal conflict. A more detailed discussion of stress management training (i.e., cognitive-behavioral interventions) for headache management can be found in Holroyd and Andrasik (1982).

Minimal-Contact Treatment Format

In a minimal-contact or "home-based" treatment format, self-regulation skills (relaxation, thermal biofeedback, stress management) are introduced in periodic clinic sessions, and written materials and audiotapes are used to guide the patient's training at home (Holroyd, French, Nash, Tobin, & Echelberger-McCune, 1995; McGrath, Cunningham, Lascelles, & Humphreys, 1990; Nash & Holroyd, 1992; Penzien & Rains, in press; Penzien, Rains, & Holroyd, 1992; Rowan & Andrasik, 1996). Examples of minimal-contact treatment protocols for combined relaxation/stress management training and combined relaxation/thermal biofeedback training are presented in Table 9.5. Only three to four monthly clinic sessions may be required to complete minimal-contact behavioral treatment, in contrast to the 10 or more (often weekly) clinic sessions usually recommended for therapist-administered or clinic-based treatment. By decreasing the number of clinic visits, these treatments can be made more widely available and less costly than other treatment methods. Certainly, if therapist contact could be completely eliminated, treatment cost could be further reduced and treatment made even more widely available; however, completely self-administered treatments have been plagued by poor compliance and modest treatment results (Kohlenberg, 1984; Larsson, Melin, & Döberl, 1990). It appears that some therapist contact is necessary to motivate patients and to optimally address problems that inevitably arise in learning and using self-regulation skills, especially for patients with more difficult headache problems.

Small-Group Treatment

Administration of behavioral treatment in groups is a widely recognized method of reducing the cost of behavioral treatments. Relaxation and stress management therapies have proven effective in reducing tension headaches when administered in small groups (e.g., Chesney & Shelton, 1976; Holroyd & Andrasik, 1978; Rains, Penzien, & Holroyd, 1993). In addition, one study has found that thermal biofeedback training can be as effectively adminis-

TABLE 9.5   The Structure of Minimal-Contact Treatment

		Tension-Type Headache	*Migraine*
1	1st clinic session (50-75 minutes)	Patient is oriented to self-management approach. Treatment rationale is explained. Progressive muscle relaxation is induced.	Same
2	No contact	Briefer forms of relaxation are introduced.	Muscle discrimination training is introduced.
3	Phone consultation (15 minutes)	Difficulties in home relaxation training are addressed. Cue-controlled relaxation, relaxation by recall, and autogenic procedures are introduced. Begin monitoring headache-related stresses.	Difficulties in home relaxation training are addressed. Briefer forms of relaxation training are introduced.
4	No contact	Muscle tension discrimination procedures are introduced. Relaxation skills are applied in daily activities.	Briefer forms of relaxation training continue to be introduced. Cue-controlled and relaxation-by-recall procedures are introduced.
5	2nd clinic session (50-75 minutes)	Headache-relevant stresses are identified, and stress management (cognitive coping or problem solving) strategies are introduced.	Thermal biofeedback procedures are introduced and practiced.
6	No contact	Stress management strategies are applied.	Thermal biofeedback procedures are practiced. Relaxation skills are applied in daily activities.
7	Phone consultation (15 minutes)	Difficulties in application of stress-management skills are addressed. Additional strategies may be introduced if indicated.	Difficulties in thermal biofeedback training are addressed; practice is continued.
8	No contact	Headache management strategies continue to be applied.	Thermal biofeedback and relaxation skills are applied.
9	3rd clinic session (50-60 minutes)	Useful headache management strategies are identified and reinforced. Current and anticipated future problems are addressed.	Most useful relaxation and hand-warming skills are identified and reinforced. Current and anticipated future problems are addressed.

tered to migraine sufferers in small groups as individually (Gauthier, Cote, Cote, & Drolet, in press). Where patient flow is adequate, it should be feasible to reduce the cost of treatment and to make efficient use of health professionals' time by administering treatment in small groups rather than individually. However, this requires not only that health professionals be adept at administering behavioral treatments but also that they be skilled at handling problems that arise in group treatment.

Modification of Headache Precipitants

The occurrence of headaches can sometimes be reduced by avoiding or modifying headache precipitants. Precipitants may include a variety of behavioral, hormonal, environmental, and dietary factors (Blau & Thavapalan, 1988; Radnitz, 1990; Rains, Penzien, & Hursey, 1996; Rasmussen, 1993). Precipitants most frequently identified by headache sufferers are listed in Table 9.6. Behavioral or lifestyle factors (stress and worry, sleep difficulties) and hormonal factors are the most commonly identified triggers and should be discussed with patients. Significant headache improvement sometimes results from teaching patients to avoid, modify, or cope more effectively with headache precipitants. Headache precipitants are not universal and do not necessarily precipitate an attack on every exposure.

Behavioral or Lifestyle Factors. The most frequently identified headache trigger is stress (Nikiforow & Hokkanen, 1978; Rains et al., 1996; Rasmussen, 1993). Although recurrent headache sufferers and matched controls do not differ with regard to the number or types of major life stressors that they experience, recurrent headache sufferers do report more minor daily stressors than controls (e.g., DeBenedittis & Lorenzetti, 1992; Holm, Holroyd, Hursey, & Penzien, 1986). Some findings also suggest that individuals with recurrent headache disorders use coping strategies of avoidance and self-blame more frequently and seek social support less frequently in response to stress than do controls (e.g., DeBenedittis & Lorenzetti, 1992; Edhe & Holm, 1992; Holm et al., 1986). However, it is unclear whether these often maladaptive coping strategies are a consequence or a contributor to recurrent headache problems, or both. In any case, stress management interventions that teach patients to modify their

TABLE 9.6   Precipitating Factors for Headache Identified by Patients

Stress:
   During stress
   After stress (i.e., "let-down headache")

Lack of food:
   Fasting
   Insufficient food
   Delayed or missed meals

Specific foods:
   Alcoholic beverages
   Chocolate
   Aged cheese
   Aged meats
   Monosodium glutamate (used in Chinese restaurants, many processed foods, seasonings)
   Aspartame (sugar substitute found in diet foods)
   Caffeine (coffee, tea, cola)
   Nuts

Physical exertion

Fatigue

Sleep:
   Excessive sleep
   Unrefreshing sleep
   Insufficient sleep
   Sleep problems
         Delayed onset
         Restless sleep

Hormones (females only):
   Menstrual period (before, during, after)
   Postmenopausal changes
   Oral contraceptives
   Hormone supplements
   Pregnancy

Environment:
   Exposure to vapors or chemicals
   Weather changes
   Heat
   Cold
   Bright light, glare
   Noise

Smoking (including passive smoking)

SOURCE: Adapted from Blau & Thavapalan, 1988; Radnitz, 1990; Rasmussen, 1993.

response to headache-related stressors and to headaches themselves have the potential to play a role in headache management.

Prolonged or unusually deep sleep may precipitate headaches in some individuals (Sahota & Dexter, 1990). Other individuals identify insufficient or unrefreshing sleep as a precipitant (Rasmussen, 1993). Patients who identify sleep difficulties as headache precipitants should be instructed in sleep hygiene and should be advised to maintain regular sleep schedules. For some, headaches may arise as a consequence of a sleep disorder that merits evaluation by a sleep specialist (Paiva, Batista, Martins, & Martins, 1995).

Hormonal Factors. Reproductive hormones are associated with headache disorders, particularly migraine (see Holroyd & Lipchik, 1997, and Silberstein & Merriam, 1993, for reviews). Hormonally related headaches (e.g., headache specifically related to menarche, menstruation, pregnancy, menopause, or hormone supplements) deserve careful evaluation. Some recent evidence suggests that behavioral treatment can be more effective in managing these headaches than was previously thought (for review, see Holroyd & Lipchik, 1997).

Environmental Factors. Patients should be instructed to avoid or restrict their exposure to various environmental factors identified as headache triggers. This can often be accomplished with little lifestyle disruption.

Dietary Factors. Individuals who identify lack of food as a headache trigger can be encouraged to eat meals at regular intervals. If a patient has difficulty maintaining a regular meal schedule, high-protein, low-carbohydrate snacks can be carried as meal substitutes. Headache patients sometimes report that their headaches follow the ingestion of certain foods or beverages, most notably alcohol (see Table 9.6); few double-blind studies of these triggers have been conducted, however, and the available data come from surveys and clinical reports. Clinical opinions differ regarding the benefits to be expected from dietary alterations (e.g., Blau & Thavapalan, 1988; Medina & Diamond, 1978). Patients often already are avoiding obvious dietary triggers when they seek treatment. If a patient is convinced that headaches are diet related but the offending substances have not been identified, a diet that eliminates possible dietary precipitants can serve as an assessment device (Rapoport & Sheftell, 1996).

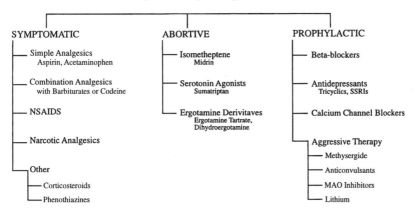

Figure 9.1. Types of Drugs Employed in Migraine Therapy

Pharmacological Interventions

Pharmacological interventions are of three types: prophylactic, abortive, and symptomatic (see Figure 9.1). Prophylactic or preventive medication is taken daily with the goal of preventing headaches. Abortive medication is taken once a headache has begun with the goal of aborting or decreasing the severity and duration of the attack, as well as the associated symptoms of nausea and vomiting. Symptomatic or analgesic medication is taken to reduce pain. The major classes of drugs used as preventive, abortive, and symptomatic therapies for recurrent headache disorders are presented in Figure 9.1. A brief overview of drug therapy follows below.

Migraine

Preventive Therapy. Preventive or prophylactic therapy is likely to be the treatment of choice in one of the following circumstances: (a) Migraines occur frequently, once a week or more; (b) migraine attacks occur less frequently but are prolonged and disabling or refractory to acute or abortive therapy; or (c) a time period can be identified when the likelihood of migraines is sufficiently high to justify preventive therapy during this period (e.g., onset of menstruation; Baumel, 1994). A wide variety of preventive medications are available. First-line therapies include beta blockers, calcium channel blockers, tricyclic antidepressants, serotonin-reuptake inhibitors, and nonsteroidal anti-inflammatory drugs (NSAIDs). When headache problems are refractory to first-line therapies, MAO inhibitors, lithium, serotonin-receptor antagonists/agonists, and anticonvulsants may also be tried. Strong evidence of effectiveness is available from controlled clinical trials for beta blockers and to a lesser extent for calcium channel blockers (Holroyd, Penzien, & Cordingley, 1991; Holroyd, Penzien, Rokicki, & Cordingley, 1992); well-controlled evaluations of the remaining medications are quite limited in number.

Abortive Therapy. Abortive agents include sympathomimetic agents, NSAIDs, ergotamine derivatives, and new serotonin-receptor agonists/antagonists. Abortive medications, particularly ergotamine and combined analgesic/sympathomimetic agents, must be used infrequently following preset guidelines because their frequent use can cause rebound headache.

Analgesic Therapy. Medications prescribed to reduce pain primarily include NSAIDs, mixed barbiturate or narcotic analgesics, and narcotics. The use of narcotic and mixed analgesics must be limited because overuse can cause rebound headaches and even addiction. NSAIDs are probably less likely to induce rebound headaches but should nevertheless be used in moderation.

Medication Treatment Algorithm. Figure 9.2 presents a medication treatment algorithm for the sequential use of abortive and prophylactic drugs for migraine. This algorithm is based largely on clinical opinion because empirical support from clinical trials is limited. In practice, treatment strategies will vary with the professional expertise and opinion of the practitioner. More detailed discussions of drug treatment strategies can be found in Baumel (1994), Davidoff (1995), Olesen, Tfelt-Hansen, and Welch (1993), and Saper, Silberstein, Gordon, and Hamel (1993).

Tension-Type Headache

Preventive Therapy. Preventive therapy is increasingly the treatment of choice as tension-type headaches occur more frequently. Tricyclic antidepressants (especially amitriptyline) provide the first line of preventive therapy for frequent tension-type headaches, though serotonin-specific

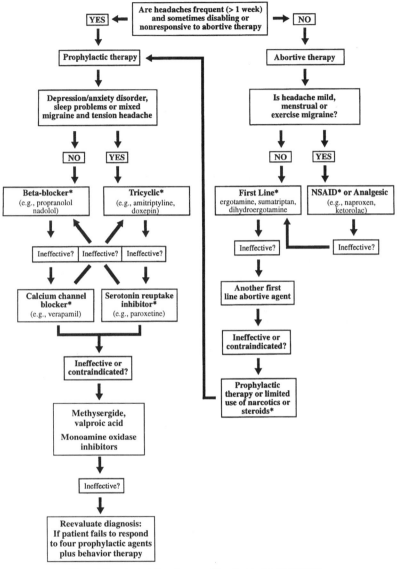

*If coexisting physical disorder or problem does not contraindicate.

Figure 9.2. Treatment Algorithm for the Administration of Abortive and Prophylactic Agents in the Management of Migraine

reuptake inhibitors (SSRIs) are increasingly receiving attention. NSAIDs also are used preventively, though it is advisable to avoid their prolonged use for safety reasons. Evidence for the effectiveness of antidepressants, even amitriptyline, is quite limited in light of the widespread use of these drugs in the management of tension-type headaches around the world. When headaches prove refractory to antidepressants, the preventive therapies used with migraine may be tried. However, support for the latter therapies with tension-type headache is largely anecdotal.

Abortive Therapy. Although patients may use NSAIDs and analgesics early in the onset of a tension headache to prevent pain from becoming severe, there are no true abortive agents for tension-type headache analogous to ergotamine or sumatriptan for migraine.

Analgesic Therapy. Mild tension-type headaches are frequently relieved with nonprescription medications such as acetaminophen and aspirin. NSAIDs such as naproxen or ibuprofen and various analgesic-sedative combinations are also used to treat episodic headaches. However, analgesics or sedatives must be used cautiously because these agents may induce rebound headaches. In fact, chronic use of any of the analgesics or analgesic-sedative combinations, whether nonprescription or prescription medications, can induce daily headaches in some individuals.

Empirical Status of Behavioral Treatments

The most widely used relaxation and biofeedback therapies have been evaluated in over 100 studies, so a substantial body of evidence is available on which to judge the effectiveness of these therapies. However, available studies have been conducted primarily in headache clinics or in specialized university or medical school settings and have generally been small, averaging 20 patients per treatment group in migraine studies and only about 10 patients per treatment group in tension-type headache studies (Holroyd & Penzien, 1986, 1990). Information about outcomes that can be expected when behavioral therapies are integrated into busy primary care or general neurology settings is thus limited.

TABLE 9.7   Average Improvement by Type of Treatment and Type of Headache

Type of Treatment	Average % Improvement	Treatment Groups (n)	Improvement Range (%)
Tension-Type Headache			
Combined EMG biofeedback and relaxation training	57	9	29 to 88
EMG biofeedback training	46	26	13 to 87
Relaxation training	45	15	17 to 94
Placebo control (noncontingent biofeedback)	15	6	−14 to 40
Headache monitoring control	−4	10	−28 to 12
Migraine			
Combined relaxation training and thermal biofeedback	56	35	11 to 93
Relaxation training	37	38	5 to 81
Thermal biofeedback training	35	14	−8 to 80
Cephalic vasomotor biofeedback training	34	11	2 to 82
Placebo control (medication placebo)	12	20	−23 to 32
Headache monitoring control	3	15	−30 to 33

NOTE: All relaxation and biofeedback therapies produced significantly larger improvements than placebo and headache monitoring controls. Combined relaxation training and thermal biofeedback also produced larger improvements in migraine than relaxation or thermal biofeedback training alone.

SOURCE: Holroyd and Penzien (1986); Holroyd, Penzien, and Cordingley (1991); Penzien et al. (1985).

Relaxation and Biofeedback Therapies

Average percentage reductions in headache activity reported with the most commonly used relaxation and biofeedback therapies calculated in recent meta-analytic (statistical) reviews are summarized in Table 9.7. It can be seen that in the treatment of tension-type headache, relaxation and EMG biofeedback therapies have each yielded about a 50% reduction in headache activity. In the treatment of migraine, relaxation training combined with thermal biofeedback training also has yielded about a 50% reduction in migraine activity, but relaxation training and biofeedback training procedures alone have yielded somewhat smaller improvements. Nonetheless, improvements reported with relaxation and biofeedback therapies have been at least three times as large as improvements reported with medication placebo control treatments (Table 9.7). Considerable evidence is thus available indicating that improvements observed with relaxation/biofeedback therapies produce clinically significant improvements in headache activity.

In the treatment of tension-type headache, individual studies that have directly compared the effectiveness of relaxation training, EMG biofeedback, and the combination of these two interventions, and meta-analytic reviews that have combined results from a larger universe of studies, have concluded that relaxation training, EMG biofeedback, and the combination of these two interventions are equally effective (e.g., Blanchard, 1992; Holroyd, 1993a; Holroyd & French, 1995; Holroyd & Penzien, 1986).

Results are less clear in the treatment of migraine. Meta-analytic reviews of the treatment literature suggest that the combination of relaxation and thermal biofeedback training may be more effective than either relaxation training or thermal biofeedback by itself (see Table 9.7). However, the few individual studies that have directly compared the effectiveness of combined relaxation training and thermal biofeedback to either relaxation training alone or biofeedback alone have not consistently supported the superiority of combined relaxation and thermal biofeedback training (see Blanchard & Andrasik, 1987, for a review). The utilization of different treatment protocols and different patient populations across studies may have obscured differences in treatment efficacy; some studies also appear to have included too few patients to possess adequate statistical power or to have included a significant number of patients unlikely to benefit from behavioral treatment (e.g., patients with chronic substance-induced headache). Thus, the hypothesis that combined relaxation/thermal biofeedback training is more effective than either relaxation training or biofeedback training alone must be considered tentative.

Even where relaxation and biofeedback therapies do produce similar outcomes, it does not necessarily imply that these therapies are interchangeable. Some patients who fail to respond to relaxation training will benefit from subsequent biofeedback training (Blanchard et al., 1982). There is no evidence, however, to indicate there is an advantage for beginning treatment with one, rather than another, of these interventions.

Stress Management Training
(Cognitive-Behavioral Therapy)

Stress management training appears to be particularly effective in managing recurrent tension-type headaches. A recent meta-analysis of a subset of studies meeting stringent research design and data-reporting criteria reported, on average, a 53% improvement in tension headache activity; this improvement figure compares quite favorably to the 32% improvement figure reported for relaxation training (McCrory, Penzien, Rains, & Hasselblad,

1996). Individual studies also have found that the addition of stress management interventions can enhance the effectiveness of relaxation training alone for a significant number of patients (for review, see Blanchard, 1992; Holroyd & French, 1995). This may occur primarily where psychological or environmental problems (e.g., chronic daily stress, depression, other adjustment problems) not effectively addressed by relaxation/biofeedback therapies aggravate headaches or prevent patients from effectively using self-regulation skills. Thus, patients exhibiting high levels of daily life stress (as assessed by the Hassles Scale; DeLongis, Coyne, Dakof, Folkman, & Lazarus, 1982) were unlikely to benefit from relaxation training alone but were likely to benefit when stress management interventions were added to relaxation training in one study (Tobin, Holroyd, Baker, Reynolds, & Holm, 1988).

Migraineurs also may benefit from stress management training; at present, however, there is no empirical support for the contention that stress management interventions enhance the effectiveness of relaxation/thermal biofeedback therapies in the treatment of migraine. In the subset of studies included in the McCrory et al. (1996) meta-analysis, stress management training yielded improvements in migraine activity that were very similar in magnitude to improvements reported with relaxation and thermal biofeedback therapies alone. Studies that have been designed to determine if the addition of stress management interventions enhance the effectiveness of relaxation or thermal biofeedback training also have found no evidence of an additive effect (see Blanchard, 1992, for review). One limitation of these studies is that stress management procedures were adopted largely unchanged from those originally developed for the management of tension-type headache. Somewhat different and more effective interventions might possibly be developed specifically for migraine, where, for example, relationships between daily life stresses and headache onset are typically less obvious than in tension headache. However, there is no evidence that currently available stress management interventions can improve on results obtained from relaxation/biofeedback therapies alone.

Alternate Treatment Delivery Formats

For many patients, treatment procedures can be effectively administered in minimal-contact or group treatment formats. In the studies that have directly compared the effectiveness of the same interventions administered in individual therapy format, and in a minimal-contact treatment format, these two treatment formats have yielded similar outcomes (see reviews by Nash & Holroyd, 1992; Rowan & Andrasik, 1996). The limited available evidence also suggests that group treatment can be as effective as individual treatment, even with interventions such as biofeedback (e.g., Gauthier et al., in press). A recent meta-analysis of this literature also has concluded that behavioral treatments administered in minimal-contact and group treatment formats have been as effective as more therapist intensive treatment formats (Rains et al., 1993). These alternate treatment delivery formats thus appear to be a cost-effective method of providing treatment for many patients. Some proportion of patients will, of course, continue to require more therapist-intensive treatment. Individuals who excessively use analgesic medication, are clinically depressed, or suffer from particularly refractory headache problems may be particularly likely to require more therapist attention. Other patients simply do not persist in efforts to learn or apply self-regulation skills without regular contact with a health professional.

Maintenance of Improvements

It is well established that improvements achieved with behavioral treatments tend to be maintained at least for the 3-to 9-month follow-up periods that have most frequently been evaluated. For example, improvements reported at such short-term follow-up evaluations have been larger than improvements observed at immediate post-treatment evaluations in 65 patient samples included in two meta-analytic reviews (Holroyd & Penzien, 1986; Penzien, Holroyd, Hursey, Holm, & Wittchen, 1985).

Positive but less definitive statements can be made about the long-term (greater than 1 year) maintenance of improvements. At least 45% of reductions in headache activity also have been reported in 14 of 15 studies that used daily headache recordings to assess improvement 1 to 3 years following behavioral treatment and in three studies that assessed improvement 5 to 7 years following treatment (see Blanchard, 1992, Blanchard, Appelbaum, Guarnieri, Morrill, & Dentinger, 1987, and Holroyd & French, 1995, for reviews). The problem in interpreting long-term follow-up data is that a significant proportion of patients are typically lost during follow-up, and other patients may have initiated medical treatment during the follow-up period. However, even in the subset of studies that have addressed these methodological problems (e.g., Gauthier & Carrier, 1991), long-term follow-

TABLE 9.8   Average Percentage Improvement in Migraine Headache for Treatment and Control Groups

	Treatment Conditions			
	Relaxation/ Biofeedback	*Propranolol*	*Placebo*	*Untreated*
Average patient improvement (%)	55	55	12	1
Range of scores (%)	11 to 93	26 to 84	−23 to 32	−30 to 33

SOURCE: Holroyd and Penzien (1990).

up results have been quite positive. Thus, it appears that improvements achieved with behavioral treatments are frequently well maintained.

Behavioral Versus Drug Therapy

Surprisingly little information is available about the comparative effectiveness of behavioral and drug therapies (see Holroyd, 1993b, for review). Because only a few studies have directly compared the effectiveness of these two therapeutic modalities, the best way to estimate the comparative effectiveness of drug and behavioral therapies is to use meta-analysis to compare the outcomes that have been reported in studies evaluating each type of treatment. Accordingly, average improvements in migraine reported with the most widely used preventive drug (propranolol HCl; 25 clinical trials) and nondrug (relaxation/thermal biofeedback; 35 clinical trials) therapies are reported in Table 9.8. Similar results have been reported with these two therapies, with each therapy yielding a 55% reduction in migraine activity in the typical patient on average. Relatively little information is available on the effectiveness of prophylactic agents other than propranolol; however, other agents have generally proven no more effective than propranolol in direct comparisons (Holroyd et al., 1991). Prophylactic drug and behavioral therapies thus appear to be equally viable treatment options. Unfortunately, we have no way of determining whether a given individual is more likely to respond to relaxation/biofeedback training or to propranolol; therefore, other factors, such as cost and availability of treatment, response to previous treatments, medication side effects, and patient preference should be considered in initial treatment selection. In a subsequent section, we outline clinical criteria that might be used in integrating drug and nondrug therapies.

The comparative effectiveness of preventive drug and behavior therapies in the management of tension-type headache has been addressed in only one study; in this study, stress management training was observed to be slightly more effective than the most widely used preventive drug therapy (amitriptyline HCL) in controlling tension-type headaches (Holroyd et al., 1991). More information is clearly needed. However, these initial findings suggest that behavioral therapies merit consideration as a first-line treatment for recurrent tension-type headaches.

Although pharmacologic and nonpharmacologic therapies are frequently administered conjointly in specialized headache treatment centers, only three studies have examined the effectiveness of such combined treatments. Two of these studies found the combination of propranolol and relaxation/thermal biofeedback training to be highly effective in managing recurrent migraines (yielding more than a 70% headache reduction on average; Holroyd, France, et al., 1995; Mathew, 1981). This combination of drug and behavioral therapies proved significantly more effective than relaxation/biofeedback training alone. In the only study that has examined the long-term effects of a combined therapy, amitriptyline initially enhanced the effectiveness of biofeedback training (Reich & Gottesman, 1993). However, beginning at Month 8 and continuing through the 24-month observation period, results achieved with biofeedback training alone were superior to those obtained with the combination of amitriptyline and biofeedback training. It is not clear why poorer results were obtained with the combined treatment than with biofeedback alone in this study. Several investigators have cautioned, however, that patients who receive combined pharmacologic/nonpharmacologic treatment often attribute improvement to drug therapy and discontinue or limit their use of self-regulation skills, thereby limiting the efficacy of the combined treatment (e.g., Hollon & DeRubeis, 1981). It is frequently assumed that individuals with near-daily headaches are likely to require preventive medication in addition to behavior therapy, although this hypothesis has yet to be tested formally.

Clinical Issues in Behavioral Treatment

Although behavioral interventions target both the frequency and the severity of headaches, these interventions emphasize prevention of headaches rather than the palliation of pain once an episode has become severe. It is clearly preferable to prevent or abort headaches early on rather than to attempt to ameliorate a headache once it has taken hold. Although pain-coping skills taught in stress management training may be of benefit to patients when they experience a headache, the most severe headaches may prove unyielding to even highly potent analgesics. Following behavioral treatment, patients frequently also show reductions in headache-related psychological distress and general somatic complaints as well as a new confidence that they can manage their headaches (Penzien et al., 1993). For some patients, these latter benefits may be appreciated as much as or more than reductions in headache activity.

Medical Evaluation

A careful headache and medical history must be obtained before initiating behavioral treatment; sufficient physician involvement in the evaluation should be ensured to rule out headaches secondary to a disease state or structural abnormality (see Diamond & Dalessio, 1992; Rapoport & Sheftell, 1996; Saper et al., 1993). Careful medical evaluation or reevaluation is critical for those patients (a) whose headaches are of recent or sudden onset ("first or worst headache"), (b) who have experienced recent head trauma, (c) who exhibit changing or progressive symptoms, or accompanying neurological symptoms (other than the focal neurological symptoms associated with migraine aura), or (d) with fever or other signs of infection. For patients over 50 years of age, disorders that increase in frequency in older patients and cause head pain should be ruled out, such as cervical spondylosis (arthritis of the cervical spine) and giant cell arteritis. Furthermore, older patients' use of medications that might aggravate depression or headaches should be assessed. In addition to excessive use of analgesics or abortive medications (see below), attention should be paid to the use of sedatives and ataraxics (particularly barbiturates, phenothiazine derivatives, and benzodiazepines).

Evaluating Outcomes

In recent years, health care providers have witnessed increasing calls from managed-care organizations and other third-party payers, as well as from accrediting organizations (e.g., Commission on Accreditation of Rehabilitation Facilities; Joint Commission on Accreditation of Healthcare Organizations), to document the effectiveness of their interventions. Careful documentation of disease severity both before and after treatment is thus increasingly necessary. For headache patients, pre- and post-treatment assessment should address not only headache activity but also headache-related functional impairment.

Headache Activity. Self-reports of headache activity routinely are employed in formulating headache diagnoses and headache treatment plans, and they constitute the clinician's principal means for evaluating treatment progress. Though daily recordings of headache activity are considered the optimal measure for assessing treatment outcome, clinicians sometimes rely on more global, retrospective self-reports derived from questionnaires or patient interviews (see Penzien & Rains, in press, for examples of daily and global measures and scoring). Unfortunately, the relationship between daily recordings of headache activity and more global self-reports is not strong, and thus these two types of measures cannot be considered equivalent (Penzien et al., 1994). Relative to daily recordings, global measures tend to overestimate headache activity (Penzien et al., 1994) and may overestimate headache improvement (Holroyd et al., 1991; Penzien et al., 1985).

Patients may be asked to complete daily headache recordings for a minimum of 2 and up to 5 weeks before initiating therapy. In addition, patients generally self-monitor their headaches daily for at least 1 month following treatment. Typically, a patient is considered a de facto "treatment responder" if he or she shows at least a 50% reduction in headache activity.

Headache-Related Functional Impairment. At present, researchers and clinicians rely most heavily on patients' reports of pain severity when assessing the severity of the patient's headache problem and when judging headache treatment efficacy. The relationship between pain severity and functional impairment is imperfect, however (Stewart, Shecter, & Lipton, 1994). Measures of functional capacity (i.e., impairment or disability) or quality of life provide a better index of the impact of headaches on the individual's life than do measures of headache frequency, severity, or duration. The assessment of functional impairment and quality of life can (a) allow evaluation of the headaches' disruptive impact on the patient's life (i.e., work, family, recreational and social activities), (b) provide an additional index of treatment efficacy, and (c) aid in the assessment of the cost-effectiveness of treatments. Assessment instruments for assessing the impact of headaches include (a) questionnaires that assess functioning without specific reference to headaches, such as the Medical Outcomes Study Short Form Health Survey (SF-20 and SF-36; Osterhaus et al., 1994; Solomon, Skobieranda, & Gragg, 1993) or the Sickness Impact Profile (Pollard, Bobbitt, Bergner, Martin, & Gilson, 1976); (b) questionnaires designed specifically to assess the impact of headaches, such as the Recurrent Illness Impairment Profile-Headache Version (Wittrock, Penzien, Mosley, & Johnson, 1991) and the Henry Ford Hospital Headache Disability Inventory (Jacobson, Ramadan, Aggarwal, & Newman, 1994); and (c) measures that require the patient to record the impact of headaches each week, such as Illness Impact Recordings (French, Holroyd, Rokicki, & France, 1994).

Commonly Encountered Clinical Problems

In this section, we discuss clinical problems that are likely to be encountered during behavioral treatment.

Rebound Headache. If headaches are aggravated by analgesic or ergotamine use, effective treatment requires withdrawal of these medications (see the section "Headache Associated With Substances or Their Withdrawal," above). Though medication withdrawal usually can be accomplished on an outpatient basis, inpatient management occasionally may be necessary. Table 9.9 outlines circumstances that may require inpatient withdrawal or unusually close supervision of outpatient withdrawal. Physician supervision of the withdrawal process is necessary.

On abrupt medication withdrawal (or when medications that are being tapered reach a critically low blood level), it is commonplace to observe an initial worsening of headache and gastrointestinal upset, followed by an improvement in symptoms within the ensuing 2 weeks. However, a period of 8 to 12 weeks may be required to fully complete the drug washout period (Rapoport & Sheftell, 1993). A variety of medications may assist in the management of severe rebound headaches or other withdrawal symptoms (Rapoport & Sheftell, 1996). Initiating preventative therapy with prophylactic pharmacotherapy and/or behavioral therapy may also make withdrawal more tolerable and facilitate the management of headaches that continue to occur following the withdrawal of offending medications.

Patients should be educated about rebound headaches, and clear guidelines for the use of medications that can produce the rebound phenomenon

TABLE 9.9   Considerations for Inpatient Treatment

Intractable disabling headache is unresponsive to outpatient treatment.
   Disabling headaches fail to respond to aggressive outpatient therapies.
   Frequent emergency room visits are not reduced with outpatient therapies.

Withdrawal of rebounding agents is risky or otherwise not feasible on an outpatient basis.
   Barbiturates, ergotamine, benzodiazepines, or opiates are used at levels that require
      close monitoring of withdrawal.
   Toxicity from offending medications (renal impairment, gastrointestinal bleeding,
      evidence of liver toxicity) necessitates close medical monitoring during withdrawal.
   Patient is unable to reduce use of offending agents on outpatient basis even after
      repeated attempts.

*Comorbid medical or psychiatric problem requires close monitoring or treatment during
initiation of drug therapy for headaches.*
   Medical disorder (e.g., coronary artery disease, uncontrolled hypertension, ulcer
      disease, renal or hepatic dysfunction, uncontrolled asthma) is present.
   Protracted nausea, vomiting, or diarrhea has produced dehydration that necessitates
      intravenous fluid replacement.
   Psychiatric disorder (e.g., severe depression, alcohol/drug abuse or thought disorder)
      renders outpatient management problematic.

SOURCE: Adapted from Rapoport and Sheftell (1996).

should be provided. It also may prove beneficial to develop individualized plans for managing severe headaches that can include a card describing appropriate emergency room headache management procedures, thereby helping patients to obtain optimal treatment if they seek emergency room care.

Chronic Daily Headaches. Even when excessive medication use is not an aggravating factor, near-daily, sometimes disabling headaches are less responsive to relaxation or biofeedback therapies than more episodic headaches. For example, Blanchard and colleagues (Blanchard, Appelbaum, Radnitz, Jaccard, & Dentinger, 1989) found that patients who recorded near-daily (one or fewer headache-free days during a 4-week baseline), at times intensely painful headaches were less likely to benefit from relaxation or EMG biofeedback than were patients with more episodic headaches (two or more headache-free days per week). Whereas 13% of the former patients showed at least a 50% reduction in headache activity, more than 50% of the latter patients showed this level of improvement. Because only about 10% of the patients with near-daily headaches in this study met criteria for excessive medication use, near-daily headaches for the most part could not be assumed to be a product of medication overuse.

Clinicians commonly assume that patients with chronic daily headache require aggressive multimodal therapy that may include multiple prophylactic medications and behavioral treatment; controlled clinical trials in this population are, however, scarce. Behavioral interventions with near-daily headaches focus on pain management, on the reduction of pain-related disability, and on preventing mild pain from progressing to a disabling pain because these patients may only rarely experience a headache-free period. If prophylactic medication produces even occasional pain-free periods, behavioral skills for preventing headaches can then be incorporated into treatment. Unremitting pain often contributes to sleep disturbances and family problems as well as psychological distress and demoralization; when present, these problems should be addressed.

Comorbid Psychiatric Disorder. Although epidemiological findings have revealed an association between migraines and both anxiety and mood disorders, psychiatric disorders are not frequent in the general population of recurrent headache sufferers (e.g., Andrasik et al., 1982; Breslau, Merikangas, & Bowden, 1994; Penzien et al., 1993; Silberstein, Lipton, & Breslau, 1995). Although numerous studies have reported that headache patients differ from control samples on measures of psychological symptoms, significant psychopathology is typically not present. For example, in virtually all studies reporting Beck Depression Inventory (BDI) scores, average headache patients' pretreatment scores have fallen in the "nondepressed" range.

Because headache patients, by and large, present with a generally normal psychological adjustment, psychological testing that focuses on the identification of adjustment problems is typically unnecessary. Rather, a brief psychological screening should be sufficient to identify the subgroup of patients who require a more comprehensive psychological evaluation. When psychological evaluation suggests the presence of a more significant psychological disturbance, numerous potential associations between headache and psychopathology need to be considered. For example, anxiety and depression can precipitate or exacerbate headache episodes in headache-prone patients. Psychological symptoms (especially depression) also can result as a consequence of living with chronically disabling headaches. In other instances, headaches may be better understood as a manifestation of a primary psychological disturbance (e.g., when headache is one of a long list of presenting physical complaints, a somatization disorder diagnosis may be warranted). Significant psychopathology also may be unrelated to the headache disorder and may have little or no impact on headache treatment (e.g., when a patient presents with schizophrenia or a bipolar disorder that is well controlled). Finally, personality disorders can seriously complicate headache evaluation and treatment because of these patients' difficult interpersonal style (e.g., histrionic patients may greatly exaggerate symptom complaints; borderline patients may be inappropriately manipulative; passive/dependent patients may excessively rely on the health care provider).

No matter what the association, significant psychopathology may contribute to a poor response to both pharmacologic and nonpharmacologic headache therapies. When patients exhibit significant psychological symptoms, combined psychological and pharmacological treatment should be considered (see below). In most instances, traditional psychotherapy is not indicated; rather, brief, focused attention to the specific adjustment problems that precipitate or exacerbate headache episodes, interfere with treatment compliance, or interfere with the use of self-regulatory skills often is sufficient.

Patients who present with a medical problem may not be open to discussion of mental health problems. In such instances, psychotropic medications commonly used at low doses for headache prophylaxis (e.g., amitriptlyine, imipramine) may prove helpful at higher doses for both reducing pain and managing psychological symptoms. Behavioral interventions, particularly biofeedback training, also can introduce patients to the process of psychological treatment in a nonthreatening way and thus help them to acknowledge psychological difficulties and accept psychological treatment.

Age. Retrospective analyses of clinical outcome data (Blanchard, Andrasik, Evans, & Hillhouse, 1985; Blanchard, Andrasik, Evans, Neff, et al., 1985; Diamond & Montrose, 1984) and a meta-analytic review of results from 37 studies (Holroyd & Penzien, 1986) initially suggested that age and treatment outcome with relaxation and EMG biofeedback therapies were negatively correlated. For example, in one retrospective analysis, it was observed that tension-type headache sufferers over 55 years of age rarely benefited from either relaxation or EMG biofeedback therapies. However, in recent prospective studies in which treatment procedures were adjusted to suit older adults, quite positive outcomes were reported, particularly with combined relaxation/stress management training (e.g.,

Arena, Hannah, Bruno, & Meador, 1991; Mosley, Grotheus, & Meeks, 1995). For example, Mosley et al. (1995) treated patients who ranged from 60 to 78 years of age (mean of 68 years) and found that 64% of patients who received 12 sessions of combined relaxation/cognitive-behavioral therapy showed clinically significant improvements in tension-type headache activity. In this study, audiotapes and written materials designed to assist acquisition of self-regulatory skills were provided, and weekly phone contacts following each session to answer questions and identify problems were included in treatment procedures. These findings suggest that by including more detailed verbal and written explanations of treatment procedures, frequent reviews of the material covered, and additional time to practice elementary skills before more advanced skills are introduced, the age effect observed in earlier studies may be completely eliminated (Arena et al., 1991; Arena, Hightower, & Chong, 1988; Kabela, Blanchard, Appelbaum, & Nicholson, 1989).

Preventing Problems

A number of problems can interfere with the successful acquisition of self-regulation skills or the application of skills that are acquired during training. Fortunately, most of these problems can be prevented or effectively managed. This section provides basic information about the nuts and bolts of treatment, emphasizing the prevention of commonly encountered problems and ways of responding to problems that inevitably do arise. This is not a substitute for training in the clinical application of relaxation, biofeedback, or stress management training. Rather, it is intended to assist clinicians who have already received this training to apply these techniques effectively in the treatment of headache patients. Additional clinical tips can be found in Andrasik (1986), Arena and Blanchard (1996), Blanchard and Andrasik (1985), Holroyd and Andrasik (1982), Holroyd, Holm, and Penzien (1988), Penzien and Holroyd (1994), Penzien and Rains (in press), and Schwartz and Associates (1995).

Treatment Rationale. Patients often view their headaches as outside their control ("Headaches just happen") or as reflecting a personal deficiency ("It must be my fault I have headaches"). Either belief will undermine the individual's ability to understand his or her headaches and take action to limit their occurrence. To combat common misconceptions about headache problems, we present a psychobiological model that conceptualizes headaches as a consequence of environmental, biological or physical, and psychological factors, with no factor regarded as the primary or sole cause (Bakal, 1982). This model helps patients to understand the relevance of psychological/behavioral interventions without necessarily attributing their headaches to psychological disturbances. With this model, relaxation or biofeedback training is introduced as a method for reducing physical arousal and muscle tension that lead to headaches. Stress management interventions (i.e., cognitive-behavioral strategies) are introduced as methods to reduce psychological reactions to stress that may trigger, aggravate, or maintain headaches.

The psychobiological conceptualization of headache is introduced during initial treatment planning with the patient. Then at each treatment session, a more specific rationale for interventions to be introduced in that session is offered, and what will be required of the patient is carefully outlined. It is helpful to tailor the rationale to the individual—for example, when introducing stress management therapy, to offer concrete examples of stress-generating thoughts and to illustrate how these thoughts can distort one's perspective and lead to physical changes that can trigger headaches. Specific examples from the patient's experience or from your own experience can make the principles of treatment concrete. It is important that the patient understand the nature of treatment and be willing and able to make a commitment to take an active role in his or her treatment.

Homework Assignments. Homework is probably central to the success of behavioral interventions. Therefore, we typically begin the initial session with an emphasis on activities that will occur outside therapy. We collaborate with the patient to structure two types of activities. One type of activity is designed to yield information that will be needed in subsequent sessions. For example, we ask patients to monitor thoughts, emotions, and physical reactions to stress. This information is then used in teaching headache management skills. The second type of activity is designed to try out the skills learned in relaxation, biofeedback, and stress management training so that problems encountered in using these skills can be addressed.

We begin treatment with easy-to-complete homework assignments. This often helps overcome patients' initial resistance to complete homework assignments and provides an opportunity for success experiences that can increase patients' confidence in their ability to complete more difficult homework assignments as treatment progresses. For example, we begin therapy with the assignment of practicing the relaxation skills (from the first session) at home in a comfortable chair in the absence of headache. This is likely to promote successful skill learning and a sense of mastery. To facilitate skill learning, we provide patients with audiotapes and manuals designed to repeat and extend what is learned in session to situations in which headaches occur.

Patients occasionally encounter problems that interfere with completion of homework assignments. Perhaps the most common problem is the patient's lack of time. We suggest working with the patient in establishing priorities and approaching problems as difficulties to be overcome. For example, if a patient reports that interruptions interfere with the completion of homework assignments, we suggest problem solving with the patient to identify a time that can be set aside and kept relatively free from distractions. If a patient frequently forgets to practice homework tasks, develop environmental and subjective cues to assist the patient in remembering and initiating homework assignments.

Therapist Attitude. Patients' confidence in their ability to manage their headaches can be more important than their abilities to regulate specific physiological responses (Blanchard, Kim, Hermann, & Steffek, 1993; Holroyd & Penzien, 1983; Holroyd et al., 1984). Therefore, it is important for the therapist to attend to patients' perceptions of their performance as well as to their actual performance during skill training. Most patients require encouragement. We recommend that the therapist review the patient's performance with optimism, initially magnifying small successes and approaching problems as normal and manageable phases of treatment.

Responses to Problems
That Arise During Treatment

Despite the above efforts to prevent problems from arising, patients are likely to experience difficulties in acquiring headache management skills. The obstacles that therapists most frequently encounter in relaxation and biofeedback training arise in three principal areas: (a) the patient's attitudes and beliefs regarding treatment, (b) environmental events and experiences that interfere with learning skills, and (c) maintenance or generalization from the clinic to the home environment. Obstacles commonly encountered in stress management training similarly arise in understanding the therapy rationale, monitoring headache-related stresses and identifying a target problem, and acquiring and applying stress and headache coping skills. Tables 9.10, 9.11, and 9.12 outline a number of these commonly encountered problems and offer strategies that may be useful in responding to them.

Beyond Empirically Validated Treatments

An empirical treatment approach requires not only individual treatments that have been empirically validated but also empirically validated treatment algorithms that can guide the selection of the most appropriate intervention for a particular patient at a particular point in therapy. As described above, many efficacy studies have furnished empirical support for individual headache therapies; most studies have investigated the effectiveness of isolated interventions under well-controlled conditions with well-defined patient populations. The knowledge that a particular treatment has empirically proven to be more effective than a control condition provides little guidance in selecting one or a combination of treatments. Unfortunately, a strong empirical foundation has not yet been established for many aspects of routine clinical decision making in the treatment of headache patients. Thus, empirically validated algorithms are not available to guide a clinician in deciding, for example, whether a patient with chronic tension-type headaches who has failed to benefit from systematic efforts to modify triggers and brief relaxation training should be provided with more intensive relaxation training, EMG biofeedback training, stress management training, amitriptyline, or some combination of these therapies. We need answers to such questions as "In what order should amitriptyline, relaxation training, EMG biofeedback training, and other therapies be administered?" and "Does a failure to respond to EMG biofeedback training imply that a patient is a good candidate or a poor candidate for amitriptyline or for stress management training?"

Several of these clinical questions could be addressed in efficacy studies designed to assess a stepped-care approach to headache treatment. For example, are chronic tension-type headaches that fail to respond to amitriptyline more likely to respond to stress management training or to an SSRI? However, questions that are further downstream in the treatment algorithm will be more difficult or expensive to address in efficacy studies. In the absence of controlled studies, preliminary answers to these latter questions

TABLE 9.10 Relaxation Training: Problems and Solutions

Problems	Solutions
A. Patient's Attitude	
1. Patient is self-critical or hesitant during training.	Identify self-critical thoughts and help patient to challenge them. Offer reassurance.
2. Patient is overly concerned about performance.	Suggest that trying hard is counterproductive; instruct in alternative attitude of passive volition.
3. Patient is hesitant to relinquish control.	Discuss fears about loss of control; explain that novelty of sensations of relaxation may be triggering anxiety.
B. Learning the Skill	
1. Patient falls asleep when practicing relaxation.	Do not schedule relaxation practice just after meals or before bedtime. Practice seated rather than lying down.
2. Patient's concentration is disturbed by distracting thoughts or feelings.	Use imagery techniques (e.g., placing interfering thoughts in an imaginary trunk or closet) or autogenic phrases (e.g., *peaceful, calm*) to focus attention. Don't fight thoughts, but let them pass through mind.
3. Certain muscles are difficult to relax.	Repeat tensing-relaxing sequence with specific muscles; use muscle stretching exercises before relaxation practice.
C. Maintenance and Generalization	
1. Patient reports no carryover effect after relaxation.	Introduce brief cue-controlled relaxation techniques to use periodically throughout the day. Identify thoughts or situations that evoke arousal.
2. Patient has difficulty detecting difference between sensations of tension and relaxation.	Use partial tensing of muscles (discrimination training) to help patient identify subtle cues of relaxation.

SOURCE: Adapted from Holroyd, Holm, and Penzien (1988).

might be obtained from studies in which the effectiveness of various treatment sequences are monitored in naturalistic clinical settings. Until such questions have been addressed, however, any treatment algorithm must be based as much on clinical opinion as on empirical data.

Nonetheless, even a partially validated treatment algorithm can be useful in clarifying treatment options and in guiding clinicians at important decision points as well as in suggesting clinically relevant research questions. It needs

TABLE 9.11 Biofeedback Training: Problems and Solutions

Problems	Solutions
A. Patient's Attitudes and Beliefs	
1. Patient is intimidated by equipment or biofeedback task.	Begin with easy-to-master responses (e.g., forearm flexor or frontal EMG).
2. Patient perceives the biofeedback task as an achievement challenge.	Allow patient to practice without therapist. Encourage attitude of playful experimentation.
B. Learning the Skill	
1. Patient is unable to alter feedback signal or believes changes in signal are unrelated to his or her actions.	Alternate direction of feedback (e.g., increase rather than decrease EMG or temperature). Reduce signal threshold to make task easier. Alter feedback signal. Have patient experiment with a variety of mental strategies (e.g., imagery, focus on sensations).
2. The physiological parameter changes in the wrong direction.	Patient may be perceiving task as a performance challenge. In thermal biofeedback, consider using short training periods (15 minutes or less) because autoregulatory mechanisms may oppose vasodilatation after 15 to 20 minutes.
3. Lack of variability in physiological parameter makes learning difficult.	Investigate possible interfering effects of medications (e.g., ergotamine, sumatriptan). Alternate direction of feedback.
C. Maintenance and Generalization	
1. Patient shows inconsistency in controlling physiological response from session to session.	Emphasize home practice. Examine use of medications or other interfering agents (e.g., caffeine, nicotine) before session.
2. Patient has difficulty recognizing subjective cues and continues to rely on feedback signal to indicate control of physiological response.	Gradually fade feedback during training session. Have patient record subjective cues during day to heighten awareness of cues. Rehearse recognizing and controlling physiological response in imagination.
3. Patient controls response during session but reports being unable to control response in natural environment.	If daily life stress disrupts patient's performance, consider stress management. Encourage patient initially to attempt to control response in "easy" situations with few distractions or pressures.

SOURCE: Adapted from Holroyd, Holm, and Penzien (1988).

to be kept in mind that in the absence of adequate data, a number of different but equally valid treatment algorithms can be formulated. Figures 9.3 and

TABLE 9.12 Stress Management Therapy: Problems and Solutions

Problems	Solutions
A. Treatment Rationale	
1. Patient does not see his or her behavior as influencing stress responses or headaches.	Use personal examples to illustrate how cognitions influence stress responses. Review rationale, using concrete examples.
B. Monitoring Stress and Identifying a Target Problem	
1. Patient presents a large number of stressful situations.	Be alert to common themes that cut across multiple problems. List problems from largest to smallest. Choose manageable problem as an initial focus. Structure session to maintain focus on selected problem.
2. Headaches are not clearly stress related, or patient is unable to identify stress-related thoughts.	Review headache records and analyze situations associated with headache. First, use physical cues or stressful events or times associated with headaches to recognize onset of episode, then identify concrete thoughts present before onset. Use events that occur in therapy as opportunity to identify automatic thoughts occurring in the "here and now."
3. Headache is always present.	Identify factors associated with exacerbation rather than onset of headache. Consider focusing on potential aggravating factors (e.g., chronic stress, depression).
4. Patient's and therapist's preferred target problems differ.	Openly discuss difference of opinion; defer to patient if patient's preference strongly held.
C. Coping Skills Training and Application	
1. Patient does not attempt or attempts but "fails" homework assignment.	Examine patient's thoughts about homework assignment for clues to maladaptive thoughts/beliefs. Frame assignments as opportunity to learn. Break assignment into easier tasks.
2. Patient believes that external pressures prevent change (e.g., inflexibility in job situation).	Be alert to thoughts or beliefs that prevent patient from seeing alternatives. Experiment with small change (e.g., muscle stretching during bathroom break). Examine persons whom the patient identifies as effective copers for models of feasible change. Brainstorm without requiring that alternatives generated be perceived as feasible.
3. Maladaptive thoughts seem self-evidently true to patient.	Offer variety of alternative explanations of same "facts." Reverse roles with patient.
4. Friction or difficulties are present in therapeutic alliance.	Openly discuss conflict. Be alert to possibility that difficulty provides information about patient's coping. Admit errors.

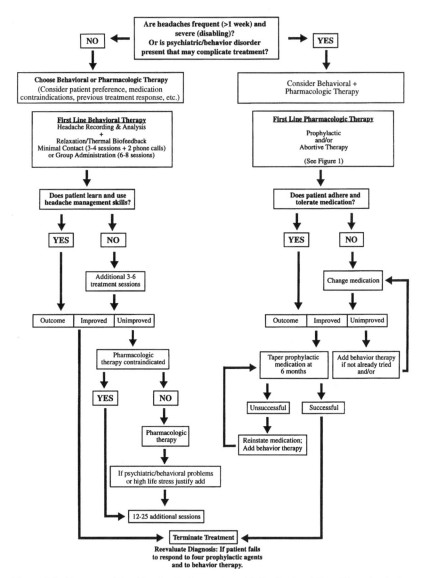

Figure 9.3. Treatment Algorithm for the Integration of Behavioral and Drug Therapies in the Management of Migraine

9.4 outline treatment algorithms for the integration of drug and nondrug therapies in the management of recurrent migraine and recurrent tension-type headache respectively. These algorithms are consistent with currently

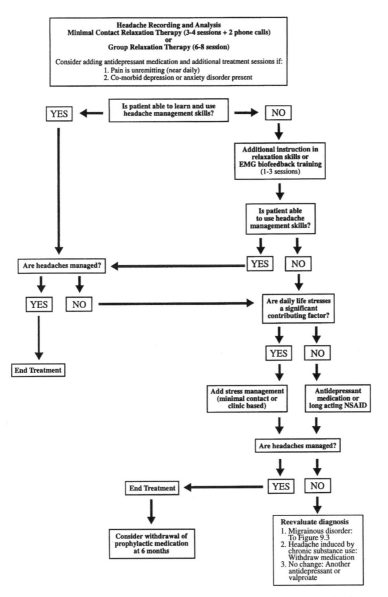

Figure 9.4. Treatment Algorithm for the Integration of Behavioral and Preventative Drug Therapies in the Management of Tension-Type Headache

available empirical data and, we believe, outline a cost-effective approach to treatment. They necessarily also reflect our clinical preferences.

Migraine Treatment Algorithm

Conjoint behavior and drug therapy is suggested when migraines or migrainous headaches are frequent and severe or when psychological problems complicate headache treatment (Figure 9.3). If migraines are less frequent and are uncomplicated by psychological problems, behavioral and drug therapies are equally viable treatment alternatives. Patient preference, treatment costs, previous experience with behavior or drug therapy, and the presence of medication contraindications (e.g., "Is it likely that the patient will become pregnant or be breast-feeding?") might then influence the treatment modality chosen. Typically, patients will have a preference for one or the other treatment modality; the alternate treatment modality can then be substituted or added if the patient does not benefit from the initial modality chosen.

For many patients, behavior therapy can be introduced in a stepped fashion, minimizing the cost and professional time required. For example, if a patient is unable to learn or to use headache management skills following either group or minimal-contact relaxation/thermal biofeedback training, three to six individual relaxation training sessions might be scheduled. Similarly, if a patient does not adhere to or tolerate the initial drug regimen, adherence problems need to be addressed or alternate drug therapies tried (see Figure 9.2). For a patient who has responded to prophylactic drug therapy, medication may be tapered after 6 months. If efforts to taper prophylactic medication are unsuccessful, behavior therapy may also be added to the treatment regimen, with efforts to taper medication being repeated following behavioral treatment.

Tension-Type Headache Treatment Algorithm

In the treatment of tension-type headaches, behavior therapy is considered the treatment of choice unless unremitting pain or comorbid depression or anxiety disorder indicates that antidepressant medication should be added (see Figure 9.4). Again, relaxation therapy may be offered in a minimal-contact or group format, with more intensive relaxation instruction reserved for patients who require additional therapist attention. In instances in which daily life stressors contribute to headache problems or prevent patients from effectively using relaxation skills to manage their headaches, stress management training can be combined with or added to relaxation training. If behavioral treatment is ineffective in controlling headaches within 4 months, we suggest that antidepressant medication be added to the treatment regimen.

FUTURE DIRECTIONS

The cost-effective management of chronic disorders in general and recurrent headache disorders in particular requires not only empirically based clinical guidelines or treatment algorithms but also a health care delivery system structured to implement these guidelines consistently and appropriately. Deficiencies in the delivery of health care services to individuals with chronic disorders, whether the disorder is depression, headaches, or diabetes, are now widely recognized. These deficiencies result, in large part, because the health care system is organized primarily to diagnose and treat acute illness (Holroyd & Creer, 1986; Levin & Idler, 1981; Wagner, Austin, & von Korff, 1996). As a result, it often fails to deliver services effectively to individuals with chronic disorders. Such individuals benefit when educational/psychosocial and medical interventions are integrated, when regular monitoring of signs and symptoms is integrated into proactive follow-up care, and when health care teaches and supports the performance of disorder management skills.

We are in the midst of a transition as major experiments in the delivery of health care services are underway. Emerging evidence from these experiments suggests that changes that are likely to be required for effective delivery of services to individuals with chronic disorders (see Wagner et al., 1996, for an overview). The majority of individuals with recurrent headache disorders, or for that matter other chronic disorders, are seen in primary practice, not in medical specialty, behavioral medicine, or mental health settings. The 15-minute primary care visit undoubtedly will need to be restructured to effectively incorporate educational and psychosocial interventions and proactive follow-up monitoring of patients into primary practice care. Current experiments in this area include increased use of proactive phone contacts to identify and address clinical problems early and the use of miniclinics in which patients with the same or related disorders are periodically scheduled for the same time period so that educational and psychosocial services delivered by nurses, health educators, or psychologists can be more readily integrated into primary care visits. Clinic information systems, which now serve primarily medical record-keeping and scheduling functions, also will need to be restructured to better support effective care for chronic conditions. Future information systems might identify patients in need of special attention, who, for example, are using analgesics excessively or who are currently depressed; at the same time, these systems could present information from relevant empirically based clinical guidelines directly to the primary care physician to encourage the use of empirically based treatments. New ways of incorporating expertise in psychosocial interventions into primary practice will also be needed. Current experiments in this area include the creation of expert teams of nurses, health educators, and psychologists who are available for immediate phone consultation during the patient visit or who are periodically available in the primary practice setting to see patients with the primary care physician. These consultation procedures, unlike more traditional consultation services that often produce little more than a written report with recommendations, will, over time, increase primary care physicians' knowledge of psychosocial assessment and treatment procedures.

It is important that behavioral scientists/clinicians be actively involved in current efforts to restructure health care delivery. Effective use will need to be made of existing behavioral science knowledge if we are to develop interventions that help patients successfully carry out sometimes difficult disorder management activities over extended periods of time. Behavioral scientists/clinicians will need to rethink the way that psychosocial treatment is administered; psychosocial interventions in primary practice are likely to take a different form than psychosocial interventions administered in a specialty behavioral medicine or mental health setting. Behavioral science knowledge also will need to be incorporated into the design of medical information systems if these information systems are to support health care providers and patients effectively in their disorder management activities. If clinician/scientists focus on maintaining their traditional roles and prerogatives, ignoring or fighting current changes in the health care system, others will fill the new professional roles that will be created in the process of solving these problems.

REFERENCES

Andrasik, F. (1986). Relaxation and biofeedback for chronic headaches. In A. D. Holzman & D. C. Turk (Eds.), *Pain management: A handbook of treatment approaches.* New York: Pergamon.

Arena, J. G., & Blanchard, E. B. (1996). Biofeedback and relaxation therapy for chronic pain disorders. In R. J. Gatchel & D. C. Turk (Eds.), *Psychological approaches to pain management: A practitioner's handbook.* New York: Guilford.

Andrasik, F., Blanchard, E. B., Arena, J. G., Teders, S. J., Teevan, R. C., & Rodichok, L. D. (1982). Psychological functioning in headache sufferers. *Psychosomatic Medicine, 44,* 171-182.

Arena, J. G., Hannah, S. L., Bruno, G. M., & Meador, K. J. (1991). Electromyographic biofeedback training for tension type headache in the elderly: A prospective study. *Biofeedback and Self-Regulation, 16,* 379-390.

Arena, J. G., Hightower, N. E., & Chong, G. C. (1988). Relaxation therapy for tension headache in the elderly: A prospective study. *Psychology of Aging, 3,* 96-98.

Bakal, D. A. (1982). *The psychobiology of chronic headache.* New York: Springer.

Baumel, B. (1994). Migraine: A pharmacological review with newer options and delivery modalities. *Neurology, 44*(Suppl. 3), S13-S17.

Benson, H. (1975). *The relaxation response.* New York: William Morrow.

Bernstein, D. A., & Borkovec, T. D. (1973). *Progressive relaxation training: A manual for the helping professions.* Champaign, IL: Research Press.

Blanchard, E. B. (1992). Psychological treatment of benign headache disorders. *Journal of Consulting and Clinical Psychology, 60,* 537-551.

Blanchard, E. B., & Andrasik, F. (1985). *Management of chronic headaches: A psychological approach.* New York: Pergamon.

Blanchard, E. B., & Andrasik, F. A. (1987). Biofeedback treatment of migraine. In J. P. Hatch, J. G. Fisher, & J. D. Rugh (Eds.), *Biofeedback: Studies in clinical efficacy* (pp. 1-79). New York: Plenum.

Blanchard, E. B., Andrasik, F., Evans, D. D., & Hillhouse, J. (1985). Biofeedback and relaxation treatments for headache in the elderly: A caution and a challenge. *Biofeedback and Self-Regulation, 10,* 69-73.

Blanchard, E. B., Andrasik, F., Evans, D. D., Neff, D. F., Appelbaum, K. A., & Rodichok, L. D. (1985). Behavioral treatment of 250 chronic headache patients: A clinical replication series. *Behavior Therapy, 16,* 308-327.

Blanchard, E. B., Andrasik, F., Neff, D. F., Arena, J. G., Ahles, T. A., Jurish, S. E., Pallmeyer, T. P., Saunders, N. L., Teders, S. J., Barron, K. D., & Rodichok, L. D. (1982). Biofeedback and relaxation training with three kinds of headache: Treatment effects and their prediction. *Journal of Consulting and Clinical Psychology, 50,* 562-575.

Blanchard, E. B., Appelbaum, K. A., Guarnieri, P., Morrill, B., & Dentinger, M. P. (1987). Five-year prospective follow-up on the treatment of chronic headache with biofeedback and/or relaxation. *Headache, 27,* 580-583.

Blanchard, E. B., Appelbaum, K. A., Radnitz, C. L., Jaccard, J., & Dentinger, M. P. (1989). The refractory headache patient. I. Chronic, daily, high intensity headache. *Behavior Research and Therapy, 27,* 403-410.

Blanchard, E. B., Kim, M., Hermann, C., & Steffek, B. D. (1993). Preliminary results of the effects on headache relief of perception of success among tension headache patients receiving relaxation. *Headache Quarterly, 4,* 249-253.

Blau, J. N., & Thavapalan, M. (1988). Preventing migraine: A study of precipitating factors. *Headache, 28,* 481-483.

Breslau, N., Merikangas, K., & Bowden, C. L. (1994). Comorbidity of migraine and major affective disorders. *Neurology, 44*(Suppl. 7), S17-S22.

Chesney, M. A., & Shelton, J. L. (1976). A comparison of muscle relaxation and elec-tromyogram biofeedback treatments for muscle contraction headache. *Journal of Behavior Therapy and Experimental Psychiatry, 7,* 221-225.

Davidoff, R. A. (1995). *Migraine: Manifestations, pathogenesis, and management.* Philadel-phia: F. A. Davis.

De Benedittis, G., & Lorenzetti, A. (1992). Minor stressful life events (daily hassles) in chronic primary headache: Relationship with MMPI personality patterns. *Headache, 32,* 330-332.

DeLongis, A., Coyne, J. C., Dakof, G., Folkman, S., & Lazarus, R. S. (1982). Relationship of daily hassles, uplifts, and major life events to health status. *Health Psychology, 1,* 119-136.

Diamond, S., & Dalessio, D. J. (1992). *The practicing physician's approach to headache* (5th ed.). Baltimore: Williams & Wilkins.

Diamond, S., & Montrose, D. (1984). The value of biofeedback in the treatment of chronic headache: A four-year retrospective study. *Headache, 24,* 5-18.

Diener, H. C. & Tfelt-Hansen, P. (1993). Headache associated with chronic use of substances. In J. Olesen, P. Tfelt-Hansen, & K. M. A. Welch (Eds.), *The headaches* (pp. 721-728). New York: Raven.

Diener, H. C., & Wilkinson, M. (Eds.). (1988). *Drug induced headache.* New York: Sprin-ger-Verlag.

Edhe, D. M., & Holm, J. E. (1992). Stress and headache: Comparison of migraine, tension, and headache-free subjects. *Headache Quarterly, 3,* 54-60.

French, D. J., Holroyd, K. A., Rokicki, L., & France, J. L. (1994). Assessing quality of life and disability in recurrent headache patients: Illness impact recordings. *Headache, 34,* 307.

Gauthier, J. G., & Carrier, S. (1991). Long-term effects of biofeedback on migraine headache: A prospective follow-up study. *Headache, 31,* 605-612.

Gauthier, J. G., Cote, G., Cote, A., & Drolet, M. (in press). Group versus individual thermal biofeedback in the treatment of migraine: A comparative outcome study. *Headache.*

Hollon, S. D., & DeRubeis, J. (1981). Placebo-psychotherapy combinations: Inappropriate representations of psychotherapy in drug-psychotherapy comparative trials. *Psychol-ogy Bulletin, 90,* 467-477.

Holm, J. E., Holroyd, K. A., Hursey, K. G., & Penzien, D. B. (1986). The role of stress in recurrent tension headache. *Headache, 26,* 160-167.

Holroyd, K. A. (1993a). Behavioral treatment strategies. In J. Olesen & J. Schoenen (Eds.), *Tension-type headache: Classification, mechanisms, and treatment.* New York: Ra-ven.

Holroyd, K. A. (1993b). Integrating pharmacologic and non-pharmacologic treatments. In C. D. Tollison & R. S. Kunkel (Eds.), *Headache: Diagnosis and treatment* (pp. 309-320). Baltimore: Williams & Wilkins.

Holroyd, K. A., & Andrasik, F. (1978). Coping and the self-control of chronic tension headache. *Journal of Consulting and Clinical Psychology, 5,* 1036-1045.

Holroyd, K. A., & Andrasik, F. (1982). A cognitive-behavioral approach to recurrent tension and migraine headache. In P. E. Kendall (Ed.), *Advances in cognitive-behavioral research and therapy.* Orlando, FL: Academic Press.

Holroyd, K. A., & Creer, T. L. (1986). *Self-management of chronic disease: Handbook of clinical interventions and research.* New York: Academic Press.

Holroyd, K. A., France, J. L., Cordingley, G. E., Rokicki, L. A., Kvaal, S. A., Lipchik, G. L., & McCool, H. R. (1995). Enhancing the effectiveness of relaxation/thermal biofeedback training with propranolol hydrochloride. *Journal of Consulting and Clinical Psychology, 63,* 327-330.

Holroyd, K. A., & French, D. (1995). Recent advances in the assessment and treatment of recurrent headaches. In A. J. Goreczny (Ed.), *Handbook of health and rehabilitation psychology.* New York: Plenum.

Holroyd, K. A., French, D., Nash, J. M., Tobin, D. L., & Echelberger-McCune, R. L. (1995). *Stress management for tension headaches.* Athens: Ohio University/National Institutes of Health.

Holroyd, K. A., Holm, J. E., & Penzien, D. B. (1988). Clinical issues in the treatment of recurrent headache. In P. Keller & S. Heyman (Eds.), *Innovations in clinical practice: A sourcebook* (Vol. 7). Sarosota, FL: Professional Resource Exchange.

Holroyd, K. A., & Lipchik, G. L. (1997). Recurrent headache disorders. In S. J. Gallant, G. P. Keita, & R. Royak-Schaler (Eds.), *Psychosocial and behavioral factors in women's health care: A handbook for medical educators, practitioners, and psychologists.* Washington, DC: American Psychological Association.

Holroyd, K., & Penzien, D. B. (1983). EMG biofeedback and tension headache: Therapeutic mechanisms. In K. Holroyd, B. Schlote, & H. Zenz (Eds.), *Perspectives in research on headache.* New York: C. J. Hogrefe.

Holroyd, K. A., & Penzien, D. B. (1986). Client variables and the behavioral treatment of recurrent tension: A meta-analytic review. *Journal of Behavioral Medicine, 9,* 515-536.

Holroyd, K. A., & Penzien, D. B. (1990). Pharmacological and nonpharmacological prophylaxis of recurrent migraine headache: A meta-analytic review of clinical trials. *Pain, 42,* 1-13.

Holroyd, K. A., Penzien, D. B., & Cordingley, G. E. (1991). Propranolol in the management of recurrent migraine: A meta-analytic review. *Headache, 31,* 333-340.

Holroyd, K. A., Penzien, D. B., Hursey, K. G., Tobin, D. L., Rogers, L., Holm, J. E., Marcille, P. J., Hall, J. R., & Chila, A. G. (1984). Change mechanisms in EMG biofeedback training: Cognitive changes underlying improvements in tension headache. *Journal of Consulting and Clinical Psychology, 52,* 1039-1053.

Holroyd, K. A., Penzien, D. B., Rokicki, L. A., & Cordingley, G. E. (1992). Flunarizine vs. propranolol: A meta-analysis of clinical trials. *Headache, 32,* 256.

Jacobsen, E. (1938). *Progressive relaxation* (2nd ed.). Chicago: University of Chicago Press.

Jacobson, G. P., Ramadan, N. M., Aggarwal, S. K., & Newman, C. W. (1994). The Henry Ford Hospital Disability Inventory (HDI). *Neurology, 44,* 837-842.

Kabela, E., Blanchard, E. B., Appelbaum, K. A., & Nicholson, N. (1989). Self-regulatory treatment of headache in the elderly. *Biofeedback and Self-Regulation, 14,* 219-228.

Kohlenberg, R. J. (1984, August). *Self-help treatment of migraine headache: An outcome study.* Paper presented at the American Psychological Association Convention, Washington, DC.

Larsson, B., Melin, L., & Döberl, A. (1990). Recurrent tension headache in adolescents treated with self-help relaxation training and a muscle relaxant drug. *Headache, 30,* 665-671.

Levin, L. S., & Idler, E. L. (1981). *The hidden health care system: Mediating structures and medicine.* Cambridge, MA: Ballinger.

Lipton, R. B., Stewart, W. F., Celentano, D. D., & Reed, M. L. (1992). Undiagnosed migraine headaches: A comparison of symptom-based and reported physician diagnosis. *Archives of Internal Medicine, 152,* 1273-1278.

Markley, H. G. (1994). Chronic headache: Appropriate use of opiate analgesics. *Neurology, 44*(Suppl. 3), S18-S24.

Mathew, N. T. (1981). Prophylaxis of migraine and mixed headache: A randomized controlled study. *Headache, 21,* 105-109.

Mathew, N. T. (1990). Drug-induced headache. *Neurologic Clinics, 8,* 903-912.

Mathew, N. T. (1993). Transformed migraine. *Cephalalgia, 13*(Suppl. 12), 78-83.

Mathew, N. T., Reuveni, U., & Perez, F. I. (1987). Transformed or evolutive migraine. *Headache, 27,* 102-106.

McCrory, D. C., Penzien, D. B., Rains, J. C., & Hasselblad, V. (1996). Efficacy of behavioral treatments for migraine and tension-type headache: Meta-analysis of controlled trials. *Headache, 36,* 272.

McGrath, P. J., Cunningham, S. J., Lascelles, M. A., & Humphreys, P. (1990). *Help yourself: A treatment for migraine headache.* Montreal: Morin.

Medina, J. L., & Diamond, S. (1978). The role of diet in migraine. *Headache, 18,* 31-34.

Mosley, T. H., Grotheus, C. A., & Meeks, W. M. (1995). Treatment of tension headache in the elderly: A controlled evaluation of relaxation training and relaxation combined with cognitive-behavior therapy. *Journal of Clinical Geropsychology, 1,* 175-188.

Nash, J., & Holroyd, K. A. (1992). Home-based behavioral treatment for recurrent headache: A cost-effective alternative. *American Pain Society Bulletin, 2,* 1-6.

Nikiforow, R., & Hokkanen, E. (1978). An epidemiological study of headache in an urban and a rural population in northern Finland. *Headache, 18,* 137-145.

Olesen, J. (Chair). (1988). Classification and diagnostic criteria for headache disorders, cranial neuralgias, and facial pain: Headache Classification Committee of the International Headache Society. *Cephalalgia, 8*(Suppl. 7).

Olesen, J., & Rasmussen, B. K. (1996). The International Headache Society classification of chronic daily and near-daily headaches: A critique of the critique. *Cephalalgia, 16,* 407-411.

Olesen, J., Tfelt-Hansen, P., & Welch, K. M. A. (Eds.). (1993). *The headaches.* New York: Raven.

Osterhaus, J., Gutterman, D. L., & Plachetka, J. R. (1992). Healthcare resource and lost labour costs of migraine headache in the United States. *PharmacoEconomics, 2,* 67-76.

Osterhaus, J. T., Townsend, R. J., Gandek, B., & Ware, J. E. (1994). Measuring the functional status and well-being of patients with migraine headache. *Headache, 34,* 337-343.

Paiva, T., Batista, A., Martins, P., & Martins, A. (1995). The relationship between headaches and sleep disturbances. *Headache, 35,* 590-596.

Penzien, D. B., & Holroyd, K. A. (1994). Psychosocial interventions in the management of recurrent headache disorders—II: Description of treatment techniques. *Behavioral Medicine, 20,* 64-73.

Penzien, D. B., Holroyd, K. A., Hursey, K. G., Holm, J. E., & Wittchen, H. U. (1985, November). *Behavioral treatment of recurrent migraine: A meta-analysis of over five-dozen group outcome studies.* Paper presented at the meeting of the Association for Advancement of Behavior Therapy, Houston, TX.

Penzien, D. B., Johnson, C. A., Seville, J., Rubman, S., Boggess, J. T., & Rains, J. C. (1994). Interrelationships among daily and global self-report measures of headache. *Headache Quarterly, 5,* 8-14.

Penzien, D. B., & Rains, J. C. (1995). Migraine diagnosis using the IHS criteria: Characterization of atypical migraine (IHS 1.7) patients. *Headache, 35,* 285.

Penzien, D. B., & Rains, J. C. (in press). *Self-management training program for chronic headache: Therapist manual.* Sarasota, FL: Professional Resource Press.

Penzien, D. B., Rains, J. C., & Holroyd, K. A. (1992). A review of alternative behavioral treatments for headache. *Mississippi Psychologist, 17,* 8-9.

Penzien, D. B., Rains, J. C., & Holroyd, K. A. (1993). Psychological assessment of the recurrent headache sufferer. In C. D. Tollison & R. S. Kunkel (Eds.), *Headache: Diagnosis and treatment* (pp. 39-49). Baltimore: Williams & Wilkins.

Pryse-Phillips, W., Findlay, H., Tugwell, P., Edmeads, J., Murray, T. J., & Nelson, R. F. (1992). A Canadian population survey on the clinical, epidemiological and societal impact of migraine and tension-type headache. *Canadian Journal of Neurological Sciences, 19,* 333-339.

Pollard, W. E., Bobbitt, R. A., Bergner, M., Martin, D. P., & Gilson, B. (1976). The Sickness Impact Profile: reliability of a health status measure. *Medical Care, 14,* 146-155.

Radnitz, C. L. (1990). Food-triggered migraine: A critical review. *Annals of Behavioral Medicine, 12,* 51-65.

Rains, J. C., Penzien, D. B., & Holroyd, K. A. (1993). Meta-analysis of alternative behavioral treatments for recurrent headache. *Headache, 33,* 271-272.

Rains, J. C., Penzien, D. B., & Hursey, K. G. (1996). Precipitants of episodic migraine: Behavioral, environmental, hormonal, and dietary factors. *Headache, 36,* 247-275.

Rains, J. C., Penzien, D. B., Lofland, K. R., Bruehl, S. P., Semenchuk, E. M., & Hursey, K. G. (1994). Chronic daily headache: Examination of diagnosis, symptom patterns, and medication in a large clinical sample. *Headache, 43,* 295-296.

Rapoport, A. M., & Sheftell, F. D. (1993). Headache associated with medication and substance withdrawal. In C. D. Tollison & R. S. Kunkel (Eds.), *Headache: Diagnosis and treatment* (pp. 227-231). Baltimore: Williams & Wilkins.

Rapoport, A. M., & Sheftell, F. D. (1996). *Headache disorders: A management guide for practitioners.* Philadelphia: W. B. Saunders.

Rasmussen, B. K. (1993). Migraine and tension-type headache in a general population: Precipitating factors, female hormones, sleep pattern and relation to lifestyle. *Pain, 53,* 65-72.

Rasmussen, B. K., Jensen, R., & Olesen, J. (1992). Impact of headache on sickness absence and utilization of medical services: A Danish population study. *Journal of Epidemiology and Community Health, 46,* 443-446.

Rasmussen, B. K., Jensen, R., Schroll, M., & Olesen, J. (1991). Epidemiology of headache in a general population: A prevalence study. *Journal of Clinical Epidemiology, 44,* 1147-1157.

Reich, B. A., & Gottesman, M. (1993). Biofeedback and psychotherapy in the treatment of muscle contraction/tension-type headache. In C. D. Tollison & R. S. Kunkel (Eds.), *Headache: Diagnosis and treatment* (pp. 167-180). Baltimore: Williams & Wilkins.

Ries, P. W. (1986). *Current estimates from the National Health Interview Survey, United States, 1984* (Vital and Health Statistics, Series 10, No. 156 [PHS 86-1584]). Washington, DC: Department of Health and Human Services, National Center for Health Statistics.

Rowan, A. B., & Andrasik, F. (1996). Efficacy and cost-effectiveness of minimal therapist contact treatments of chronic headaches: A review. *Behavior Therapy, 27,* 207-234.

Sahota, P. K., & Dexter, J. D. (1990). Sleep and headache syndromes: A clinical review. *Headache, 35,* 80-84.

Sanin, L. C., Mathew, N. T., Bellmeyer, L. R., & Ali, S. (1994). The International Headache Society (IHS) Headache Classification as applied to a headache clinic population. *Cephalalgia, 14,* 443-446.

Saper, J. R., Silberstein, S., Gordon, C. D., & Hamel, R. L. (1993). *Handbook of headache management: A practical guide to diagnosis and treatment of head, neck, and facial pain.* Baltimore: Williams & Wilkins.

Schulz, J. H., & Luthe, V. (1969). *Autogenic training* (Vol. 1). New York: Grune & Stratton.

Schwartz & Associates. (1995). *Biofeedback: A practitioner's guide* (2nd ed.). New York: Guilford.

Silberstein, S. D., Lipton, R. B., & Breslau, N. (1995). Migraine: Association with personality characteristics and psychopathology. *Cephalalgia, 15,* 358-369.

Silberstein, S. D., Lipton, R. B., Solomon, S., & Mathew, N. T. (1994). Classification of daily and near-daily headaches: Proposed revisions to the IHS criteria. *Headache, 34,* 1-7.

Silberstein, S. D., & Merriam, G. R. (1993). Sex hormones and headache. *Journal of Pain and Symptom Management, 8,* 98-114.

Solomon, G. D., Skobieranda, F. G., & Gragg, L. A. (1993). Quality of life and well-being of headache patients: Measurement by the Medical Outcomes Study instrument. *Headache, 33,* 351-358.

Stang, P. E., & Osterhaus, J. T. (1993). Impact of migraine in the United States: Data from the National Health Interview Survey. *Headache, 33,* 29-35.

Stang, P. E., Osterhaus, J. T., & Celentano, D. D. (1994). Migraine: Patterns of healthcare use. *Neurology, 44*(Suppl. 4), S47-S55.

Stewart, W. F., Lipton, R. B., Celentano, D. D., & Reed, M. L. (1992). Prevalence of migraine headache in the United States: Relation to age, income, race, and other sociodemographic factors. *Journal of the American Medical Association, 267,* 64-69.

Stewart, W. F., Shecter, A., & Lipton, R. B. (1994). Migraine heterogeneity: Disability, pain intensity, and attach frequency and duration. *Neurology, 44*(Suppl. 4), S24-S39.

Tobin, D. L., Holroyd, K. A., Baker, A., Reynolds, R. V. C., & Holm, J. E. (1988). Development and clinical trial of a minimal contact, cognitive-behavioral treatment for tension headache. *Cognitive Therapy and Research, 12,* 325-339.

Wagner, E. H., Austin, B. T., & von Korff, M. (1996). Improving outcomes in chronic illness. *Managed Care Quarterly, 4,* 12-25.

Wittrock, D. A., Penzien, D. B., Mosley, T. H., & Johnson, C. A. (1991). The Recurrent Illness Impairment Profile: Preliminary results using the headache version. *Headache Quarterly, 2,* 138-139.

10

Alcohol Abuse and Dependence

THE PROCESS OF EMPIRICAL VALIDATION

MARK S. GOLDMAN

The empirical validation of treatments for any disorder is a process and therefore is never fully completed. Hence, the existing empirical base for any treatment can only represent a point along the validation continuum, with continued validation not only possible but necessary to increase confidence in the continued use of the treatment. Even very well-established medical treatments are subject to this constraint. Well-established antibiotics, for example, may be supplanted by newer, more potent, variants or may even lose potency in the face of more resilient bacteria. Newer antibiotic variations that target a broader spectrum of vulnerable bacteria, are cheaper, are easier to administer, and have fewer side effects are also always possible.

Most psychological treatments, even those included in the Division 12 Task Force review, have yet to achieve a high level of empirical validation in all the areas necessary to ensure confidence in their widespread use. Hence, we would do well to understand the topic to be addressed by this book

AUTHOR'S NOTE: Preparation of this chapter was supported in part by National Alcohol Abuse and Alcoholism Grant R37 AA08333.

as "treatments that have begun the process of empirical validation" rather than as a review of treatments for which empirical validation is conclusive. Even treatments that have received the most methodologically rigorous validation (given the current state of the art) are still subject to considerable controversy. Such controversy represents a natural part of the validation process. Witness the recent discussion of the interpretation of findings from the National Institute of Mental Health Treatment of Depression Collaborative Research Program (TDRCP; see "Special Feature," 1996). Despite this study's standing as close to the state of the art for treatments of depression, the exact meaning of the results has been debated, refined, and reinterpreted since the findings first became available (e.g., Jacobson & Hollon, 1996; Klein, 1996).

It is laudable that we have embarked on this process in the field of psychotherapy for reasons cited elsewhere in this book. And it is laudable that Division 12 set up a task force to begin compiling a list of treatments that have received some measure of empirical validation (Task Force on the Promotion and Dissemination of Psychological Procedures, 1995). It is important to appreciate, however, that the Division 12 Task Force made a number of assumptions about how to begin this process and that these assumptions, in essence, constituted a template for the process of empirical validation. This template has not been without critics, however, as can be seen in some of the reports in this volume. For example, the requirement for just two studies that are superior to placebo may leave us with a myriad of validated treatments, given that nonspecific effects account for so much of treatment outcome variance. In other cases, criticisms have arisen because of dimensions of empirical validation that the Division 12 guidelines do not consider at all (e.g., cost, acceptability to clients, disseminability).

Some of these points of contention may be reduced with more extensive consideration of all the relevant dimensions along which empirical validation must take place. Some of these additional dimensions have been recently considered and reported by another task force of the American Psychological Association (APA) that operated concurrently with the Division 12 Task Force but that remains less well known. This committee was constituted above the division level by representatives of the practice and science directorate. The purpose of this committee was also different, as shall be explained below. This chapter shall first review the major points of this APA task force report on the development of guidelines for empirical validation of treatments, to provide a "road map" for the later consideration of the work that already has been done in this regard for alcohol abuse and dependence. Because the process of developing, refining, and validating treatments is always best informed by consideration of what is known about the etiology of the disorders involved, the etiology of alcohol abuse and dependence shall then be briefly reviewed. The implications of etiology for current strategies of treatment will be highlighted. Finally, the current status of the validation process for treatments of alcohol abuse and dependence will be reviewed in light of the new task force template for development of guidelines. The actual application of these guidelines to these treatments has yet to be completed and is beyond the scope of this chapter, but the implications of the guidelines will be made explicit. Because the etiology and treatment of other substance abuse are too extensive to include in a single chapter with some of the general points to be made here, this chapter will focus on alcohol alone, with occasional mention of other substances.

TEMPLATE FOR DEVELOPING GUIDELINES: INTERVENTIONS FOR MENTAL DISORDERS AND PSYCHOSOCIAL ASPECTS OF PHYSICAL DISORDERS

On February 22, 1995, the APA's Council of Representatives approved a template for developing treatment guidelines that had been put together by a task force of the Board of Professional Affairs (BPA), the Board of Scientific Affairs (BSA), and the Committee for the Advancement of Professional Practice (CAPP) of the APA (APA, 1995).[1] (Task force members were David Barlow, chair; Susan Mineka and Elizabeth Robinson, cochairs; Daniel Abrahamson, Sol Garfield, Mark Goldman, Steven Hollon, and George Stricker.) The task force was formed after discussions in the BPA about how the APA might respond to guidelines that were being offered from a number of public and private sources and most immediately by the Agency for Health Care Policy and Research (AHCPR) of the federal government. The challenge was that each organizational entity was using different rules for constructing guidelines, ranging from empirical to political to economic. As a consequence, guidelines for treatment of the same disorder might vary from entity to entity, and different disorders might have treatments judged using entirely different conceptual schemes. Therefore, the task was to generate a set of ground rules or a template that all groups could follow for developing guidelines.

The two most significant differences between the conceptual framework of the "template" task force and that of the Division 12 Task Force were (a) the recognition that recommendations need to be made for some treatments before full empirical validation is available and that there is, therefore, a legitimate place for professional judgment (applied systematically) in the validation process; and (b) the recognition that there are many differences between the kind of evidence that one can obtain for *efficacy* of a treatment using traditional research criteria and evidence for a treatment's *clinical utility* in real-world settings. Efficacy, of course, is what the Division 12 Task Force is referring to exclusively when it speaks of empirical validation—that is, the application of the most rigorous research methodology for reaching a logical conclusion that the application of a particular treatment reliably produces a particular outcome. The fact that a particular treatment can reliably produce an outcome in a carefully controlled experimental study does not ensure, however, that the same treatment will reliably produce that outcome in real-world clinical settings, given a host of unpredictable and difficult-to-control influences that impinge on actual clinical settings. Empirical investigation of real-world outcomes and the factors that may influence these outcomes establishes clinical utility (when the Division 12 Task Force considers promotion and dissemination, it is addressing portions of clinical utility, although not in relation to each specific treatment). It is evident that both efficacy and clinical utility must be considered in connection with any treatment offered for amelioration of human problems. Many of the issues raised in this volume in connection with the Division 12 report fall in the realm of clinical utility. Included below is a brief review of the efficacy and clinical utility dimensions included in the APA Template for Guidelines.

Efficacy

The efficacy domain consists of one asymmetrical, bipolar dimension, with anchor points as follows: *contradictory evidence, strongly negative clinical consensus, mixed clinical consensus, strongly positive clinical consensus, quantified clinical observations, randomized controlled trial (RCT)—better than no therapy, RCT—better than nonspecific therapy,* and *RCT—better than alternative therapy.* Obviously, confidence in the efficacy of a treatment increases as one moves up the scale from *contradictory evidence* to *RCT—better than alternative therapy.* And the quality of the studies on which judgments are made contributes to confidence in efficacy. Both these considerations are noted in the template.

It is, however, critical to recognize that although the confidence in the efficacy of a treatment increases as the scale is ascended, evidence for the potency of a treatment does not. These considerations are too often confused. A new and not yet evaluated treatment may be far more active (curative) than a well-established treatment. Efficacy studies can only supply evidence that a treatment can be reliably used to affect a specified condition or disorder (i.e., that it is valid for that condition). Hence, advocates of unvalidated treatments may legitimately argue that validated treatments are not necessarily "better" than their preferred treatment. They are, however, obligated to begin the process of validation for the treatment that they support.

Note that the efficacy dimension includes a role for informed judgment by researchers and clinicians in the early stages of validation. It is recognized that many current treatments have no empirical validation and that new treatments will have no research-based validation as they are being introduced. Hence, the template recommends the convening of panels of experts in the target condition to consider the confidence that may be placed in a particular treatment until research-based results are available. Implicit in the use of expert panels is that individual clinicians are discouraged from making idiosyncratic decisions about the utilization of a treatment just because they personally approve of it. Although it is understood that in the earliest phases of development of a new treatment there is little information of any kind available on which to make a decision, decisions about the general utilization of a particular treatment should never be left entirely to the individual practitioner.

Even at these early stages of treatment validation, quantified clinical observations are possible and to be encouraged. That is, a practitioner should collect systematic data on the outcomes associated with particular treatments, and mechanisms for compiling these data with data from other clinicians using the same treatments should be arranged. Short of controlled clinical trials, even very limited data collection is the best way of ensuring that clinicians are not continuing to make treatment decisions on the basis of illusory correlations. The tendency for clinicians to selectively recall only successes while minimizing recollection of less-than-successful applications is well known (see Chapman & Chapman, 1967; Golding & Rorer, 1972).

Ultimately, efficacy validation must move into randomized controlled trials, with comparisons of newer treatments to previously established treatments as the ideal. Randomization of patient assignment, and control groups that allow for logical parsing of effects not specifically attributable to the new treatment (and for ensuring that the new treatment does not do damage), are the most confidence-inspiring methods for evaluating treatments. It is not the purpose here to review all the ancillary methodology necessary to make the trials "state of the art," but of course the inclusion of methods for making treatment constant across patients (some form of treatment manuals) is essential, despite the concerns raised elsewhere in this volume about them.

There are, of course, many additional concerns associated with tightly controlled efficacy evaluations besides the effects of manuals. As noted earlier, these limitations are not addressed in the Division 12 scheme, but in each case, these concerns are reflected in the clinical utility portion of the template to be discussed next. Among these factors that may influence conclusions in efficacy studies are:

1. Patients often feel part of something special.
2. Financial resources available in funded efficacy studies are often greater than would be available to ordinary clinicians for provision of treatment.
3. In addition to the clinicians providing treatment, RCTs often include administrative, assessment, and oversight personnel, some of whom are in contact with patients.
4. Because attrition severely impairs the ability to draw conclusions, extensive efforts are made to keep patients in treatment and in follow-up assessments.
5. The extensive assessments may themselves be reactive or even seen by patients as part of the treatment and may boost treatment effects.
6. The typical location for RCTs is a university or university-based hospital or clinic; such settings may increase patient confidence as compared to a small, out-of-the-way clinician's office.
7. Because the effort and cost of conducting RCTs is high, personnel are usually selected to be high quality and to maintain a high level of engagement in the project.
8. Besides the use of manuals, other efforts are made to ensure treatment integrity. Sometimes such efforts can be damaging to treatment outcome due to rigidity of the protocol that does not allow for handling of unanticipated events.

The total list of possibilities is too extensive to be fully addressed here.

Clinical Utility

For many reasons, some already cited, the APA task force on the template extensively addressed issues associated with extending empirical validation to treatments as they are provided in the real world of clinical service. Three dimensions addressing these issues fell generally under the heading "Clinical Utility (External Validity)." The first of these dimensions, *feasibility,* addressed the general question of whether a treatment could practically be used in day-to-day practice. For example, a treatment might be very effective for a minor disorder but be very expensive or risky. Would people avail themselves of brain surgery for infrequent minor headaches, no matter how effective? As part of feasibility, guideline developers were directed to consider patient acceptability (cost, pain, duration, side effects, etc.); patient choice in the face of relatively equal efficacy; probability of compliance; and ease of disseminability, such as the availability of clinicians with competence in the treatment, requirements and opportunities for training, and need for expensive technologies or support personnel.

The second dimension of clinical utility reflected the self-evident question of *generalizability.* Would treatments shown to have efficacy in rigorous studies work equally well in different patient groups (gender, cultural, age/developmental level, etc.); for all therapists, regardless of their characteristics; and in practice settings using different time frames and settings?

The third dimension to be considered by developers of guidelines was the obvious question of *costs and benefits;* not only should the costs of service delivery be considered but also the estimated cost of withholding a service. It would be foolish, for example, to withhold even relatively expensive prevention efforts if the cost to society of the eventual disorder was even higher (this aspect of cost/benefit assessment is often referred to as *cost offset*). Consider the cost of polio vaccine or the cost of psychological interventions if the disorders that they address result later in even more debilitating physical or psychological conditions.

These three dimensions of clinical utility are not meant to be considered by guideline developers merely through consensus or opinion. The template specifically calls for "systematic and objective methods and strategies for assessing these characteristics of treatment as they are applied in actual practice" (APA, 1995, Table 1, p. 30). It is conceivable that the methodology of RCTs could even be applied in the appropriate settings and with the appropriate dependent variables. The template does note, however, that more often these data will come from quantified clinical observations or the methods of econometrics as applied to the health sphere.

ALCOHOL ABUSE AND DEPENDENCE

Alcohol dependence as described in the fourth edition of the *Diagnostic and Statistical Manual of Mental Disorders* (*DSM-IV;* American Psychiatric Association, 1994) presents an interesting extreme case of the difference between efficacy and clinical utility. It is well known that by far the most frequently used treatment is Alcoholics Anonymous (AA), either as a stand-alone (i.e., attendance at meetings), or as part of a more general hospital- or clinic-based treatment. Yet AA, for a variety of reasons, has received very little formal efficacy validation. In contrast, however, consider the dimensions of clinical utility. It is obviously quite feasible; patients accept it; in its pure form it is essentially cost-free; it is easily disseminated; and it is often the treatment of choice by patients. It has spread into almost all cultures, ethnic groups, and nations; hence, it is apparently generalizable. At the societal level, it is relatively low cost as well. And, if we are to accept the recent survey results of *Consumer Reports* magazine ("Psychotherapy," 1995), patients report that they feel it is successful for them.

Even the soon-to-be-released findings from Project MATCH (see below) include only a manualized variant of a 12-step approach and not AA treatment as commonly delivered. In contrast, cognitive-behavioral treatments have received considerable efficacy validation but little validation of clinical utility. It is evident that both efficacy and clinical utility must be considered if we are to have confidence that a treatment is truly empirically validated.

ETIOLOGY

Although not explicitly considered as part of either efficacy or clinical utility, advances in medicine indicate that treatments are best considered in light of known parameters of etiology. Unfortunately, the frequent demonstration of the power of common, nonspecific influences in psychological treatment has tended to deemphasize etiology in the consideration of treatment planning. Such information is only beginning to be considered in the context of matching studies, which may include putative etiological factors as matching variables. Although the results are far from complete in relation to these kinds of matching variables, it seems that advances in treatment can ultimately come from knowledge of etiological processes. For this reason, we will now briefly review those etiological variables in the alcohol dependence field that seem most likely to relate to treatment planning. This material currently must fall within the realm of clinical consensus, rather than on the continuum of truly empirically validated treatments, because the treatment outcome data are just beginning to arrive on these variables.

These variables may be generally grouped as being of biological origin, psychosocial origin, or some combination of the two. Within the category of biologically based variables, the early investigation of the etiology of alcoholism emphasized a search for a specific biological characteristic or process that led to alcohol abuse and dependence and to no other condition. Although some recent reports continue to come out of this tradition, most researchers now believe that there may be genetically transmitted biological characteristics that increase risk for alcohol dependence but that these mechanisms are more generalized and lead to a variety of behavioral patterns, of which excessive alcohol use is just one (see review by Sher, 1991). The currently favored specific pathways are theorized to be connected with an individual's intrinsic tolerance for alcohol. Some researchers suggest that high-risk individuals are less responsive to the effects of alcohol (Schuckit, 1987) and so must drink more to achieve the same effect as others. These individuals come to be at higher risk due to their higher consumption. Other researchers suggest instead that high-risk individuals have greater reactivity to alcohol and are at higher risk due to their more intensive experience of alcohol effects (see Sher, 1991). And finally, others indicate that both characteristics are present in high-risk individuals, with more intensive reactions occurring as alcohol levels are increasing in the body and fewer aversive effects experienced as alcohol is being eliminated (i.e., during what is sometimes referred to as acute withdrawal; Newlin & Thomson, 1990).

Of the more generalized inherited mechanisms, some researchers take an agnostic position about the characteristics that influence drinking patterns and just refer to these variables as "genetic/family history variables." Other researchers go further and discuss paths of influence that derive from variations in personality/temperament (see Sher, 1991). As we shall see below, it is these generalized mechanisms that have more obvious implications for treatment planning.

Behavioral Undercontrol

By far, the most often cited generalized set of variables thought to be linked to alcohol abuse and dependence has fallen generally under the umbrella term of *behavioral undercontrol* (Sher & Trull, 1994). Among these variables have been included sensation or thrill seeking, impulsivity, conduct disorder and/or delinquency in children and adolescents, and at the most extreme, antisocial personality characteristics. Sometimes these variables are conceived to be comorbid conditions: that is, two or more separate but coincidentally occurring conditions that, taken together, increase risk. Others contend that the underlying brain mechanisms that are thought to produce these conditions result in a pattern of behavior that itself increases risk for alcohol abuse and dependence—that is, that these behavior patterns are but separate manifestations of the same underlying condition. For example, of considerable current interest is a set of brain structures that are known to transmit impulses using the neurotransmitter dopamine. Animal researchers have identified these areas to be related to the mechanisms that cause organisms to move ahead in their environment, seeking reinforcement. For example, brain systems such as Wise's (Wise, 1988; Wise & Bozarth, 1987) dopaminergic ventral tegmental/nucleus acumbens system, Panksepp's (1990) foraging/expectancy system, Gray's (1990) behavioral activation system, and the incentive system of Stewart, deWit, and Eikelboom (1984) are variants on such mechanisms. At the human level, similar mechanisms have been related to thrill seeking, impulsive behavior, and even antisocial behavior, and more molecular dopaminergic characteristics (e.g., receptor types) have been suggested as one genetically influenced characteristic that may mediate expression of these behavioral patterns (see discussion by Zuckerman, 1994).

It is readily apparent how these behavioral patterns might relate to treatment outcome, either as separate comorbid conditions or as manifestations of the same brain mechanisms. To the extent that alcohol abuse (or other substance abuse) is accompanied by impulsive, irresponsible behavior, both getting individuals into treatment and maintaining them on a treatment program may be a considerable challenge. Furthermore, it is of course likely that other aspects of their lives will have been heavily influenced by these same behavior patterns, mostly in the negative direction. So, for example, an individual who is not receiving rewards from school and job success, from social relationships, from family, and so on and who may be overcoming problems from other kinds of deficit-inspired actions (problems with the law, in work settings, etc.) has considerably more to overcome, and possibly to be treated for, than just the excessive use of alcohol or other substances. The presence of these characteristics should probably also be taken into account when empirical validation is carried out; outcomes for these collections of problems may understandably not be the same as for purer instances of alcohol consumption problems.

Negative Affectivity

A second behavioral pattern thought to increase risk for alcohol abuse and dependence is negative affectivity, which consists of uncomfortable anxiety and possibly depression, or both together. This affective pattern is also thought to be regulated by a separate brain system that has some degree of genetic loading for its intrinsic level of activation (Gray, 1990). Individuals with higher levels of negative affectivity may use alcohol (or other drugs) primarily for their palliative effects. These characteristics are more likely to be viewed as comorbid with alcohol use, rather than as due to a common substrate, simply because this behavioral pattern is thought to lead, not to undercontrolled behavior, but instead to overcontrolled behavior. Hence, the use of substances is seen a means of achieving relief from discomfort. Variants of this "tension reduction" view are among the earliest psychological explanations for alcohol risk (Conger, 1956). Alcohol, however, has not been uniformly found to be a tension-reducing agent, although the parameters of its tension-reducing or "stress response-dampening" effects (Sher, 1987) are still being investigated. More molecular versions of these ideas are currently being investigated in relation to particular receptor systems (GABA and NMDA receptors) that may mediate some pleasure and fear reduction systems in the brain.

Once again, the treatment implications of these systems are obvious. Contrary to intuition, however, therapeutic techniques for reducing anxiety have not been terribly effective in treatment for alcohol abuse and dependence, perhaps because they have not been targeted to the correct patient groups. Reducing anxiety for individuals having impulse control problems might be contraindicated, or at least unhelpful.

Psychosocial Factors

Among the psychosocial risk factors that might be most important to consider in treatment planning are community norms for consumption practices and peer group influences. It would clearly be more difficult to modify drinking patterns in the context of a community that regarded alcohol use as not only acceptable but even required for social functioning. There are clear differences between various ethnic and religious groups as to these norms. For adolescents in particular, the more restricted version of the community— namely, the peer group—may exert the same sorts of influence. In these instances, successful treatment might require a social group shift.

OTHER ASSESSMENT ISSUES

A number of other issues that may relate to treatment planning must be considered in the early evaluation of the alcohol abuser or dependent individual. First, of course, is the severity of the problem. Individuals who are drinking almost constantly and who show the least ability to refrain from use even long enough to permit treatment may need a period of detoxification, perhaps followed by an inpatient stay. It must be remembered, however, that outpatient treatment has worked for even highly dependent individuals.

The time frame of the problem or, more important, the extent to which use has become an integrated portion of that individual's entire existence is also critical. The more that alcohol use has crowded out other life events, the more care must be taken to incorporate these events back into that person's life. Simply put, if an individual does not have much to do when not drinking, it will be more difficult for him or her to refrain from relapsing.

Because excessive alcohol use can result in cognitive impairment, individuals may not be in the best position to profit from the new learning required by treatment shortly after they cease drinking (Goldman, 1995). Waiting a few days after drinking ceases, particularly for older individuals, may prove useful (providing that abstention can be maintained). It has also been recently suggested that cognitive rehabilitation may add to the patient's ability to profit from treatment (Goldman, 1995). Evaluating a patient's own expectations about which treatments are likely to prove effective may be important. An individual who expects AA-type treatment as the most likely to be successful for him or her may do less well with a cognitive-behavioral program, for example.

An area of assessment that has received a good deal of attention in recent years is that of readiness for change. It has been suggested that individuals go through stages that represent their level of preparedness to engage in whatever may be necessary to achieve treatment success (Miller, 1995; Prochaska, DiClemente, & Norcross, 1992). The stages are *precontemplation*—the time before the person is even considering change; *contemplation*—the first dawning awareness that change may be necessary, along with a resistance to the requirements for change; *determination*—the point at which the internal debate tips in favor of change; *action*—the process of beginning to actually take steps to support the intention for change; *maintenance*—the most difficult and perhaps most long-lasting stage, during which the difficult process of resisting pressures to return to the abusive lifestyle must be continually maintained; and, finally, *relapse*—the process of slipping back to the problem lifestyle if maintenance fails. Hopefully, at this point, the individual returns to the beginning of the change process. Although this system by which change can be characterized has proven to be a useful heuristic for clinicians, it is not clear that there are clearly definable stages of change: That is, aspects of these supposedly distinct thought processes may overlap. More important, it remains unclear how to move an individual along the stages in this process. The reader is advised to consult Prochaska et al. (1992) for details about stages of change that go beyond the scope of this chapter.

EMPIRICALLY VALIDATED TREATMENTS
FOR ALCOHOL ABUSE AND DEPENDENCE

We now turn our attention to existing reviews of the empirically validated treatment literature in the field of alcohol abuse and dependence. It is not the intention of this review to provide a new evaluation of the treatment literature in light of either the criteria used by the Division 12 Task Force or the perspective of the APA Task Force on development of treatment guidelines. Reviews of this body of literature using the Division 12 criteria are currently being undertaken. In addition, as current president of Division 50 (Addictions), I have initiated an ongoing committee that will begin to evaluate all addiction treatments in accord with the APA template.

An additional reason for not attempting a definitive review at this point is that the results of Project MATCH will very shortly become available (see Donovan & Mattson, 1994). Project MATCH is a recently completed multisite consortium study that compares three treatment approaches for alcohol dependence, each as used in a full outpatient setting or as the aftercare strategy following standard inpatient or intensive day treatment. A version of AA-type treatment (12-step facilitation) was compared with cognitive-behavioral coping skills training and a motivational enhancement approach. All treatments were carefully manualized and carried out for 12 weeks at five outpatient settings and four aftercare sites. This project was funded by and designed in close collaboration with staff of the treatment research branch of the National Institute of Alcohol Abuse and Alcoholism (NIAAA) to represent state-of-the-art treatment and treatment evaluation. The intent was to collect data on sufficient numbers of participants so that the best matches between patient characteristics and treatment types could be evaluated on a post hoc basis: That is, patients were assigned to treatments randomly and not via a matching strategy. These treatments will be further discussed below. Given the scope of this project, there will undoubtedly be continued analysis and discussion over the next few years that will help refine our understanding of the best treatment approaches in the alcohol abuse and dependence field, and it would be premature at this time to draw conclusions based solely on the existing body of literature.

What is necessary to discuss at this point is two characteristics of Project MATCH that are present in an inconsistent fashion in those studies that make up the previously existing body of literature. These characteristics need to be considered carefully as part of the evaluation of the current status of empirical validation in this field. The first consideration is the use of highly detailed treatment manuals. If a broad definition of treatment manuals is permitted, many existing treatments may be considered manualized (consider, e.g., books closely associated with AA and the 12-step approach). Nevertheless, agreement about consistency of treatment would be difficult to reach within the current body of treatment research because of the variations in specificity of these "manuals." The second consideration is the comparison between alternative treatments, rather than just comparison to no-treatment controls. Because most treatments compare favorably to no treatment, empirical validation against an existing treatment is considerably more confidence inspiring, providing that the existing treatment has already received empirical support (otherwise, both treatments may be doing undetected harm). Within the alcohol abuse and dependence treatment literature, a number of treatments reach the level of evidence required by the Division

12 guidelines, and some have even been considered along the dimensions included as part of the clinical utility axis of the APA Template for Guideline Development.

Before reviewing some of the most validated treatments, it is important to make four points. First, the reader is advised to consult other recent reviews in this field that have been undertaken independently of either the Division 12 guidelines or the APA task force template (e.g., Emrick, Tonigan, Montgomery, & Little, 1993; Holder, Longabaugh, Miller, & Rubonis, 1991; Miller & Hester, 1986, 1989; Miller et al., 1995). Quite a large body of treatment evaluation literature now exists in this field, and these reviews have been carried out using systematic schemes for aggregating findings. Although these schemes do not match precisely the Division 12 or APA systems, they are quite informative as to the current state of the field. Second, the present review will not include treatments for which the body of findings is negative or nonexistent. Given the customary practice of more behaviorally oriented clinicians to carry out treatment evaluation research as a natural part of treatment development, more studies are available on these types of treatment. This tendency leaves room, however, for an important source of bias in the treatment research literature. Treatments tend to be empirically supported when research is undertaken by believers in that treatment. Such "allegiance effects" ultimately demand that evaluations be undertaken by researchers who are neutral or who even fall in a different treatment camp. This requirement appears in neither empirical validation system discussed in this chapter, but it is implicit in the clinical utility portion of the APA template. Third, although a treatment may be called by a particular name and may have many similarities to a treatment that appears in another validation study under the same name the specifics of those treatments may vary with the different investigator groups. Last—and this is true of all treatment research as it is currently performed—there is no guarantee that everyone who tries to use a particular treatment, even in manualized form, is necessarily good at it. Thus, for example, there may be highly effective medical-surgical treatments that in the right hands are quite successful but that in the wrong hands are unhelpful or even dangerous, even if described in detail in books. We currently do not evaluate the competence of particular providers to offer qualified treatment, and combining results from various groups may be unfair to some treatments. Of course, treatments with high reported rates of success may be sufficiently robust to overcome these differences between providers.

Brief Intervention

Among the more remarkable findings in the alcohol treatment literature is the observation that, contrary to intuition and most prevailing treatment practice up until very recently, treatment for alcohol dependence does not have to be carried out in an inpatient setting and does not need to be very extensive to have therapeutic impact (Miller & Hester, 1986). In fact, even extremely limited interventions carried out by primary care physicians during office visits for medical consultations have been shown to have significant effects (Heather, 1995).

Brief interventions typically include a comprehensive assessment, which not only gives treatment personnel the information on which to base the intervention but also renders the treatment personnel credible in the eyes of the treatment recipient. That is, feedback to the client, based on the information that the client just provided, has therapeutic salience. Following information gathering and feedback, the remainder of that single session may be used to define goals in life areas related to the drinking problem. It is then best if some follow-up system, even one as limited as mail inquiries or telephone calls, is used to remind the client of the plan. Such interventions make the most sense after detection of a problem in primary care settings and are not viable options in all cases. For example, they may not be useful when there is a need for detoxification, when there is other physical illness, or when the individual circumstances are potentially life threatening. Brief interventions would appear to rate high in clinical utility, although systematic evaluation of these dimensions has not been carried out except in relation to cost (Holder et al., 1991; Miller et al., 1995).

A variant on the brief intervention strategy is based on the recognition that many therapeutic procedures could assist individuals with alcohol problems if these individuals would only employ the procedures and stay with them. That is, if the individual's motivation for change could be enhanced, the specific treatment strategy might become less important. In fact, with sufficient motivation, the individual might develop his or her own strategies, as do the many individuals who stop drinking or other substance use (e.g., smoking) without any intervention. In many ways, the techniques associated with motivational enhancement are similar to traditional forms of therapy, in which relationship building, rapport enhancement, and learning to give feedback to the client in a way that could be accepted have always been central elements. In the alcohol field, however, the therapeutic approach traditionally has been to confront denial, sometimes in a rather harsh fashion. Such "interventions" have become common practice in alcohol treatment, even though they are contraindicated by the research findings (see Miller, 1995).

Social Skills Training

Social skills training is predicated on the notion that excessive drinkers often turn to alcohol in social situations because they do not know how to interact in such situations in the absence of alcohol and because they do not know how to say "no" to individuals in such circumstances who offer alcohol or even try to "force" alcohol on them. Hence, this approach emphasizes drink refusal skills, giving and receiving positive feedback and criticism (including about drinking itself), listening skills, conflict resolution skills, and developing social supports, as well as other skills of effective inter-personal interaction. These programs are usually delivered in a very structured manner (see Monti, Rohsenow, Colby, & Abrams, 1995). Overall, the empirical evidence for these approaches is quite strong from an efficacy point of view (Miller et al., 1995). They have not been sufficiently reviewed from the perspective of clinical utility.

Community Reinforcement

Community reinforcement refers to the enlistment of a drinker's entire social and work environment so as to provide rewards for behavior that does not include drinking and nonreinforcement of drinking behavior (Smith & Meyers, 1995). This is not a therapeutic approach that resembles classical therapy but rather is an environmental manipulation that alters the drinking context. A small number of studies support this approach from an efficacy perspective (see Miller et al., 1995), but the clinical utility of this strategy seems limited because it is very costly and difficult to carry out for most drinkers in the real world (i.e., it is difficult to reorder most environments to the extent necessary for successful outcomes).

Behavioral Techniques

A number of techniques typically included within the general category of behavioral approaches have received some support (see Miller et al., 1995, for review). Behavior contracting, or the establishment of specific goals and the reinforcement of successive approximations to these goals, has been supported, as has the use of self-help manuals that codify many cognitive-behavioral approaches in a form that the drinker can use directly. The closely related approach of behavioral self-control training has received support, although it has not always been found to be more effective than briefer approaches. Aversive procedures such as covert sensitization and nausea aversion have received mixed support, but electrical aversion has received sufficient instances of negative findings so as to be recommended for discontinuation. Relapse prevention, or the application of largely behavioral techniques toward the goal of anticipating and minimizing the negative effects of slips and lapses, has also received mixed support, as has more purely cognitive therapy, in the form recommended by Beck, Wright, Newman, and Liese (1993). Behaviorally oriented marital therapy has received mixed support, although the preponderance of evidence has been positive; marital therapy that is not based on behavioral techniques has not been supported.

Not all behavioral techniques have been supported, however. For example, relaxation training performed in the absence of a more comprehensive treatment program has not been supported. Interestingly, the exclusive use of antianxiety medication has also not been supported. Evidently, anxiety reduction alone is not sufficient to treat alcohol problems, despite common conceptions of alcohol abuse and dependence as related to the negative affectivity dimension described earlier.

Client-Centered Therapy

Interestingly, classical Rogerian client-centered therapy has received support, perhaps for the same reasons that motivational enhancement approaches have had success (Miller et al., 1995). That is, both approaches are based on building a trusting and supportive relationship with the drinker and allowing the drinker's motivation to emerge from the therapeutic interaction. These approaches contrast with the confrontational approach implicit in the concept of the "intervention."

Other Treatments

A number of other treatments have been investigated for alcohol abuse and dependence but have received decidedly mixed or negative reviews.

Some other treatments have not yet reached the Division 12 criterion of two positive studies performed by independent investigators. As noted by Miller et al. (1995), it is remarkable that the list of treatments reported to have little effect includes those that are dispensed to the vast majority of treated individuals in the United States. Included in this group are studies on AA itself (Miller et al., 1995, listed only two studies on AA, which turned out to be nonsupportive of this approach) and treatments commonly administered by alcohol and drug treatment agencies, which are most often highly associated with AA principles. As noted earlier, this inconsistency represents the clearest form of conflict between efficacy validation and validation of clinical utility. Many reasons for this inconsistency can be imagined, some having to do with the much greater room for variation in technique that could be called AA based, or "standard alcoholism treatment." Because those providing these services are not likely to also be researchers (as are many of those who have offered and tested cognitive-behavioral treatments), allegiance effects could be an important source of inconsistency. Perhaps the soon-to-be-available findings of Project MATCH will prove helpful in this regard, but it can be anticipated that there will also be questions that will underscore the difficulty of trying to design single studies, no matter how large or carefully executed, to provide definitive answers. Recent controversy over the findings of the national collaborative study on depression is a case in point (see Jacobson & Hollon, 1996).

The field looks forward to the results of Project MATCH with great anticipation, and undoubtedly more definitive statements about efficacy will be made on the release of these findings. But we may also anticipate some of the major sources of controversy that underscore the limitations of any single study, regardless of scope, as it must be carried out in the real world. Leaving aside some of the common debates about treatment studies of this type (e.g., awkwardness of manualized treatments, statistical vs. clinical significance, site differences), some characteristics particular to treatment in the alcohol field are worthy of note. First, unlike treatments for anxiety and depression, in which patients are most often eager participants, the key element in treatment for alcohol problems centers on engagement of the patient in treatment (note the core premise of motivational enhancement). Major studies of this type are filled with repeated assessments carried out by research personnel, include procedures designed to help retain patients to reduce attrition, and have personnel who feel part of a special, important project and whose casual contact with patients is, in many ways, dictated as part of the patient protocol. Hence, a much richer form of all treatments is provided than is typically available in real-world settings. Second, because these treatments were offered in sites that provided treatment independently of the study, there was most likely already a treatment ambiance in some or all sites that included AA-based philosophy. Hence, the 12-step treatment might be enhanced by the background availability of a consistent treatment philosophy, and the other treatments might be at some conflict with this ambiance. On the other hand, some important aspects of the AA approach (the spiritual component and the urging of mutual help and fellowship) are difficult to manualize, in comparison to the more definable components of the other two approaches. And, perhaps most important, the 12-step treatment in Project MATCH was delivered on an individual basis, unlike the group format that is almost the defining characteristic of the AA approach. Hence, regardless of how the results turn out, proponents of any of the approaches will have a reason to question the results.

CONCLUSION

This chapter, and the other reviews referenced in this chapter, can provide an immediate guideline for practitioners looking for empirically validated treatments of alcohol abuse and dependence. On the basis of the review conducted in this chapter, which was in large part based on ongoing reviews by Miller and his colleagues (see Miller et al., 1995), practitioners working with alcoholic patients can have some confidence in the following treatment models: brief intervention, social skills training, motivational enhancement, community reinforcement, behavior contracting, aversion therapy (nausea), client-centered therapy, relapse prevention, self-help manuals, and cognitive therapy. The treatments least supported by currently available evidence are educational lectures/films, alcoholism "counseling," unspecified "psycho-therapy," confrontational counseling, relaxation training (in the absence of other treatment components), video self-confrontation, and unspecified "standard" treatment. Of course, the field awaits further evidence in the form of the Division 12 report on validated treatments for these conditions, as well as the results of Project MATCH, to help advance the process of validation. Review of these treatments in accord with the APA Task Force criteria also is essential.

NOTE

1. This report is available from the Practice Directorate at the American Psychological Association, 750 First Street, NE, Washington, DC, 20002-4242.

REFERENCES

American Psychiatric Association. (1994). *Diagnostic and statistical manual of mental disorders* (4th ed.). Washington, DC: Author.

American Psychological Association. (1995, July). *Template for developing guidelines: Interventions for mental disorders and psychosocial aspects of physical disorders.* Washington, DC: Author.

Beck, A. T., Wright, F. D., Newman, C. F., & Liese, B. S. (1993). *Cognitive therapy of substance abuse.* New York: Guilford.

Conger, J. J. (1956). Reinforcement theory and the dynamics of alcoholism. *Quarterly Journal of Studies on Alcohol, 17,* 296-305.

Chapman, L. J., & Chapman, J. P. (1967). The genesis of popular but erroneous psychodiagnostic observations. *Journal of Abnormal Psychology, 72,* 193-204.

Donovan, D. M., & Mattson, M. E. (1994). Alcoholism treatment matching research: Methodological and clinical issues. *Journal of Studies on Alcohol, 55*(Suppl. 12), 5-14.

Emrick, C. D., Tonigan, J. S., Montgomery, H., & Little, L. (1993). Alcoholics Anonymous: What is currently known? In B. S. McCrady & W. R. Miller (Eds.), *Research on Alcoholics Anonymous: Opportunities and alternatives* (pp. 41-76). New Brunswick, NJ: Rutgers Center of Alcohol Studies.

Golding, S. L., & Rorer, L. G. (1972). Illusory correlation and subjective judgment. *Journal of Abnormal Psychology, 80,* 249-260.

Goldman, M. S. (1995). Recovery of cognitive functioning in alcoholics: The relationship to treatment. *Alcohol Health and Research World, 19,* 148-154.

Gray, J. A. (1990). Brain systems that mediate both emotion and cognition. In J. A. Gray (Ed.), *Psychobiological aspects of relationships between emotion and cognition* (pp. 269-288). Hillsdale, NJ: Lawrence Erlbaum.

Heather, N. (1995). Brief intervention strategies. In R. K. Hester & W. R. Miller (Eds.), *Handbook of alcoholism treatment approaches: Effective alternatives* (2nd ed., pp. 105-122). Needham Heights, MA: Allyn & Bacon.

Holder, H., Longabaugh, R., Miller, W. R., & Rubonis, A. V. (1991). The cost-effectiveness for treatment of alcoholism: A first approximation. *Journal of Studies on Alcohol, 52,* 517-540.

Jacobson, N. S., & Hollon, S. D. (1996). Cognitive-behavior therapy versus pharmacotherapy: Now that the jury's returned its verdict, it's time to present the rest of the evidence. *Journal of Consulting and Clinical Psychology, 64,* 74-80.

Klein, D. F. (1996). Preventing hung juries about therapy studies. *Journal of Consulting and Clinical Psychology, 64,* 81-87.

Miller, W. R. (1995). Increasing motivation for change. In R. K. Hester & W. R. Miller (Eds.), *Handbook of alcoholism treatment approaches: Effective alternatives* (2nd ed., pp. 89-104). Needham Heights, MA: Allyn & Bacon.

Miller, W. R., Brown, J. M., Simpson, T. L., Handmaker, N. S., Bien, T. H., Luckie, L. F., Montgomery, H. A., Hester, R. K., & Tonigan, J. S. (1995). What works? A methodological analysis of the alcoholism treatment outcome literature. In R. K. Hester & W. R. Miller (Eds.), *Handbook of alcoholism treatment approaches: Effective alternatives* (2nd ed., pp. 12-44). Needham Heights, MA: Allyn & Bacon.

Miller, W. R., & Hester, R. K. (1986). Inpatient alcoholism treatment: Who benefits? *American Psychologist, 41,* 794-805.

Miller, W. R., & Hester, R. K. (1989). Inpatient alcoholism treatment: Rules of evidence and burden of proof. *American Psychologist, 44,* 1245-1246.

Monti, P. M., Rohsenow, D. J., Colby, S. M., & Abrams, L. (1995). Coping and social skills training In R. K. Hester & W. R. Miller (Eds.), *Handbook of alcoholism treatment approaches: Effective alternatives* (2nd ed., pp. 221-241). Needham Heights, MA: Allyn & Bacon.

Newlin, D. B., & Thomson, J. B. (1990). Alcohol challenge with sons of alcoholics: A critical review and analysis. *Psychological Bulletin, 108,* 383-402.

Panksepp, J. (1990). Gray zones at the emotion/cognition interface: A commentary. In J. A. Gray (Ed.), *Psychobiological aspects of relationships between emotion and cognition* (pp. 289-302). Hillsdale, NJ: Lawrence Erlbaum.

Prochaska, J. O., DiClemente, C. C., & Norcross, J. C. (1992). In search of how people change: Applications to addictive behaviors. *American Psychologist, 47,* 1102-1114.

Psychotherapy: Does it work? (1995). *Consumer Reports, 60,* 734-739.

Schuckit, M. A. (1987). Biological vulnerability to alcoholism. *Journal of Consulting and Clinical Psychology, 55,* 301-309.

Sher, K. J. (1987). Stress response dampening. In H. T. Blane & K. E. Leonard (Eds.), *Psychological theories of drinking and alcoholism.* New York: Guilford.

Sher, K. J. (1991). *Children of alcoholics: A critical appraisal of theory and research.* Chicago: University of Chicago Press.

Sher, K., & Trull, T. (1994). Personality and disinhibitory psychology: Alcoholism and antisocial personality disorder. *Journal of Abnormal Psychology, 103,* 92-102.

Smith, J. E., & Meyers, R. J. (1995). The community reinforcement approach. In R. K. Hester & W. R. Miller (Eds.), *Handbook of alcoholism treatment approaches: Effective alternatives* (2nd ed.). Needham Heights, MA: Allyn & Bacon.

Special feature. (1996). *Journal of Consulting and Clinical Psychology, 64,* 74-108.

Stewart, J., deWit, H., & Eikelboom, R. (1984). Role of unconditioned and conditioned drug effects in the self-administration of opiates and stimulants. *Psychological Review, 91,* 251-268.

Task Force on Promotion and Dissemination of Psychological Procedures. (1995). Training in and dissemination of empirically-validated treatments. *Clinical Psychologist, 48*(1), 3-23.

Wise, R. A. (1988). The neurobiology of craving: Implications for the understanding and treatment of addiction. *Journal of Abnormal Psychology, 97,* 118-132.

Wise, R. A., & Bozarth, M. A. (1987). A psychomotor stimulant theory of addiction. *Psychological Review, 94,* 469-492.

Zuckerman, M. (1994). *Behavioral expressions and biological bases of sensation seeking.* New York: Cambridge University Press.

11

Empirically Validated Treatments for Sexual Dysfunction

JULIA R. HEIMAN

CINDY M. MESTON

Although there might be a number of reasons to identify and evaluate empirically validated treatments, the two most obvious have to do with developing standards of practice and addressing political and economic expediencies. Both of these reasons have mixed implications for the treatment of sexual dysfunctions. With respect to clinical standards, clinicians and researchers have a responsibility to stimulate new ideas for treatment, particularly for those dysfunctions that are poorly researched, while being careful about accepting fringe treatments simply because they are new and unusual. An example of the latter might be that for some time during the 1970s it was recommended that walking nude in the desert and picking out desirable fruit could be therapeutic (Hartman & Fithian, 1970, 1971). Regarding the second point of political or economic pressures to develop

AUTHORS' NOTE: This chapter is based on material presented at the Banff Conference, Best Practice: Developing and Promoting Empirically Validated Interventions, Banff, Alberta, Canada. March 17 to 20, 1996.

259

validated treatments, if sexual dysfunctions are considered unimportant health issues, insurance policies certainly will not provide resources for supporting patients to receive treatment for these disorders. The valuation of sexual disorders directly and indirectly affects funding for research, which in turn affects the availability of controlled studies.

OVERVIEW: EMPIRICAL VALIDATION OF SEXUAL DYSFUNCTION TREATMENTS

If we use the definition of empirically validated treatments given by the American Psychological Association (APA) Task Force (APA, 1995), almost no treatments for sexual dysfunctions conform to all of the criteria of "well-established treatments": (a) group studies by different investigators demonstrating efficacy by comparison to pill or psychological placebo or (b) a large series of well-designed single-case studies demonstrating efficacy, with (c) treatment manuals and (d) clear specification of client samples. The specific weaknesses in sexual dysfunction research fall into predictable areas. One problem is that treatment manuals are rather uncommon for the treatment of sexual problems, at least in the form that we have come to know them. A second reason for the lack of empirically validated treatment is the lack of control groups. Clinical researchers have, for ethical reasons, preferred waiting-list controls over placebos, and reasonably efficacious alternative treatments have not been available for most of the dysfunctions. A third issue is the overwhelming and widespread impact of the Masters and Johnson (1970) text. More controlled research was delayed by the fact that there were no readily comparable treatments with competitive success rates, except for systematic desensitization, that seemed legitimate to offer as serious alternatives to Masters and Johnson's approach. Never before or since have so many individuals ($N = 792$) with sexual problems been treated with such clearly described treatment techniques and with such a high success rate (overall 15% failure rate), including a 5-year follow-up (Masters & Johnson, 1970). Though methodological problems are clearly present in Masters and Johnson's work, particularly the use of only one therapist-generated nonstandardized item to measure outcome, its impact truly brought sexual dysfunction research into the forefront so that increasingly systematic research could eventually be designed.

An additional issue that has affected the engagement of researchers in controlled outcome studies in sexual dysfunction is the availability of funding for research. Sexual disorders, with the possible exception of violent sexual offender treatment, have not been a priority for funding, particularly at the costly level of outcome research projects. As a result, projects more modest in size and design complexity dominate the outcome literature.

The present chapter evaluates the status of sexual dysfunction treatments with respect to the evidence for validation. The text provides a discussion of treatment comparison and own-control studies and summarizes the results, and the tables specify study details. We have included as many studies as we could locate that have been published in English. With this material, we intend for the reader to become well informed regarding the strength and weaknesses of the research on treatment effectiveness for sexual dysfunction, and we hope to stimulate new approvals and further documentation of treatment effectiveness.

RATES OF SEXUAL DYSFUNCTION

Sexual dysfunctions are relatively common, though studies documenting their prevalence using random sampling techniques are scarce. The Laumann, Gagnon, Michael, and Michaels (1994) study is the only national random U.S. probability sample available on this topic. Selected results are presented in Table 11.1.

Known as the National Health and Social Life Survey (NHSLS), the Laumann et al. study was based on a sample size of 3,432 men and women aged 18 to 59 and a response rate of nearly 80%. A combination of face-to-face interviews and self-administered questionnaires (for very sensitive questions and reliability checks) were administered to assess sexual problems within the past 12 months. The sample's most common problems for women were lack of sexual interest (33%, figures rounded) and inability to orgasm (24%). For men, climaxing too early (29%), anxiety about performance (17%), and lack of sexual interest (17%) were the most frequently reported problems. Age effects were apparent, though less dramatic than expected: There was little age-related increase or decrease between ages 18 and 59 among men who reported climaxing too early or orgasmic inability; for women, there was little change in lack of sexual interest or in orgasmic inability. Increased education was typically associated with fewer sexual

TABLE 11.1 Sexual Dysfunction Percentages, Based on a Random Sample of 3,432 Individuals, Aged 18 to 59, Interviewed Between 1991 and 1992

	Sexual Dysfunction (Men/Women)							
	Pain During Sex	Sex Not Pleasurable	Unable to Orgasm	Lacked Interest in Sex	Anxiety About Performance	Climax Too Early	Unable to Keep an Erection (Men)	Had Trouble Lubricating (Women)
Overall (N = 1,346/1,622)	3.0/14.4	8.1/21.2	8.3/24.1	15.8/33.3	17.0/11.5	28.5/10.3	10.4	18.8
Marital Status (N = 1,341/1,613)								
Married	2.8/14.4	6.0/20.5	7.7/21.9	11.8/29.4	13.9/9.7	30.2/9.2	9.6	21.6
Never married	2.8/14.9	9.7/23.0	8.7/26.6	20.0/37.3	18.5/15.3	25.7/13.4	9.9	15.0
Divorced	3.8/13.9	11.4/22.2	9.1/28.6	18.2/39.4	27.4/13.1	32.5/10.8	14.6	16.6
Education (N = 1,342/1,614)								
Less than HS	4.6/16.1	14.7/25.8	12.7/30.0	22.3/43.2	23.2/16.2	36.0/17.4	15.4	14.0
HS graduate	4.1/16.8	5.7/22.2	8.2/28.0	13.2/35.4	17.3/11.8	32.5/11.7	9.5	19.5
Finished college	2.2/9.6	6.6/18.4	6.5/19.1	15.7/27.9	10.9/8.3	25.8/6.2	9.1	19.3
Master's/adv. deg.	1.7/9.3	5.2/16.5	6.8/13.3	13.3/23.4	14.5/13.3	24.1/4.1	9.3	23.7
Race/Ethnicity (N = 1,342/1,623)								
White	3.0/14.7	7.0/19.7	7.4/23.2	14.7/30.9	16.8/10.5	27.7/7.5	9.9	20.7
Black	3.3/12.5	15.2/30.0	9.9/29.2	20.0/44.5	23.7/14.5	33.8/20.4	14.5	13.0
Hispanic	2.0/13.6	8.2/19.8	10.9/20.3	16.7/34.6	7.1/11.7	25.0/18.4	8.9	12.0
Income (N = 1,098/1,297)								
Poor	5.5/16.2	15.3/23.3	15.9/27.4	25.4/39.7	20.5/20.0	29.7/18.2	14.0	13.9
Middle	2.8/14.5	6.0/21.5	7.2/23.6	13.0/32.0	15.3/10.2	28.0/10.6	9.1	19.0
Rich	1.9/11.4	9.1/17.3	6.1/20.8	15.0/27.5	14.2/11.7	30.3/4.4	11.3	23.7

SOURCE: Adapted from Laumann et al. (1994).

problems, with the exception of lubrication disorders in women, for which fewer symptoms were associated with less education. With respect to race/ethnicity, a higher percentage of black men and women reported dysfunctions compared to other groups, with the exception of fewer difficulties for black men and women on orgasm variables and fewer lubrication problems for black women (see Laumann et al., 1994, pp. 368-374, for more details).

SEXUAL DYSFUNCTIONS
REPORTED BY WOMEN

Orgasmic Dysfunctions

As is evident from the preceding section citing the NHSLS, orgasmic disorders are common conditions among women and remain fairly constant across each 5-year age group between 18 and 59 (with a range from 19% at ages 45 to 49 to 28% at ages 30 to 34). By contrast, data from the same national sample showed that 29% of the women reported always being orgasmic with their partner, 41% reported being extremely physically satisfied with their partner, and 39% reported being extremely emotionally satisfied with their partner (Laumann et al., 1994). Although previous studies have not consistently shown socioeconomic status to be related to women's orgasmic experiences, the NHSLS found that low-income women were somewhat more likely to report inability to orgasm than those classified as high income (27% vs. 21%) and that women with less than a high school education reported greater orgasmic incapacity than those who had finished college (30% vs. 19%). Master's-level and advanced-degree women reported a comparably low orgasmic inability of 13%. One must be cautious about interpreting these results as indicative of only primary orgasmic dysfunction. The question posed was whether, in the past 12 months, there had ever been a period of several months or more when the inability to have an orgasm had been a problem. Because some of the women concerned may have had orgasms before the 12-month point, it is likely that this category includes women with both primary and secondary anorgasmia.

Several other sources corroborate the point that primary and secondary orgasmic disorders are common among women (Hawton, 1982; Heiman & Grafton-Becker, 1989; Spector & Carey, 1990). Here we shall use *primary anorgasmia* to refer to lifelong and global anorgasmia and *secondary anorgasmia* to refer to situational or acquired lack of orgasm. This terminology is comparable to that of the fourth edition of the *Diagnostic and Statistical Manual of Mental Disorders* (*DSM-IV;* American Psychiatric Association, 1994), with the addition of the use of *primary* and *secondary* as summary labels.

Treatments for primary anorgasmia appear to fulfill the criteria of "well established," whereas secondary anorgasmia studies fall into the "probably efficacious" group. Table 11.2 summarizes the research that we located on this topic, including case studies, single-group designs, own-control and wait-list control group designs, and treatment comparison studies. We will discuss primary and secondary anorgasmia separately, though several studies combine the two groups.

Primary anorgasmia has been most frequently treated with the techniques of sensate focus, desensitization, and/or directed masturbation exercises. Before the interventions developed in the last 30 years, there is no research documentation that psychoanalytically oriented psychotherapy was successful in treating this problem. *Sensate focus* exercises were the development of Masters and Johnson (1970) and consist of exchanging physical caresses, moving from nonsexual to increasingly sexual touching of one another's bodies over the course of assigned sensual experiences at home. These techniques are described in Masters and Johnson's 1970 book. Conceptually, sensate focus exercises can be seen, though the authors did not so label them, as a modified *in vivo* desensitization using relaxation to counter anxious feelings and gradually introducing more sexually arousing actions. Masters and Johnson reported an 84% success rate among 193 primary anorgasmic couples (note that they actually reported the converse 16% "failure rate") who experienced orgasm at the end of 14 sessions. The success rate dropped to 82% at 5-year follow-up.

A number of controlled studies have used *systematic desensitization* to treat primary anorgasmia. This intervention is typically used when anxiety plays a significant role in maintaining the sexual disorder. As can be seen from Table 11.2, sexual anxiety typically decreases with the administration of systematic densensitization without a subsequent increase in orgasmic capacity. This effect suggests that in most cases anxiety does not necessarily play a causal role in orgasmic disorders.

Treatments involving *directed masturbation* consist of a series of at-home exercises that begin with visual and tactile total body exploration and move

(text continues on page 273)

TABLE 11.2 Orgasmic Dysfunction

Study	N	Subject Characteristics	Treatment Type	No. of Sessions	Outcome	Follow-up
Treatment Comparison Controlled Outcome Studies						
Husted (1972, 1975)	30	Mixed sexual dysfunction; all with partners; sexual anxiety	SD: Imaginal (I) vs. (C); vs. *in vivo* (I) vs. (C) vs. no-treatment control	Imaginal, *M* = 8 sessions; *in vivo*, *M* = 13 sessions	SD: decreased anxiety, increased coital frequency and orgasmic ability with masturbation; no difference (I) vs. (C) or imaginal vs. *in vivo*	
Obler (1973)	37	Mixed sexual dysfunction; marital status matched across groups; absence of psychopathology	SD with videotapes (I) vs. psychoanalytic tx with videotapes (G) vs. WL	SD: 15 45-min sessions; Psychoanalytic: 10 75-min sessions	SD: 85% orgasmic Psychoanalytic: 36% orgasmic WL: 23% orgasmic SD > psychoanalytic, WL on decreased anxiety	
Heinrich (1976)	44	*M* age = 25; prim; 20 married, 24 with regular partner	DM (G) vs. DM bibliotherapy (I) vs. WL	DM: 10 sessions/5 wk; DM bibliotherapy: 1 session		2 mo: DM: 100% om, 47% co. DM bibliotherapy: 47% om, 13% co. WL: 21% om, 0% co. No difference between groups on self-esteem, marital adjustment
Mathews et al. (1976)	18	*M* age = 28; 13 prim, 5 sec; 17/18 low sexual desire/arousal	SD, sexual tx (C) vs. SF, sexual tx (C) vs. SF, bibliotherapy (C)	10 sessions; 3 sessions and 10 wk mailing for SF, bibliotherapy	2/18 increased orgasmic ability; no difference between groups	4 mo: no difference between groups
Wincze & Caird (1976)	21	18-38 yo; 16 prim, 5 sec; married; sexual anxiety; absence of psychopathology or medical problems	SD: Imaginal (I) vs. SD video (I) vs. WL	*M* = 10 sessions/ 2-7 wk	SD: 18% orgasmic, decreased anxiety; no difference between imaginal/video	1-3 mo: 25% orgasmic

265

(continued)

TABLE 11.2 Continued

Study	N	Subject Characteristics	Treatment Type	No. of Sessions	Outcome	Follow-up
Carney et al. (1978)	32	19-36 yo; sec; sexual anxiety	SF weekly: testosterone (T) vs. diazepam (C) vs. SF monthly: T vs. diazepam (C)	SF weekly: 16 sessions SF monthly: 5 sessions	No difference in orgasmic ability between weekly vs. monthly T > diazepam frequency of orgasm, vaginal lubrication, sexual satisfaction	6 mo (after drug discontinuation): gains maintained
Nemetz et al. (1978)	22	21-39 yo; 7 prim, 15 sec; sexual anxiety; all with regular partners	SD (I) vs. SD (G) vs. control	5 sessions/3 wk	SD (G) > SD (I), control on decreased anxiety; no difference between groups on orgasmic ability	3 wk; 1 yr: gains maintained
O'Gorman (1978)	40	M age = 36; low sexual desire/arousal, some dysparuenia/vaginismus	SD, sex education (G), partner-only discussion groups vs. SD, intravenous methoxitone sodium to induce relaxation (I with partner participation)	SD (G) 20 1-hr sessions; SD (I) 15 10-min sessions/10 wk	SD, sex education (G): 63% successful; SD, methoxitone sodium (I): 47% successful	
Riley & Riley (1978)	37	M age = 26; prim; married	DM and SF (C) vs. SF (C)	6 weekly and 6 bimonthly sessions	DM and SF: 18/20 orgasmic; SF: 8/15 orgasmic	1 yr: gains maintained
McMullen & Rosen (1979)	60	M age = 29; prim 30 married, 30 single	DM bibliotherapy (I) vs. DM instructional videotape (I) vs. WL	6 sessions/6 wk	Bibliotherapy: 65% orgasmic with masturbation (om), 50% coitally orgasmic (co). Instructional: 55% om, 30% co. WL: 0% om, 0% co	1 yr: gains maintained/improved

Study	n	Subject characteristics	Treatment	Duration	Results	Follow-up
Andersen (1981)	30	M age = 25; prim; 25 married, all with regular partners; some sexual aversion	SD (G) vs. DM (G) vs. WL	10 sessions/5 wk	No difference between SD and DM on self-acceptance, sexual anxiety; DM > SD, WL on orgasmic response	6 wk: SD > DM on self-acceptance; DM > SD on orgasmic response
Fichten et al. (1983)	23	M age = 33; sec; M yr married = 10	Sexual information, relaxation, Kegel ex, DM, SF, sexual communication training, ban on si: (C) vs. (G) vs. minimal contact bibliotherapy	14 wk	SF: significant increase in enjoyment of noncoital sexual caressing and si, no change in orgasmic responsiveness	
Kilmann et al. (1986)	55	M age = 33; sec; 51 married; all with partners; no dyspareunia or vaginismus, no premature ejaculation in partners	2 2-hr sessions sex education followed by communication skills (C/G) vs. sexual skills (C/G) vs. WL vs. attn-placebo		Communication and sexual skills > controls: increased frequency si and sexual satisfaction; no difference between groups	6 mo: gains decreased; no difference between groups
Morokoff & LoPiccolo (1986)	43	M age = 30; prim; M yr married = 9; no male sexual dysfunction, no psychosis or depression	Minimal therapist contact (MTC; n = 14) (C) vs. full therapist contact (FTC; n = 29) (C)	MTC: 4 sessions FTC: 15 sessions	Increased orgasmic ability during masturbation and si, increased sexual satisfaction; MTC > FTC on increased frequency orgasm during masturbation	
Kilmann et al. (1987)	11	M age = 30; 10 married; sec; no premature ejaculation in partners	2 2-hr sessions sex education followed by communication and sexual skills vs. WL vs. attn-placebo		Tx > WL, attn-placebo: significant increase in orgasmic ability	

(continued)

TABLE 11.2 Continued

Study	N	Subject Characteristics	Treatment Type	No. of Sessions	Outcome	Follow-up
Milan et al. (1988)	38	M age = 33; sec: M yr relationship = 10; regular sexual partners with no sexual dysfunction	Sex education plus either communication skills vs. sexual skills vs. condensed sex and communication skills vs. didactic lecture vs. WL	10 2-hr sessions/5 wk		2-6 yr: no difference between treatment groups, WL on sexual or relationship functioning
Hurlbert & Apt (1995)	36	M age = 28: 6 prim, 30 sec: M yr married = 5	Coital alignment technique (CAT) (C) (n = 19) vs. DM (C) (n = 17)	4 30-min sessions plus 4 10-min telephone contacts	CAT: 56% increased orgasmic ability during si; DM: 27% increased orgasmic ability during si	
Own-Control or Wait-List Controlled Outcome Studies						
Munjack et al. (1976)	22	12 prim, 10 sec	SD, DM, assertiveness training, modeling, sexual education (I/C) vs. WL	22 weekly sessions	Tx > WL orgasmic ability; no difference between prim and sec	
Sotile & Kilmann (1978)	22	M age = 27; 8 prim, 14 sec; all with partners; sexual anxiety	Sexual education followed by SD (G) or WL	16 sessions/ 8 wk	Decreased sexual anxiety, increased sexual satisfaction, increased noncoital orgasmic frequency; sec > prim orgasmic frequency	6 wk: orgasmic gains maintained, sexual satisfaction decreased
Heiman & LoPiccolo (1983)	41	M age = 30; 25 prim, 16 sec, absence of psychosis, depression, or severe marital distress	CBT, communication training, DM, SF, systems conceptualization (C) vs. WL	15/1-hr sessions	Prim and sec: increased duration foreplay and si; Prim: increased frequency si, increased orgasmic response during masturbation and si; Sec: increased orgasmic response during si, increased initiation of sexual activity	3 mo: prim: gains maintained sec: orgasmic gains maintained, decreased duration foreplay and si

Study	N	Sample	Treatment	Sessions	Results	Follow-up
LoPiccolo et al. (1985)	31	M age = 35; 12 prim, 19 sec; M yr married = 13	CBT sexual therapy (LoPiccolo & Hogan, 1979) vs. WL (C)	15 1-hr sessions	Prim and sec: significant increase in orgasmic ability with masturbation	3 mo: gains maintained/improved

No-Control Outcome Studies

Study	N	Sample	Treatment	Sessions	Results	Follow-up
Lazarus (1963)	16	M age = 25; married; some decreased desire/arousal	SD (I)	M = 29 sessions/6 mo	9/16 "nearly always achieve orgasm"	15 mo (4 patients): gains maintained or improved
Cooper (1970)	50	Coitally anorgasmic	In vivo SD, sex education, psychotherapy (I)	21 sessions/1 yr	24/50 coitally orgasmic 26/50 unchanged or worse	
Masters & Johnson (1970)	342 (1959-1964)	193 prim; 11 masturbatory dys; 106 coital dys; 32 random	Sex education, SF, communication training, in vivo SD (C)	14 sessions/daily	Prim: 83% orgasmic; masturbatory: 91% orgasmic; coital: 80% orgasmic; random: 63% orgasmic	5 yr: prim 1% relapse; sec 2% relapse
Jones & Park (1972)	55	Prim; anxiety; sexual shame	SD with Brevital injections to induce relaxation (I with partner participation)	M = 14 sessions	82% orgasmic, decreased sexual anxiety; increased sexual communication	Anxiety returned to pretreatment levels
LoPiccolo & Lobitz (1972)	8	Prim; married	DM (I)	15 sessions	8/8 orgasmic with masturbation; 6/8 coitally orgasmic	6 mo: gains maintained
Lobitz & LoPiccolo (1972)	13	Prim; married	DM (I with partner participation)	15 sessions	13/13 orgasmic with masturbation; 13/13 coitally orgasmic 50% of time	
Barbach (1974)	83	19-48 yo	DM (G)	10 sessions/5 wk	91% orgasmic with masturbation	
Wallace & Barbach (1974)	17 (of the 83 above)	M age = 27; 11/17 married; all with partners	DM (G)	10 sessions/5 wk	100% orgasmic with masturbation; 87% orgasmic with partner	8 mo: gains maintained

(continued)

TABLE 11.2 Continued

Study	N	Subject Characteristics	Treatment Type	No. of Sessions	Outcome	Follow-Up
McGovern et al. (1975)	12	6 prim, 6 sec	Sexual and communication skills training, anxiety reduction, DM	15 sessions	Increased sexual and marital satisfaction, prim: 6/6 increased orgasmic ability, sec: no change in orgasmic ability	
Schneidman & McGuire (1976)	20	10 < 35 yo, 10 > 35 yo; prim	Variation of Masters & Johnson (sexual education, group discussions, DM, couples tx) (C)	10 wk	< 35 yo: 70% orgasmic during masturbation, 0/10 coitally orgasmic; > 30 yo: 40% orgasmic during masturbation, 1/10 coitally orgasmic	6 mo: < 35 yo: 80% orgasmic during masturbation, none orgasmic during si; > 30 yo: 60% orgasmic during masturbation, 1/10 orgasmic during si
Kirkpatrick et al. (1977)	4		DM (G)		4/4 orgasmic during masturbation, 3/4 coitally orgasmic	
Leiblum & Ersner-Hershfield (1977)	16	23-43 yo; 12 married	DM (G)	8 sessions/8 wk	80% orgasmic with masturbation, increased assertiveness, body attitude	
Sotile et al. (1977)	6	3 prim, 3 sec	Sexual and communication skill training, sexual education, SF, DM, Kegel ex, role-play orgasm (C)	6 1½-hr sessions	Decreased sexual anxiety, increased sexual communication	
Ersner-Hershfield & Kopel (1979)	22	M age = 26	DM: spaced vs. massed sessions (GI) vs. DM: spaced vs. massed sessions (GC)	10 sessions/5 wk	91% orgasmic with masturbation, 73% orgasmic with partner; no difference GI vs. GC or spaced vs. massed sessions	10 wk: 82% orgasmic with partner

270

Study	N	Subject characteristics	Treatment	Duration	Outcome	Follow-up
Barbach & Flaherty (1980)	26	Sec	DM, communication training (I)	10 1½-hr sessions		1-2 yr: 60% increased orgasmic frequency with partners
Kuriansky et al. (1982)	19	M age = 30	SD, DM, assertiveness training (GI)	10 sessions/5 wk	18/19 orgasmic	2 yr: 16/19 orgasmic
Kilmann et al. (1983)	48	M age = 33; sec; M yr married = 9	Sexual education (C)	2 2-hr sessions	Significant increase in orgasmic frequency, decreased sexual anxiety	
De Amicis et al. (1985)	22	M age = 34; M yr married = 13; 13 prim, 9 sec	Sensual awareness, SF, DM, communication training, modification of sexual interactions (C)	15-20 sessions	No significant change in orgasmic ability, significant increase in sexual satisfaction	3 yr: prim: significant increase in orgasmic ability with genital caress, increased marital and sexual satisfaction; sec: some increase in orgasmic ability during masturbation, increased sexual satisfaction
Case Studies						
Brady (1966)	5	17-30 yo; married; anxiety and dysparuenia	SD with Brevital injections to induce relaxation (I)	10-14 sessions/ 3-14 wk	4/5 coitally orgasmic	3-8 mo: gains maintained
Kraft & Al-Issa (1967)	1	25 yo; prim; divorced; sexual aversion; anxiety	SD with hypnotic induction (I)	84 sessions	Decreased sexual anxiety	9 mo: gains maintained
Madsen & Ullmann (1967)	1	"Young"; prim; married; coital anxiety	SD and conjoint therapy (I with partner participation)	12 sessions	Coitally orgasmic	9 mo: gains maintained

(continued)

TABLE 11.2 Continued

Study	N	Subject Characteristics	Treatment Type	No. of Sessions	Outcome	Follow-Up
Ince (1973)	1	21 yo; prim; married; low sexual desire; dyspareunia	In vivo SD (I)	1 mo	Coitally orgasmic	
Caird & Wincze (1974)	1	24 yo; prim; married; sexual aversion	SD	7 sessions/2 wk	Coitally orgasmic, decreased anxiety	6; 9 mo: gains maintained
Kohlenberg (1974)	3	28-33 yo; married	DM (C)	10 sessions/10 wk	3/3 orgasmic with masturbation; increased sexual arousal	6 mo: coitally orgasmic
Reisinger (1974)	1	23 yo; single	DM (I)	8 sessions	Orgasmic with masturbation	6 mo: coitally orgasmic
Snyder et al. (1975)	1	Sec	Sexual techniques training, marital tx (C)	17 sessions/15 wk	Significant increase in sexual and marital satisfaction	3 mo: gains maintained

NOTE: SD = systematic desensitization, DM = directed masturbation, SF = sensate focus, CBT = cognitive-behavioral therapy; WL = wait-list, (I) = individual therapy, (C) = couples therapy, (G) = group therapy, (GI) = group/individual therapy, (GC) = group/couples therapy, prim = primary orgasmic dysfunction, sec = secondary orgasmic dysfunction, si = sexual intercourse, tx = treatment, yo = years old, om = orgasmic with masturbation, co = coitally orgasmic.

toward increased genital stimulation with the eventual optional use of a vibrator. LoPiccolo and Lobitz (1972) and Lobitz and LoPiccolo (1972) established masturbation as an effective technique with 21 women who were able to become orgasmic in 15 individual sessions. Barbach (1974) extended this approach to a 10-session, women-only group model, resulting in 92% of the women becoming orgasmic with masturbation. Evidence for generalization to interpersonal orgasm (e.g., manual, oral, coital) has been less consistent and, except for coital orgasm, is often not mentioned in individual studies. Exceptions include Wallace and Barbach (1974), who reported that 87% of their sample were orgasmic during partner-related sexual activity after the 10-session women-only group therapy. Ersner-Hershfield and Kopel (1979) found that 73% of their sample of 22 women were orgasmic during partner activities after 10 sessions of group therapy using Barbach (1974) and Heiman, LoPiccolo, and LoPiccolo (1976) as written guides during their treatment.

Several studies have looked at different presentations of directed-masturbation materials. Heinrich (1976) compared a one-session introduction to directed masturbation using bibliotherapy to group treatment and to a wait-list control. At follow-up 2 months later, 100% of the group therapy, 40% of the bibliotherapy, and 21% of the wait-list controls were orgasmic during masturbation, whereas 47%, 13%, and 0%, respectively, were orgasmic during coitus. McMullen and Rosen (1979) compared texts on becoming orgasmic to a series of weekly 20-minute videotapes that portrayed the weekly assignments. Compared to no change in orgasmic status for the wait-list control group, 65% of the text and 55% of the video group became orgasmic during masturbation. In addition, 50% of the text and 30% of the video group became orgasmic during intercourse.

Heiman and LoPiccolo (1983) examined primary anorgasmic dysfunction in an own-control design using 15 sessions of treatment that included sensate focus, directed masturbation, and other cognitive-behavioral home assignments. At post-treatment, 25 previously anorgasmic women reported a significant increase in masturbatory orgasm (from 0% to 63%), in manual orgasm (to 43%), in coital orgasm (to 25%), and in sexual satisfaction. These changes were either maintained or increased at the 3-month follow-up. The wait-list analysis revealed that waiting approximately 3 months for therapy to begin resulted in a significant decrease in global sexual dissatisfaction for all the women in this study (the primary anorgasmic women were not analyzed separately) and greater marital happiness. These changes were not accompanied by resolution of sexual symptoms during the same time period.

We could locate no studies that compared some type of active treatment to a placebo. Five studies were found that compared different types of psychological interventions. Of these, only one compared group systematic desensitization with group directed masturbation (Andersen, 1981). After 10 biweekly sessions, Andersen found the changes in orgasmic response at post-testing were modest: 10% of the desensitization, 20% of the masturbation, and 10% of the wait-list control subjects became orgasmic. However, by the 6-week follow-up, an additional 20% of the directed masturbation subjects became orgasmic. In addition, after later receiving directed masturbation, 66% of the wait-list control subjects became orgasmic. Overall, directed masturbation was superior to the other conditions in increasing orgasmic responses. Directed masturbation and systematic desensitization groups were found to be equal on the self-acceptance scale of the Sexual Interaction Inventory (LoPiccolo & Steger, 1974) and showed no changes on measures of sexual anxiety.

Two other studies have compared systematic desensitization with an alternative treatment (Mathews et al., 1976; Obler, 1973). In both cases, approximately 15 hours of therapy were offered over approximately 10 to 15 weeks, using videotapes with both treatments. Unfortunately, both primary and secondary anorgasmic women were included in the analysis, with no subanalysis of each group. Obler (1973) is the only study to compare individual systematic desensitization with group psychoanalytic treatment, though he combined primary and secondary anorgasmic women. The results showed that 85% of the desensitization subjects, 36% of the psychoanalytic subjects, and 23% of the control group members experienced orgasm for the first time (or during the specifically desired situation) during the course of the treatment.

Mathews et al. (1976) followed 18 anorgasmic women, 13 of whom were primary anorgasmic. Seventeen of the 18 women also reported low desire and arousal. Comparisons were made between 10 weekly sessions of systematic desensitization combined with counseling on sexual attitudes; conjoint sensate focus sessions, which also included some counseling on sexual attitudes; and sensate focus plus bibliotherapy for three sessions, with 10 weekly mailings. There were no differences between the groups on ratings of the couples' general and sexual relationships. By comparison, Riley and Riley (1978) selected 37 primary anorgasmic women and compared conjoint sensate focus therapy to conjoint sensate focus plus directed masturbation sessions. Six weekly and six bimonthly sessions were offered. They found that the directed masturbation plus sensate focus group improved more than the sensate focus group alone, with 90% of the former and 53% of the latter patients achieving orgasm by the end of treatment. In addition, coital orgasm was attained by 47% of the sensate focus group and 85% of the directed masturbation plus sensate focus group.

Morokoff and LoPiccolo (1986) compared 14 couples who received minimal therapist contact (MTC, four 1½-hour therapy sessions once a month) to 29 couples who received full treatment contact (FTC, fifteen 1- to 1½-hour sessions, occurring weekly). Both groups read *Becoming Orgasmic* (Heiman et al., 1976; now Heiman & LoPiccolo, 1988) and saw the accompanying video. The following percentages are estimates taken from the graphed material in Morokoff and LoPiccolo (1986). Compared to FTC, the MTC group showed a greater (nonsignificant) frequency of masturbatory orgasm (approximately 73% vs. 45%) and manual or vibrator orgasm (approximately 76% vs. 25%). These changes were maintained at the 3-month follow-up. Lower percentages were found for orgasm from partner stimulation (approximately 25% in both groups at post-treatment and 3-month follow-up), coital orgasm (5% FTC and 12% MTC at post-treatment, rising to 12% and 25% at follow-up), and coital orgasm with additional stimulation (30% MTC, 15% FTC at post-treatment, increasing to over 40% and 20% at follow-up). Thus, MTC claimed comparable success—better in the case of masturbatory orgasm and coital orgasm with additional stimulation—to the full 15-session therapy format.

To briefly summarize the outcomes of the comparative treatment studies of primary anorgasmia, it appears that directed masturbation sustains good outcomes over systematic desensitization and enhances or is enhanced by the effects of sensate focus interventions. In fact, directed masturbation fits the criteria for an empirically validated treatment for primary orgasmic disorders. Overall, however, controlled conditions are underutilized, interventions differ somewhat in intensity even within the same study, and multiple disorders are sometimes combined under the rubric of orgasmic dysfunctions. In addition, primary and secondary orgasmic disorders are sometimes combined, making results difficult to evaluate precisely.

Secondary orgasmic dysfunction, the infrequency or restrictiveness of an orgasmic pattern, is a common complaint with a generally less optimistic prognosis than primary anorgasmia.

In a study by Carney, Bancroft, and Mathews (1978), sensate focus treatment was combined with either testosterone or diazepam in treating orgasmic disorder and "general sexual unresponsiveness." Weekly and monthly treatments were equally effective for the 32 women and their partners assigned to these treatments. However, testosterone appeared to be asso- ciated with significant gains that were maintained at follow-up 6 months af- ter the drug was discontinued. This is one of the few studies that combined drug therapy and psychotherapy to examine how they might augment one another. For this particular study, it was difficult to tell if diazepam might have had a negative impact on sexual responsiveness, thus apparently enhancing testosterone's effect. In fact, that interpretation was supported by a later study that compared sex therapy with testosterone or placebo to testosterone alone; there were no differences between the sex therapy groups, and there was no superiority of those groups over testosterone alone (Dow & Gallagher, 1989; see also Mathews, Whitehead, & Kellett, 1983).

The Heiman and LoPiccolo (1983) own-control outcome study used Masters and Johnson's approach, as well as other directive cognitive-behavioral approaches, with 16 couples who reported secondary anorgasmia in the female partner. They reported highly significant improvements from pre- to post-therapy on sexual and marital satisfaction but a nonsignificant increase, from 12% to 30%, in orgasmic ability from manual stimulation and a significant but clinically modest increase from 12% to 30% in orgasmic ability during coital experiences. Changes were maintained at the 3-month follow-up.

Other studies have compared different therapy formats. For example, Libman et al. (1984) found that a standard couple format resulted in more positive change on subjective satisfaction and behavioral measures than did group therapy or minimal contact bibliotherapy. The importance of both members of a couple being present for treatment is also suggested by the McGovern, Stewart, and LoPiccolo (1975) study, which compared outcomes of six primary and six secondary anorgasmic women. Whereas the former improved dramatically, the latter did not. Consequently, the authors suggested that future work might combine marital therapy and sex therapy to treat secondary inorgasmic disorder.

Kilmann and colleagues (Kilmann et al., 1987; Kilmann, Mills, et al., 1986) appeared to recognize the value of working with couples issues by examining the impact of four different kinds of treatment components typically used to treat women with secondary anorgasmia. In the 1986 study, all couples received 4 hours of basic sex education before they were assigned to one of six groups: communication skills training, sexual skills training, a condensed combination of communication (C) and sexual skills (S) training presented in two different orders (S/C and C/S), an attention-placebo control consisting of a series of didactic lectures of the material presented in the combined treatment condition, and a wait-list control. Although there were no outcome differences between treatment components at post-treatment, the treated couples, when compared to controls, reported less sexual dissatisfaction, greater harmony, and a greater number of women attaining coital orgasm during at least 50% of coital experiences. In the follow-up study (Kilmann et al., 1987), 11 new couples were used to compare the two sexual communication skills sequences of the combined treatment to the nine no-treatment and 11 attention-placebo individuals of the earlier study. Treatment was 2 hours twice a week in group format (S/C = seven couples, C/S = four couples). Women in the treatment group were significantly more coitally orgasmic at post-test than women in the control group, though these gains were lost at follow-up. The results showed greater coital orgasm frequency gains in the S/C group compared to either control group, whereas the C/S group did not make significant gains over either control group. However, the S/C women showed a significant decline at follow-up, and the attention-placebo control group showed a significant increase. The extremely small sample size limits the discussion of the impact of the study, but it does suggest that combined communication and sexual skills training can be a useful group intervention.

To summarize the treatment perspective for women with secondary anorgasmia, some combination of sex education, sexual skills training, communication on general and sexual issues, body image and, perhaps, directed masturbation appears to be helpful. Gains are somewhat fragile long term, however. Given that secondary orgasmic disorder can take so many different forms (e.g., complete lack of coital orgasm, vibrator/masturbatory-only orgasm, general low frequency of orgasm), it may be that interventions have not been adequately tailored to individual needs, except perhaps at the case study level.

Vaginismus

Vaginismus is involuntary spasmic contraction of the vaginal musculature that interferes with or prevents coitus. Although there are no reliable estimates of its prevalence in the general population, it is a rather frequent problem, accounting for 12% to 17% of women presenting to sex therapy clinics (Hawton, 1982; Spector & Carey, 1990).

There are no controlled or treatment comparison studies of vaginismus (Table 11.3). In fact, it is questionable whether the extant clinical research qualifies vaginismus treatment as "probably efficacious." With some reservations, we include it here on the basis of the evidence that therapy that involves insertion training appears to be very effective, with an unusually clear outcome measure—the ability to have sexual intercourse. There have been several case studies, including those described by Masters and Johnson and other authors. Comparison studies have not been done and are unlikely given the rarity of this diagnosis, the lack of a clearly viable alternative, and the hesitation that clinical researchers feel about putting these patients in a placebo group given the distress that the problem causes to relationships. An own-control study could be a valuable alternative.

There is general agreement that repeated daily use of dilators or the insertion of some objects of graduated size, such as fingers, is important in treating vaginismus. Masters and Johnson (1970) combined dilators with the physical demonstration of the involuntary spasm to both partners. The male initiated the dilator use with the woman's control and guidance. Their success rate, after 14 sessions of treatment, was high: 29 out of 29 cases were able to have sexual intercourse, and these gains were maintained at 5-year follow-up. Fuchs et al. (1973) combined systematic desensitization, vaginal dilators, and hypnotic techniques. Over 8 to 10 sessions, 37 (86%) of the patients were able to have intercourse. Hawton and Catalan (1986) used a combined Masters and Johnson, sex education, and psychotherapy approach over an average of 15 sessions of couples treatment. Although three cases showed no improvement, most (80%) were either resolved or largely resolved.

Other clinicians have incorporated a broader range of interventions, including Kegel exercises, with the emphasis on first the woman (rather than her partner) using dilators or fingers, and the use of films of intercourse (e.g., Leiblum, Pervin, & Campbell, 1989). Active ingredients of treatment are unknown at this point, although the behavioral intervention of gradual insertion, possibly combined with *in vivo* desensitization and active therapeutic processing of difficulties, appears to be important. Little is known about the treatment ingredients required of the therapeutic interactions that might help patients and partners continue to remain motivated and overcome their fears. Couple treatment appears to predominate in the reports of suc-

TABLE 11.3 Vaginismus

Study	N	Subject Characteristics	Treatment Type	No. of Sessions	Outcome
No-Control Outcome Studies					
Masters & Johnson (1970)	29 cases (11 yr)	Many cases of sexual trauma, male sexual dysfunction, religious orthodoxy	Demonstration of involuntary nature of spasms & vaginal dilators (C)	14 sessions	29/29 able to have si
Hawton & Catalan (1986)	26	*M* age = 33	Homework assignments (as outlined by Masters & Johnson, 1970), sexual education, psychotherapy (C)	*M* = 15 sessions	12 resolved, 9 largely resolved, 2 some improvement, 3 no change
Case Studies					
Ellison (1968)	100	14 < 20 yo, 66 21-50 yo, 17 31-40 yo, 3 > 40 yo; *M* yr married = 2.5	Insight therapy & vaginal dilators (in some patients)	3-10 hr psychotherapy	87/100 able to have si, 5/100 not able to have si, 8/100 not known
Lerner (1971)	1	Patient also dyspareunia	Roger's client-centered psychotherapy		able to have si
Fuchs et al. (1973)	9 (1968—1970)	Severe vaginismus 2-5 yr	*In vitro* "hypno-SD" (I)	6-8 sessions	6/9 able to have si; gains maintained at 1-3 yr

(continued)

TABLE 11.3 Continued

Study	N	Subject Characteristics	Treatment Type	No. of Sessions	Outcome
Fuchs et al. (1973)	34 (1965-1970)	Severe vaginismus > 2 yr	In vivo SD & vaginal dilators (I)	8-10	31/34 able to have si; gains maintained at 1-5 yr
Kaplan (1974)	1	30 yo; history sexual abuse; married 4½ yr	Psychotherapy; finger insertion by husband (C)	12 sessions/6wk	Able to have si
Gottesfeld (1978)	1	20 yo; history physical abuse; married 1 yr	Psychotherapy & hypnosis (I)	2 yr	Able to have si; gains maintained at 2 yr
Leiblum & Rosen (1989)	2	24-25 yo; married	SD, Kegel exercises, sensate focus, finger insertion (I/C)	12-15 sessions	1 able to have si, 1 able to engage in partial penetration
Wincze & Carey (1991)	1	History of sexual abuse; borderline; married 4 yr	Couples therapy; gradual penile insertion (I/C)	1½ yr (I); 3 mo (C)	Able to have si

NOTE: SD = systematic desensitization, (I) = individual therapy, (C) = couples therapy, si = sexual intercourse, yo = years old.

cessful outcome, though there is no indication that individual treatment could not be effective. In treatment-resistant cases, perineometer biofeedback has been tried clinically with some success, but we could not locate studies that might substantiate this approach for vaginismus.

To summarize, vaginismus appears to be successfully treated if repeated practice with vaginal dilators is included in the treatment. Most applications of the method also include relaxation, Kegel exercises, and both individual and partner involvement in the exercises, though the weight of each of these factors has not been researched.

SEXUAL DYSFUNCTIONS
REPORTED BY MEN

Erectile Disorder

Although not the most prevalent men's sexual disorder in the general population (Laumann et al., 1994), the largest group of men seeking clinical services for sexual problems are those having difficulties with erection (Hawton, 1982; Spector & Carey, 1990; U.S. Department of Health and Human Services, 1987). One study confined to a cross-sectional sample of 40- to 70-year-old healthy men found that 52% of the sample reported some level of erectile problem (Feldman, Goldstein, Hatzichristou, Krane, & McKinlay, 1994).

A wide variety of treatments are available for erectile disorders, in part because of a proliferation of assessments and interventions that focus on physiological causes and medical-surgical treatments. For example, the use of sleep measures of erection, cavennosography, and vasoactive injections into the corpora are commonly used for diagnoses. Although a detailed review of biomedical interventions is beyond the purpose of the present chapter, a few comments are in order (see Rosen & Leiblum, 1995). The least invasive of the medical interventions is the vacuum device and constriction ring. Althof and Turner (1992) found lower attrition rates with a vacuum tube compared to the intracorporal injections but equal partner acceptability across methods. There has been increasing interest in oral pharmacological treatment of erectile problems. In one placebo-controlled study, yohimbine hydrochloride, a centrally acting alpha$_2$ adrenoceptor antagonist, was found to increase erections in men, although, perhaps because of inadequate dosage or the mixture of organic and psychogenic erectile problems in the sample, less than half of the sample reported adequate erections for intercourse (Riley, Goodman, Kellett, & Orr, 1989). Although other pharmacological avenues are being pursued, there are no clearly identified well-established treatments for erectile dysfunction as of this writing.

Intracorporal injection of vasoactive drugs whose primary effect appears to be the relaxation of corporal smooth muscle tissue have had an efficacy rate of about 80% (Linet & Neff, 1994). The most common vasoactive drugs currently used are papavarine and prostaglandin E_1, with the latter being the only one currently approved for this purpose in the United States by the Federal Drug Administration. Side effects, including occasional priapism and fibrotic nodules, are greater than the side effects of the vacuum device.

All of the above treatments may be used for both psychogenic or organic forms of erectile dysfunction. The only biomedical intervention that is currently restricted to organically based erectile dysfunction patients is penile implants, either the inflatable prosthesis or the semirigid silicone rods. Though nearly three times the price and associated with more significant surgical complications than the semirigid model, the inflatable device results in higher partner satisfaction (Tiefer, Pederson, & Melman, 1988).

The pattern of increased medicalization with the interventions for erectile dysfunction has been noted by other researchers, with some concern for the meaning of the shift and the impact on sexual values (e.g., Bancroft, 1990; Hawton, Catalan, & Fagg, 1992; Tiefer, 1994). Still, it is understandable that people may want to find a solution quickly with what appears to be certainty, which medical interventions are better at promising.

The key therapeutic ingredients for psychological interventions are similar to orgasmic disorders: sensate focus and systematic desensitization. In addition, many interventions include interpersonal and sexual communication, sensory awareness training, and masturbation exercises. The interventions are typically multimethod and are not easily separated from an integrated package or tested by components.

Among the five psychological treatment comparison controlled outcome studies located, there were several repeated patterns of results (see Table 11.4). Treatment occurred in a relatively brief format of 5 to 20 sessions. Systematic desensitization for individuals or groups was an effective intervention, superior to interpretive or psychoanalytic treatment and to an attention placebo (Auerbach & Kilmann, 1977; Lazarus, 1961; Obler, 1973). In addition, systematic desensitization was found equal to "routine treat-

(text continues on page 290)

TABLE 11.4 Erectile Failure

Study	N	Subject Characteristics	Treatment Type	No. of Sessions	Outcome	Follow-Up
Treatment Comparison Controlled Outcome Studies						
Obler (1973)	27	Sec ed; absence neurotic or psychotic disorders; mixed pe	SD and assertiveness training (I) (*n* = 9) vs. psychoanalytic (G) (*n* = 9) vs. no-treatment control (*n* = 9)		SD: 80% improvement (increased sexual performance and decreased sexual anxiety) vs. 15% of other 2 groups	1½ yr: gains maintained
Kockott et al. (1975)	24	Ed min 6 mo.; *M* age = 31	SD (*n* = 8) vs. Routine tx (standard psychiatric advice and medication) (*n* = 8) vs. WL (*n* = 8). Groups matched on age, prim/sec ed, IQ, neuroticism (I)	14 sessions SD; 4 sessions Routine tx; 16 wk WL	SD and Routine tx: increased quality and quantity of sexual behavior vs. WL. SD: decreased sexual anxiety vs. WL or routine. No difference between groups on plethysmograph ratings or in ability to maintain erection > 1 min during si.	
Auerbach & Kilmann (1977)	16	Sec ed	SD (G) (*n* = 8) vs. attention-placebo control (relax training alone) (*n* = 8). Groups matched on age, education, severity and duration of disorder, marital status, number of sexual partners, and partner cooperation	15 3/4-hr sessions	Tx: 40% improved in frequency of successful si Placebo: 3% improved in frequency success si	3 mo: gains maintained
Reynolds (1980)	30	17 married; 13 single	Erectile biofeedback training vs. control (I)		17/30 some improvement in erectile function; 7/30 considerable improvement in erectile function	1 mo: no difference tx vs. control

(continued)

283

TABLE 11.4 Continued

Study	N	Subject Characteristics	Treatment Type	No. of Sessions	Outcome	Follow-Up
Takefman & Brender (1984)	16	Sec ed min 6 mo.; M age = 48; absence of psychopathology or marital dysfunction; M yr. married = 20	No si and communication training vs. communication training alone (tx administered primarily via written instruction) (C)	1 mo	Significant improvement in erectile ability and marital adjustment for both groups; no difference between groups	
Sonda et al. (1990)	33	Prim ed min 3 mo	Yohimbine (5.4 mg 3/day) vs. yohimbine + placebo vs. placebo. Double-blind, cross-over design; 4-wk drug administration, 1 wk between study phases (I)		Improvement in subjective erectile function: yohimbine (11/33); yohimbine + placebo (5/33); placebo (5/33); no change (12/33)	
Own-Control or Wait-List Controlled Outcome Studies						
Price et al. (1981)	21	Sec ed; M age = 45; none with sexual partners	Didactic presentations and discussions, DM bibliotherapy (G) vs. WL	8 2-hr sessions	Tx: 64% increased satisfaction of erectile function; 36% complete improvement WL: no change	6 mo: gains maintained
Heiman & LoPiccolo (1983)	19	M age = 32; absence of psychosis, depression, or severe marital distress	CBT, communication training, SF systems conceptualization vs. WL (C)	Tx: 15 1-hr sessions WL: 1-2 mo.	Significant increase in sexual and marital satisfaction, sexual contact, foreplay and si duration, and frequency of orgasm during masturbation, no sig. change in attaining or maintaining erections	3 mo: significant decrease in patient and partner sexual satisfaction

Study	N	Sample	Treatment	Duration	Outcome	Follow-up
Munjack et al. (1984)	16		RET focusing on performance anxiety vs. WL	6 wk	RET vs. control: increased frequency si; decrease sexual anxiety	6 mo: relapsed
Flaherty (1989)	29	Sec ed	Sex education, behavioral assignments, DM, SF, sexual and communication skills (G) vs. WL (post-test only)	10½-hr sessions/5-6 wk	Tx vs. control: increased frequency sexual activity, increased sexual satisfaction, lower frequency ed, increased sexual arousal, decreased sexual anxiety	

No-Control Outcome Studies

Study	N	Sample	Treatment	Duration	Outcome	Follow-up
Wolpe & Lazarus (1966)	31	Mixed sexual dysfunctions	SD		21/61 "achieved entirely satisfactory sexual performance"; 6/31 "sufficiently improved"	
Friedman (1968)	10	24-50 yo; 2 single, 8 married	SD & intravenous methohexital to maximize muscular relaxation (I)	$M = 9$ sessions	8/10 ability to have si without ed or ejaculation problems; 2/10 improved	12 mo: gains maintained
Masters & Johnson (1970)	245 (1959-1970)	32 prim ed; 213 sec ed	Educational presentations, therapy discussions, SF (C)	daily/2 wk	59% success for prim ed 74% success for sec ed	5 yr: prim ed 0/7 relapsed, sec ed 9/90 relapsed
Jones (1973)	7		SD & methohexital	$M = 7$ sessions	6/7 "restored to coital competence"	

(continued)

285

TABLE 11.4 Continued

Study	N	Subject Characteristics	Treatment Type	No. of Sessions	Outcome	Follow-Up
Lobitz & LoPiccolo (1972)	6		Modification of Masters & Johnson, daily monitoring of sexual feelings/behavior, interpersonal sexual skills, some classical conditioning of sexual arousal (C)	15 sessions/ 15 wk	4/6 partner satisfied min 50% of si	
Meyer et al. (1975)	7	Mixed sexual dysfunction	Variation of SF (C)	10 sessions/ 10 wk	5/7 complete relief; 2/7 "equivocal improvement"	7 mo: 3/4 gains maintained
Csillag (1976)	12	6 ed min 6 mo., 6 controls; 18-38 yo	Erectile biofeedback training (I)	16 sessions/ 8 days	5/6 patients improved erectile ability outside of laboratory; 0/6 controls improved	
Levine & Agle (1978)	16	Sec ed min 6 mo.; M age = 41; 6 subjects also had pe: absence of psychopathology; M yr. married = 14	SF; psychotherapy for performance anxiety and interpersonal issues (C)	8-26 sessions/ 6-48 wk	6/16 consistently potent; 14/16 ability to attain erection during foreplay	3 mo: 6/6 potency maintained; 12 mo: 69% improved vs. pre-treatment; 75% declined vs. post-tx measures
Lobitz & Baker (1979)	9	3 prim ed, 6 sec ed; M age = 31; 4 single; psychopathology	In vivo SD, communication training, sexual education, sensory awareness exercises, sexual fantasy training, stop and start (G)	12 90-min sessions	Significant decrease incidence ed, sig. increase in sexual sat and sexual fantasy (TAT)	9 mo: gains maintained

286

Study	N	Sample	Treatment	Sessions	Outcome	Follow-up
Reynolds et al. (1981)	11	Sec ed: M age = 50; 8 divorced; none with steady partners	Dating skills, sexual communication skills, role play, sexual therapy, bibliotherapy (G)	10 sessions	Significant decrease in ed and social anxiety	6 mo: gains maintained
Everaerd et al. (1982)	13	8 prim ed, 3 sec ed, 2 pe and sec ed; M age = 30	RET (G), social skills training, SF, DM	18-21 2-hr sessions	9/13 ability to maintain erection	2 mo: 6/15 "complete cure," 3/15 slight improvement
Kuruvilla (1984)	13	Single	SD, DM, sex education		9/13 full erection during masturbation, 4/13 partial erection during masturbation	2 yr: 7/11 con't improvement
LoPiccolo et al. (1985)	16	M age = 38; M yr. married = 13	CBT (LoPiccolo & Hogan, 1979) (C)	15 1-hr sessions	Significant increase in ability to attain and maintain erection	3 mo: gains maintained
DeAmicis et al. (1985)	15	M age = 38; M yr. married = 13	Sensual awareness exercises, SF, communication training, modification of sexual interactions (C)	15-20 sessions	Significant increase in length of foreplay and ability to maintain erection during si, sig. increase in sexual satisfaction	3 yr: ability maintain erection during si, no change in ability to attain erections prior to si
Hawton & Catalan (1986)	34	M age = 33	Homework assignments (Masters & Johnson, 1970), sexual education, psychotherapy (C)	M = 15 sessions	14 resolved, 9 largely resolved, 5 some improvement, 5 no change, 1 worse	
Hawton et al. (1992)	36	34 sec ed, 2 prim ed; M age = 39; married; M duration ed = 5 yr.	SF; DM (C)	M = 12 sessions	15 complete resolution; 10 marked improvement; 11 little or no change	3 mo: marked/complete resolution declined to 20

(continued)

287

TABLE 11.4 Continued

Study	N	Subject Characteristics	Treatment Type	No. of Sessions	Outcome	Follow-Up
Case Studies						
Lazarus & Rachman (1957)	1	Prim ed	SD	8 sessions	Ability to maintain erection	17 mo: gains maintained
Wolpe (1958)	7		In vivo SD	M = 31 sessions/10 mo	6/8 "cured"; 1/8 "much improved"	
Lazarus (1961)	5		SD (G) (n = 2) vs. interpretive tx designed to explore emotions, interpersonal relationships and their relation to ed (G) (n = 3)	20 sessions/3 wk	SD: 2/2 complete recovery Interpretive tx: 0/3 recovery	
Cooper (1968)	31		Relaxation training, sex education, psychotherapy (I/C)	20 sessions/1 yr	13/31 cured/improved	
Cooper (1969b)	49		In vivo SD, sex education, psychotherapy (I)	M sessions = 24	7/49 recovered; 12/49 improved/ 21/49 unchanged; 9/49 worse	
Salzman (1969)	1	Prim ed; 33 yo; married 10 yr.	SD	49 sessions	Ability to maintain erection during si	1 yr: gains maintained
Masters & Johnson (1970)	28	19 prim ed; 9 sec ed	Sexual surrogate (C)		Prim ed: 63% success sec ed: 88% success	
Bass (1974)	1	24 yo; single	SD (I)	5 50-min sessions	Able to maintain erection during si	6 mo: gains maintained

Study	N	Sample	Treatment	Duration	Results	Follow-up
Herman & Prewett (1974)	1	Prim ed: 51 yo	Erectile biofeedback training (I)	16 sessions	Increase in erectile ability outside of laboratory	7 mo: relapsed
Glick (1975)	1	36 yo; married 6 yr.	Relaxation training; SD	68 sessions/ 2 yr	Able to maintain erection during si	
Lansky & Davenport (1975)	3		SF	11 sessions	1 total improvement; 2 no improvement but noncompliant	
Davis & Davis (1980)	1	48 yo	Nocturnal penile tumescence conditioning (C)	5 sessions	Able to maintain erection during si	2 yr: gains maintained
Apfelbaum (1984)	407 (1971-1981)	19-83 yo; mixed sexual dysfunctions	SF, sexual surrogate	Daily/ 2-3 wk	29% completely successful; 40% largely successful; 21% moderately successful; 7% no change; 1% worse	
Stravynski (1986)	1	54 yo	*In vivo* SD, social skills training	6 wk	No ed during si, decreased anxiety	
Dauw (1988)	311 (1970-1980)	*M* age = 49; 55 prim ed; 256 sec ed	Bibliotherapy, sex education, social skills, DM, sexual surrogate		98% success for prim ed 85% success for sec ed	3 mo: gains maintained

NOTE: SD = systematic desensitization, SF = sensate focus, DM = directed masturbation, WL = wait-list, CBT = cognitive behavioral therapy, prim ed = primary erectile dysfunction, sec ed = secondary erectile dysfunction, pe = premature ejaculation, si = sexual intercourse, tx = treatment, yo = years old, (I) = individual therapy, (C) = couples therapy, (G) = group therapy.

ment" (Kockott, Dittmar, & Nusselt, 1975). There was also a suggestion that communication training was helpful (Takefman & Brender, 1984). Importantly, only one of the treatment comparison studies used couples, and none directly compared systematic desensitization with sensate focus. Among the wait-list control or own-control studies, behavioral assignments, masturbation, sex education, and communication skills resulted in increased satisfaction with erectile functioning that was maintained at 6 months (Price, Reynolds, Cohen, Anderson, & Schochet, 1981). In addition, these components increased frequency of sexual activity, sexual satisfaction, and decreased erectile dysfunction and sexual anxiety (Flaherty, 1989).

The only wait-list own-control study that involved couples used cognitive-behavioral treatment homework assignments, sensate focus exercises, and communication training (Heiman & LoPiccolo, 1983). Significant changes in sexual and marital satisfaction were achieved by the 19 couples. In addition, there were changes in foreplay and intercourse duration, but there was only a nonsignificant improvement of erectile problems. Interestingly, the wives of men with erectile dysfunction reported significant improvement in their partners' ability to achieve and maintain erections. At the 3-month follow-up, sexual satisfaction decreased significantly in both males and females despite coital erection problems having remained the same as post-test levels (problems during 30% to 35% of contacts).

Among group uncontrolled studies, five used systematic desensitization as all or part of the treatment, with generally positive results of between 30% and 85% improvement. Higher levels of improvement and better maintenance of gains occurred when systematic desensitization was combined with other interventions such as communication training, education, or directed masturbation (Friedman, 1968; Jones & Park, 1972; Kuruvilla, 1984; Lobitz & Baker, 1979; Wolpe & Lazarus, 1966). Similarly, the treatments that included sensate focus found significant decreases in erectile problems, though three of the studies found some decrease in functioning or satisfaction at follow-up (Hawton et al., 1992; Levine & Agle, 1978; Masters & Johnson, 1970). This pattern was generally similar to that found among the case studies.

In summary, there is more evidence for systematic desensitization's than for sensate focus's effectiveness in treating erectile disorders, though no direct comparisons have been made within the same study. Other therapeutic ingredients such as behavioral assignments, sex education, and communication training appear to contribute to better erectile functioning and general sexual satisfaction. Partner data and couples treatment in controlled studies are too limited to make firm conclusions.

Premature Ejaculation

As indicated by the Laumann et al. (1994) study, premature ejaculation is an extremely common phenomenon. The pattern of premature ejaculation is subjectively and individually defined, in that it typically refers to persistent or recurrent ejaculation before, at, or shortly after penetration and before the person wishes it. Another aspect of the definition is that often partners will complain that the time before ejaculation is too short, causing impairments in their own sexual response.

The treatment approaches for premature ejaculation have included behavioral approaches such as the squeeze technique developed by Semens (1956) and made popular by Masters and Johnson (1970), cognitive-behavioral interventions (Zilbergeld, 1992), and, more recently, the use of various pharmacological agents. The only controlled outcome studies that have included a placebo or comparison treatment have been two studies involving medications (Althof et al., 1995; Segraves, Segraves, & Maguire, 1993). In both studies, clomipramine, a serotonergic antidepressant, was compared with a placebo and found to be effective in controlling premature ejaculation. The men selected for the Althof et al. study were 15 men with a history of se- vere premature ejaculation who had not done well with other treatments. A higher (50-mg) dosage level of clomipramine was compared with a lower (25-mg) dosage and was found to be more helpful in delaying ejaculation (see Table 11.5).

Whether pharmacological agents such as serotonin-reuptake inhibitors or alpha-adrenergic antagonists should be encouraged as first-line treatment interventions (as opposed to being interventions primarily for treatment-resistant patients) remains to be evaluated. Although these medications are a simple and, if not used for a lifetime, cost-effective treatment for premature ejaculation, there are some limitations to their widespread use. First, providing a systemic drug for a specific problem may be unnecessary, given fairly good outcomes from behavioral interventions. Second, the serotonergic drugs have been associated with diminished desire and, in some cases, diminished arousal (Gitlin, 1997; Meston & Gorzalka, 1992). Therefore, these drugs would not be recommended for patients who also have low sexual desire or erectile dysfunction. Third, they would not be recommended for

TABLE 11.5 Premature Ejaculation

Study	N	Subject Characteristics	Treatment Type	No. of Sessions	Outcome	Follow-Up
Treatment Comparison Controlled Outcome Studies						
Obler (1973)	27	Absence of neurotic or psychotic disorders; mixed ed	SD and assertiveness training (I) (n = 9) vs. psychoanalytic (G) (n = 9) vs. no treatment control (n = 9)		SD: 80% improvement (increased sexual performance, decreased sex anxiety) vs. 15% other 2 groups	1½ yr: gains maintained
Segraves et al. (1993)	20	M age = 45; absence of psychiatric disorders or other sexual dysfunctions; 8 lifelong pe	25 mg clomipramine 6 hr prior to si vs. placebo 6 hr prior to si. Double-blind design.	10 trials	sig. increase in ejaculatory latency	
Althof et al. (1994)	15		25 mg/day clomipramine vs. 50 mg/day clomipramine vs. placebo. Double-blind cross-over design		Clomipramine: increased sexual satisfaction among patient and partners	
Own-Control or Wait-List Controlled Outcome Studies						
Heiman & LoPiccolo (1983)	21	M age = 32; absence of psychosis, severe depression, or marital distress	CBT, communication training, systems conceptualization, pause and squeeze, SF vs. WL (C)	Tx: 15 1-hr sessions WL: 1-2 mo.	Increased duration of foreplay and si; increase in partner-initiated sexual activity	3 mo. decreased duration si (still sig. increase from pre tx) sexual satisfaction maintained
No-Control Outcome Studies						
Masters & Johnson (1970)	186 (1959-1970)		Pause and squeeze		182/186	5 yr.: 1/74 relapsed

Study	N	Sample	Treatment	Sessions	Outcome	Follow-up
Lobitz & LoPiccolo (1972)	6		Modification of pause and squeeze, communication training (C)	15 sessions	6/6 cured	6 mo.: gains maintained
McCarthy (1973)	14	Mixed pe/erectile dysfunction	Modification of pause and squeeze (C)	10-15 sessions/ 10-15 wk	12/14 "marked improvement"	
Yulis (1976)	37		Homework assignments (Masters & Johnson, 1970); 3 men also assertiveness training	18 sessions/ 3wk	80%-100% ejaculatory controlled encounters	6 mo: 33/37 ejaculatory control
De Amicis et al. (1985)	20	M age = 38; M yr. married = 13	Sensual awareness, communication training, modification of sexual interactions (C)	15-20 sessions/ 15-20 wk	Significant increase in duration of foreplay and si	3 mo. & 3 yr.: decreased duration si, sexual and marital satisfaction
LoPiccolo et al. (1985)	21	M age = 38; M yr. married = 13	CBT (LoPiccolo & Hogan, 1979) (C)	15 1-hr sessions	Significant increase in duration of foreplay and si	3 mo.: gains maintained
Hawton & Catalan (1986)	14	M age = 33	Homework assign-ments (Masters & Johnson, 1970), sex education, psychotherapy (C)	M = 15 sessions	4 resolved, 5 largely resolved, 1 some improvement, 3 no change, 1 worse	
Case Studies						
Cooper (1968)	10		Stop and start, relaxation exercises, sexual education, couples interview, individual tx	Minimum 20 sessions	1/10 improved	

(continued)

TABLE 11.5 Continued

Study	N	Subject Characteristics	Treatment Type	No. of Sessions	Outcome	Follow-Up
Cooper (1969a)	30	(I)	*In vivo* SD, sexual education, psychotherapy	Minimum 20 sessions	13/30 improved; 15/30 unchanged; 2/30 worse	
Ince (1973)	1		SD, thought stopping, masturbation prior to si			
Tanner (1973)	2	1 patient psychotic	Pause and squeeze (C)		Increased duration si, increased sexual satisfaction	9 mo (1 patient): gains maintained
Kaplan et al. (1974)	4		Sexual techniques training, stop-start (C)	6 45-min sessions	Ejaculatory control	4 mo: gains maintained
Zeiss (1978)	6		Sexual and communication training, ban on si (C)	6 sessions	4/6 ejaculatory control	8 mo: 3/4 gains maintained
Assalian (1988)	5	26-52 yo; chronic pe	25 mg/day clomipramine		5/5 ejaculatory control within 2 days	12/18 mo (2 patients): gains maintained
Dauw (1988)	127 (1970-1980)	M age = 28	Bibliotherapy, sex education, social skills training, masturbation exercises, sexual surrogate	Daily 2-3/wk	122/127 ability to maintain erection during si minimum 10 min before ejaculation	

NOTE: SD = systematic desensitization, WL = wait-list, CBT = cognitive behavioral therapy, si = sexual intercourse, pe = premature ejaculation, tx = treatment, yo = years old, (I) = individual therapy, (C) = couples therapy.

294

patients with an undiagnosed bipolar disorder because they may significantly increase the likelihood of onset of a manic episode. There are also minor side effects that accompany any drug use and should be examined in terms of patient tolerance. Finally, there are no current long-term follow-up studies for the ongoing use of these medications.

Further work would be helpful to see if a brief trial of pharmacological intervention could be used only short term to initiate the change toward a less anxious and more extended sexual experience. Relatedly, one could imagine combining medication with a brief behavioral intervention, but as yet no studies have been done to compare the usefulness of pharmacological versus behavioral treatments versus a combination of the two interventions.

The primary psychological intervention that has been used for premature ejaculation is some version of the squeeze technique (also referred to as the pause-and-squeeze) (Masters & Johnson, 1970; Semens, 1956). This technique involves stimulating the penis to full erection and close to the point of ejaculation ("moment of inevitability") and then applying a firm squeeze on either side of the penis, usually just under the glans. Typically, this procedure is repeated twice before the person is allowed to ejaculate. A typical modification of this procedure includes having the person first practice it during masturbation (Lobitz & LoPiccolo, 1972) and then transfer the skill to a partner.

The only controlled study that has tested this procedure has been Heiman and LoPiccolo (1983). In an own-control design, the effectiveness of 15 sessions using cognitive-behavioral treatment, including the squeeze technique, was tested. Heiman and LoPiccolo found that foreplay duration increased from 7 to 10 minutes to 11 to 15 minutes and intercourse duration from 1 to 2 minutes to 5 to 8 minutes; both of these increases were significant effects. However, at 3 months following the end of therapy, there was a decrease in duration of intercourse. Other research from the same clinical center found similar changes immediately post therapy but different responses at follow-up (De Amicis, Goldberg, LoPiccolo, Friedman, & Davies, 1985; LoPiccolo, Heiman, Hogan, & Roberts, 1985). The LoPiccolo et al. study found that most gains were maintained at 3 months, whereas the De Amicis et al. study found that at 3-month and 3-year follow-ups there was a decreased duration of sexual intercourse.

The largest study was Masters and Johnson's (1970), for whom the main intervention was the squeeze technique. They reported a 98% cure post treatment and a 97% cure at 5-year follow-up. Unfortunately, a comparison control group was not included. Yulis (1976) combined Masters and Johnson's approach with assertiveness training and found that 33 of 37 men reported ejaculation control on 80% to 100% of their sexual encounters.

Overall, the squeeze technique has demonstrated marked improvement for premature ejaculation, with some exceptions (Hawton & Catalan, 1986). It also appears that a pharmacological intervention may be very helpful for a subgroup of men experiencing premature ejaculation.

CONCLUDING OBSERVATIONS

What can we say with some conviction? Empirically validated psychological treatments for several dysfunction exist, "well established" in the case of primary anorgasmia in women and erectile failure and "probably efficacious" for secondary anorgasmia in women, premature ejaculation, and perhaps vaginismus. Outcome studies in this area have dropped off since the mid-1980s, although we can anticipate an increasing rate of research using pharmacological agents. There is inadequate support for effective treatments for hypoactive sexual desire, sexual aversions, dyspareunia, and delayed orgasm in men. Desire disorders and dyspareunia describe many different types of disorders under one label and will need further diagnostic conceptualization if tailored treatments are to be proposed.

Perplexing and valuable issues remain to be examined. One is the comparison between couple and individual interventions. Of the treatment control and wait-list control studies located, few were studying couples; approximately 57% for orgasmic disorders in women, 0% for vaginismus, 20% for erectile disorders, and 25% for premature ejaculation. These figures are striking given that the largest noncontrolled study was with couples (Masters & Johnson, 1970), with a clear philosophy that the solution to these disorders required couple involvement. In addition, it is clear that these diagnoses are interpersonally defined and experienced. When couple treatment studies are done, the partner's data are underutilized.

Another issue is the need to examine *both* short- and long-term effects of given treatments. This factor becomes increasingly important when one is comparing psychological and medical (e.g., pharmacological) treatments because short-term gains may fade differentially by modality. Particularly underresearched are comparisons of psychological, pharmacological, and combined treatments. Designs similar to those used in depression or anxiety outcome research, examining both pharmacological and psychotherapeutic effectiveness, have potential value in sexual dysfunction treatment evaluations.

Methodological issues are not unique to this area but deserve mention: (a) Controlling for or matching subjects on group variables (e.g., age, years of disorder, marital status) would help interpretation; (b) measures for both client and therapist and measures including changes in the target symptom as well as overall sexual and relationship satisfaction would be informative; (c) long-term follow-up evaluations; and (d) qualitative methods, tapping on aspects of treatment that clients find most and least helpful, could contribute to our understanding of therapeutic change and its maintenance.

REFERENCES

Adelson, E. R. (1974). Premature ejaculation. *Medical Aspects of Human Sexuality, 8,* 83-85.

Althof, S. E., Levine, S. B., Corty, E. W., Risen, C. B., Stern, E. B., & Kurit, B. A. (1995). A double-blind crossover trial of clomipramine for rapid ejaculation in 15 couples. *Journal of Clinical Psychiatry, 56,* 402-407.

Althof, S. E., & Turner, L. A. (1992). Self-injection therapy and external vacuum devices in the treatment of erectile dysfunction: Methods and outcome. In R. C. Rosen & S. R. Leiblum (Eds.), *Erectile disorders: Assessment and treatment* (pp. 283-312). New York: Guilford.

American Psychiatric Association. (1994). *Diagnostic and statistical manual of mental disorders* (4th ed.). Washington, DC: Author.

American Psychological Association. (1995). Training in and dissemination of empirically-validated psychological treatments: Report and recommendations. *Clinical Psychologist, 48*(1), 3-24.

Andersen, B. L. (1981). A comparison of systematic desensitization and directed masturbation in the treatment of primary orgasmic dysfunction in females. *Journal of Consulting and Clinical Psychology, 49,* 568-570.

Annon, J. S. (1973). The therapeutic use of masturbation in the treatment of sexual disorders. In R. D. Rubin, J. P. Brady, & J. D. Henderson (Eds.), *Advances in behavior therapy* (Vol. 4). New York: Academic Press.

Apfelbaum, B. (1984). The ego-analytic approach to individual body-work sex therapy: Five case examples. *Journal of Sex Research, 20,* 44-70.

Assalian, P. (1988). Clomipramine in the treatment of premature ejaculation. *Journal of Sex Research, 24,* 213-215.

Auerbach, R., & Kilmann, P. R. (1977). The effects of group systematic desensitization on secondary erectile failure. *Behavioral Therapy, 8,* 330-339.

Bancroft, J. (1990). Man and his penis: A relationship under threat? *Journal of Psychology and Human Sexuality, 2,* 6-32.

Barbach, L. G. (1974). Group treatment of preorgasmic women. *Journal of Sex and Marital Therapy, 1,* 139-145.

Barbach, L., & Flaherty, M. (1980). Group treatment of situationally orgasmic women. *Journal of Sex and Marital Therapy, 6,* 19-29.

Bass, B. A. (1974). Sexual arousal as an anxiety inhibitor. *Journal of Behavior Therapy and Experimental Psychiatry, 5,* 151-152.

Brady, J. P. (1966). Brevital-relaxation treatment of frigidity. *Behaviour Research and Therapy, 4,* 71-77.

Caird, W. K., & Wincze, J. P. (1974). Videotaped desensitization of frigidity. *Journal of Behavior Therapy and Experimental Psychiatry, 5,* 175-178.

Carney, A., Bancroft, J., & Mathews, A. (1978). A combination of hormonal and psychological treatment for female sexual unresponsiveness. *British Journal of Psychiatry, 133,* 339-346.

Cooper, A. J. (1968). A factual study of male potency disorders. *British Journal of Psychiatry, 114,* 719-731.

Cooper, A. J. (1969a). Clinical and therapeutic studies in premature ejaculation. *Comparative Psychiatry, 10,* 285-295.

Cooper, A. J. (1969b). Disorders of sexual potency in the male: A clinical and statistical study of some factors related to short-term progress. *British Journal of Psychiatry, 115,* 709-719.

Cooper, A. J. (1970). Frigidity, treatment and short-term prognosis. *Journal of Psychosomatic Research, 14,* 133-147.

Csillag, E. R. (1976). Modification of penile erectile response. *Journal of Behavior Therapy and Experimental Psychology, 7,* 27-29.

Dauw, D. C. (1988). Evaluating the effectiveness of the SECS surrogate-assisted sex therapy model. *Journal of Sex Research, 24,* 269-275.

Davis, R., & Davis, T. (1980). Treatment of erectile impotence using a nocturnal penile tumescence conditioning procedure. *Journal of Behavior Therapy and Experimental Psychiatry, 11,* 63-65.

De Amicis, L., Goldberg, D. C., LoPiccolo, J., Friedman, J., & Davies, L. (1985). Clinical follow-up of couples treated for sexual dysfunction. *Archives of Sexual Behavior, 14,* 467-489.

Dow, M., & Gallagher, J. (1989). A controlled study of combined hormonal and psychological treatment for sexual unresponsiveness in women. *British Journal of Clinical Psychology, 28,* 201-212.

Ellison, C. (1968). Psychosomatic factors in the unconsummated marriage. *Journal of Psychosomatic Research, 12,* 61-65.

Ersner-Hershfield, R., & Kopel, S. (1979). Group treatment of preorgasmic women: Evaluation of partner involvement and spacing of sessions. *Journal of Consulting and Clinical Psychology, 47,* 750-759.

Everaerd, W., Dekker, J., Dronkers, J., van der Rhee, K., Staffeleu, J., & Wiselius, G. (1982). Treatment of homosexual and heterosexual sexual dysfunction in male-only groups of mixed sexual orientation. *Archives of Sexual Behavior, 11,* 1-10.

Feldman, H. A., Goldstein, I., Hatzichristou, G., Krane, R. J., & McKinlay, J. B. (1994). Impotence and its medical and psychosocial correlates: Results of the Massachusetts male ageing study. *Journal of Urology, 151,* 54-61.

Fichten, C. S., Libman, E., & Brender, W. (1983). Methodological issues in the study of sex therapy: Effective components in the treatment of secondary orgasmic dysfunction. *Journal of Sex and Marital Therapy, 9,* 191-202.

Flaherty, M. Y. (1989). *Group treatment of men with erectile dysfunction: An outcome study using physiological, behavioral, and psychological assessments.* Unpublished dissertation, Pacific Graduate School of Psychology.

Friedman, D. (1968). The treatment of impotence by Brietal relaxation therapy. *Behaviour Research and Therapy, 6,* 257-261.

Fuchs, K., Hoch, Z., Paldi, E., Abramovici, H., Brandes, J. M., Timor-Tritsch, I., & Kleinhaus, M. (1973). Hypno-desensitization therapy of vaginismus. *International Journal of Clinical and Experimental Hypnosis, 21,* 144-156.

Gitlin, M. J. (1997). Psychotropic medication: Induced sexual dysfunction. In D. Dunner (Ed.), *Current psychiatric therapy* (2nd ed., pp. 385-389). Philadelphia: W. B. Saunders.

Glick, B. S. (1975). Desensitization therapy in impotence and frigidity: Review of the literature and report of a case. *American Journal of Psychiatry, 132,* 169-171.

Gottesfeld, M. L. (1978). Treatment of vaginismus by psychotherapy with adjunctive hypnosis. *American Journal of Clinical Hypnosis, 20,* 272-277.

Hartman, W. A., & Fithian, M. A. (1970). Desert retreat. In J. Robbins (Ed.), *An analysis of human sexual inadequacy.* New York: Signet.

Hartman, W. A., & Fithian, M. A. (1971). Enhancing sexuality through nudism. In H. Otto (Ed.), *The new sexuality.* Palo Alto: Science and Behavioral Books.

Hawton, K. (1982). The behavioral treatment of sexual dysfunction. *British Journal of Psychiatry, 140,* 94-101.

Hawton, K., & Catalan, J. (1986). Prognostic factors in sex therapy. *Behaviour Research and Therapy, 24,* 377-385.

Hawton, K., Catalan, J., & Fagg, J. (1992). Sex therapy for erectile dysfunction: Characteristics of couples, treatment outcome, and prognostic factors. *Archives of Sexual Behavior, 21,* 161-176.

Heiman, J. R., & Grafton-Becker, V. (1989). Orgasmic disorders in women. In S. R. Leiblum & R. C. Rosen (Eds.), *Principles and practice of sex therapy: Update for the 1990s* (pp. 51-88). New York: Guilford.

Heiman, J. R., & LoPiccolo, J. (1983). Clinical outcome of sex therapy. *Archives of General Psychiatry, 40,* 443-449.

Heiman, J. R., & LoPiccolo, J. (1988). *Becoming orgasmic: A sexual and personal growth program for women.* New York: Simon & Schuster.

Heiman, J., LoPiccolo, L., & LoPiccolo, J. (1976). *Becoming orgasmic: A sexual growth program for women.* Englewood Cliffs, NJ: Prentice Hall.

Heinrich, A. G. (1976). The effect of group and self-directed behavioral-educational treatment of primary orgasmic dysfunction in females treated without their partners (Doctoral dissertation, University of Colorado at Boulder, 1976). *Dissertation Abstracts International, 37,* 1902B. (University Microfilms No. 76-23)

Herman, S. H., & Prewett, M. (1974). An experimental analysis of feedback to increase sexual arousal in a case of homosexual and heterosexual impotence: A preliminary report. *Journal of Behavior Therapy and Experimental Psychiatry, 5,* 271-274.

Hurlbert, D. F., & Apt, C. (1995). The coital alignment technique and directed masturbation: A comparative study on female orgasm. *Journal of Sex and Marital Therapy, 21,* 21-29.

Husted, J. R. (1972). The effect of method of systematic desensitization and presence of sexual communication in the treatment of female sexual anxiety by counter-conditioning (Doctoral dissertation, University of California at Los Angeles, 1972). *Dissertation Abstracts International, 33,* 1.

Husted, J. R. (1975). Desensitization procedures in dealing with female sexual dysfunction. *Counseling Psychologist, 5,* 30-37.

Ince, L. P. (1973). Behavior modification of sexual disorders. *American Journal of Psychotherapy, 27,* 446-451.

Jones, G. S. (1973). Treatment of single-partner sexual dysfunction. *Current Medical Dialog, 40,* 471-472.

Jones, W., & Park, P. (1972). Treatment of single partner sexual dysfunction by systematic desensitization. *Obstetrics and Gynecology, 39,* 411-417.

Kaplan, H. S. (1974). *The new sex therapy.* New York: Brunner/Mazel.

Kaplan, H. S., Kohl, R. N., Pomeroy, W. B., Offit, A. K., & Hogan, B. (1974). Group treatment of premature ejaculation. *Archives of Sexual Behavior, 3,* 443-452.

Kilmann, P. R., Milan, R. J., Boland, J. P., Mills, K. H., Caid, C., Davidson, E., Bella, B, Wanlass, R., Sullivan, J., & Montgomery, B. (1987). The treatment of secondary orgasmic dysfunction. *Journal of Sex and Marital Therapy, 13,* 93-105.

Kilmann, P. R., Mills, K. H., Bella, B., Caid, C., Davidson, E., Drose, G., & Wanlass, R. (1983). The effects of sex education on women with secondary orgasmic dysfunction. *Journal of Sex and Marital Therapy, 9,* 79-87.

Kilmann, P. R., Mills, K. H., Caid, C., Davidson, E., Bella, B., Milan, R., Drose, G., Boland, J., Follingstad, D., Montgomery, B., & Wanlass, R. (1986). Treatment of secondary orgasmic dysfunction: An outcome study. *Archives of Sexual Behavior, 15,* 211-229.

Kirkpatrick, C., McGovern, K., & LoPiccolo, J. (1977). Treatment of sexual dysfunction. In G. G. Harris (Ed.), *The group treatment of human problems.* New York: Grune & Stratton.

Kockott, G., Dittmar, F., & Nusselt, L. (1975). Systematic desensitization of erectile impotence: A controlled study. *Archives of Sexual Behavior, 4,* 493-500.

Kohlenberg, R. J. (1974). Directed masturbation and the treatment of primary orgasmic dysfunction. *Archives of Sexual Behavior, 3,* 349-356.

Kraft, T., & Al-Issa, I. (1967). Behavior therapy and the treatment of frigidity. *American Journal of Psychotherapy, 21,* 116-120.

Kuriansky, J. B., Sharpe, L., & O'Connor, D. (1982). The treatment of anorgasmia: Long-term effectiveness of a short-term behavioral group therapy. *Journal of Sex and Marital Therapy, 8,* 29-43.

Kuruvilla, K. (1984). Treatment of single impotent males. *Indian Journal of Psychology, 26,* 160-163.

Lansky, M. R., & Davenport, A. E. (1975). Difficulties in brief conjoint treatment of sexual dysfunction. *American Journal of Psychiatry, 132,* 177-179.

Laumann, E. O., Gagnon, J. H., Michael, R. T., & Michaels, S. (1994). *The social organization of sexuality.* Chicago: University of Chicago Press.

Lazarus, A. A. (1961). Group therapy of phobic disorders by systematic desensitization. *Journal of Abnormal and Social Psychology, 63,* 504-510.

Lazarus, A. (1963). The treatment of chronic frigidity by systematic desensitization. *Journal of Nervous and Mental Diseases, 136,* 272-278.

Lazarus, A. A., & Rachman, S. (1957). The use of systematic desensitization in psychotherapy. *South Africa Medical Journal, 31,* 934-937.

Leiblum, S. R., & Ersner-Hershfield, R. (1977). Sexual enhancement groups for dysfunctional women: An evaluation. *Journal of Sex and Marital Therapy, 3,* 139-152.

Leiblum, S. R., Pervin, L. A., & Campbell, E. H. (1989). The treatment of vaginismus: Success and failure. In S. R. Leiblum & R. C. Rosen (Eds.), *Principles and practice of sex therapy: Update for the 1990s.* New York: Guilford.

Leiblum, S. R., & Rosen, R. C. (Eds.). (1989). *Principles and practice of sex therapy: Update for the 1990s.* New York: Guilford.

Lerner, M. (1971). Un caso grave de dispaureunia y vaginismo neurotico. *Acta Psiquiatrica y Psicologica de America Latina, 17,* 19-32.

Levine, S. B., & Agle, D. (1978). The effectiveness of sex therapy for chronic secondary impotence. *Journal of Sex and Marital Therapy, 4,* 235-258.

Libman, E., Fichten, C. S., Brender, W., Burstein, R., Cohen, J., & Binik, V. M. (1984). A comparison of three therapeutic formats in the treatment of secondary orgasmic dysfunction. *Journal of Sex and Marital Therapy, 10,* 147-159.

Linet, O. I., & Neff, L. L. (1994). Intracavernous prostaglandin E1 in erectile dysfunction. *Clinical Investigation, 72,* 139-149.

Lobitz, W. C., & Baker, E. L. (1979). Group treatment of single males with erectile dysfunction. *Archives of Sexual Behavior, 8,* 127-138.

Lobitz, W. C., & LoPiccolo, J. (1972). New methods in the behavioral treatment of sexual dysfunction. *Journal of Behavior Therapy and Experimental Psychiatry, 3,* 265-271.

LoPiccolo, J., Heiman, J. R., Hogan, D. R., & Roberts, C. W. (1985). Effectiveness of single therapist versus cotherapy teams in sex therapy. *Journal of Consulting and Clinical Psychology, 53,* 287-294.

LoPiccolo, J., & Hogan, D. R. (1979). Multidimensional behavioral treatment of sexual dysfunction. In O. Pomerlieu & J. P. Brady (Eds.), *Behavioral medicine* (pp. 177-204). Baltimore: Williams & Wilkins.

LoPiccolo, J., & Lobitz, W. C. (1972). The role of masturbation in the treatment of orgasmic dysfunction. *Archives of Sexual Behavior, 2,* 163-171.

LoPiccolo, J., & Steger, J. C. (1974). The Sexual Interaction Inventory: A new instrument for assessment of sexual dysfunction. *Archives of Sexual Behavior, 3,* 585-595.

Masters, W. H., & Johnson, V. E. (1970). *Human sexual inadequacy.* Boston: Little, Brown.

Mathews, A., Bancroft, J., Whitehead, A., Hackmann, A., Julier, D., Bancroft, J., Fath, D., & Shaw, P. (1976). The behavioral treatment of sexual inadequacy: A comparative study. *Behaviour Research and Therapy, 14,* 427-436.

Mathews, A., Whitehead, A., & Kellett, J. (1983). Psychological and hormonal factors in the treatment of female sexual dysfunction. *Psychological Medicine, 13,* 83-92.

McCarthy, B. W. (1973). A modification of Masters and Johnson sex therapy model in a clinical setting. *Psychotherapy Theory, Research and Practice, 10,* 290-293.

McGovern, K. B., Stewart, R. C., & LoPiccolo, J. (1975). Secondary orgasmic dysfunction: 1. Analysis and strategies for treatment. *Archives of Sexual Behavior, 4,* 265-275.

McMullen, S., & Rosen, R. C. (1979). Self-administered masturbation training in the treatment of primary orgasmic dysfunction. *Journal of Consulting and Clinical Psychology, 47,* 912-918.

Meston, C. M., & Gorzalka, B. B. (1992). Psychoactive drugs and human sexual behavior: The role of serotonergic activity. *Journal of Psychoactive Drugs, 24,* 1-40.

Meyer, J. K., Schmidt, C. W., Lucas, M. J., & Smith, E. (1975). Short-term treatment of sexual problems: Interim report. *American Journal of Psychiatry, 132,* 172-176.

Milan, R. J., Kilmann, P. R., & Boland, J. P. (1988). Treatment outcome of secondary orgasmic dysfunction: A two-to six-year follow-up. *Archives of Sexual Behavior, 17,* 463-480.

Morokoff, P. J., & LoPiccolo, J. L. (1986). A comparative evaluation of minimal therapist contact and 15-session treatment for female orgasmic dysfunction. *Journal of Consulting and Clinical Psychology, 54,* 294-300.

Munjack, D., Cristol, A., Goldstein, A., Phillips, D., Goldberg, A., Whipple, K., Staples, F., & Kenno, P. (1976). Behavioral treatment of orgasmic dysfunction: A controlled study. *British Journal of Psychiatry, 129,* 497-502.

Munjack, D. J., Schlaks, A., Sanchez, V. C., Usigli, R., Zulueta, A., & Leonard, M. (1984). Rational-emotive therapy in the treatment of erectile failure: An initial study. *Journal of Sex and Marital Therapy, 10,* 170-175.

Nemetz, G. H., Craig, K. D., & Reith, G. (1978). Treatment of female sexual dysfunction through symbolic modeling. *Journal of Consulting and Clinical Psychology, 46,* 62-73.

Obler, M. (1973). Systematic desensitization in sexual disorders. *Journal of Behavior Therapy and Experimental Psychiatry, 4,* 93-101.

O'Gorman, E. C. (1978). The treatment of frigidity: A comparative study of group and individual desensitization. *British Journal of Psychiatry, 132,* 580-584.

Price, S. C., Reynolds, B. S., Cohen, B. D., Anderson, A. J., & Schochet, B. V. (1981). Group treatment of erectile dysfunction for men without partners: A controlled evaluation. *Archives of Sexual Behavior, 10,* 253-268.

Reisinger, J. J. (1974). Masturbatory training in the treatment of primary orgasmic dysfunction. *Journal of Behavior Therapy and Experimental Psychiatry, 5,* 179-183.

Reynolds, B. S. (1980). Biofeedback and facilitation of erection in men with erectile dysfunction. *Archives of Sexual Behavior, 9,* 101-113.

Reynolds, B. S., Cohen, B. D., Schochet, B. V., Price, S. C., & Anderson, A. J. (1981). Dating skills training in the group treatment of erectile dysfunction for men without partners. *Journal of Sex and Marital Therapy, 7,* 184-194.

Riley, A. J., Goodman, R. E., Kellett, J. M., & Orr, R. (1989). Double blind trial of yohimbine hydrochloride in the treatment of erection inadequacy. *Sexual and Marital Therapy. 4,* 17-26.

Riley, A. J., & Riley, E. J. (1978). A controlled study to evaluate directed masturbation in the management of primary orgasmic failure in women. *British Journal of Psychiatry, 133,* 404-409.

Rosen, R. C., & Leiblum, S. R. (1995). Treatment of sexual disorder in the 1990's: An integrated approach. *Journal of Consulting and Clinical Psychology, 63,* 877-890.

Schneidman, B., & McGuire, L. (1976). Group therapy for nonorgasmic women: Two age levels. *Archives of Sexual Behavior, 5,* 239-247.

Segraves, R. T., Saran, A., Segraves, A. S., & Maguire, E. (1993). Clomipramine versus placebo in the treatment of premature ejaculation: A pilot study. *Journal of Sex and Marital Therapy, 19,* 198-200.

Semens, J. (1956). Premature ejaculation. *Southern Medical Journal, 49,* 352-358.

Snyder, A., LoPiccolo, L., & LoPiccolo, J. (1975). Secondary orgasmic dysfunction II. Case study. *Archives of Sexual Behavior, 4,* 277-283.

Sonda, L. P., Mazo, R., & Chancellor, M. B. (1990). The role of yohimbine for the treatment of erectile impotence. *Journal of Sex and Marital Therapy, 16,* 15-21.

Sotile, W. M., & Kilmann, P. R. (1978). The effects of group systematic desensitization of orgasmic dysfunction. *Archives of Sexual Behavior, 7,* 477-491.

Sotile, W. M., Kilmann, P. R., & Follingstad, D. R. (1977). A sexual enhancement workshop: Beyond group systematic desensitization for women's sexual anxiety. *Journal of Sex and Marital Therapy, 3,* 249-255.

Spector, I. P., & Carey, M. P. (1990). Incidence and prevalence of the sexual dysfunctions: A critical review of the empirical literature. *Archives of Sexual Behavior, 19,* 389-408.

Stravynski, A. (1986). Indirect behavioral treatment of erectile failure and premature ejaculation in a man without a partner. *Archives of Sexual Behavior, 13,* 355-361.

Takefman, J., & Brender, W. (1984). An analysis of the effectiveness of two components in the treatment of erectile dysfunction. *Archives of Sexual Behavior, 13,* 321-340.

Tanner, B. A. (1973). Two case reports on the modification of the ejaculatory response with the squeeze technique. *Psychotherapy Theory, Research and Practice, 10,* 297-300.

Tiefer, L. (1994). The medicalization of impotence: Normalizing phallocentrism. *Gender and Society, 8,* 363-377.

Tiefer, L., Pederson, B., & Melman, A. (1988). Psychosocial follow-up of penile prosthesis implant patients and partners. *Journal of Sex and Marital Therapy, 14,* 184-201.

U.S. Department of Health and Human Services. (1987). *National Center for Health Statistics: Detailed diagnoses and procedures for patients discharged from short stay hospitals: United States, 1985.* Hyattsville, MD: Author.

Wallace, D. H., & Barbach, L. G. (1974). Preorgasmic group treatment. *Journal of Sex and Marital Therapy, 1,* 146-154.

Wincze, J. P., & Caird, W. K. (1976). The effects of systematic desensitization in the treatment of essential sexual dysfunction in women. *Behavior Therapy, 7,* 335-342.

Wincze, J. P., & Carey, M. P. (1991). *Sexual dysfunction: A guide for assessment and treatment.* New York: Guilford.

Wolpe, J. (1958). *Psychotherapy by reciprocal inhibition.* Stanford, CA: Stanford University Press.

Wolpe, J. A., & Lazarus, A. A. (1966). *Behaviour therapy techniques: A guide to treatment of neurosis.* Oxford: Pergamon.

Yulis, S. (1976). Generalization of therapeutic gain in the treatment of premature ejaculation. *Behavior Therapy, 7,* 355-358.

Zeiss, R. A. (1978). Self-directed treatment for premature ejaculation. *Journal of Consulting and Clinical Psychology, 16,* 275-281.

Index

About the Editors

Kenneth D. Craig, PhD, is Professor of Psychology in the Department of Psychology at the University of British Columbia, where he has also served as Director of the Graduate Programme in Clinical Psychology on two occasions. His teaching currently focuses on abnormal psychology and health psychology at the undergraduate level and psychological assessment and supervision in the Psychological Clinic at the graduate level. He has authored numerous research papers and chapters on the psychology of pain and on anxiety disorders. His research has won a number of awards, including the Canada Council Killam Research Fellowship. He has been the editor of the *Canadian Journal of Behavioural Science* and currently is an associate editor of the journal *Pain*. He has coedited the following books: *Anxiety and Depression in Adults and Children*; *Health Enhancement, Disease Prevention and Early Intervention: Bio-Behavioral Perspectives*; and *Advances in Clinical Behavior Therapy*. He is a Fellow of the Canadian Psychological Association, the American Psychological Association, and the Society for Behavioral Medicine; a founding member of the International Association for the Study of Pain; and a member of the Academy of Behavioral Medicine Research. His service for scientific and professional organizations has included terms as President of the Canadian Psychological Association, President of the British Columbia Psychological Association, and Treasurer of the Social Science Federation of Canada. He currently is President of the Banff International Conferences on Behavioural Science and President of the Canadian Pain Society.

Keith S. Dobson, PhD, is Professor of Psychology of the University of Calgary, where he was formerly Director of the Programme in Clinical Psychology. He is a Professional/Scientific Member of the Department of Psychiatry at Foothills Hospital and a Staff Psychologist at Wilson/ Banwell and Associates, Calgary. His research interests center on the issues of cognition and psychopathology (particularly anxiety and depression), gender issues in psychopathology, cognition and interpersonal relationships, cognitive-behavioral therapies, and professional issues in psychology. He is the editor or coeditor of several volumes, including the *Handbook of Cognitive-Behavioral Therapies, Psychopathology and Cognition*, and *Professional Psychology in Canada.* In addition to his research interests, he has been active in professional psychology and has served on many committees of several organizations. Among other roles, he was formerly Chair of the National Professional Psychology Consortium and President of the Canadian Psychological Association.

About the Contributors

Kent W. Anderson, PhD, currently works in a group private practice setting in Logan, Utah; is a staff psychologist at the regional hospital; is a consulting psychologist for the inpatient drug and alcohol treatment facility; and is Adjunct Assistant Professor at Utah State University. He received his master's and doctoral degrees in clinical psychology from Utah State University and completed his internship training at the University of Oklahoma Health Sciences Center from 1993 to 1994. He subsequently completed a 2-year postdoctoral fellowship at the Anxiety Disorders Unit at the University of British Columbia in Vancouver, Canada. His research interests involve comparative treatments for depression and anxiety disorders and the personality correlates that influence psychopathology and treatment outcome.

Mary Baker, MA, received her master's degree in counseling psychology and is currently in a counseling/clinical/school psychology doctoral program emphasizing clinical psychology at the University of California, Santa Barbara. She has published and/or presented papers in the areas of empirically validated treatments, managed health care, and social interactions in children with autism. She has special interests in patient treatment matching for psychiatric disorders, childhood disorders (primarily autism), and families with developmentally disabled children.

Larry E. Beutler, PhD, is Professor and Director of the Counseling/ Clinical/School Psychology Program at the University of California, Santa Barbara. He obtained his PhD from the University of Nebraska in 1970 and subsequently served on the faculties of Duke University Medical School, Stephen F. Austin State University, Baylor College of Medicine, and the University of Arizona. He is a Diplomate of the American Board of Professional Psychology (ABPP), a past international President of the Society for Psychotherapy Research (SPR), past President of the Division of Psychotherapy (American Psychological Association), and a past editor of the *Journal of Consulting and Clinical Psychology*. He is co-editor of the *Journal of Clinical Psychology*.

Andrew Christensen, PhD, is Professor of Psychology at the University of California, Los Angeles. He received his PhD in clinical psychology from the University of Oregon and completed his internship at Rutgers Medical School. His special area of research and clinical interest is couples conflict and couples therapy. With Neil Jacobson, he has developed a new treatment for couples therapy and received funding from the National Institute of Mental Health to evaluate that treatment. That treatment is described in their chapter in this volume.

Paul Crits-Christoph, PhD, is currently Associate Professor and Director of the Center for Psychotherapy Research in the Department of Psychiatry at the University of Pennsylvania. He received his PhD in clinical psychology from Yale University in 1984. He is Principal Investigator of the only National Institute of Mental Health-funded Clinical Research Center that has a focus on psychotherapy. In addition to publishing more than 100 articles and chapters, he is an editor (with Jacques Barber) of the *Handbook of Short-Term Dynamic Psychotherapy* and *Dynamic Therapies for Psychiatric Disorders: Axis 1*.

Anna Beth Doyle is Professor of Psychology, Member of the Centre for Research in Human Development and Director of Clinical Training at Concordia University in Montreal. She obtained her PhD from Stanford University and her clinical training as a postdoctoral fellow at McGill University and the Montreal Children's Hospital. Her current research areas are family and peer influences on minority and majority children's adjustment and the development of prejudice in children.

Shirley M. Glynn, PhD, is Clinical Research Psychologist at the West Los Angeles VA Medical Center and an Assistant Research Psychologist in the

Department of Psychiatry and Biobehavioral Sciences at the University of California at Los Angeles (UCLA) Neuropsychiatric Institute and Hospitals. After completing her PhD in social/clinical psychology at the University of Illinois at Chicago, she completed her doctoral internship at Camarillo (CA) State Hospital and then accepted a position as the staff psychologist at the UCLA Mental Health Clinical Research Center's inpatient unit at Camarillo State Hospital. She subsequently joined the Research Service at the West Los Angeles VA Medical Center, where she has conducted empirical investigations on the development and evaluation of psychological interventions for schizophrenia and chronic post-traumatic stress disorder. She is a licensed psychologist in California and has published extensively on family and behavioral interventions for serious psychiatric illnesses.

Mark S. Goldman is Distinguished Research Professor and Director of the Alcohol and Substance Abuse Research Institute and was Director of Clinical Psychology Training (1985-1995) at the University of South Florida (USF). He received his PhD in 1972 from Rutgers University and has been on the faculties at Wayne State University and USF (since 1985). He is a fellow of Divisions 3, 12, 28, and 50, is a member of Divisions 6 and 40, and is board certified (American Board of Professional Psychology) in clinical psychology. In addition to research and clinical work in the addictions field since 1969, he has served as Psychology Field Editor for the *Journal of Studies on Alcohol*, member and then Chair of the Psychosocial Study Section of the National Institute on Alcohol Abuse and Alcoholism (NIAAA), member of the Board of Professional Affairs of the American Psychological Association (APA), member of the Task Force on Psychological Intervention Guidelines (APA), and President of Division 50 of APA (1995-1996). In 1992, he received a MERIT Award from the NIAAA.

Steven C. Hayes, PhD, is currently Nevada Foundation Professor and Chair in the Department of Psychology at the University of Nevada. He received his PhD in clinical psychology from West Virginia University in 1977 and did his internship at Brown University. He is currently President-Elect of the Association for Advancement of Behavior Therapy and was formerly President of the American Association for Applied and Preventive Psychology, President of Division 25 (Experimental Analysis of Be-

havior) of the American Psychological Association, and Secretary-Trea-
surer of the American Psychological Society. An author of more than a
dozen books and nearly 200 scientific articles, his interests cover verbal
regulatory processes, behavioral assessment, psychological acceptance,
rule governance, and other topics. In 1992, his work was listed by the
Institute for Scientific Information as having the 30th highest citation
impact in the world within psychology as a whole.

Julia R. Heiman, PhD, is currently Professor of Psychiatry and Behavioral Sciences at the University of Washington, where she directs the
Reproductive and Sexual Medicine Clinic, an interdisciplinary clinic to
study and treat sexual disorders. She received her PhD in clinical psychology from the State University of New York (SUNY) at Stony Brook,
followed by a postdoctoral fellowship and faculty position in the SUNY
Stony Brook Medical School and a Research Scientist position at Long
Island Research Institute. Her research has examined the psychophysiology of sexual arousal in men and women, the effectiveness of sex therapy,
and psychological correlates of medical conditions with sexual consequences. Her current research is directed at conceptualizing and differen-
tiating early physical and sexual abuse on later sexual and relationship
patterns.

Kenneth A. Holroyd, PhD, is Professor of Clinical and Health Psychology, Director of the Headache Clinic, and Associate Director of the Institute of Health and Behavioral Sciences at Ohio University. His interests
are in the psychobiology and clinical management of chronic pain disorders, particularly the integration of psychosocial and drug therapies. He is
on the editorial boards of several professional journals, a member of the
Agency for Health Care Policy Clinical Guidelines Panel on Headache,
and advisor to the World Health Organization Psychosocial Interventions
in Support of Health. He has published over 80 articles and chapters in
professional journals and two books, including (with Tom Creer) *Self-
Management of Chronic Disease: Handbook of Clinical Interventions and
Research.*

Neil S. Jacobson, PhD, Professor at the University of Washington, has
published more than 200 books and articles on marital and couples therapy, domestic violence, depression, and related topics. His books include

Marital Therapy (written with Gayla Margolin), *Clinical Handbook of Couple Therapy* (edited with Alan Gurman), and *Integrative Couple Therapy* (written with Andrew Christensen). He has completed one trade publication, *When Men Batter Women: New Insights Into Ending Abusive Relationships* (coauthored with John Gottman). He received his PhD from the University of North Carolina, Chapel Hill. He has received numerous grants and research awards, including the prestigious MERIT Award and Research Scientist Award from the National Institute of Health. He has also been honored for his distinguished lifetime contributions to family therapy research by the American Association for Marriage and Family Therapy and the American Family Therapy Academy. He was formerly President of the Association for the Advancement of Behavior Therapy and the American Psychological Association's Society for a Scientific Clinical Psychology.

Gay L. Lipchik, PhD, is Assistant Professor of Research in Psychology at Ohio University and Project Manager of a National Institutes of Health clinical trial of drug and nondrug therapies for headache. She received her PhD in clinical psychology from Ohio University and was a predoctoral resident in health psychology at the University of Mississippi Medical Center. She is a recent recipient of a Research Award from the American Association for the Study of Headache for her investigation of physiological mechanisms involved in chronic tension-type headache. Her primary research and clinical interests have been in the fields of health psychology and behavioral medicine, with a particular interest in the psychophysiology of headache disorders and the evaluation of nondrug treatments of pain disorders. She is a member of the American Psychological Association, the Society of Behavior Medicine, and the American Association for the Study of Headache.

Peter D. McLean, PhD, is Professor in the Department of Psychiatry, University of British Columbia, Vancouver, Canada, and is Director of the Anxiety Disorders Unit, Vancouver Hospital and Health Sciences Centre. He is best known for his studies of the relative short- and long-term utility of behavioral therapy for the treatment of depression as well as factors predictive of outcome in the treatment of depression. More recently, he and his team have studied the efficacy of cognitive-behavioral therapy for the treatment of depression and panic disorder when these disorders pre-

sent both individually and concurrently. He has long been an advocate of
the belief that our value in the prevention and treatment of mental disorders
is improved to the extent that we evolve and practice empirically derived
psychological interventions.

Cindy M. Meston, PhD, is currently Assistant Professor of Psychology at
the University of Texas at Austin. She received a PhD in clinical psychology from the University of British Columbia in 1995 and completed a
Senior Postdoctoral Fellowship in sexual and reproductive medicine at the
University of Washington School of Medicine in 1996. Her primary research focus has been on understanding the role of the sympathetic nervous
system in female sexual arousal. Secondary interests include serotonergic
influences on sexual behavior, the influence of acculturation on sexuality,
social desirability influences on self-reported sexual behavior, and the
relation between early abuse and adult sexuality.

Kim T. Mueser, PhD, is a licensed clinical psychologist and Professor in
the Departments of Psychiatry and Community and Family Medicine at
the Dartmouth Medical School in Hanover, New Hampshire. He received
his PhD in clinical psychology from the University of Illinois at Chicago
in 1984, completed his psychology internship training at Camarillo State
Hospital in 1985, and was on the faculty of the Psychiatry Department at
the Medical College of Pennsylvania in Philadelphia until 1994, when he
moved to Dartmouth Medical School. His clinical and research interests
include the psychosocial treatment of schizophrenia and other severe
mental illnesses, and post-traumatic stress disorder. He has published
numerous articles, books, and book chapters. Recent books that he has
published include *Behavioral Family Therapy for Psychiatric Disorders*
(with Shirley Glynn), *Coping With Schizophrenia: A Guide for Families*
(with Susan Gingerich), and *Social Skills Training for Schizophrenia* (with
Alan Bellack, Susan Gingerich, and Julie Agresta).

Donald B. Penzien is a clinical psychologist specializing in assessment
and treatment of recurrent headache. He is a fellow of the American
Association for the Study of Headache (AASH) and Diplomats of the
American Academy of Pain Management. He is Associate Professor of
Psychiatry at the University of Mississippi Medical Center (UMC) and
Director of the UMC Head Pain Center. He has published numerous

research articles and book chapters on headache, and his research has been supported by the National Institute of Health and private foundation grants. He serves on advisory committees for the AASH, the American Council for Headache Education, and the American Academy of Neurology, and he has been actively involved in the Agency for Health Care Policy and Research Headache Treatment Guidelines Project. At the invitation of the World Health Organization, he recently coauthored *Self-Management of Recurrent Migraine and Tension-Type Headache,* and his nondrug treatment program manual *Self-Management Training Program for Chronic Headache* is in press.

John R. Weisz, PhD, is currently Professor at the University of California at Los Angeles, where he has also served as Director of Clinical Training. He received his BA from Mississippi College. After college, he was a Peace Corps volunteer in Kenya. He later received his PhD in clinical and developmental psychology from Yale University. He has held faculty positions at Cornell University and the University of North Carolina at Chapel Hill. His research addresses child and adolescent psychopathology and psychotherapy. He is the author, with Bahr Weiss, of *Effects of Psychotherapy With Children and Adolescents* (Sage Publications).